Predators, Prey,
and Other Kinfolk

Predators, Prey, and Other Kinfolk

Growing Up in Polygamy

DOROTHY ALLRED SOLOMON

W. W. NORTON & COMPANY   New York • London

For information about permission to reproduce selections from this book,
write to Permissions, W. W. Norton & Company, Inc.
500 Fifth Avenue, New York, NY 10110

Manufacturing by The Courier Companies, Inc.
Book design by Dana Sloan
Production manager: Amanda Morrison

LIBRARY OF CONGRESS CATALOGING-IN-PUBLICATION DATA
Solomon, Dorothy Allred.
Predators, prey, and other kinfolk : growing up in polygamy / by
Dorothy Allred Solomon.— 1st ed.
p. cm.
Includes bibliographical references.
ISBN 0-393-04946-9
1. Solomon, Dorothy Allred. 2. Mormons—United States—Biography.
3.Polygamy—Religious aspects—Mormon Church.
4. Polygamy—United States. I. Title.
BX8695.S755A3 2003
289.3'092—dc21
2003001044

W. W. Norton & Company, Inc.
500 Fifth Avenue, New York, N.Y. 10110
www.wwnorton.com

W. W. Norton & Company Ltd.
Castle House, 75/76 Wells Street, London W1T 3QT

1 2 3 4 5 6 7 8 9 0

This book is dedicated to the children,
shapers of the future, especially
Denise, Layla, Jeff, and Laurie
and their children

The events and dates in this book are true, so far as I know them to be, but some names and some details have been changed in order to protect the privacy of persons, particularly my relatives.

Contents

Note to the Reader

 PERCHED ON THE WASATCH FAULT-LINE at the foot of Mount Olympus in Salt Lake City, Utah, stands the compound where I was born, an outlaw by birth. I descend from four generations of polygamy, beginning with my great-great-grandfather, William Moore Allred, a bodyguard to the Prophet Joseph Smith, founder of the Church of Jesus Christ of Latter-day Saints (often called LDS or "Mormon"). Joseph Smith had received a revelation regarding the Principle of Plural Marriage, and he gave my ancestor and many others permission to take plural wives. In 1890, after five decades of polygamy, the Church of Jesus Christ of Latter-day Saints responded to intense political pressure by adopting the 1890 manifesto that abolished polygamy. But even with this ecclesiastical release, my great-grandfather, my grandfather, and then my father, Dr. Rulon C. Allred, lived the Principle of Plural Marriage as a matter of religious conscience. My family paid a high price to practice plural marriage, yet I broke away from my father's religious group, abandoning the way of life that engendered me.

I broke away because I wanted to be the only wife in my marriage and because I wanted equality. I broke away because I could not reconcile the contradiction of keeping the laws of God while breaking the laws of State. I did not know how to be honest while conforming to a fundamentalist view—a vision that urged me to see the evil in the outside world while blinding myself to evil within or close at hand.

My family's presence in Utah might best be compared to the deer herds that populate the Wasatch mountains above the Salt Lake valley. For the most part, we were shy, gentle creatures who kept to ourselves, ruminants chewing on our private theology, who dealt with aggression by freezing or running. As with the deer herd where several females precede the male into the meadow, my father's wives ventured into the fields of the wicked world—the neighborhood, the public school, the grocery store—drawing fire in behalf of their shared, stately husband. The mothers were vigilant and hardworking, raising the young and enduring every type of hardship with courage and grace. They hid themselves during pregnancy and after giving birth, keeping the babies quiet so that enemies would not find us—those prying neighbors who might turn us in, those social workers and state police and federal agents who might interfere with our home.

Since public exposure could destroy our family, we stayed aloof and alert at school or work. We learned to blend in and vanish at the first hint of discovery. Despite our caution we often became victims and were unsurprised by our suffering, for we had been warned to expect persecution and were promised that those who die for the Gospel of Jesus Christ are granted eternal life. My father's price for living the Principle—losing part of his family, his good citizenship, and his professional status—were seen as martyr's wounds, and we were expected to make similar sacrifices.

We regarded ourselves as "Mormon fundamentalists" since we lived the early tenets of the Church of Jesus Christ of Latter-day Saints, including the Principle of Plural Marriage as well as the United Order, a system where everyone gives to the common store for distribution according to need, and the Law of Consecration, where all that we are, do, and have is given freely to God for the building up of His Kingdom.

Fundamentalists stake their lives on being right, which catalyzes a transmogrification from mild amity to predatory behaviors ancient as an eye for an eye. When hearts are broken or blood spilled, feuds spring up. Some leaders take an aggressive stance, insisting that others conform to their point of view and lapsing into outlaw behavior. When fundamentalist leaders become tyrants, women and children suffer most, but peaceful patriarchs are also targets, especially since support from law enforcement officers is not always available to those living outside the law.

In the polygamous culture, personal identity is hard to come by. Social boundaries around the religious group keep out the larger world, but inside the group, personal boundaries are discouraged and readily breached. The secrecy imposed by an illegal lifestyle further undermines individual development, increasing the likelihood of abuse and exploitation. Focus on the self is actively discouraged, but as my mother's only girl and a favorite of my father, I didn't absorb the constant reminder "Don't be selfish." Keenly aware of myself, of my thoughts, feelings, and appetites, I felt driven to express them. I wanted friends who had been raised in monogamous households, who could tell the truth about their parents. I wanted that life over there.

Some years after my father's death, I did express myself and published a book. It ended with his death, and chronicled my life as I perceived it until then. In *In My Father's House* I walked a tightrope between the idealism I had grown up with and a developing sense of reality that I could not fully identify or interpret. Frequently, what I came to realize did not align with my father's estimation that we were "a good and saintly people."

That first book no longer adequately represents me. Along the fault-line of my personal history, I now feel my polygamous childhood shift against my monogamous life. With each shift in perspective, forgotten things are brought to light. Personalities I thought would stand forever have turned to salt while others have emerged with substance and meaning. Influences I once thought were wholesome have yielded poisonous fruit, while influences I considered poisonous have made me stronger. Marriage, childbirth, death—all seem different when the childhood in polygamy is stacked against the gradient of monogamy. Old injustices deepen and reveal themselves in a new generation, demanding reconciliation for the sake of my daughters and son, and for the children of my brothers and sisters. With each passing year, I find it harder to sustain secrets, more compelled to tell the truth. My hope is that these pages offer something redemptive, honest, and close to home.

Dorothy Allred Solomon

ONE

The Mark of My Ancestors

 I AM THE ONLY DAUGHTER of my father's fourth plural wife, twenty-eighth of forty-eight children—a middle kid, you might say, with the middle kid's propensity for identity crisis. My sprawling family shares a birthmark, the light hair of many of my father's children barely concealing a small reddish swirl like a fingerprint or a bruise at the base of the skull. Our grandmother had the mark, and our children have inherited it, as have the grandchildren. Once, when I was young and my father read to us from Genesis about the mark of Cain, I asked if Cain had the same birthmark we did. In a frosty tone my father replied that Cain was marked on the forehead by the evil he had done, while our birthmark signified that we were members of a good family. Knowing that my father had traced our lineage back to Adam, I then wondered if our family birthmark came from Abel and if a blow to the back of the head that ended his life was proof of his goodness. Since as an adult I don't live polygamy, I sometimes worry about my place in the family and I'm unreasonably grateful for the proof of belonging at the nape of my neck.

"Remember who you are," my father used to tell us. These may be the first words I heard him say, and he said them often. There was no irony in his tone, although he had fathered so many, and each of us believed that the message was intended specifically for us. He always spoke the words in a preaching voice that rippled with significance, as though he was both declaring our value and defining our identity. But it was a feat to remember who I was while keeping the fact of our burgeoning family a secret from the outside world.

I was, myself, a carefully kept secret. When my mother was expecting me, she went into hiding as soon as she started "showing" until June of 1949, when I was born in the bedroom of the grey house at the south end of our Great Salt Lake Valley compound. The other mothers weren't in the room that morning, despite the tradition of sister-wives supporting each other during labor and delivery. Only my father, a naturopathic physician, attended my birth. Perhaps his presence sparked the extraordinary arc between us, a different kind of energy from my connection with my mother. After I was tightly swaddled (according to fundamentalist practice) my father showed me to a few of the older children who promised to keep the new baby a secret. No birth certificate was filled out, and the family went on as if nothing had happened, nothing alive and wriggling that could be used as evidence that my father lived polygamy.

In keeping with our fundamentalist ritual, when I was eight days old I received a name and a blessing, but mine was a private ceremony that included only my father, the seven mothers, and a few of the older children in the family. The other members of our religious community were not invited and for months they did not know I existed. But my mother's oldest son, Saul, knew about me, and so did her sister's son, Isaac. The two boys were sometimes mistaken for twins, which was no surprise since they had been born three months apart to twin sisters married to my father. Tall, with light hair and light eyes, Saul and Isaac taught me to walk and talk and count as they led me down the steps of the grey house, each of them holding a hand as we crossed the graveled yard to the big white house where the family met for prayers morning and night. Saul and Isaac set the standard for the younger boys, so my second and third brothers, Jake and Danny, recited with me my ABCs, breath by breath, step by step, and they let me tag along behind them as they launched into games and adventures. I much preferred the world of my brothers, with its mud and blood and dank odors and rough talk, to the clean, quiet world of the mothers and sisters. Not the least of attractions to the society of men was my father, who took my brothers on outings and taught them all the important things. When my father headed an excursion, he talked about the workings of God and nature, about what could heal and what could kill, about what lived in heaven and what lived on earth. It was clear that he knew about life, and that he knew he mattered—to himself, to us, and to God.

"You boys must remember who you are," my father said as he surveyed the fields beyond the compound where we lived. He reminded us that we should strive to be "saints" in accordance with the official Church of Jesus Christ of Latter-day Saints from whence we had sprung.

I was very small when I established the habit of tagging along as my father led my brothers through the gate and across the east field to Big Cottonwood Creek to fish. The meadow opened before us, ripples of wheat grass, prickles of purple-blooming Russian thistle, sunflowers staring up like large, unblinking eyes. Crusty cow pies lured us into their stink unless we had the legs to step over them. I stopped to scrape my feet and pick cockleburs from my socks, then ran to catch up. As we drew near the stream we could hear a rush rather than the roar of April, and we breathed air cool and damp and sharp with the bite of watercress and mint. My father cautioned me not to scare the fish, to stay very still and watch while he taught the boys how to rig their rods. The older, more experienced ones—Saul and Isaac and Jake—helped the younger boys get their poles ready. They knew how to use an inflating needle to make a good firm knot between line and leader, knew how to attach the hook without snagging their skin on the barb.

"Fish are smart," my father said as they worked. "It takes some genius to fool them." With nimble fingers, he tied a dry fly above his spinner. He'd been born ambidextrous, and enhanced the gift by learning to knit while studying to be a doctor, so that when he had to perform precise surgical tasks, his hands would be quick and sure. As it was, he could rig his line without thinking about it, and he paused to point out riffles and eddies where the biggest trout hid. He shook his head sadly and predicted that Cottonwood Creek would one day be channeled in viaducts that would change the habitat and spoil the fishing. It took wild rivers and streams to preserve native trout, he said, just as it took pure waters of fundamentalism to provide shallows and depths, hiding places and rapids for protecting and strengthening ancient bloodlines. My brothers nodded as if they knew exactly what he meant, and they probably did since they accompanied him to priesthood meetings every week, where they learned more secrets of the universe than I could count. As a mere girl, I was privileged to eavesdrop on their conversation. The best way to insure my continued presence was to be silent, and so when the things he said provoked questions, I suppressed them and floated on the sound of my father's voice, following its ebb and flow and the exultant rush when a fish took the line.

Sometimes I saw through the fish's eyes, looking up through the glare, everything above me distorted into monstrous or heroic proportion, everything painful and beautiful and bright. Sometimes when I watched my father, his countenance at once intense and serene, his shirt so white even when fishing, I was surprised to remember that even though he was a doctor, he was also considered a criminal. I knew that beyond our chainlink fence, people called us bastards, dismissing our right to be alive, much less our citizenship. When my brothers raised questions about our legitimacy, my father referred to scripture to justify our lives. "In the beginning was the Word and . . . and the Word was God," my father recited from John 1. Then calling on his photographic memory, he'd choose a section of the *Doctrine and*

Covenants, a book of commandments appended to the *Book of Mormon*, ". . . and whatsoever you bind on earth in my name and by my word . . . it shall be eternally bound in the heavens." This was the scriptural foundation of our family kingdom, the source of five generations of patriarchal polygamy. A corollary in Genesis bound me to ancestors as far back as Abraham: "And this shall be your promise," my father recited. He stooped to sift white sands from the shallows of the stream, and we saw our place in the grand design: one of many stars in the sky, one grain of sand in the sea of human souls, chosen by God.

As the family patriarch and the leader of our religious group, my father was next to the godhead in our eyes. He looked like Heavenly Father, with his crown of silver-blond hair, his long straight nose, his piercing blue eyes. And when he spoke, his teeth biting each pronouncement, we felt the precision of his authority. Once God had spoken the world into being; now my father declared our day-to-day reality, and it materialized.

One May morning, just after family prayers, my father announced, "It's Memorial Day. My office is closed, so we'll go fishing." He raised his voice in a rally-cry. "Every man in the yard at ten minutes past seven!" I was there, doing my best to look like one of the boys. And every male who could walk by himself showed up except for Aunt Rose's son, Malcolm. Even though he was the oldest of my father's children on the compound, Malcolm always hid when my father conducted outdoor lessons. But even Malcolm could not escape family or religious meetings. When my father said, "We will have Home Evening at seven o'clock," we gathered in the parlor of the white house just before seven, the children with clean faces, the mothers with freshly braided hair. His word was the only hold he exercised on his wives, and the only legitimacy beyond his love that he could grant his children. Everyone in the family called him "Daddy"—even his wives, who only called him "Rulon" when they wanted to suggest a private connection with him. Daddy was the patriarch, governing the household and all within it. Only God was greater.

That morning, as my father led us along the bank, he pointed out stinging nettle with a warning that we'd itch all afternoon if we touched it, then explained that nettles make a wonderful tea for curing stomach ills. He picked a sprig of belladonna, saying that the delicate purple flowers could put a person in a coma deep enough to kill him, but delivered in proper doses, could relieve pain and insomnia. He held up the seed of the wild geranium, in appearance like the seed that fertilized a human egg, and showed how its tail twisted as it dried, screwing itself into the earth. And when Danny discovered a cotton-tail rabbit, still alive although its innards had been gnawed by a fox, my father said that the rabbit had been too young to flee, and as we sadly gazed at the creature's dimming eyes, he explained that this was the way of nature, for the presence of predators made prey swifter and more aware. The rabbits carrying disease would lag behind, and the next generation of rabbits would be hardier, smarter, and faster.

He defined good and evil for us, reciting scripture to prove that the Lord used the greatest evils to accomplish the highest good. He told how the first killer had been set apart to do his grisly deed, proof that in the face of evil, we all require a savior. But Cain, sent away from his family and condemned by God to roam the earth, had nothing in common with our family. Evil lived outside, in the wicked world. Good, which lived inside, included the people in our family and the members of our religious group who believed, as we did, in the Principle of Plural Marriage. Outsiders—those who were not with us—were against us. We must use this knowledge, he said, to make ourselves better than those who mocked and persecuted us, so that we would be beyond reproach.

He swept his arm, taking in the fields, the mountains, the stream. "God created this beautiful world for us. And He sent His Son to atone for our sins so that we can have eternal life. That is our Heavenly Father's plan." My father exhorted his sons to be good examples, to live as representatives of Christ. "You must do your part, keep the commandments. You must be willing to die for what you believe."

None of us wanted to hear about dying, not even when we thought of our benevolent Heavenly Father, our loving Lord and Savior. We especially did not want to think of dying as we stood at the rim of the gold and green meadow with the sunlight washing over us. Death seemed like something imaginary, not part of our lives, so why was our father bringing it up? He threw his line out to where trees cast a shadow over a deep pocket. As the spinner sank and the dry fly settled, he warned us that all true believers would be tested, and my brothers had those pained smiles, torment lurking at the corners of their eyes; they already knew about commandments and sacrifice: "Don't hurt people. Don't kill animals unless you intend to eat them. Don't yell. Don't swear. Don't think about yourself all the time." He adjured us to give, as God gives: continuously, abundantly, without any expectation of return. He encouraged us to sing a primary song as we trekked behind him, smelling fishy and sweaty, tired and ready for dinner. But my father was just getting started.

> *Give said the little stream.*
> *Give, oh give, give, oh give.*
> *Give, said the little stream*
> *As it hurried down the hill.*
> *I'm small, I know, but wherever I go*
> *The fields grow greener still.*

I sang at the top of my lungs until Danny told me to shut up.

"Shut up's a swear word," I said.

"Stop that fighting!" My father elevated his voice just enough to let us know we were on treacherous ground. "As if we don't already have enough to contend with. We don't need contention among ourselves."

Contention with the outside world was my family's constant challenge, a struggle that refined and distorted our perception. We lingered in the shadow of secrecy, yet hungered for light. Our best shot was to spring straight for heaven and hope that a divine hook would yank us up, out of the small corridor of our fundamentalist existence into the freedom of eternal life.

How could we, as children in such a setting, see the gap between idealism and day-to-day reality? How could we know concepts like "paranoia" and "delusion"? Since we dared not trust the world, we trusted my father as surveyor and purveyor of truth, and the way he saw it was the way it was. He was the center of gravity from which balance was struck. He established our definition of "sane." His encyclopedic memory freely unfolded when he took us into the fields or the mountains, where his nature lessons might expand beyond the secrets of trout-fishing into descriptions of timber-wolf hierarchy.

My brother Danny was always into some mischief or another, tormenting me or getting his shoes wet or tangling someone else's fishing line. My father gave him a disappointed look, then urged his boys to put their energy into constructive activity. Saul put the preaching into practice. He motioned Danny close and taught him to cut a green willow whistle, showed him where to notch it and how to loosen the sheath of bark so that it would slide. Danny blew his whistle until everyone's head ached, and my father took it away. He challenged his sons to carve vessels of the spirit, to master the impulses of the flesh. Fishing trips were as good as weekly priesthood meetings for teaching the mysteries of the Gospel. He told us about the Three Nephites who were granted immortality by Jesus Christ when he visited the New World upon his resurrection. These three men walked the earth performing miracles, and would do so until Christ came again, he said. He told us about the City of Enoch, a city so righteous it was lifted into the heavens to dwell near Kolob, the home of Our Father in Heaven. My father told us of the seerstones called the Urim and Thumim which Joseph Smith had used to translate ancient writings inscribed on the golden plates of Mormon. At the age of fourteen, Joseph Smith had knelt in the woods to ask which church was true and he experienced theophany—a personal visit from Heavenly Father and His Son, Jesus Christ. A few years later, Joseph was directed by an angelic presence named Moroni to dig into the Hill Cumorah, in New York State, and there he found them—plates of brass and plates of gold containing the record of a people who traveled from Jerusalem to the New World about six hundred years before Christ was born. This history had been abridged by Moroni's father, a prophet and general called Mormon who passed the responsibility for the plates to his son. By this process we were given the *Book of Mormon*, containing the restored Gospel of Jesus Christ. My father also talked about more earthly matters such as temperance and obedience, about mucking stalls instead of losing one's temper, about the wanton act of spilling one's seed on the ground instead of waiting to plant in the proper season when married for time and all eternity.

Every spring he helped his sons till and plant the vegetable garden. In the summer he would make hay with them, in the autumn they would prune fruit trees, and in the winter they would chop wood together. He helped them to whitewash the stucco house, to repair the shingles of the grey house, and to caulk the stone foundation of the cottage. He supervised construction of a cinder-block swimming pool where each child would be baptized as he or she turned eight years old, the Mormon age of accountability. He milked the cows every morning, then scraped the manure from his shoes and polished them before heading out to his doctor's office. When he came home from work, he helped get supper on the table and, often as not, helped with the dishes.

He often combined his love of fishing with his house-calls to patients in remote towns and ranches—to the northern reaches of Utah, or east to Neola in dinosaur country, or southwest to the Deep Creek Mountains along the Utah-Nevada border. But the particular season I am remembering he stayed close to home, as if standing watch. As the Memorial Day morning wore on, he lapsed into silence and seemed freighted with worry. Some of the boys went home for lunch, but Saul, Isaac, Jake, Danny, and I stayed on, waiting for him to catch something or say something that would lend meaning to the day. Isaac stood quietly at my father's right hand. My father towered above the willows, waving his fishing rod like a choirmaster. Isaac imitated him. Before long, Isaac had hooked a trout. My father struggled to get a net under it and shouted for Isaac to reel it in. "Look! I do believe it's a Utah cutthroat!" My father swept the fish into the net and turned it over, shaking his head in disappointment. "Nope. Only a hybrid. Not the pure breed."

He showed us the faint pink under its lower jaw. "Since before the Flood, there has been a fish with a red throat like this, but the pure strain has a blood-red line—as though it had been cut from gill to gill. That's why it's called the cutthroat trout."

My father slipped the fish into his creel and untangled the line. Then he handed the creel to Saul and told him to clean the fish downstream. As Saul gutted the fish, my father explained that ancient Lake Bonneville had once covered most of Utah and Nevada. Holding his arm as wide as he could reach, "In those days the cutthroat was huge—it weighed as much as sixty pounds. When the waters receded and left the Great Salt Lake, the Utah cutthroat was trapped in the little brooks of the Upper Deep Creek Mountains. Now it's not much bigger than a fingerling. About as big as you, princess," he said, brushing the tip of my nose with his knuckle. And in response to the question we hadn't asked, "The water's too cold and the Deep Creek too narrow for it to thrive the way it did in the days of Lake Bonneville."

By then the boys were tired of his lecture, and they gave each other sidelong grins as they flexed their milking muscles, bulges in their forearms rippling like small trout beneath their skin as they contested who had the biggest. My father gave them the eye, and waited for their attention to return to him before explaining that the native trout sometimes jumped the rapids and slipped over the waterfall into the wider, deeper streams below. There, the fish spawned with rainbow and German brown and brook trout. The ancient bloodline was quickly absorbed and the cutthroat marking faded.

He compared the Utah cutthroat to those of us born into the Principle. "Satan will try to lure you over the falls," he said, looking at each of us. "You must resist temptation. Stay in the pure spiritual waters of the family until you find someone worthy of you."

He grimaced, perhaps thinking of his great losses and of being branded "outlaw" and "adulterer" by the president of the Church of Jesus Christ of Latter-day Saints, Heber J. Grant. President Grant (my father declared) had once lived the Principle himself, in the days before the Manifesto of 1890 abolished plural marriage. And yet President Grant had played a part in our persecution and pain.

As we made our way upstream, he reminded us that we owed our lives to the Principle. "Even in the days when the Church openly practiced plural marriage, it was reserved for those who were worthy to live it." He stopped abruptly and we stopped, too, gazing up at him. "You children come from five generations of polygamy. You chose before the world was created to keep the Principle alive until Christ comes to set things in order. Remember who you are."

I did not know for sure who I was. Yes, I was my father's daughter. I was my mother's only girl. But when I closed my eyes, it seemed I came from a distant place beyond the clouds, a place of white light and blue air beyond the gold field humming with grasshoppers, beyond these willows teeming with yellow jackets.

My father looked over my head at his sons—slender blond zealots, younger versions of himself. "Abraham lived the Principle, as did Isaac and Jacob," my father told them. "The Lord promised that their seed would outnumber the stars. When Christ's true church was restored to the earth, the promise of the Principle was extended to the Prophet Joseph Smith. Now the promise is yours. You will be blessed beyond your wildest dreams if you stay true to your heritage." He moved down the bank and cast his line again.

I watched my father's line settle on the clear stream, watched the fly drift on the current. No ripple broke the surface, and I wondered where the fish had gone. Perhaps I was standing too close and had scared them away. As I gazed at my reflection in the water, I wondered if I would be one of those to desert the noble line, to head into the rapids and jump into deeper, wider streams below the fall. It was an exciting and terrifying thing to imagine.

At the time, I felt wrong for having such rebellious thoughts. But my willful spirit may have been inherited, too. Rugged individuals who had carved their own destinies stared up at me from daguerreotypes in my Grandmother Evelyn's photograph album. All the big portraits were of men. To find a woman, you had to turn to the snapshots too small to reveal faces. I didn't like it, the men getting all the close-ups. I didn't like how quiet my mother was or how clean she wanted me to be. As if to emphasize this unfairness, my older brother Danny turned his back on me, unzipped, and sent a sparkling arc into the center of a cow-pie. I glanced up at my father, who paid no attention to the display of immodesty. Danny looked over his shoulder and gave me a knowing grin, and I thought of how smug he had been when he came home from his first priesthood meeting, all puffed up with secret knowledge. Pointing through a frosty window, he said. "That's the North Star. You know who lives there?" Of course I didn't, and then he told me that it was a secret for the men to know. I was sick of secrets, and I protested, "Why can't I know too?" And Danny said, so smug, so superior, "Because you're just a girl. You don't know and you won't ever know. You don't have the priesthood."

Now Danny zipped himself up and sauntered downstream with his fishing rod. I didn't have a fishing rod either. Girls didn't get to fish— didn't need to, Danny said, because the men would do the fishing. I gazed at the blue-black water and then up at the empty sky. That's what I feared most—slipping into something so empty—a sky of perfect truth or endless lies. If I floated away, would God catch me? If I slipped into some blue-black hole would God fish me out? I needed strong words and loving hands, I needed swaddling and sweet lullabies to remind me of who I am.

As I heard more and more stories, whether of ancestors or immediate relatives, I felt overwhelmed by those who set the standard I was expected to achieve. How would I distinguish myself while honoring such a stringent legacy? How would I catch enough sun to grow among these long-legged icons? Gradually I began to realize that the need for distinction and, conversely, for belonging, was not exclusive to me. All of us lived in the paradox of too much expectation crowded into too little space. We were tightly swaddled in ritual and doctrinally protected from ourselves; still we were charged to "remember who you are" while fenced off from the outside world. We had no way of learning how to be at once individuals and part of the greater whole. As we ventured into adulthood, we lost our way and became strangers to each other and to ourselves.

I find myself wishing for a shaman like my father to define the world and bring us back together, although I know about life's uncompromising demand that we find our own way. In those times when the predator stalks gentle things, I yearn for that crowded, sturdy nest that was home. And I'm stunned to realize that a few fragile words can carry me back to the place and the people I love.

Jewels in a Heavenly Crown

ONLY THE LAND COULD contain us, so many were we, thirty or more of my father's children and his seven wives living with him on the farm where I spent my early years in Salt Lake County, Utah. The majority of us were born at the compound, full of spunk despite the fundamentalist rigor that bound us to home and pulled us skyward. Lovely land it was, too, twenty acres in the shadow of Mount Olympus with ferocious Big Cottonwood Creek nearby, and willow-lined Spring Run rippling through it, plus a sleigh-riding hill, two ponds and an acre of leech-ridden, frog-happy swamp to ballast the asphalt roar of the highway. Near the road a large garden stretched beside the orchard, and along the lane a chainlink fence was twined with grapevines bearing fruit as bitter as Satan's lips. Animals milled here and there: a rust and white Brittany spaniel named King; a Hereford cow named Bossy and a Jersey cow named Red; a pair of stout mountain horses, several generations of chickens, ducks, geese; and various unnamed hogs (heeding Old Testament law, we sold the pork rather than eat it ourselves). Among the scrub oak and cotton-wood, you could spot raccoons, porcupines, and a deer or two wandering down from the foothills of the Wasatch Mountains. In the streams, you could find water snakes, water skaters, and a variety of trout. To my father and the mothers, home with its teeming life meant responsibility and a lot of work. To us children, it was paradise.

An oasis of rural life in the growing metropolis of Salt Lake City, our home was insulated by poplar and black walnut trees from the surrounding community. The two-story stucco farmhouse built in the 1880s during Utah's polygamous epoch had once housed all the mothers and their children. The architecture emphasized harmony and conviviality, and my father's wives met form with function, each wife accepting the assignment to keep up her bedroom and a portion of the household. With three or four women pregnant at the same time, the family grew in quantum leaps, and by the end of World War II we overflowed "the white house." The brethren in our religious group constructed the grey house where I was born, and soon after that we acquired a small cottage on adjoining property. Regardless of who lived where, all of the homes were open to us children at least some of the time.

I wandered through the compound unchallenged, for I was favored by my father, and I enjoyed benign attention from most of the mothers. But I spent a good deal of time in the grey house close to my own mother, about whom I felt protective. She was my father's fourth wife, a high-strung and sensitive woman who didn't stand up for herself. I knew that if she couldn't stand up for herself, neither could she stand up for me.

One June morning the year I turned five stands out in my memory. I had been watching my mother since breakfast, noting her pained expression, her full lips compressed as she gathered laundry, dumping it in the white wringer washer, swinging wide the bar with its bright red rollers that squeezed water and air from the clothes. She saw me hovering and cautioned me not to stick my hand in the wringer or it could swallow my arm and break it. I argued with her, recalling an instance when I'd gotten my arm caught and only been bruised, and she reminded me that I'd broken the wringer, and she'd had to wring the clothes by hand, and wasn't she already having a rough enough time of it today without me adding a problem to a day already full of them?

"Why are you having a rough time?" I asked, but she wouldn't give me a straight answer, just said that her back hurt.

"Why?" I asked, sensing that something unseen was happening.

"From lugging these clothes up and down the stairs."

I left then, telling her to take care of herself, that I'd be right back. I actually said those words, and I am now aware that this was not a normal way for a five-year-old to talk to her mother, but this was how it was with us, for there was something in my mother that was more childlike than I would ever be. I clumped down the front steps and went straight across the yard to get Aunt LaVerne.

Aunt LaVerne was one of the mothers who actually told me to go away if she didn't feel like having me around. But today she listened, big hands on broad hips, gold-flecked eyes flashing as I told her about my mother's aching back. "Just like Ella to suffer in silence!" she exclaimed. In her clipped way, she told me to wait while she took off her apron and exchanged her house-slippers for shoes. I liked Aunt LaVerne's bustling way and the fact that she could be counted on to speak her mind. The other mothers would gasp and mutter to each other behind their hands when Aunt LaVerne said something shocking. But even if Aunt LaVerne had been as mild as milk, her civil marriage to my father would have been resented by those wives married only in spiritual ceremonies.

When the plural wives and their children moved out of the white house into the grey house, Aunt LaVerne, as my father's legal wife, remained the unchallenged matron of the family, filling the front door with her imposing presence when people walked from the highway to take the census or sell vacuum cleaners. When patients came by, hoping to get the doctor's attention after office hours, she fielded their questions and decided whether or not to send them away. As I waited in Aunt LaVerne's kitchen that morning I could see the dining room, large enough to seat the whole family, and I was delighted with the imperious chiming of the grandfather clock she had inherited from her parents.

Aunt LaVerne reappeared and I followed her across the graveled yard. My mother had lugged a basket of wet clothes outside and was about to hang them on the line.

"Ella, stop!" Aunt LaVerne shouted. My mother stopped, alarmed. "You can't lift your arms so high, not as close as you are!" She went to my mother, took away the clothespin apron and lifted a heavy swath of sheet. "Just count your contractions. I'll get these hung in no time."

I could feel my mother's resentment, the feeling that often filled the air when Aunt LaVerne started bossing people around. LaVerne had rules for everyone, including how often people should go to the bathroom in order to avoid disease. She was the one who told my mother she mustn't kiss my father in front of the other wives. She was the one who told Aunt Sally to stop behaving like a teenager when "Daddy" was in the room. She told the mothers when they could open a new jar of strawberry jam and when they needed to clean their cupboards. At first, the young wives had tolerated her managerial ways, but they had grown weary of her interference. Still, they said nothing when Aunt LaVerne barked orders. My mother stood by and watched as LaVerne hung the laundry, then began to speak softly about the new, relaxed method of childbirth my father wanted her to try, recounting how he had said it was better to keep on moving right up to the time the baby was born. Muttering around the clothespin in her mouth, LaVerne wanted to know when was the last time my father gave birth to a baby. She went on hanging and pinning until all the wet sheets were swaying in the morning sunshine, fresh and sweet as sego lilies.

"How can I ever thank you enough?" my mother said. "I hate to impose."

"It's not imposing to get help when you need it," Aunt LaVerne said, although everyone knew *she* would rather die than ask for help. This was one of the games the mothers played, each one trying to out-martyr the other.

My mother went back inside, and I followed her down the stairs to the laundry room in the basement. She paused and leaned her head against the cement wall, then scooped steaming clothes from the washtub, passing them through the wringer into the cool blue rinse water. Then she put them through the wringer again, stopping to rub her back and close her eyes, sometimes leaning against the washing machine. "Shall I go get Aunt LaVerne?"

"No!" she spoke sharply. Then softer, "I'm all right."

She hung these whites on the clotheslines in the basement, long-legged, long-armed underwear made of soft silky material dangling ghostly in the dark room. These were her temple garments and she always hung them inside so that strangers would not see and make a mockery of God. Meanwhile a batch of towels was agitating in the washer. "I just hope I can get the towels and the boys' clothes done in time."

I wanted to ask in time for what but didn't. We went upstairs to the kitchen where she cleared away the breakfast dishes and began washing them in the sink. She stopped more frequently to close her eyes and count, and her breath came fast and hard. "I'll get Aunt LaVerne," I said.

"No. She's busy . . . and I don't like to feel obligated."

Back down the stairs, stuffing towels through the wringer, into the rinse water, and out the wringer into the basket. Then up the stairs into the blinding sun and the clothesline. She set the basket down and said, "I suppose I'll be in trouble with LaVerne if I hang these."

Just then Aunt Sally, my father's fifth wife, banged the door of the cottage that we called "the Jewkes place" and started across the graveled yard. She carried a bread pan covered with a white dishtowel, and she smiled broadly, round cheeks glowing. She called, "Hey, Ella, you enjoying those labor pains yet?" My mother gave an exasperated sigh. "Not as much as you are, Sally," she muttered under her breath.

Aunt Sally had grown tired of living in the same house as the other wives and their children. Even though she got along famously with "the twins," (my mother and Aunt Emma) she didn't like living in the basement of the grey house, always hearing our footsteps overhead. She didn't like living in the upstairs apartment of the white house either, with noise and odors wafting from downstairs. When the Jewkes family had realized that their new neighbors were polygamists, they put their cottage on the market, but what they were asking was well beyond our means. Aunt Sally went over there a few times with her pecan rolls and her rosy cheeks, and soon my father was buying that little cottage for half its value. Aunt Sally moved in, quick as a heartbeat, and set about making it hers. But she made it clear that her door was always open. She treated all us children as though we belonged to her—recipients of her love and her discipline alike. She would take a hairbrush to the seat of Danny's pants as quickly as she did to her own son's, yet she was just as quick to read a sad countenance and offer a comforting hug.

Aunt Sally regarded my mother carefully. "You shouldn't be working so hard today, Ella. You won't have any energy left for labor."

My mother went on flopping towels over the line, trying to keep her arms low as possible. Aunt Sally sighed. "Here, take this inside and get the bread in the tins. I'll pin these towels on the line."

By the time my mother had the bread-tins greased and the loaves rising, Aunt Sally had spooned up bowls of apricots and fixed a plate of bread and butter. We sat down for lunch, but my mother didn't eat. "You know how the contractions make you nauseous."

Aunt Sally nodded cheerfully. "I remember better than you do. It's only been four years since Alma was born. And it would be all right with me to wait another year or two. Five years seems an ideal distance between babies. I'm just glad we women get our say about it."

Aunt Sally was referring to "the Law of Chastity" that governs sexual relations in plural marriages. To the extent that it is practiced, the Law of Chastity keeps the fires of jealousy banked and also gives women some measure of choice about the use of their bodies. Since the purpose of the Principle of Plural Marriage is procreation, not recreation, the Law of Chastity proscribes sexual relations when a woman is nursing, pregnant, menopausal—and when she doesn't want to conceive.

My mother blushed as if Aunt Sally's implication was an accusation. "I can't say I was that deliberate. Rulon does say its up to us—and God—to decide when we're ready. But how can we know if enough time has gone by . . . or too much?"

"It's like making good bread, I guess," Aunt Sally said. "You have to feel your way."

I must have known by then that my mother was going to have another baby, but still she had not said so, and something in me did not want to believe that she would push me aside for a squalling stranger. I was her darling, the center of her universe, just as my father was the center of mine. When Aunt Sally returned to her own home, my mother went back to her laundry, gathering the clean, dry sheets off the line and making her bed with them. Then upstairs to the attic, to make my brothers' beds, then down to the main floor to make Aunt Emma's.

One reason my mother worked so hard, even on a day such as this, was that she shared the grey house with her twin sister, Emma. Aunt Emma had high standards and a strong conviction that a house of God was a house of order; according to Aunt Emma, there was a place for everything and everything should be in its place, and there was no reason we couldn't keep the grey house in perfect order, especially since it was brand-new when we moved in. After all, my mother was home all day, with nothing to do but keep up the house, while Aunt Emma worked as the nurse and receptionist in my father's office.

The grey house was sweet, with clean lines and the smell of new wood. My mother had the bedroom with rose-sprigged wallpaper, pink curtains frothing with each breeze that blew over the Great Salt Lake. Aunt Emma opted for the room across the hall with east sunlight and white wallpaper laced in tiny ferns, a cool green enclave by noon and a place I was forbidden to enter except upon Aunt Emma's invitation. "Now don't go into Aunt Emma's room," my mother frequently said.

"Why don't you have nice things, like Aunt Emma?" I once asked my mother.

"I have my children instead of nice things," my mother said.

I wondered, did this mean that we children were not nice things? Or that we were more desirable than other kinds of possessions? Such fundamental confusions created a marsh below the surface of our lives. Aunt Emma often lost her temper, wondering why we couldn't keep things clean or put away. But I sensed that her frustration came from my mother having so many children while Aunt Emma seemed to have stopped at two. As I grew older, I understood that in our way of life, a woman had to produce a big family or she felt pressured to prove her worth in other ways.

Around four o'clock, Aunt Sally came to get the bread from the oven and took one look at my mother. "Ella, you need to get into the bathtub and then into bed." She steered my mother toward the bathroom and spoke over her shoulder to me. "Tell Aunt LaVerne to call your father. Your mother's baby is coming!"

From behind the bathroom door, I could hear my mother shriek, a panicked, piercing cry. I ran across the yard and pounded on the door of the white house, where Aunt LaVerne went to the only phone on the compound, then took off her apron, replacing her house-slippers with sturdy brown shoes. Meantime, she sent me upstairs to Aunt Rose's apartment, saying I needed to stay out of the grey house for a while.

Aunt Rose, my father's second plural wife, and her ten children shared the five-room apartment in the upstairs of the white house with Aunt Melissa, my father's seventh wife. Aunt Melissa had two little children and was expecting another; she currently lived in the walled-off front porch, although it was freezing in the winter and stifling in the summer. For Aunt Melissa, living in this uncomfortable room was another opportunity to prove that righteousness and suffering are one and the same. As the youngest of my father's wives, previously the mothers' favorite babysitter, Aunt Melissa was always being moved from one household to another. I'd heard my mother and Aunt Emma whisper about how Melissa had asked to come into the family, even though my father hadn't said anything about taking another wife. Then her father, who was on the Priesthood Council, said that it was time Rulon completed "his Quorum" of wives to seal his standing as a patriarch.

The marriage was conducted hastily one night, just after Melissa had finished her homework. Her father, a lantern-jawed, stubborn man, whisked her away to my father's naturopathic office. Since Melissa had dressed for bed, she wore an old flannel nightgown and her hair was braided with rag curlers, but her father would not stop so she could change her clothes. "Do you want to get married, girl, or do you not?" he whispered. Her mother could not be told because the woman wouldn't keep a secret. Of all the sacrifices on her wedding day, the one thing Aunt Melissa couldn't forgive was that my father forgot to kiss her until she called after him; then he hurried back and gave her a perfunctory smack on the lips. She had confided to my mother once that she didn't believe "Daddy" loved her, and my mother had said, "Of course, he does, he loves each of us," but Aunt Melissa shook her head, smiling in her sad way. His relationship with her did seem more like that of a father to his daughter than husband to wife. As I came to the top stair, I saw Aunt Melissa through the big windows that separated the porch from the rest of the apartment, a dark ringlet falling across a pink cheek, smiling in her familiar pained way as she bent over her embroidery.

I went looking for Aunt Rose and at first I couldn't find her, which seemed strange since her rooms were nearly bare of furnishings. Her many children ate meals at the kitchen counter, slept on mattresses tossed on the floor, and spent most of their time outside. The apartment had the look of recent abandonment, as of a ghost town. It gave me the same haunted feeling I got from Aunt Rose's eyes when she turned from the living-room window, where she merged with the afternoon light.

Rose had been slated to marry my father first, which would have given her "the right of Sarah" to reject or choose any subsequent wives, and a chance at being the legal wife, married to Rulon in a civil ceremony. But LaVerne met my father, expressed her interest in him, and preempted Rose by three days. My father had talked the matter over with Joseph Musser, who was his priesthood leader, and the two decided that LaVerne should marry Rulon first. As a mature woman and a legal secretary with considerable experience in the world, LaVerne would be better prepared to meet the public as the doctor's wife than would Rose who was barely fifteen, reared and sparsely educated in the dusty fundamentalist village of Short Creek, Arizona. Brother Musser charged LaVerne with responsibility "to give Rulon all the wives he has coming to him," a duty she assumed like her life depended on it. LaVerne legally married my father and thereafter went out on his arm to his professional meetings and to other public events, even though, as time went on, he was also married to Rose and Emma and to my mother, Ella. LaVerne's three sons now enjoyed the advantage of being legitimate; unlike the rest of us, they didn't need to wonder about their place in the family.

"My mother's going to have a baby," I told Aunt Rose. She smiled and motioned me to sit beside her on the bare wood of the window seat. She was a small, squat woman; even her face seemed pushed-down, as though a heavy hand had weighed there. She let me lean against her and we sat that way for awhile, not speaking. I drifted with her in a netherworld peculiar to Aunt Rose, not quite present, not quite gone.

"Maybe you won't feel so special if you're not the baby?" She asked the question kindly. "I know how that is. Your mother will understand, too. She knows how it feels to be looked down on."

"Who? Who looks down?"

"Well, Emma, for one."

Aunt Rose's words startled me. Everyone felt beholden to Aunt Emma because she ran my father's doctor's office, went to work every day, and roused herself in the middle of the night to attend baby cases with him.

Aunt Emma, my mother's twin, was my father's third plural wife and had married a year ahead of my mother, even though she was younger by eight minutes. Aunt Emma frequently pointed out that she married him before my mother did, and my mother privately wondered why things had gone contrary to scripture. Jacob in the Old Testament had to marry Leah, the older sister first, even though it was the younger, Rachel, he wanted. I wanted to believe that my father, like Jacob, had to marry the stern, hardworking sister first so that he could have the musical, laughing one, the one he really wanted.

As if summoned by my thoughts, the Hudson bearing my father and Aunt Emma rattled down the lane. I ran from Aunt Rose's apartment, stumbled down the steps, and threw myself into my father's arms. He nuzzled me quickly, smelling of fresh air and a hint of disinfectant soap. His brilliant blue eyes met mine as he hugged me, then set me down. He moved fast, long lean legs crossing the yard to the grey house in a few strides.

I followed, slipping in the back door, and sat at the kitchen table, waiting. Soon the air was filled with the sound of rusty hinges opening and closing. Then Aunt Emma came out of my mother's room carrying the noise—my baby brother, a red-faced, skinny creature who seemed outraged to be born. My father, right behind her, took the baby and plunked him down in front of me on the table. He pulled back the blankets. The baby was bloody and white-filmed, and he shuddered pathetically. My father seized his right foot, which crooked out at a right angle, and twisted it firmly until the little foot pointed forward. The baby screamed. My father worked with the foot a little longer and we heard a tiny pop, like a soap bubble bursting, and the baby stopped crying. My father wrapped him, gave him back to Aunt Emma, then hurried back to the bedroom and my mother.

Even though it was a summer evening, Aunt Emma had lit the oven and opened its door to make the room warm for the baby. Now she took him to the sink, her mouth soft, her eyes gentle in spite of the baby's cries, her fingers slow and deliberate as she dipped a washcloth in the warm water and wiped away the white down. She massaged olive oil into his many creases, then wrapped the blue-green stub of the cord with a white flannel binder. She diapered him and dressed him in a white nightgown that covered his hands and tied at his feet. Then she swaddled him tightly in a blue flannel receiving blanket and brought him to me. It hadn't occurred to me that Aunt Emma would let me hold him, but she did. I remember that we exchanged a look and an understanding passed between me and Aunt Emma, who had never liked me. Something about having to share a loved one.

I was outdoors most of that prolonged summer until the days melded into autumn. My little brother, Thomas, seemed to grow inches overnight, perhaps because I saw so little of him. My mother kept him to herself, and when I saw her she was distracted or tearful, as though the baby took all her joy. I felt like an intruder on their sad communion and gave up being my mother's companion to find comfort in the garden, the orchard, the stream running through the field beyond our house.

"Come inside!" That summer the mothers always had to call us indoors to eat, to bathe, to pray. We were drinking in nature, drinking it as though this was our last hour in Eden. And the mothers worked hard to reclaim us from the wild swamps and streams and meadows, trying to keep us civilized within our insular world. "Cleanliness is next to godliness," they said as they scrubbed our ears and elbows. For every religious precept cut by the men, a gem of dutiful homemaking was polished by the women. A few months after my baby brother was born, I noticed that it was always Aunt Emma who called us to come home. She had taken over many of my mother's homemaking duties.

Home, where we were conceived and born and bathed and fed and dressed and tucked in and prayed over, had more to do with shaping us than our religious beliefs. Most of the mothers kept the upper hand, even with the male children in our patriarchal society. The one predictability in a plural wife's day was the ongoing responsibility of children and home: her husband would come and go as would her feelings of being important or treasured, but every morning brought its maternal duties and rewards: prayers, breakfast, dishes, kisses good-bye. These carried resonant meaning, and in the absence of radial power, daily tasks such as ironing or cooking took on overweening significance for the women, especially if they pertained to my father.

Each wife had her night scheduled in my father's appointment book as the last notation of his busy day so that he'd know where he was headed when he left the office. (How convenient to have a wife for each night of the week!) Still, one never knew where he might end up spending the night, when birthdays or anniversaries came up and special dispensations were requested. He might be headed to my mother's and Aunt Emma's for the evening until Aunt LaVerne would stop him in the yard and remind him about the Naturopathic Physicians Association meeting that night, or Aunt Sally might coax him to come to dinner because her sister was in town. My mother and Aunt Emma, whose high standards escalated the night my father came to dinner, blinked tears and choked back resentful remarks when the order of things was interrupted.

The women in my father's household rarely quarreled—the emphasis being on harmony—but I still remember the upset about my father's new white shirt. He'd spent the night with Aunt Sally, and rose to milk the cows before dawn. After he'd poured the milk into pans so that the cream could rise, he returned to Aunt Sally's to bathe and dress for work. But his new white shirt—one Aunt Sally had bought him with her allowance—had mysteriously disappeared. A search ensued in the most likely place, Aunt LaVerne's bedroom, since she generally assumed that anything that belonged to Rulon belonged to her. Aunt LaVerne endured the search with dignity. Aunt Sally then checked the hook on the back of Aunt Rose's door since she didn't have a closet and everyone knew she didn't like to iron. My mother and Aunt Emma got grilled about the white shirt as well, before one that was suspiciously similar was found in Adah's closet. Aunt Adah was a nearsighted, waspish woman, my father's sixth plural wife born to aristocrats of polygamy who had lived the Principle, passing it down from father to son since the early days of the church. Aunt Adah's people prided themselves on being more righteous than any other family, and she was outraged at the implication that she would stoop to steal.

"Stranger things have happened," Aunt Sally said, happy to have found the shirt. To soften the situation, she reminded Adah of the time when Rulon had given in to so many requests and birthday invitations that the schedule was hopelessly tangled. That night, he went from one house to another, but each of the women had other plans, and no one invited him in. One by one his wives had kissed him good night and urged him on his way. He spent the night at his office, sleeping on the examination table. Though Aunt Sally hooted with laughter, remembering the incident, Aunt Adah didn't smile.

"If the truth were known, I quite enjoy it when he's away. I like having my time to myself."

"The truth *is* known, Adah," Aunt Sally said. "But is it that you like being by yourself, or that you'd rather be with your brother and his wives? I notice they come for dinner every time Rulon spends the night with someone else."

Everyone knew that Aunt Adah's family thought they were better than any of us. They always seemed to be competing with the Allreds. Some suspected that Adah thought more highly of her brother than she did of our father. Still, Sally knew they were supposed to "love one another" and she would do her best even though the relationship with Adah was strained.

Looking back, it seems curious to me that no one thought to hold

my father responsible for the shirt "fiasco" and other incidents like it.
Undoubtedly, on his night with Aunt Adah, he had taken off his shirt
and put on a clean one in the morning without thinking to return the
new shirt to Sally. After all, they were *his* shirts, weren't they? Mostly,
he ignored the furor his absentminded congeniality caused. While he
was torn by the jealousies of his wives whenever they broke the
smooth surface of daily life, I think he secretly liked the hubbub of
women fighting over him, just as he enjoyed the drama of childbirth.
Whenever such challenges arose, my father's eyes would sparkle and
he'd rub his hands together swiveling his head this way and that, his
profile lean and sharp as an eagle's. But for the women, such battles
were more than theater. They were gut-wrenching wars of body,
mind, and spirit.

～

A few months after my baby brother was born, my mother failed to go
to Sunday school. At one time, we had met in the white house parlor,
but now spies were watching our house too closely, so we traveled to
Midvale, on the outskirts of Salt Lake City, where two of my father's
younger brothers, Anthus and Lawrence, lived. My mother said she
was too tired for the drive across town where she'd have to sit for long
hours in Uncle Anthus's garage. It was unusual for her to skip religious
devotion, but she was too tired, she said.

It was strange to be in Sunday school without my mother, odd not
to see her sitting at the piano playing a perfect prelude, to see instead
Aunt LaVerne's bristly hair and broad back, her ample bottom rocking
the piano bench as she raced through a hymn. Aunt LaVerne prided
herself on being able to do everything—a sort of renaissance woman.
She knew how to play the piano (although not with my mother's virtu-
oso touch), she knew how to take shorthand (although not with the
swift accuracy of Aunt Adah), and she knew how to cook (but always
fell short of Aunt Sally's culinary magic). Once she'd tried to horn in
on Aunt Emma's territory, ordering uniforms and setting one day a

week for herself in my father's office, but Aunt Emma sent the uniforms back before Aunt LaVerne could wear them.

Now on this Sunday morning, Aunt Emma had marched me forward to the front row facing my father and the other members of the Priesthood Council. Aunt Emma had taken over for my mother. Earlier she braided my hair so tightly my eyes slanted, then pulled over my head a peach organdy dress that she had finished because my mother had suddenly lost the patience to sew. She sat me on one of the little chairs in front.

"Be good," she ordered, and went to sit with the other wives. "Rulon's girls" as people called them, sat in the center section of chairs, wiping their children's noses and straightening their sashes, shushing and bussing in a flurry to get everything in order before the meeting began. My father kissed each of his wives, exchanging a word or two, then went forward to sit on the priesthood bench facing the congregation. The faint hum of the crowd stopped, heads bowed, and the prelude rushed to a conclusion. My father stood.

"Brothers and sisters," he began as he always did. The greeting was quite literal, for almost everyone in the group was related, not simply through our lineage to Adam, but through blood or marriage. My father smiled, and a light shone from him that seemed to embrace everyone in the room. He talked about how much he loved the people, about how blessed he was to share his life with them, and for that moment we were one people connected to each other through him.

"We ask for your prayers and fasting for dear Ella. We miss her lovely piano music, but she is suffering with her nerves." A murmured assent from the congregation. Then he announced the page of the opening hymn.

"Catch the sunshine though it flickers through a dark and dismal cloud," we sang, as if my mother could hear us over the miles. We had a prayer and then it was time to take the sacrament, the pieces of coarse wheat bread on a chipped plate, the Mason jar of sacramental water, a few crumbs floating on its surface. Afterward, my father invited people to bear their testimonies, a time when women as well as men could speak. One woman stood immediately and held forth about the Principle of Plural Marriage. Like many of the women in the group, she wore no makeup and her hair and dress seemed to come from the previous century. "We all have faults," she said. "God has given us the Principle to refine ourselves so that we might return to His presence." She sighed deeply. "We must forgive the flaws in others and ask for forgiveness for our own. Thus we may enjoy the blessings of eternal marriage—our lives going on and on together." Then she was sitting down and Aunt Sally was standing, smiling and crying at the same time, talking about her father and mother and her sisters who could not understand why she would get mixed up with these polygamists. "I pray that the Lord has a plan to bring us all together." She paused, her lips trembling. "If families are eternal, that means everybody's family. Otherwise there is no happiness, and no heaven."

As if this spark had lit everyone's candle of filial loyalty, Aunt Adah stood, her mouth compressed tight as the little black bun that perched at the crown of her head. Aunt Adah's brother was a leader in another fundamentalist sect. It had been formed from the original fundamentalist gathering after the 1890 Manifesto abolished polygamy, when die-hard polygamous patriarchs banded together, unified by their belief in plural marriage as well as their hardships. Now that their persecutors had retreated, the group had divided. Aunt Adah's mouth pinched tight. "I might remind you that the men of the Short Creek group were here before most of the people in this room." She spoke directly to my father and the brethren on the priesthood bench: "You received your callings and authority through the same lines. If they are wrong, so are the brethren here." Aunt Adah said she knew the Gospel was true, in the name of Jesus Christ, Amen. People were murmuring to each other, their faces very flushed or very white, and the air in the room was turgid, as though something was about to die or be born.

My father's brother Uncle Lawrence stood, his shoulders bent from arthritis, though he was younger than my father. He said in his humble way that if we were to receive celestial blessings, we must behave in celestial ways. Before anyone else could speak, my father stood and said it was time we adjourned for Sunday school classes.

The children my age filed from the garage into Uncle Anthus's house where we occupied a bedroom crowded with small metal chairs. When the scraping, scuffling, and twitching had stopped, Aunt Emma closed the door. She looked so much like my mother, with her chestnut chignon, her hazel eyes, and wide smile. But she was so different in temperament.

"Today we are going to learn a song. Songs are nice, but they can also teach us lessons. The song we are going to learn today teaches us not to say things to hurt each other."

> *Angry words, oh let them never*
> *From the tongue unbridled slip*
> *Let the heart's best impulse ever*
> *Check them ere they soil the lip.*

I was still thinking about the earlier meeting, where Aunt Adah and everyone else got angry. I already knew a little about the quarrel over who was in charge of the fundamentalist group—my father or Aunt Adah's brother. Everyone seemed angry about it except my father, and he didn't seem to know what they were talking about. Aunt Emma, who was telling us not to speak angry words, sometimes shouted "Pigs!" or "Filthy animals!" at us. I hadn't figured out what made Aunt Emma so angry, and at the time I had no frame of reference, no indication that it wasn't normal to be as obsessively organized as Aunt Emma was, everyone sitting in the same place at the dinner table, her insistence that the wash be done on Monday, the ironing on Tuesday, the floors on Wednesday, the grocery shopping on Thursday, and so on. We were always being cautioned, in the scriptures and from the pulpit, not to speak in anger, yet Aunt Emma's anger seemed to make her more powerful. Some of the other mothers—Aunt LaVerne, Aunt Adah, even jolly Aunt Sally—got angry from time to time, and they, too, seemed to grow stronger, while my mother, who never got angry, was sick. It made me think that her nervous breakdown wasn't my baby brother's fault.

~

Perhaps this Sunday school lesson provoked me to study my father's wives, observing how they related to each other and noticing when they gained or lost energy. I wanted to know what made them do what they did, and what they got from their behavior. I paid close attention to little stories, tidbits of information, photographs and knickknacks, heirlooms and furnishings. Despite some residual shame, I sifted through what I knew and spied for more information, like an investigator at the scene of a crime. Over time, I learned how each of the mothers came to be in my father's family, but my primary interest was my mother and Aunt Emma.

My mother and her twin had grown up in the official Church of Jesus Christ of Latter-day Saints, their parents joined in a loving monogamous marriage marred by financial loss and the declining health of my grandfather. When the twins were twelve, their family had moved to Hollywood, California, hoping that the sea air would relieve their father's congestive heart and tubercular lungs. In 1935, when they were sixteen and students at Hollywood High, my father was the featured speaker at a "cottage meeting" where a handful of Church members gathered to discuss religious doctrines. The twins attended at the request of their father, who wanted them to know "the fullness of the Gospel"—which, the handsome speaker proclaimed, included plural marriage. The young doctor was thin and sad, speaking of the price he'd had to pay for his testimony of the Principle. My father was always charismatic, and at thirty years old, he must have seemed larger than life to the young women as he declared his belief in the Principle.

My mother was shy and she already had a suitor who was pressing her to marry him as soon as she finished high school. She was so unassuming that she did not think of the young doctor as being available to her, anymore than she would entertain such thoughts about movie idols Nelson Eddy or Ramon Navarro. As the twins walked down Sunset Boulevard and past Hollywood High School, a yearning to talk about the speaker waxed with the ascending moon.

"He was so handsome . . . and so tall!" my mother exclaimed, just as she would when telling me the story twenty years later. She murmured her sympathy for the young doctor.

Emma turned and gave her a sharp look. "What if Curtis heard you talking like that! He'd be heartbroken." After letting the rebuke sink in, Emma added, "You know, the doctor's married."

"Yes," my mother bowed her head. And a thought, "but he believes in plural marriage!" riffled the placid surface of my mother's mind, but she said nothing. Being agreeable was very important to my mother.

"He's wonderful. The most wonderful man I've ever met," Aunt Emma said fervently.

"Yes," my mother nodded. "He's wonderful."

The next night, Emma fussed at Ella for staying out too late too many nights in a row. It was a role they had played since they were six and Ella had been confined to bed with rheumatic fever, Emma always the strong one, and Ella the one who was fragile. Emma went to the next cottage meeting alone while my mother stayed home, nursing her health.

My father doted on both young women, but in the brotherly way that made him everybody's friend. My mother, who had a horror of imposing, kept her distance even after the family followed the young doctor's advice and moved from Hollywood to northern Arizona, joining other fundamentalists in the tin-roof settlement where dust was always blowing and where children played in the Short Creek instead of going to school.

On Christmas day in 1935, my grandfather's heart acted up, and my father made a house call at the family shack. Only a thin drape separated the sick room from the living quarters, and the twins and their mother could hear the low murmur of male voices. While my father attended to my grandfather, he asked to marry "one of your twins." He knew that my grandfather's heart was failing, and that the older man wanted to complete his duties as a father before he left this life, so Rulon probably felt confident of the outcome. Still, it must have been daunting for him, already married to LaVerne and Rose, to be asking for another woman's hand in marriage and more daunting yet to hear my grandfather's reply: "If you take one, you have to take them both." Whether stunned or truly delighted, my father answered without skipping a beat: "That suits me just fine!"

My grandfather coughed and clutched at his congested heart. "Which one first?" he asked.

And my father said, "The one who sits by LaVerne in the choir." When the doctor left, Emma, who sang alto, was called to her father's side, and asked if she was prepared for marriage. Behind the curtain, my mother bowed her head, and a voice shouted in her mind, "But I love him!" A few days later, during choir practice, LaVerne invited Emma into the doctor's family. Some months later, around the time he married Emma, my father formally asked my mother to marry him. He chose the shelter of a cornfield south of Short Creek, taking her by the hand and leading her deep into the rows. He kissed her once before proposing. She was both disturbed and delighted and before she could answer, he was exulting, deciding that they would marry as soon as he established his naturopathic practice in Salt Lake City.

My grandfather died before my father and mother could marry, and the remnant of my mother's family moved to St. George, Utah, where my mother supported her widowed mother and her younger brother by waitressing. This she did until the day my father came to take her on their only date, to a local theater. The next day, they were wed in a place known as the "McClain House." By that time, my father had been married to Emma for nine months, to Rose for twenty-two months, and to LaVerne for twenty-two months and three days.

My mother made up for being married after Aunt Emma by having children. Given her thoroughbred temperament, her health and her musical gifts suffered under the demands of motherhood combined with Aunt Emma's exacting standards. What began as simple "baby blues" turned into a "nervous breakdown" that lasted seven years. It often took my mother away from me to my father's office where two or three times a week she received mysterious treatments: sessions under the black mitts of a diathermal machine, or naked in a green steam tent or sweating beneath an infrared lamp.

In our polygamist world, a woman's purpose was to "raise up a righteous seed unto the Lord," with emphasis placed on quantity even more than quality. The more righteous seeds raised up, the better. Children became the estimate of a woman's worth and her ticket to fulfillment. And since nothing more important than the birth of a child could happen on the compound, each of my father's wives rose to participate in the occasion. You could feel the gathering of expectancy every time a birth was imminent, the crackle and pop of something momentous, as in the air before a thunderstorm. Paradoxically, I also associated "birth energy" with the swell of change in the air that preceded various disasters in our lives, probably because of my mother's postpartum depression.

Aunt Emma's heartache had also been Aunt LaVerne's, who prayed for children of her own yet remained childless for many years. As she waited for motherhood, Aunt LaVerne turned her vast energies to organizing my father's household and the lives of each member of his family. She earned the nickname "Boss Two" but some people suspected that she, and not my father, was "Boss One." She took an avid interest in rearing the children of her sister-wives, sometimes taking them in and teaching them skills she thought important to successful living. For twelve years she tried to be content with managing other people's lives, always praying that she would become "a mother in Israel." By the time she gave birth to her sons, she was raising four of Aunt Rose's daughters.

"Rose can't take care of them and she can't stop having them," Aunt LaVerne would explain when people asked why Rose's daughters lived with LaVerne. She took care of Aunt Rose's girls the way she did everything—enthusiastically. She made them take music lessons and do their homework and clean house. She made them wash their hair and curl it. She made them learn to cook and sew. Aunt Rose mourned the loss of her daughters, and the girls didn't seem too happy either, but strangely, my father supported the arrangement. When Aunt LaVerne wanted something, everyone complied.

One afternoon when my father and Aunt Emma were attending a baby case, Aunt LaVerne came to watch over my mother and ordered her to get back into bed, speaking to her like she was one of Aunt Rose's daughters. "Stop worrying, Ella. Have a little faith."

My mother's voice shimmered. "I try to have faith." Her voice broke with unshed tears. She cried often these days, covering her face at the breakfast table, sprinkling tears on the shirts she ironed for a dollar a basket, weeping into the baby's bathwater. I had once burst into tears, too, not knowing what else to do, and after that she crept into the linen closet, where she wept into the clean sheets and towels.

My mother cleared her throat and spoke to Aunt LaVerne with a trace of her former dignity. "I just wish I'd get well, that's all. In fact, I'm starting to feel better right now. I must get up and fix dinner while Emma is on this baby case." Through the door I watched her sit up and swing her feet to the floor.

Aunt LaVerne pushed her back onto the pillows. "Ella, do what you're told. We have enough to do without you falling apart."

My mother smiled sadly to herself. She and Aunt LaVerne spoke wistfully about the woman in the group who would soon be a new mother. "I wonder how long it will last for her, the feeling of being special? It doesn't seem to last long enough."

Aunt LaVerne shook her head. "In this way of life you can't be special all the time, Ella. You should know that."

～

Perhaps my own need to be special made me ill-at-ease around my family. As I learned to identify my feelings, I realized that I scarcely knew what I wanted. Mainly I knew what I didn't want: I didn't want the emotional pain of my mother, with its giddy highs and devastating depressions. Neither did I want the peculiar need to control others that I saw in Aunt Emma, bossing my mother in the name of love. But what kind of woman would I be instead? Certainly I did not want to be like Aunt Rose, who doubted everything about herself, who could not summon enough presence to hold onto her children or teach them how to live. Nor did I want to be like Aunt LaVerne, needing to be in charge all the time. I did not want to be like them, the persecuted and the persecutor.

I admired rosy-cheeked, sharp-eyed Aunt Sally who said, "Happiness is a do-it-yourself project." But I didn't want to lose one family to gain another, as she had. Neither did I want to be like Aunt Adah who eventually left us for the other group, taking her children (who were some of my favorite playmates as well as my brothers and sisters). I also didn't want to be like Aunt Melissa who saw the Devil at every turn. When she was only fifteen, she engineered the marriage to my father, perhaps thinking that she would be safe in the household of the group's spiritual leader; then she spent the rest of her days wondering if he really loved her.

I once asked my father which of his wives he loved the most. He grinned and said, "Each of my wives is a queen, a jewel in my heavenly crown." I wondered aloud how they could be at once jewels in his crown and queens with crowns of their own. "You children are *their* jewels. And they love each of you as I love each of my wives." Then, searching my eyes, he said, "You must never give up your quest for queenhood, darling. It is your birthright and your destiny." I suspect he meant I should become one of many wives, content to have power through my husband's priesthood authority. But even when I was young, I sensed that "queenhood" could be a hollow title, the booby prize in the great and passionate tableau of life.

Vase with Flowers

WITH SEVEN MOTHERS, I had seven sets of choices about how to be a woman. Perhaps each of his wives was, as my father said, a queen in her own right, but I was reluctant to adopt Aunt LaVerne's brusque way of directing people, Aunt Adah's paucity of spirit, or Aunt Emma's desperate need to control. I could see homilies and good humor in Aunt Sally, but nothing that would bear the weight of big decisions. My own mother avoided making choices altogether, and struggled to maintain her point of view by keeping her opinions covert, often contradicting what she said in public with private observations. Aunt Rose and Aunt Melissa exercised little power, usually in opposition, standing against rather than for something.

So I did not want the queenly examples of my seven mothers to shape my character, being more inclined to identify with my father. But one woman, my father's mother, Grandmother Evelyn, stood apart from the others in the family and I was strongly attracted to her. What was it in her that I admired? As a child I did not have the words for it, but I felt an openmouthed yearning to know her better. She had a recipe for survival that I craved—a mix of power and wisdom. She alone could teach me how to be a woman in a manner that reflected my father. She alone seemed to have the means of commanding respect for womanhood in a patriarchal culture.

Before I was born, Grandmother Evelyn had moved to our compound, installing herself in the log cabin we called "the well-house." The mechanism that pumped water from the artesian well was hidden beneath the pine slabs and you could hear the gears whirring and groaning, an ancient presence that made me feel that those settlers who first lived on the farm were speaking to us through the floorboards.

Grandmother Evelyn was a high-minded woman who drummed her fingers on the tabletop while waiting for people to play their cards at pinochle—a game where the only way to beat double royal families is to shoot the moon. Impatient with people who weren't quick enough to keep up with her, Grandmother revealed her frustration by demanding responsiveness from life itself. She harped at the ducks' slow waddle across the yard and she prodded the radish sprouts to hurry. The sound of her cane rapping against my mother's bedroom window summoned us to come do her bidding and do it immediately. She inspired urgency and respect in everyone, including my father, who was her oldest living son.

Grandmother would come to the door of her cottage when we children sailed past on the way to the swings, calling after us to pipe down. I might have been the only one to notice, since I didn't always play with the other children. I remember a moment of watching her watching the children play on the swings, her tall body steady and straight as a pine overlooking the confusion of our compound. Unlike the soft roundness of my mother's mother, Grandmother Evelyn made right angles with the earth, her prim blouse and black skirt hanging neatly on her thin frame. Her roving gaze took me in, and I raised my hand in a timid wave.

It was a moment of hunger, of longing to know her better. I could not have articulated the longing then, but I sensed that she had secrets and knew things about life I needed to know. I wondered how she came by the courage to skip religious meetings. How did she dare to openly contradict my father? How did she keep living so many years after her own husband, my Grandfather Harvey, had died? She knew hidden truths about the way we lived, knew things about my father as a boy, knew about being a woman of strength in the presence of men who were patriarchs and leaders. Her challenges were my challenges. I wanted her to take me in, hold me, teach me—especially in the days after my mother got sick. I stood at the edge of the garden wishing that Grandmother would wave in return. How my heart pounded when she called me over! I had picked and eaten a ripe tomato, heavy and warm from the sun, and I licked the juice from my hands, trying to conceal the evidence of my theft.

"Don't stand there with your fingers in your mouth, child. Come in."

I peered into the cool interior of the cottage. There were none of the knickknacks or doilies other grandmothers seem to collect. Only the lace curtains and a black handmade vase painted with three flowers attested to her feminine side. A strange absence of warm smells gave the air a feel of clean bedsheets.

"Sit down. I will make us some Brigham tea." She indicated a teakettle on the stove.

"Mama told me never to drink tea."

"Oh, she did? And why not?"

We both knew it was part of the religion, and I wanted to defend my mother. "It's against the Word of Wisdom; she said tea will make me sick."

"Nonsense. The Word of Wisdom warns against black tea—and coffee, of course, as well as tobacco and alcohol. But herbal teas can do you good." Grandmother moved slowly but steadily as she unhooked plain white cups and poured the steaming yellow-green tea. She held the handle until all my fingers had circled the cup, then sat in her black rocking chair and watched as I sipped a liquid that tasted like the meadow.

"You're a strange one, aren't you?"

I didn't know how to answer.

"Always watching," she said.

She sat down and rocked, her eyes needling me. Finally I blurted out the only question I could think of. "Why don't you like little kids?"

She nodded and after a time she spoke. "I was your grandfather's second wife. His plural wife." She pointed at the buffet, where a tiny oval picture of a dark-haired, dark-eyed woman sat beside a large portrait of Grandfather Harvey. "That's Charlotte, his first wife—my sister-wife. She had eleven children, six boys and five girls. By the time he married me, Charlotte was worn out from having babies. But we were building up God's kingdom."

The rocking chair ground against the wood floor. "I spent my honeymoon tending her children so that she wouldn't hate me, but she was bitter anyway. Then I lost my first baby to pneumonia—a terrible way to lose a child. But any way you lose a child is terrible. It breaks a mother's heart." She stared at the floor. "That's one thing Charlotte and I had in common."

She explained that two of Charlotte's children—the oldest and the youngest—had died about the time she, Evelyn, came into the family. Later, Charlotte had died giving birth to twins and then the twins had died too. "So much heartache for all of us, especially Harvey," Grandmother said. At the age of twenty-four, Grandmother Evelyn had taken on the responsibility of raising all the children. "I mothered the seven of hers that survived, and nine of my own—sixteen children in all. I did it gladly. But I didn't count on . . . loving Charlotte's children so much. Little Rhea, Charlotte's daughter who was a few months younger than your dad—I nursed her because Charlotte didn't have enough milk. She was like my own." Sudden tears washed her sunken cheeks. "I didn't think it would hurt so much to lose them. Charlotte's boys—they turned against me. I don't know why. Maybe my tongue was too sharp. Or maybe they thought that loving me was disloyal to their own mother. But they left as soon as they were old enough. The older girls too. They took little Rhea with them, took her away from me."

She explained, with some pride, that Rhea was the only one of Charlotte's daughters to live the Principle of Plural Marriage. "Most of mine live this way. And why shouldn't they? They owe their lives to it."

She rocked for the longest time, her eyes flashing blue fire. "You children do not know—you do not appreciate—the price we paid to live the Principle." She seemed to be waiting for me to speak. "It isn't just what you believe," she said softly. "It's how you live."

A glimmer of understanding grew brighter and I felt as if a cord of light had been strung between us. The silence deepened. I pointed at the vase painted with pale flowers.

"That's pretty, Grandmother."

"Yes." She stepped to the buffet and picked it up, caressing its smooth glaze. "Your great-great grandmother made it. She was quite the artist, they say. Her daughter, your great-grandmother brought it across the ocean to Utah. How it survived when so much else was lost, I don't know." Slowly she turned the vase in her hands. "Lilies," she said. "'They toil not, they spin not; and yet I say unto you, that Solomon in all his glory was not arrayed like one of these.'" She held out the vase so I could run my hands over the smooth mound of its base. I peered beyond the lip of red earth into the slender throat. Grandmother set the vase on the buffet. "They say she loved to make things from the clay."

She sat down and looked at me. "You like the vase?" I nodded. "You'll inherit it someday." She closed her eyes as if she'd lost all desire to speak. After awhile she murmured, "Go play, child."

～

Grandmother Evelyn's health failed that year, but she insisted on being at home in her little log house. Every day she dressed in her black skirt and white blouse, combing her beautiful silver hair in an upsweep. She played pinochle in her impatient way, and rapped on my mother's window with the same urgency. She came to the white house for home evening, and at Sunday dinner she still presided at one end of the long dining table, my father at the other, as forty or more of us sat quietly waiting for our plates to be filled.

Grandmother Evelyn spoke to all of us, adults and children, about international matters as though to remind us of our responsibility to know what was going on in the wicked world. It was from Grandmother that I first heard about the Holocaust. My mother was visiting her that day, and Grandmother Evelyn had made herbal tea—"for your nerves" she told my mother.

I watched as my mother drank every drop.

"Gas chambers," my mother whispered.

Grandmother Evelyn nodded. "If people doubt that we are living in the Last Days, they should look at Hitler. An abomination. Makes Pancho Villa look like a saint."

"The Nazis starved them right down to the bones. And then, when they couldn't work anymore they shaved their heads and told them they would be deloused in the showers." My mother's voice caught. "I haven't been able to eat or think straight since I saw the pictures."

Grandmother said, "Stop reading the papers, Ella. You're in no condition to dwell on these things."

"We've suffered some, but we don't know true persecution. They marched them into gas chambers, then they put the bodies in ovens, Mother Evelyn! Stacks and stacks of them!" My mother began to weep in earnest, shaking her head. "I can't believe that human beings would do such things to one another. Or that . . . that a kind Heavenly Father would allow . . ."

Grandmother Evelyn stroked my mother's bowed head. "Human beings will do anything they can conceive of, my dear. And God gave us free agency. He won't stop us from using it for evil. You must not participate in the horror by getting discouraged, Ella." Grandmother's voice was firm. "You must be strong for the children's sake, if not your own."

My mother stopped crying and looked over at me. "I forgot . . . little pitchers have big ears." Her face flushed. "I'm . . . I don't know what got into me. . . ."

"She can handle the truth. It's the lying she has a hard time with. Isn't that right?" Grandmother touched my cheek with a long finger. She looked at my mother. "You think she hasn't seen the papers? You think she hasn't seen people be cruel? You should talk with her."

My relationship with my mother shifted that day. As we walked home, she asked me what I knew about what happened in Germany. I told her that I had seen the pictures in newspapers and magazines, but that I hadn't known why people looked like walking skeletons. I had seen the pictures of the war, pieces of arms and legs, smoking heaps of rubble, the mushroom cloud.

After that conversation my mother treated me with a new respect that became its own kind of burden. Her voice was more resonant when she spoke to me, and more often than not, she told me the truth. She began to ask me what I thought about things, and she often honored my opinions over her own. Later in life, she would heed my suggestions that she shave her legs, learn to drive, and keep the deed to her house, rather than leaving it with the priesthood council.

~

Just as I began to know Grandmother Evelyn, she went to the hospital. The last time my father drove to visit her, I rode in the cavernous back seat of the maroon and grey Hudson along with brothers and sisters near my age, hoping to get a glimpse of her. We waited in the car while he rushed inside to give her a priesthood blessing. I knew he would anoint her head with consecrated oil and he would ask for healing. If God wanted her healed, she would be healed; if it was her time, we would let her go.

"See over there." One of my sisters pointed to an unlighted window in the upper story of the hospital. "They keep crazy people locked up in there. So they won't hurt anyone."

"Is Grandmother in there?" Suddenly I was terrified. "Is she crazy?"

My sister shrugged. When my father returned to the car, he sat with his hands on the steering wheel, not moving. He seemed sad and troubled. I leaned forward and whispered, "Is Grandmother crazy?"

He turned and stared at me. "Of course not!"

Grandmother died the next morning. Her kidneys had failed. My mother explained that kidneys clean poisons from the body, and that Grandmother could no longer keep her blood clean.

The viewing was scheduled just before the funeral, and we wore our Sunday clothes. My mother and Aunt Emma dressed alike in pink silk with a pattern of gray. We stopped at Grandmother's cottage before we left for the mortuary so that Aunt Emma could wear Grandmother's cameo necklace. I pointed at the vase with flowers.

"Grandmother promised I could have that," I said.

Aunt Emma turned from rummaging through the buffet and eyed me. "Don't be silly."

My mother spoke up, her voice trembling. "Mother did say she could have it."

Aunt Emma shook her head. "The child would only break it. And it wouldn't be fair to the other children." She found the necklace and put it on. We followed Aunt Emma to the car and didn't speak on the way to the mortuary. My mother stared at the shifting landscape, a hand against her cheek.

At the funeral parlor, we walked down a long dark corridor and into a bright room, with lights shining onto Grandmother's coffin. My mother squeezed my hand. The older uncles—Charlotte's sons—stood in a group. Aunt Rhea and Aunt Olive, who were half-sisters as well as sister-wives, stood with their husband at the foot of the casket, each with a hand on the shiny surface. My father stood at the head, with people lined up to speak to him.

Grandmother lay among the tufts of satin dressed in her white temple gown. She was beautiful and empty as a big old doll. Aunt LaVerne tucked a crochet-trimmed handkerchief, white as the purest cloud, between Grandmother's long, stiff fingers.

My mother had disappeared. I searched the crowd. I couldn't see her anywhere. I thought I saw her bob of chestnut hair, but it was my father's patient, a rich woman who sent us her clothes when they were out of fashion. My eyes scanned the crowd again and in a swirl of pink silk I thought I saw her again, but it was Aunt Irene, one of Charlotte's children who had turned against Grandmother Evelyn. Aunt Irene leaned into the coffin and tenderly kissed Grandmother's cheek, but Grandmother did not know that Irene loved her.

Loss swept over me, strong enough to make me gasp. There was so much about Grandmother I did not know, so much I did not know how to ask. I saw my mother across the room, her pink-and-grey silk back turned to me. I dodged through the crowd and pulled her elbow. "Mama . . ."

Aunt Emma looked down at me. "I'm not your mother," she said.

The room seemed to shift beneath me. My father had always said we were one, all one family, each of his wives a mother to any and all his children. But it wasn't true for Aunt Emma and me anymore than it had been true for Grandmother and Rhea, or Grandmother and Irene. Through the crowd I saw my father shaking hands and smiling, the long line of people waiting to speak to him, even on the day of his mother's funeral expecting him to solve their problems. He would never have time to hear all their questions, let alone find their answers.

The flowers put too much sweetness in the air and made it hard to breathe. I fought my way through a forest of legs onto the lawn outside. The sound of a hymn reached me and I recognized my mother's touch on the piano, each note falling soft and vivid as a rose petal or a drop of blood.

My memories of Grandmother Evelyn have faded over the years, but the yearning to know her has lingered. Today, in my fiftieth year, I am at my mother's house because her knees are giving her trouble. She wants me to retrieve the furniture oil from the top shelf of her utility closet so we can polish her piano. After I tease her about wearing out her knees and God's ears with her long prayers, I drag a kitchen chair over and climb up, a precarious perch by the back door. If someone came barging in right now, they'd pitch me down the stairs into the black hole of the basement. It occurs to me that this is where I live my life—perched on the edge of disaster or discovery, always in effect of others' comings and goings. Such a posture toward life doesn't initiate stability or strength, and I wish I'd learned more about surviving well. I reach into the shadows of the uppermost shelf, pushing past Raid and rat poison, brushing aside cobwebs and my fear of spiders.

In my mother's house, my skin always crawls when I'm searching dark corners. She is a diligent housekeeper, but it's the inner house-keeping that's wanting, an unwillingness to explore shadowy rooms and puzzling facets of life. "I don't like to make trouble," my mother says, an expression I've heard from her too many times. Again I grope in the dark, trying to find the bottle of oil. Then my fingers close on something round and dusty, and even before I draw it into the light, I know that I have found an ancient treasure. After thirty years of wondering if it has been broken or buried, I am holding the vase my grandmother said would be mine someday. The glaze is cracked, and the painted flowers have chipped and faded.

I take the vase to my mother and ask if she remembers when Grandmother gave it to me. She nods. "I'm not sure how it was put up there, but you're welcome to it."

A feeling of coming home after a long absence overwhelms me. I vow to repair the crack and restore the fading flowers, but I can see that my mother does not place particular value on the vase. "I didn't have a place to put it. That's why it was in the utility closet, I expect."

"Mama, don't you understand? This is a real heirloom! My great-

great-great grandmother made it with her own hands! My great-great grandmother brought it across the ocean! She probably pulled it in a handcart across the plains."

My mother smiles patiently, as if she knows something about vases and time that I have yet to learn. "Of course I understand. Actually, it was my great-grandmother who inherited it and gave it to my mother. And she gave it to me to give to you. My mother always did dote on you."

"But I thought it was Grandmother Evelyn's!"

"We wanted her to have some nice things in her little house, so we lent it to her."

Musing on the misunderstanding I've held for so many years, I wrap the vase and place it in a box. Then I finish what I started: I find the oil with its smooth, warm scent, and pour it onto a soft cloth to shine the baby grand piano that my brothers and I bought my mother some years ago. But it is Grandmother Evelyn who occupies my thoughts. In spite of the mystery she has always been, I know that her legacy is more than the vase, more than memories. Her power rises out of the earth and connects with sky—the raw energy of giving birth and rearing children, of sharing one's husband and serving God, of being second-class and mourning what has been uncreated or stillborn or lost. Her legacy is a way of being, unspoken and unwritten, and somewhere, in the dark corners of my life, it demands to be known.

The Fullness of Times

MY LACK OF KNOWLEDGE about Grandmother Evelyn cannot be blamed on family scribes, for we have an
embarrassment of riches when it comes to personal histories. In keeping with our religion, we are a record-keeping people,
writing regularly in journals and diaries, and tracking our ancestry
with single-minded intensity. My father wrote a definitive genealogy,
The Allred Family in America, which traces our ancestry in Colonial
America, across the water and back through the centuries to find a
forefather in the Archbishop of York who crowned William the Con-
queror first King of the Britons. Family members have passed down
anecdotes and events through oral tradition and letters, which were
then recorded in autobiographies and journals. To hear my father, my
grandfathers, my great-grandfathers tell it, men lived lives that really
mattered: they grappled with politics and religion, forayed into the
wilderness, eked out a living. The women, it seems, were too busy
sewing, cooking, giving birth, and raising children; they had no time
to write their stories. Whatever they knew was told to their children
and to each other while fulfilling domestic duties, and was carried forward by their children or other women.

My mother has told me that Grandmother Evelyn's mother, Mary Catrina, turned against the Principle after spending most of her life in polygamy. When Aunt Emma and my mother married my father, they were not allowed to meet the old woman for fear she would suspect plural marriage. I have read elsewhere that Karen Sorensen, who was Grandmother Evelyn's grandmother, lived polygamy in reverse, getting married for time and all eternity to *two* men. Curious about what would create such a reversal, I began asking questions, and my queries led me to people, books, and journals I hadn't known existed. From various books of remembrance, my father's autobiography, and my Aunt Rhea's writings, I learned that Karen Sorensen, born in Denmark, was sixteen years old when she met a pair of Mormon missionaries and in the course of their teachings, was "moved by the Holy Spirit" to convert to the Church of Jesus Christ of Latter-day Saints. When her staunchly Lutheran parents learned of her baptism by Mormon elders, they were so dismayed they threw her out of the house.

There's only one photograph of Karen in the family album, a small portrait of an older woman with light hair pulled into a severe bun, chin lifted proudly, disappointment written in the downward curve of her mouth. When her parents ordered her away, Karen reached out to other converts to the Church of Jesus Christ of Latter-day Saints and in 1858 they booked her passage across the Atlantic Ocean. She boarded ship at Copenhagen with a dream of finding a new home in Zion, the place in the mountains where the missionaries promised God's kingdom would congregate. This dream, of the great gathering of the chosen people in the New World, shone through the homesickness that seized her as the vessel took her out to sea. Perhaps it was comforting to be surrounded by other Latter-day Saints who had also given up family and country to embrace the Restored Gospel of Jesus Christ. Mads Peter Rasmussen, not much more than a boy himself, had also been touched by the missionaries and had converted to the Church. He, too, was alone in the world and he felt drawn to this spirited girl with no father aboard to chaperone her. Their walks on the moonlit deck and the wagging tongues of other saints encouraged them to marry immediately. Their union took place somewhere on the Atlantic, a new life struck in salt spray.

In the spring of 1859 they sailed into New York harbor. Along with others from the ship, the newlyweds joined a wagon train. They made their way to Council Bluffs, Iowa, then crossed the Great Plains to the mountains of Utah. Karen pulled a handcart piled with their few possessions while Mads handled oxen for the wagon train. They encountered sites of massacre, charred skeletons of wagons, bodies skinned and bloated. They drank contaminated water, ate wormy roots and rancid meats. They buried victims of cholera, snakebite, and exposure, many who died as infants or in old age, and some who died in the prime of their lives. At night, fear and exhaustion preyed on them as they tended to feet blistered raw and gazed into the campfire within the circle of wagons, but the next morning they continued westward, driven by the dream of gathering with the saints and building up the Kingdom of God. If they died en route, they believed they were assured a place with the Most High, having given their lives for the Gospel, and some longed for this release from pain. Other times, the going was easier and the saints would dance and sing, celebrating another day of survival. Thus Karen and Mads arrived in Salt Lake City just twelve years after Brigham Young looked over the Salt Lake Valley and declared, "This is the place."

In 1860 they were sealed "for time and all eternity" in the newly constructed Endowment House where ordinances such as baptisms and celestial marriages were performed for people both dead and living, a place where earthly time became eternal through sacred rites performed there. With saints in farms and settlements all around, perhaps the young couple expected an illuminated, balmy life, better temperaments and kinder hearts now that the trials of the journey were over. But thrown together, day in and day out, Mads and Karen lost sight of eternity. They discovered that they did not see eye to eye, each as strong-willed as the other. No one seems to know exactly what plagued their marriage. Perhaps Karen was more industrious than Mads, or more officious. Perhaps they had married in youthful longing, then discovered that marriage is not an escape, but a commitment. They took their conflict to the bishop, who probably told them, as Mormon bishops often do, to pray and study their scriptures together and not to go to bed angry.

Ironically, as Mads and Karen quarreled in Utah, Karen's parents in Denmark were converting to the Church of Jesus Christ of Latter-day Saints. They followed their headstrong daughter across the Atlantic, but by the time Karen embraced her parents in Utah, her mother was ailing. Karen's and Mads' oldest living child, Mary Catrina, was eight years old when the grandmother moved into the tiny log house, where Karen could nurse her day and night. Mary Catrina learned to cook and bake and sew and took over most of her mother's duties while Mads worked the farm.

Perhaps Mads Peter Rasmussen struggled with being just another worker in the hive of Deseret (the name Brigham Young had given to the Mormon settlement). Perhaps he realized that an adventure in independence awaited him in this New World, and he strained against the responsibilities that tied him down. Karen was now expecting twins—her fifth and sixth child in nine years. Perhaps Mads felt that there was no place for a man in such a household—no place to rest from a day in the fields, no permission to sit by the fire and smoke. Not with the Word of Wisdom outlawing a beloved pipe and mug of ale. Not with Karen and Mary Catrina always braiding rag rugs or putting up fruit or distilling tinctures of this or that for the old woman.

Yet he was expected to climb each rung of the priesthood ladder. Some had talked to him about plural marriage, as if more responsibility would make his life easier. Is this what drove him to think of leaving and starting over somewhere else, of going to California, where gold had been discovered, or to Oregon where people said things grew overnight? Karen was left alone with a sickly mother, all those little children, and twins on the way.

In the family album there's another faded photograph, this one of Mary Catrina Rasmussen at the age of ten. The year is 1874. She sits with other members of the family before her mother's log cabin in Morgan County, Utah, light curls softening high cheekbones. She is holding a white dress that her younger sister will wear to their grandmother's funeral. Mary Catrina had made the baby's dress by tearing apart a nightshirt Mads had left behind, using her little sister's only gown as a pattern. The photograph reveals Mary Catrina's intensity. You have the clear sense that whatever else happens, this dress will be finished before the funeral, and it will fit perfectly. Mary Catrina demonstrated early what would become a prevailing character trait— that once her sights were set on something, she would do whatever she must to get it.

Mary Catrina dressed her little sister in the white dress and they attended the funeral. After the brethren in their ward had dug the grave and the women of Relief Society had brought their loaves of bread and pots of stew for the funeral supper, people seemed to forget the Rasmussen family. When Karen went into labor, only Mary Catrina was there to do what was needed as the twins came into the world. Perhaps this was her first experience of midwifery as well as her initiation into being guided by the Holy Spirit as she delivered healing aid.

Something dark must have attended Karen's marriage to Mads; perhaps abandonment gave the Church grounds for their eternal marriage to be dissolved. In those days a divorced woman in the church usually went through life alone, for if she wanted to marry again she would have to content herself with a civil marriage. Church policy rarely allowed a woman to be "released" from temple marriage unless her ex-husband was a known pervert or criminal, while in most cases the husband was allowed to remarry whether divorced, widowed, or married, and he could have many wives sealed to him. But in this instance, Karen was encouraged by ecclesiastical leaders to marry again. After three years she seems to have regarded any spouse as an improvement over single motherhood in a land of pioneers, and Karen's second eternal marriage was sealed in the same Endowment House as the first.

Mary Catrina briefly endured her mother's second marriage before deciding that something had to change. She had enjoyed suitors even before she asked the bishop for help. One of her beaux wrote that Mary Catrina "made the best bread and biscuits, and was the prettiest girl in Morgan County." By the time she was fourteen, she was long-limbed and fair-skinned, her straight nose and high cheekbones giving an impression of delicacy that contradicted her workhorse habits. No one expected her to marry so young, not when Mary Catrina loved school so much, but she came away from her meeting with the bishop strongly resolved to leave her mother's home and begin her own life. The man she wanted to marry, Arthur Benjamin Clark, an immigrant from England who believed in the Principle, was already married to a diminutive woman of refined temperament named Helen Ross.

Although Arthur was known for his gentle way with horses, at six feet four inches tall, with his dark eyes and bristly beard, he was more like a grizzly bear than a man. Mary Catrina was a tall woman, but her paleness—the sense that she could merge with sunlight—made her seem frail alongside Arthur. As they got to know each other, Mary Catrina told Arthur little of life in her stepfather's house, only that "conditions weren't good for me there."

Her virtue may have been in jeopardy, for her bishop advised Arthur to wed Mary Catrina at once, even though in terms of years, she was scarcely more than a child. The bishop did ask Arthur to wait until Mary was older before consummating the union. Arthur agreed to wait until Mary was sixteen. Until then, she would live in the Clark household and help Arthur's wife, who was plagued with morning sickness.

Meanwhile, forces conspired to make their lives more difficult. In 1862, Abraham Lincoln had been under political pressure from his party platform, which promised to "stamp out the twin relics of bar-barism—slavery and polygamy" and in 1862, he had signed the Mor-rill Anti-Bigamy Law even though it went against his grain. As president of the United States, Lincoln usually chose to leave the Mormons alone. He told Brigham Young's emissary, T.B.H. Sten-house, "When I was a boy on the farm in Illinois . . . occasionally we would come to a log . . . too hard to split, too green to burn, and too heavy to move, so we just plowed around it. That's what I intend to do with the Mormons." After Lincoln died, the antipolygamy campaign surged and in 1874 the United States Congress passed the Enabling Act, which provided that church leaders could be charged as collabo-rators in polygamy. Then the Edmunds Act of 1882 barred polyga-mists from voting or holding public office. In danger of losing all assets, Church authorities ordered polygamous patriarchs, including Arthur Clark, to move out of the territory known as Utah.

In the early 1880s the Clarks moved to Bear Lake, Idaho, to join a stronghold of polygamous refugees. Mary Catrina did her best to serve the outlawed saints, and often assisted midwives with their work. One night she was called to the bedside of a Danish immigrant, where she demonstrated her knowledge of the language as well as a healing influence upon the body. She knew that a few herbs combined with a prescription for the spirit could make all the difference in a person's desire to live or die. She learned that fulfilling a wish could save a life, that sending for the hemorrhaging woman's husband (who had been off visiting other wives) while administering blackthorn could stop the bleeding of both body and spirit. Mary found many ways to dovetail the Gospel with her growing repertoire of healing methods. For instance, an herbal tea to soothe the stomach worked well with re-baptism for cankers of the spirit. Restoring the health of the whole being became her specialty. She was never accused of overstepping her bounds as a midwife, or of taking upon herself the power reserved for the priesthood. She attributed glory where she firmly felt it belonged—to God.

Some said that a dark presence lived in the deep blue center of Bear Lake, something that rose out of the earth's core, a great serpent, maybe Satan himself. The Shoshone said the Bear Lake monster bore the spirit of the outraged bear and of something else, a creature too terrible to speak about. White trappers who claimed to have seen it called it "devil fish" and described a many-legged snake that spit fire and water. Unless a baptism was being held, and the waters had recently been dedicated, most Mormons would not enter the lake, though it was pure snowmelt, and to justify their fears they repeated what Brigham Young had once said about the Devil living in the water. Some saints would trace the sandy shore in their bare feet, but they waded only to their knees and refused to swim to the center where, they swore, every daring person disappeared forever, the soul lost along with the body.

Mary Catrina, who seems to have known something about true evil, was not so impressed with their round-eyed stories. She liked to go down to the lake on those nights when her husband visited his first wife, Helen. In the silky waters, Mary Catrina smoothed away conflicts. On Saturday afternoons when the sun warmed the sand, she taught the children to swim and then braided or trimmed their hair, preparing them for Sunday. These were the only recreations she allowed herself. She had no time for the gossip of the sisters following Relief Society—she was too busy looking after people who needed immediate relief, and she had no affection for quilting bees. She decided that she would teach her children to quilt, the boys as well as the girls. Before each of them was grown she would insist that they piece together a quilt, and then she would help them block and finish it for their wedding night. She decided that she would teach them to make bread, too, for there was no way to predict when they might need to do so.

Three years after she married, Mary Catrina gave birth to her first son, George, a sweet comfort during her nights alone. Then came the second child, Evelyn, who would be my grandmother, born at St.

Charles, Idaho. When Evelyn was two, the pressure of the Edmunds-Tucker Act threatened the existence of the entire Church of Jesus Christ of Latter-day Saints. John Taylor, the third church president and a practicing polygamist, was forced into hiding, which meant that he could no longer publically preside over his congregation. Church assets had been seized, and pressure mounted among the Latter-day Saints to bring an end to the Principle. Some of the leaders proposed a manifesto that would outlaw the practice among the church membership. President Taylor struggled with the issue, spending much of his isolation in fasting and prayer, seeking a solution. The secrecy surrounding him provided an environment for the mysterious Revelation of 1886 that would underpin fundamentalist beliefs. Some people swore that President Taylor had been visited by Joseph Smith and Jesus Christ who directed him not to sign the proposed manifesto. They testified that after his congress with divine visitors, President Taylor met with all the people in the house where he was hiding, and in their presence, pointed at the document and thundered that he would rather his arm be ripped from his body, his tongue torn from his mouth than abolish the Principle of Plural Marriage. Others said that such a meeting never took place, and used journal entries to prove that the most adamant advocates of the so-called revelation had been in another part of the state at the time of the supposed meeting.

Now that the Edmunds-Tucker Act allowed members' personal assets to be impounded (even if one did not practice polygamy), some brethren in the Church of Jesus Christ of Latter-day Saints succumbed to pressure and turned in their own brethren. The fact that any polygamist could wind up in prison motivated Arthur Clark to outstrip federal marshals by settling in the wilderness of southwestern Wyoming, where the Shoshone and Ute didn't care how many wives he had. Besides the Clarks, five other polygamous clans homesteaded in the Star Valley, establishing Afton, Freedom, and Fairview, Wyoming. Arthur became the presiding elder for the LDS Church in a land not fully mapped. He treasured the fact that the Indian tribes trusted him and his wives. He pulled their aching teeth, having apprenticed as a dentist at Bear Lake, and he invited them to visit his homes and use his whetstone. My father's half-sister, Rhea, relates in her book, *Voices of Women Approbating Celestial or Plural Marriage*, that sister-wives Helen and Mary Catrina made friends with the Indians, sharing what food they had, rather than risking offense to "these children of nature who were already being pushed off their choicest grazing areas and hunting grounds." The *Book of Remembrance of Arthur B. Clark and Descendants* reveals:

> Indians learned that they could always get a handout from "Bishop's Woman." . . . Mary early exhibited a great talent for nursing and seemed to possess a true gift of healing. She never refused to go to those in need of her care.

The Clarks established a full life of ranching and midwifery, of music and worship. Arthur, always a consummate rancher, also practiced his dentistry, a profession that engendered fear and respect wherever he traveled.

In October of 1890, Dr. Arthur Clark set off for Salt Lake City, accompanied by his wives and children. As the first Mormon bishop in southwestern Wyoming, he was guaranteed a seat in the Tabernacle at Temple Square, where the LDS faithful met for general conference. He was attended by other regional and local authorities and their families, forming a small caravan of buggies and wagons. Among them was another Wyoming resident, Byron Harvey Allred Sr.

Byron had been called to meet with the president of the Church of Jesus Christ of Latter-day Saints, Wilford Woodruff himself. This was indeed an auspicious summons, and Byron may have yearned to let the Clark family know that he had been called to meet with the living prophet of the church. Did Byron, who owned the general store in

Fairview, Wyoming, feel any affinity for this itinerant dentist, Arthur Clark, who led the choir, played the organ, and held the highest ecclesiastical authority in southwestern Wyoming? Like Arthur, Byron had moved to Wyoming to escape the political snares set for polygamous patriarchs. Both men loved horses, and Byron may have envied the well-circulated story that Arthur Clark had traded horses with Brigham Young himself.

Byron Sr. traveled to the October conference with his first wife, Irene, and his second wife, Matilda. Eliza Tracy, a small, light-haired beauty whose father languished in prison for polygamy, traveled with them, raising more than a few eyebrows. The possibility of betrayal came not only from the "gentiles"—those who were not members of the Church—but from the ranks of Mormons. The political climate required that plural marriages be held secret, so no one openly shared the suspicion that a matrimonial bond had been forged between Eliza Tracy and Byron Allred. He would have been reluctant to announce the marriage even to his closest brethren given the rumors that LDS Church President Wilford Woodruff was about to issue a manifesto abolishing polygamy. Consequently, Byron's third plural marriage was kept from most family members, all but his wives and his oldest son, Byron Harvey Allred Jr., who was called Harvey to distinguish him from his father.

Harvey knew the need for discretion. He had also been married long enough to realize some of the responsibility and sensitivity required of a good husband. He would later write his reflections on marriage in his journals, where he frequently proclaimed his love for his wife, Charlotte Susannah Pead, known to her loved ones as "Lottie."

> It then seemed and I have ever since felt that God blessed me as He had blessed very few of His sons, with one of the sweetest and purest wives ever given to men. . . .

Charlotte was a vibrant woman who loved to ride horses almost as much as she loved the Gospel, but she stiffened in the face of anything unfamiliar, and she seemed incapable of making her own decisions. Harvey noted this, but he seemed to enjoy being the protector and the decision-maker, and having exercised these quite skillfully in behalf of Charlotte and the babies, he had decided to become a lawyer. Then his horizons had expanded when he was asked to run for the first Wyoming legislature. After this church conference, he was scheduled to go to Cheyenne where he would meet with men who were forming the government of the new state.

The sight of the Salt Lake Temple never failed to bring tears to Harvey's eyes. It had been under construction for thirty-seven years and still the capstone had not been set; the stories of those who sacrificed and those who were blessed in its construction were exchanged among the company as they arrived on the temple grounds. The Allreds stopped on the east lawn, and Byron Sr. hurried inside the guard house near the temple gates to meet with Church President Woodruff and his counselor, George Q. Cannon.

An hour later the door opened and Byron came out, hatless and stumbling on the granite step. A presentiment swept over Harvey then, that something dreadful would happen to his father. Perhaps Harvey fought his doubts by remembering that Byron had survived infancy at Winter Quarters near Council Bluffs, Iowa, when thousands of other babies had died. As a child, Byron had been part of the third wagon train to make its way to Utah, withstanding Indian attacks, cholera, buffalo stampedes, and drought. In 1857, when Colonel Albert Sidney Johnston's Army marched on the Mormons, Byron was only a child, but he had accompanied his father, William Moore Allred, to run back and forth before the blazing bonfire, built to convince the invaders through the repetition of human shadows flashing against the rock wall of Echo Canyon that Colonel Johnston's troops were outnumbered. As a patriarch Byron had spurned the "test oath" (a prerequisite to voting that all Idaho citizens had to sign declaring that they were monogamous), which was designed to flush out polygamists in 1886. On more than one occasion he had eluded

Pinkerton detectives and federal agents bent on arresting polygamists. Surely he would be able to take care of himself.

Byron came to them and kissed Harvey's mother, Irene. "Are you ready for the next trial of faith?" She nodded. "Whatever the Lord wants."

Byron turned to Harvey. "I'm sorry to tell you this, son, especially since you and Lottie made the move from Idaho to live near us in Star Valley." Byron explained that President Woodruff had called him to go to Mexico and set up a colony for saints who lived the Principle. "I'm to establish a place where we can live plural marriage without breaking the law of the land," he explained. "The Brethren want me to be on my way by November. I'll be here in Salt Lake City till mid-October, which gives me half a month to raise the cash."

Byron wrote of this meeting in his journal:

> President Woodruff informed me that had not the Manifesto been published, this nation would seize the Temples and stop the work therein; also imprison the leaders for life. They informed me that I was to leave my home in Fairview, Wyoming, and move to Mexico. . . . On the morning of October 6th, the Manifesto was read and presented to the conference, and while it was being read President Woodruff wiped the tears from his face which were forced to flow to give vent to the great regret and emotion in his breast that this nation was so blind that they could not see that they were bringing the wrath of God upon them and that they were responsible for this step, and the sin should rest upon them.

The temptation to indulge in self-pity must have been overwhelming. Only the year before, Byron had moved his families from Idaho to Wyoming, in response to the "test oath" and a church calling. Perhaps he wouldn't have been charged with such a difficult mission, to establish a colony of polygamists in Mexico, if it hadn't been for his new wife, Eliza. Harvey, who had followed his father to Wyoming, had no hope of following his parents to faraway Mexico. At the time, Harvey harbored no thought of living the Principle because his wife, Charlotte, became distraught when the subject came up.

During that Sunday morning session of the October 6, 1890, conference of the Church of Jesus Christ of Latter-day Saints, President Wilford Woodruff read the Manifesto renouncing the practice of plural marriage on the grounds that it was in violation of laws enacted by the United States Congress. A sea of right hands was raised in support and my grandfather, Harvey Allred, later found significance in the fact that he was in the foyer with a crying baby, and his hand was not among those giving assent to abolish plural marriage.

Although he had not received a call to go to Mexico, Arthur Clark and his family had their share of concerns now that the Manifesto had been accepted. With the Principle officially outlawed, the Church built a large, lovely red-brick home, a dormitory of sorts on South Temple in Salt Lake City, and invited the disenfranchised wives to establish themselves there, rent-free. Only one woman ever took advantage of this offer, and she did not stay for long. Most plural wives stayed with their husbands even after they were released from their spiritual bonds. Mary Catrina was no exception.

By November 10, 1890, Byron Harvey Allred Sr. had sold everything that wasn't nailed down or needed by Matilda and Irene, the wives who would stay in the States until the Star Valley, Wyoming, property was sold. The third wife, Eliza, would accompany Byron to New Mexico by train and from there by horse and carriage to Dublan, in the province of Chihuahua, Mexico. He bought two train tickets and pocketed the remaining eighty-six dollars that would see him to his new home. As they traveled into Utah's sage and sand desert, following the Grand River into Colorado, he made frequent notes about the scenery and speculated about the adventure ahead, confiding in his journal rather than in the quiet young woman beside him. They headed through mountains and lush green valleys, following the Gunnison River south toward Pueblo, and he remarked the beauty of God's creation, his bold hand growing a little shaky as he reflected how far they would soon be from home. Eliza attended to his health, but Byron felt an acute stab of homesickness for his first wife, Irene, who knew him as no other person on earth did, and Matilda, who had borne him nine children.

> I cannot describe my feeling when I left my loved ones behind me to take such a journey and to think I was going over 1900 miles away where I could not get back if sickness came among them and neither leaving available means for them to come to me or taking means whereby I could return to them no matter if even death should be allowed to visit them. Thus I left, not for wealth, or to attempt to accumulate wealth, but sacrificed all I had and left my family in the care of God for the sake of his eternal laws.

They reached Pueblo, Colorado, at 4 A.M.

> where we had to lay over until evening. I wrote home and walked around part of the day viewing the city. In the morning a fine-dressed gentleman (so I took him to be) came to me and during the conversation he asked where I was going. I told him Deming, New Mexico. He said he was a merchant of that place and would be apt to accompany me . . . Said his name was Miller and in the afternoon he wished me to go down . . . with him while he attended to having his Mdse transferred, so I went with him.

When they reached the freight hauler, Mr. Miller was told he must pay $75 or his goods could not be moved onto the train. Miller produced a check for $1,000 but the freighter refused to accept it, saying he could not cash it. Moreover, the freighter could not wait for Miller to go to Pueblo and return with cash.

Miller glanced anxiously about, then turned to Byron. "If I don't pay my charges, I'll lose everything." He stepped over to Byron and spoke in a confidential tone. "Friend, make me a loan of $75 and I'll hurry back to the Pueblo station and cash this check. Then you shall have your money back."

Glad to have made a friend on this lonely journey, Byron Harvey Sr. took out his wallet and counted out the $75, which left him with $11. Miller then asked Byron to take care of his valise until he returned. Reassured, Byron went back to the train and sat with Eliza to await his new friend's return. When another person called to claim the valise, "it flashed on me for the first time that I had been made a victim of their deeds, and robbed," Byron wrote.

The train was delayed so that Byron could contact the law in Pueblo, but it was clearly not the first time such fraud had been committed on this railway. "You're fortunate they didn't hold you at gunpoint and take everything," the sheriff said. "Including your wife—and your life."

The deputy rode ahead to see if he could catch Miller (not at a burning pace, Byron noted, thinking perhaps the railroad, the freight line, and the town of Pueblo were in on the scheme). Meanwhile the sheriff told tales of Hole in the Rock and Robber's Roost. Perhaps he told of Butch Cassidy, a Mormon boy gone wrong, who stole from good people for the thrill of being bad. Some have theorized that it was Butch Cassidy himself who played the part of the merchandiser named "Miller." In any case, Byron counted himself lucky to be poor and alive, instead of broke and dead.

> I after wondered why I did not think far enough to resist them, but on due reflection I see I was in a place where if I had refused a lick from either of them I would have been floating down the river and I had to say, "Thank God, my life is still spared" and I have gained an experience (though sad) that I will never forget.

As Byron and Eliza went on their way, loneliness overwhelmed him again. His religion no longer sanctioned his way of life, even though it had been perpetrated by the Church. The support of the brethren was vanishing, and with it, the political leverage that had kept him out of prison. Could he expect the men who'd bought his land and animals to honor their debts now that he was beyond the influence of the Church and soon would be outside the borders of the nation? His ranch land in Wyoming could be gone without reimbursement, as well as his property near Bear Lake. Except for the eleven dollars in his wallet, his money was gone. He was not sure how he would bring Irene and Matilda to join him in Mexico. With a premonition that poverty and despair lay ahead, he turned toward Mexico.

Range Wars and Religion

 IN THE NEW STATE OF WYOMING, Harvey faced challenges of his own. The harsh winter of 1887 had nearly ruined the cattle industry, and in Johnson County a full-scale range war threatened to break out between big cattle ranchers (who were mainly Republican) and homesteaders (who were mainly Democrats). Wyoming had been granted statehood the same year that the Manifesto abolishing plural marriage was presented to the LDS congregation, and many polygamists homesteaded in places that hadn't yet outlawed polygamy. In 1892, the first Wyoming legislature convened, and among the Democrats elected to the Lower House was twenty-two-year-old Byron Harvey Allred Jr., who dreamed of home-steading and starting a ranch of his own. Various politicians took Harvey under their wing in an attempt to commandeer his vote. Church leaders exercised their influence as well, urging him to vote according to the "church interests," which were generally Republican. Harvey longed for the counsel of his parents, but his father had long-since gone to Mexico, and his mother and "Aunt" Matilda had recently joined Byron there. Deliberating in his journal, Harvey wrote that he would vote with his party unless he had some good reason to do otherwise. He saw himself as loyal, but his Democratic party, beset with internal struggles, did not trust his susceptibility to the primarily Republican influence of the LDS Church. For several weeks, the legislators battled to elect a United States senator from Wyoming, but the Democrats tied with Republicans, each party one vote shy of electing their candidate.

Amid the turmoil, Harvey was called to a late-night dinner with a powerful Democrat named John E. Baxter. On the way, two men appeared from the shadows and accompanied him along the street. Harvey had heard of church leaders charged with polygamy accosted on the street by men like these, in bowler hats and neat dark suits, detective-like in their manner. He wondered if they had mistaken him for his father, who more than once had fled out the back door or hidden in the root cellar because the law was hunting polygamous patriarchs. Surely people knew that his father had gone to Mexico. Harvey told himself he had nothing to fear. He looked at each of the men and nodded, and they nodded in return, yet continued with him, their steps purposeful until they passed the railroad yard where there was a single steam engine, puffing but with lights out. Harvey kept his dinner engagement, then returned the same way. Again the two men emerged from the darkness and walked alongside him until they had passed the puffing engine and stepped onto the well-lit main street. Then they tipped their hats and disappeared.

The next morning, as the legislature assembled, two of Harvey's colleagues whispered that they had hired these men to protect him against a Republican plot to kidnap him so that he could not cast his vote in the state legislature. Jarred by this narrow escape, Harvey decided to elect any good Democrat who would run. It isn't clear whether the Democrat Baxter made his offer that mysterious night, or whether he made it subsequently, but Harvey was faced with a dilemma. Baxter had offered to pay forty-five thousand dollars to any three representatives who would vote for him. A trusted church advisor counseled Harvey to accept the money, and agreed to personally place Harvey's third of the "reward" in an account in Salt Lake City.

In his journal, Grandfather Harvey rationalized that since he had already decided to vote for another Democrat, the money was not a bribe because it didn't change his vote. But in truth, his vote split the Democrats and thus the Republican Frank Warren was elected to the U.S. Senate, which was the Mormon objective. This was not the only time Harvey would break the law, yet he was a man of some conscience, and it didn't sit right with him. In his ruminations, he told himself that he meant well, that he had meant only to serve his church and his family, just as his father had done in Idaho after the Edmunds Bills was passed; rather than lie or sacrifice his freedom to live the Principle, Byron Sr. had proudly refused to vote. The laws of God transcended the laws of men—didn't they? The concern shows up time and again in Harvey's journal:

> This matter was a source of worry to me, for I realized that in the letter of the law, I had done a wrong, yet the spirit of the law would not condemn me. . . . President Budge told the saints in Star Valley that he had seen me tried and knew that I was an upright man in whom the people could well place their confidence. I hope and pray I may ever prove worth such commendation.

This was perhaps the first time my grandfather engaged in religious justification of his own illicit behavior. But it seems he could not make himself feel clean about it and soon became alternately self-effacing and self-righteous. As with his father, Harvey's financial life fluctuated. He was not reelected to the Wyoming legislature, so he took work as he could find it, traveling to Ogden, Utah, staying with his wife's parents and working at the meat-packing plant. He hated the bloody work of slaughtering cattle and pigs, and soon learned that if he could tell a racy joke or two, the men would do his work for him as long as he kept them entertained. When these indiscretions caught up with his conscience, he entered a period of fasting and prayer. In days to come, as Harvey became an instructor at the Brigham Young Academy and later, as an attorney, he was ill at ease with himself. He ran again for the legislature only to be overwhelmingly defeated. He thought God had served him his just deserts, that he was undeserving of victory or leadership. At night, unable to sleep, he listed his regrets.

~

A favorite Mormon aphorism holds that adversity makes us strong. That's what must have happened for Grandfather Harvey as he despaired that the Lord would ever want such an unworthy vessel to do His work. When he was called to serve a mission to preach the Gospel of Jesus Christ to the Cherokee Nation in the lands known as Indian Territory (which included Oklahoma, Kansas, Indiana, Arkansas, Louisiana, and parts of Texas), he accepted the calling without a hitch, perhaps feeling that the sacrifice and commitment would wash him clean. He left his wife and four small children in the care of friends and relatives in Wyoming. He was assigned a companion named Joseph J. Richardson, and soon they were moving among the Cherokee and Choctaw preaching the Gospel, building schoolhouses and meeting houses, and administering to the sick. He and Elder Richardson reached out to whoever would talk with them, including a desperately poor community near Blackgum, Oklahoma, where a group of emancipated slaves attempted to survive. More than once the missionaries came to the aid of women and children left unprotected by their men. Much of Indian Territory was made up of badlands and these were inhabited by renegades of every sort. Missionarying without purse or scrip required vast amounts of faith. The elders did not know from one day to next where they would eat or sleep, or whether they would be greeted with hospitality or hostility. Sometimes they were treated like young gods and on other occasions they were targets of mockery and persecution. One time, while Harvey was preaching in Kansas, the crowd got ugly and a voice yelled that they should string him up. A burly man leapt to his side, crowbar in hand, and threatened to kill anyone who touched the missionary. The crowd began to disperse. Then, as quickly as he appeared, the burly man vanished.

In the mission field Harvey lived for the occasional convert and the more frequent letters from home. After two years of serving God and fellow man in various ways, he was released from his mission. He said good-bye to his companion in El Paso, and returned home by way of Mexico, stopping in the Mormon colonies to visit with his mother and father. He was stunned by his mother's gauntness, by how dramatically his father had aged. As he heard about the illness and deprivation they had endured, he felt like weeping. He had seen much hardship in Indian Territory, but nothing that compared with his parents' plight. His father confided in a bitter undertone that some elders in the colonies thrived, yet they seemed to have no concern for their poor and starving brethren.

Harvey told his parents that he had met Loren C. Woolley while serving his mission in Indian Territory. Loren C. Woolley swore on his soul that he had been present when third LDS Church President John Taylor was visited by the resurrected Joseph Smith and the Savior, both of whom ordered President Taylor not to sign the document that would outlaw the Principle of Plural Marriage. Byron and Irene smiled fondly, perhaps thinking what a good son they had, going so far to justify their way of life. Or perhaps they sensed Harvey's new attraction to the Principle. When he left the mauve sands of Chihuahua, Harvey made a solemn promise to return to Mexico soon.

I've often wondered, what was it about Mexico that called to Harvey? Was it the fact that his parents seemed starved for human connection as well as food? Was it the appeal of wilderness and attraction to a community so newly established that a polished statesman-lawyer-teacher such as himself was bound to succeed? Or was it the call of the banished to another exiled soul? Harvey returned to Afton, Wyoming, with an inchoate burning in his heart, his thoughts revisiting his conversation with Loren C. Woolley as he wondered if the man was a liar or an apostle. The Principle of Plural Marriage was supposed to be a thing of the past, all current practitioners secured in Mexico or Canada, yet Harvey heard rumors of men who were still taking plural wives with the blessing of Church authorities.

Once he was home in Afton, Wyoming, Harvey embraced his law practice with enthusiasm, but found himself confronting the depraved and dishonest: men who stole other men's land, men who rustled other men's cattle, men who stole women's honor. In his struggle to see offenders as children of God, Harvey returned to the habits developed on his mission of fasting, praying, and studying scripture. In the course of one such spiritual exercise, he fell asleep and had a dream that he walked along a river in a land far south, where he met a beautiful blonde woman. He took her by the hand and he knew that she would be his wife. He awakened beside his dark-haired Charlotte, feeling both ashamed and exultant.

In Freedom, Wyoming, Arthur B. Clark was presiding elder of the church, yet he liked to polish his array of vocations the way some men polish their boots. He was a knowledgeable horse trader and a savvy rancher, proud of his lands green and fertile as the county of Essex, where he'd been born. He'd been the first bishop in the area, had led every choir and had played the organ for most church meetings. He could out-fiddle any fiddler in Wyoming, but these were sheer accompaniment for plying what he thought of as his profession: itinerant dentist. Through book-learning and as an apprentice, he had learned the latest methods of vulcanizing. The beginning of a new day, he called it, when people weren't forced to enter old age as soon as their teeth gave out, because with porcelain and rubber he could fix anybody with a fine set of teeth—and how appropriate that even rotted teeth could be restored as they entered the last century of an old millennium and the beginning of the Lord's dominion on earth. To make dentistry easier on his patients, Arthur used various methods of pain relief, employing ether and some of the herbal remedies known to his wife, Mary Catrina, through her midwifery and nursing. As he traveled about Wyoming, northern Utah, and southeastern Idaho on his dentistry rounds, the favorite method of fully banishing the pain inflicted by his procedures was to have the family gather around after the ordeal and sing along while he fiddled, then join him in a prayer before he hit the road again.

Arthur was used to living on the fringes, creating civility and safety on the periphery of the community. His childhood years in Essex County, England, where his family had been Mormons in a Protestant land, had acclimated him to persecution and to walking a fine edge. As a self-taught professional in a land without laws, he had practiced dentistry in Utah and Idaho and had repaired Wyoming teeth for several years before a patient sued him for practicing dentistry without a license. Since Wyoming had only begun to address issues of professional licensing, Arthur suspected that the lawsuit had nothing to do with dentistry, and he wondered if the anti-polygamy campaign had caught up with him. Sensing that the suit was based on political motives, Arthur wrote to Harvey Allred, who, he knew, had enjoyed a round of success as a barrister since returning from a mission. Arthur asked Harvey to defend him when the suit went to court, and suggested that they discuss the matter following the regional church conference in Afton, Wyoming, about twenty miles from the Clark ranch.

The day the conference began, Arthur and his family traveled a rough road through green and gold valleys, climbing to mountain passes so white and still they seemed not to have seen the sun since the last summer. The bears had just come out of hibernation, ravenous and cranky; everywhere they saw bear track—gouged in the white bark of the quaking asp and beneath broken lower branches of pine and spruce, the giant hand of the grizzly and the smaller print of the black bear. Evelyn Clark, now 16, recognized these signs and saw that her father drove the team harder than a true horse-lover like himself would normally do. She was glad to arrive at the white ward-house in Afton, and grateful that they would spend the night with saints.

The meeting had a fervent timbre, so many immigrants among them, some who'd come on overcrowded ships from Scandinavia and pulled handcarts across the plains, like her mother's people. They had survived the deep winter and spring was coming; gratitude rang from the rafters as they lifted their voices in song. When Evelyn stepped outside, the sun hit her face and mirrored the light in her heart. As she descended the steps, accompanied by her parents, she encountered a young man, vaguely familiar. He stopped and stared at her in astonishment. Evelyn realized that she had known him since her childhood— Brother Allred's son, Harvey, the politician and attorney. Too handsome for his own good. Dark, liquid eyes, dark moustache. Straight, strong nose, with a jagged scar across the bridge. A little taller than she was, thank goodness. He looked at her mother and asked, "Is this your daughter?" and Mary Catrina gave him a knowing smile, as if she were seeing straight through him. He wrote about their encounter in his journal.

> I was entering the door of our Afton Church building to attend one of the sessions of the quarterly church conference. As I ascended the steps I met, coming toward me, the same good face I had seen in my dream. I stopped almost speechless. It was the same sweet girl that afterward became my wife in that distant southland I saw in my dreams. I would not have known her had she not been with her parents, whom I knew well. I had met her before when she was a little girl. Now she had grown to beautiful womanhood in which I did not recognize the pretty little girl of a few years before. I asked Sister Clark if this was her daughter. Being somewhat confused I did not know what else to say, although I knew well that she was, before I asked. I then grasped, for the first time, the hand of my wife to be, and called her by name, Evelyn, that afterward became so dear to me.

He left in a flurry, forgetting his promise to confer with Arthur. Harvey returned later and agreed to take the case despite his plan to give up his law practice. He had seen too much of the seamy side of humanity and had decided to become the school principal. As he mulled this decision against the surprising firmness with which he accepted the Clark case, he could not stop thinking of Evelyn and his dream two years before.

Evelyn might have suspected what flustered Harvey, and that it wasn't just that he was married, or her parents eyeing him coolly as he fumbled about. Perhaps she had dreamed of him, too. Perhaps she had a sense that they had met in another reality, that she had pledged herself to him in the Pre-existence. Perhaps she believed, as do many Latter-day Saints, that such dreams come from the knowledge one's spirit carries of what one's soul has pledged. It didn't particularly bother her that Harvey was already married, even though the Manifesto outlawing the Principle of Plural Marriage had been accepted at the LDS Conference in Salt Lake City nearly ten years before; everybody knew that people in Wyoming still lived it. Her own father was married to Aunt Helen, who now lived in Mexico, and her mother, who still delivered babies in Wyoming. Recently she had overheard her parents' hushed conversations about bringing another woman into the family. Most people respected Brother Harvey's father, Byron, who had gone to Mexico to start a colony for those who would continue to "raise up a righteous seed unto the Lord" through plural marriage—in spite of the Manifesto.

～

During the journey back to Freedom, Evelyn might have wondered how this sudden romance could amount to anything, with the federal agents on the lookout for every patriarch who might show an interest in polygamy. But she was not a young woman given to daydreaming. Her life was full of work: bread-baking and fruit-bottling, gardening and quilting, meanwhile studying Shakespeare and scripture in equal parts. She turned the matter over to the Lord, determined to accept His will.

Meanwhile, Harvey wondered how he would ever explain his materialized dream of meeting Evelyn to his wife, Charlotte. He decided that until he knew he must enter the Principle, he dared not impose on Lottie's delicate temperament. He prayed and fasted and studied scripture, waiting for inspiration or some direction.

Harvey anticipated working with Arthur Clark, as much for the chance to see Evelyn as to see that justice was upheld. By asking some of his political cronies, Harvey soon learned that a powerful state senator wanted Arthur's land, and a local justice had promised to help the senator acquire it. A councilman also had it in for Arthur because of his polygamous way of life, and had paid a former patient of Dr. Clark to testify against him. Among them, these men had conspired to run Dr. Clark out of the state. Since the parties involved were not always cooperative, the trial stretched out and it sometimes became necessary for Harvey to stay overnight at the Clark home.

Evelyn was helpful in preparing legal briefs in her flowing script, and she often discussed the issues with Harvey. Despite the senator's greed for the Clark ranch, both Evelyn and Harvey were convinced that enemies of the Principle had launched this campaign against Arthur. Yet Harvey hinted that the Church was still giving some men permission to enter plural marriage and Evelyn affirmed that she knew this was happening. Harvey pressed to know how she knew. What he learned moved him to express his affection for her:

> Evelyn had attended the trial and we all rode to their home in Brother Clark's large carriage. On this journey . . . I took Evelyn's hand in mine for the purpose of expressing by touch the love I felt for her. To my joy, the confidence and token of more than friendship was returned. That evening I had the happiness of meeting her and conversing alone, while we pretended to be engaged in making out Religion Class reports.

It seems that Stake President A.V. Call (who presided over a stake, or group of wards, in the region) had also attended the trial, ostensibly to be a character witness for Brother Clark,

> but really for the purpose of asking Evelyn's hand in marriage. We both guessed his mission, but I was blessed to beat him to the coveted prize. Yet I must admit that I never realized . . . perhaps not fully for months afterward how close I came to losing the first chance, which I . . . must reluctantly admit was the only thing that enabled me to be successful.

Harvey was reluctant to have the Clark case conclude, since it had provided him with an excuse to see Evelyn without raising eyebrows in the community. But he was a winner by nature, and jubilant when the jury ruled in favor of Arthur Clark. The evening of the verdict, Harvey joined the Clarks at their home for a victory celebration, and to mark his last appearance as a barrister. In the privacy of the milk-room he caught both Evelyn's hands in his, and told her in a rush that he loved her, that he believed in the Principle but the thought of plural marriage had always disturbed his wife, Charlotte. He expressed his faith that Charlotte would rise to the challenge, if only Evelyn would be patient.

Harvey had determined that he would not enter the Principle without Charlotte's consent, although men sometimes did so, citing Joseph Smith as their example. (Most church members knew that Joseph forged ahead with the Principle even while his wife, Emma, savagely opposed it.) Unsure that church authorities would support him in plural marriage now that the Manifesto had been issued, Harvey kept postponing the difficult conversation with his wife. Yet he was nervous since more than one man in the county wanted to marry Evelyn, including Warren Longhurst, who was married to Harvey's only full sister, Myra. It was Myra who told Harvey, with some sorrow and embarrassment, that Warren had gone to Salt Lake City to get permission from church authorities to take a second wife since Myra remained childless. Harvey scarcely expressed compassion for his sister, so worried was he that Warren might beat him to the prize. To assure himself that he still had Evelyn's loyalty, Harvey invited her to visit the school where he was the newly appointed principal.

> I handed her some examination papers for inspection and while she sat near me looking them over, I whispered in her ear my anxious desire to meet and converse with her on a question near to my heart—that of marriage, and asked if she would promise fair consideration of the matter and give future opportunity to hear my cause. She gave me promise in undertone that I should have such a chance and she would in the meantime think the matter over. This could hardly be considered a proposal. I had not made sure with Lottie that it would be acceptable to her for me to proceed so far at this time, but I must make sure of my girl if possible.

When Warren Longhurst returned from Utah with a letter of permission from LDS Church authorities to enter plural marriage, he asked Evelyn for her hand in marriage, just as Harvey had suspected. When pressed for an answer, Evelyn confessed that she loved someone else and had waited in hope that this love would be returned. Later, she sent a note to Harvey, requesting a talk. Harvey drove his buggy to Myra's and asked Evelyn to accompany him to his home. The two of them rode in the spring starlight, their silence interrupted by the occasional howl of a coyote or an owl's hooting and the relentless hoofbeats of his horse. At the Allred home, Charlotte received the pair warmly. She had lit a fire and wrapped herself in her Sunday shawl, the fringe draped to minimize her swelling belly, for she would deliver her seventh child soon. The three of them sat by the fire with cups of Brigham tea and discussed the Principle in general terms. Charlotte was dignified and earnest, expressing a desire to do the Lord's will. Evelyn, too, seemed queenly and wise beyond her years. In hypothetical terms, they spoke around the matter of sharing a life, a husband. Evelyn was careful not to speak of romance or any matter that might cause Charlotte pain. Harvey later observed, writing in his journal, that both women seemed ready to sacrifice for the Principle—Charlotte willing to share her husband, and Evelyn willing to forego the courtship she might have otherwise enjoyed.

Now that Charlotte had been approached, Harvey went to his bishop to find out, face to face, if men were still embracing the Principle. Then he went to the stake president with the same question. Both church leaders affirmed that men were still being given permission by the First Presidency of the Church to enter the Principle, but on condition that they emigrate to Mexico or Canada. The stake president drafted a letter of recommendation for Harvey. With the letter in hand, Harvey approached Charlotte for her final approval.

What was Charlotte thinking, through all this? Did she hope that church leaders would deny Harvey's petition so that she would not have to speak on her own behalf? Apparently so, for when confronted with the reality of plural marriage, Charlotte wept wildly and said that she could not bear to share him with another woman. Harvey declared that he would abandon the plan and do his best to forget the dream. And then she told him he must go ahead for the sake of their eternal welfare. In his journal, Harvey wrote:

> These incidents . . . are of joy and happiness, yet joys not free from their . . . sadnesses, for while I loved this beautiful woman, I had at home another good and beautiful woman—my wife—whom I loved more than I thought it was ever possible for me to love another woman, and to know that while I was paying my respects to another good soul, it was causing my dear wife at home sorrow . . . caused in me a sorrow that only pure men, who love, can feel.
>
> When I would let my mind dwell on dear Lottie's grief, I would feel that I could not possibly carry this matter any farther and . . . that I was not fit to live this great law, calling for so much heartache

and sacrifice. Then, if I would give this thought expression before Lottie, she would . . . after controlling her grief, tell me not to stop, but to do my duty . . . to obey the law. She would try to do her part. Oh, if ever there was a blessing in store for those who sacrifice for the purpose of obeying what they believe to be the will of God, it surely awaits such noble women.

And so it continued. Harvey would return from Freedom to find Charlotte in bed suffused with grief. Harvey would vow to give up the notion of plural marriage. Then Charlotte would sequester herself in prayer, and come to him, confessing that the Lord must have high regard for them to extend such an invitation. Charlotte would speak of the children that might be born of Evelyn and Harvey, how she felt the pressure of their souls and could not stand in the way of their being. And the next time he visited the Clark household, the drama would repeat itself.

One day while visiting Harvey's sister, Myra, Evelyn said that President Call had paid another visit the evening before, and that he had proposed marriage to her again.

"What did you tell him?" Harvey asked, fearing he had lost her.

"I told him I would take the matter under advisement."

Harvey decided to confront Charlotte with new urgency and purpose. The next morning, Harvey called at his sister's house and asked Evelyn if, in her opinion, he and Charlotte should go to Salt Lake City to obtain the apostolic blessing required to enter the Principle. He was committed, he said, and so was Charlotte. But he could not speak for certain others. Evelyn told him demurely that if he were to receive such an invitation, his efforts certainly would not be in vain.

Harvey traveled again to Freedom, this time to ask Arthur Clark for his daughter's hand, detailing the encouragements he had been given. In the magnanimous style that was his hallmark, Arthur received Harvey's proposal with optimism, confessing that he would be most glad to have "dear Evelyn" in Mexico. Arthur's first wife, Helen, was already in the colonies, and Arthur's intended fourth wife, Marinda, would be leaving soon so that they could be sealed in plural marriage. Arthur would complete the move as soon as he managed to sell his ranch. Evelyn's presence in Mexico would help him to convince Mary Catrina to follow, which would greatly relieve him since, as a midwife, she had refused to leave her Wyoming patients.

This groundwork had been laid for Harvey's first legitimate meeting with Evelyn. He formally asked her to marry him, she accepted, and they kissed, a chaste and proper meeting of the lips. Perhaps in anticipating his second honeymoon, Grandfather Harvey felt compelled to explain his motives in his journals. He wrote,

> . . . if the prime factor leading men to practice plural marriage as taught by the Latter-day Saints was gratification of lustful desire . . . who would take such an expensive way, ever beset with trial, hardship and sacrifice? There is too ready at hand the common means and practice of approved society by which men can satisfy their sexual desires simply by paying a few measly dollars and the forgetting of further care and responsibility.
>
> I would not wish to pass judgement on my fellow church men, but many things have led me to believe that in the majority of cases where plural marriage has proven a failure, the desire for sexual gratification has been one of the large factors moving [the husband] to attempt its practice . . . our religion teaches that it is a gross sin to indulge in sexual relations outside the sacred marriage ties, and some of us may be fool enough to think we could afford a religious cloak to cover our desire for sinful practice.
>
> Only the purest religious motives, strengthened by deep love for wife and children will enable a man to pay the price modern civilization will exact. If one is strong enough to pay this high price, what is the reward? First, a multiplicity of offspring . . . the chief measure of our glory in the future kingdom over which righteous living will permit us to reign as kings and queens. Another reward of eternal

magnitude . . . is the development of the true spirit of charity and self-sacrifice. No other school through which the mortal can pass has the ability to develop these Godlike attributes that righteous living of the law of plural marriage will discover. . . .

On April 13, 1901, Charlotte gave birth to a baby boy. Harvey and she planned to have him blessed in Salt Lake City at the tabernacle during an upcoming youth conference, and Harvey seized this opportunity to clarify their situation.

. . . if we could obtain assurance that the Lord did not require this of us now, and would permit us because of . . . the Manifesto to have the same blessings without its practice that . . . we could have . . . by living it . . . we would not go farther. We all three felt that the living of the Law would require sacrifice too great for us to undertake if the eternal blessings could be obtained without it.

Charlotte waited on the lawn outside the Salt Lake Temple as her husband conferred with LDS Church Apostle Matthias F. Cowley, asking if he and his wife might have the eternal blessings promised without entering the Principle. Harvey wrote his memory of Apostle Cowley's reply in his journal: ". . . the law was as binding now on those who would receive the blessings the Lord had promised through its obedience as it ever was and it was my duty to obey that principle." Apostle Cowley confirmed that Harvey must also obey the laws of the land in keeping with Mormon Article of Faith #12, which meant that they would have to move to Mexico or Canada before they could enter into the covenant. Harvey had also received a letter from Church President Joseph F. Smith instructing Mexico Mission President Anthony W. Ivins to conduct a plural marriage between Byron Harvey Allred Jr. and Mary Evelyn Clark upon their arrival in Mexico. Charlotte would participate in the marriage, "giving" the young woman to her husband, in the manner described in Genesis 16 when Sarah gave her slave, Hagar, to Abraham.

Meanwhile, outside the temple, Charlotte waited, alternately praying that the bitter cup would be taken from her and praying that the Lord's will would be done. Both she and Evelyn had voiced concerns about living polygamy outside the law and about living outside the United States. The colonies were plagued by disease and banditos, by poverty and exploitation. She fervently wished that they might all be spared this trial of faith. When Harvey presented Charlotte the letter of permission,

> Her grief was something I will never forget and so great that I told her I would not cause her such sorrow; in spite of the advice given me, we would not attempt to obey that law. She felt some better, but later informed me that she would not stand in the way, and inasmuch as we had been so instructed, we would obey the law. We returned to our home and passed the balance of the season in work with mingled joys and sorrows, more sorrows than joys, by all odds.

When Charlotte and Harvey returned to Afton, Wyoming, he made arrangements to sell his farm. Then the couple prepared to make the trip to Freedom, to inform Evelyn of the necessary move to Mexico. They prayed that if it be the Lord's will that they not enter the Principle, Evelyn would refuse to move. En route, Charlotte was overcome by a headache, and the baby, Othello, screamed so relentlessly Harvey decided that the child had been overtaken by an evil spirit. Everything combined to make the visit to the Clark home harrowing and unpleasant. Observing Lottie's grief and the general ill will that surrounded them, Evelyn spoke up. Harvey wrote of the evening,

> Because of our feelings and Lottie's sorrow, Evelyn said we had better give it up and release each other from all promises made. Her

chief reason for this was Lottie's grief—it was not that she hesitated to make the sacrifice of moving away, but for fear that with the deep feeling Lottie had in the matter, we could not live the law and expect any happiness in life, and she did not wish to destroy the happiness that Lottie now enjoyed with me. She, Evelyn, felt deep sorrow that it should be so, for she loved me and had intended to make every sacrifice on her part necessary to our marriage. With a decision that it was best, I kissed her lips and thanked her for her love . . . We then parted after the most strange feeling of unrest and disturbance ever experienced by me. I felt that I now had reason for not obeying the law, but felt no ease of conscience.

Although it seemed they'd received an answer, the ill-will continued as they made the trip home. Othello cried himself into a colicky sleep, and Harvey took advantage of the silence. "I have no ease of conscience in this," he said.

"Of course you wouldn't," Charlotte sobbed. "You've lost your precious Evelyn—the girl of your dreams." At this outburst, the child awoke and stormed again.

Harvey wrote of this difficult evening,

> It was unlike anything we had ever before experienced. I blamed dear Lottie for her ill temper, and she in turn blamed me for lack of patience. So it seemed we passed from a stage of sorrow and sympathy for each other into a period of fault-finding and harsh words. I think it was unlike anything we had ever before experienced, but we now had made up our minds to forget our former ambitions along the line of plural marriage and turned our attention to some other things less harrowing.

At last, Charlotte wiped her eyes and comforted the baby. She and Harvey realized they were exactly where they'd started: facing the choice whether to live the Principle or not live it. For the remainder of the journey they sat in silence, stunned by the extremes they had endured.

The next day a special messenger delivered a letter from Evelyn recanting everything she had said the night before. She did not feel she had done right in ending their commitment. "I wish to restore our promises and fulfill our former intentions." she wrote. For once, Harvey didn't try to hide his joy that Evelyn loved him.

With that, clarity replaced confusion. Charlotte and Harvey agreed to reestablish the promise, and Harvey wrote a letter thanking Evelyn for her love and confidence and promising that their pledges would be renewed without further hesitation. They began their preparations to move to Mexico.

Because there was danger for anyone entering plural marriage, Evelyn left her home in Freedom at night, traveling with her brothers, who had agreed to take her to Montpelier, Idaho. Here she said good-bye and boarded a train bound for Logan, Utah, where she planned to attend the LDS temple to receive her endowments (a set of covenants people make with God to prepare them for missions or celestial marriage). She arrived in Logan late at night, and asked a taxi driver to take her to the home of Harvey's uncle, Alonzo Cook.

While Evelyn was traveling, Harvey was beset by nameless fears, not regarding her loyalty, but for her safety and honor. All that day and into the evening he prayed for her, but his fears persisted until sometime during the night when he had a sweet dream of rescuing angels. Later, he learned that he had good reason to fear for Evelyn.

Instead of this driver taking her as directed, he drove in another direction and so long was he in making the drive, away from town, that Evelyn knew he was going a greater distance than it would require to have taken her to my uncle's. She became alarmed and called on him to halt. He drove a little farther and then entered the cab, but through her faith . . . she compelled him through fear of exposure to release his hold on her and take his place on the driver's seat and turn back to the place he should have first delivered her. Such fear came over him, because of the way in which she resisted him and the Spirit of the Lord that was with her in answer to her cry to Him for help, that he apologized and begged that she would not expose him. She gave him no promise, but he, through fear, delivered her unharmed one block distant from my uncle's home.

The next day Evelyn reported the man to the police and to the church authorities. In the course of their investigation they learned that this taxi driver had assaulted two young women prior to his attempt on Evelyn. By the time Evelyn completed her endowment session, the taxi driver was in jail. By the time she arrived in Mexico, he had been excommunicated from the Church of Jesus Christ of Latter-day Saints and was serving a fourteen-year sentence in prison. Harvey mused over the accuracy of his premonition and the appropriateness of his recourse to prayer.

> In my fear and worry for her safety I had earnestly prayed to the Lord to protect her from harm. She had at the first instance of fear prayed the Lord to preserve her. We must say we believe it was through His blessing that she was delivered.

In the years ahead, they noted many more instances when they survived only through what seemed to be a course of miracles. But always they faced enormous tests of faith—in themselves, in each other, in the Church, and in God.

~

It has been a test of my own faith to read their histories. In the stories told by my father and his brothers, Grandfather Harvey stood tall and bright, the lantern of faith shining. They told of the miracle following disaster one day while chopping wood and an ax-head flew through the air and severed Harvey's nose, but the brethren gathered round, pressed it back in place and the bleeding stopped and it healed. They told of his being saved during a blizzard that caught up with him as he carried the U.S. mail through Sardine Canyon between Ogden and Logan, detailed how he got lost in the marsh then was led by a mysterious light back to the main road and home. They implied that Grandfather Harvey's stories of faith proved the purity of his choice to live the Principle of Plural Marriage. I do not doubt that Grandfather Harvey was a good and God-fearing man. I am grateful for the life that was given to me through his peculiar practice. But Charlotte's agony and Evelyn's various humiliations have had a distorting effect on my view of him. Seen through the lens of these women's pain, Harvey Allred seems a fat cat in a bowler hat, a smooth politician showing up for this constituency in one way, and for that constituency in another. From this perspective, my life does not seem conceived in the clouds of celestial promise, but in smoky back rooms where bad bargains are made.

In the Colonies

 GRANDMOTHER EVELYN CROSSED the border a few weeks after her encounter with the taxi driver in Logan. Clearly she was all for seeing that justice was done, but the context for justice changed when she crossed into revolutionary Mexico where she would expose herself and her future children to lawlessness. She did so with her eyes wide open, knowing through Harvey's letters that the situation in Mexico was dire. She had weighed the odds and gone to meet her future anyway, and in crossing that line brought herself and her progeny into the land of the outlaw.

Meantime, Harvey and Charlotte enjoyed a going-away party given by the saints in Wyoming. Then they traveled to Montpelier, Idaho, to begin the long train trip to Ciudad Juarez. Harvey later admitted that he'd been distracted and inattentive, worrying about Evelyn at Charlotte's expense. He'd made a promise to arrange for photographs of the children to be taken at Montpelier, then forgot to do so. On the long journey to Mexico, Charlotte alternately complained and wept, unable to explain her great sense of loss in his failure to arrange for the portraits. Harvey threw up his hands, helpless to console her. Upon arriving at the Mexican border, Harvey ran into his former missionary companion, Joseph Richardson, who invited them to rest at his home in Ciudad Juarez before they went on to Colonia Dublan in the province of Chihuahua, Mexico.

To Harvey, this chance meeting with his old friend seemed like a gift from heaven. He reasoned that a chance to recover from the long journey before crossing into Mexico would allow Evelyn to catch up with them. But their rest was cut short when Charlotte had a terrible dream that Harvey abandoned her while crossing a muddy river where their youngest and oldest children, Othello and Ezra, were lost or nearly lost. Her distracted manner and bouts of weeping weighed on his friend's hospitality, and after two days of recovery, Harvey decided it would be best to cross the Rio Grande.

He settled Charlotte and the children in a small adobe at the outskirts of Colonia Dublan, then returned to Ciudad Juarez to meet Evelyn. When the engaged couple arrived at Colonia Dublan, Evelyn could see that Charlotte had grown pale and listless, although the desert sun burned most people a rich red-brown. Evelyn suggested that they delay their marriage until Charlotte was in better health. When Evelyn spoke to her, Charlotte made no response. When Charlotte did speak, she complained about the tiny adobe shack, nothing like the fine brick home Harvey had promised her. The situation was so strained that Evelyn opted to stay at the home of "Aunt" Helen, her father's first wife.

Soon after Evelyn's arrival, the baby, Othello, came down with meningitis, and within hours was so sick that Harvey and Charlotte watched over him constantly, taking turns at the baby's bedside. Three nights into the illness, while Harvey was sitting with him, the baby suddenly stopped struggling. Harvey was about to call out to Charlotte when he saw something radiant and wondrous—the baby resurrected, reaching to him from the Other Side. Harvey experienced a deep conviction that the baby would be restored to him in the next life and would be his throughout eternity. But the baby's death broke Charlotte's heart and her faith; all she could think was that the first part of her terrible dream had become a reality, and she waited in terror for the second half to unfold. In her sorrow she sometimes believed that because of her reluctance to enter the Principle the infant's death was her fault. Other times, she blamed Harvey for everything, including the fact that she had no photograph of her baby.

The day after Othello was buried in Chihuahua's alkaline soil, Evelyn and Harvey were married in the home of Anthony W. Ivins at Colonia Dublan's twin village, Colonia Juarez. With a few loved ones attending, the three assembled before President Ivins, Charlotte alongside Harvey, speaking the words said to have been spoken by Sarai to Abrahm. Then Charlotte put Evelyn's hand in Harvey's and stepped back so that Evelyn could step forward. Harvey took Evelyn by the hand, and then Charlotte's hand was placed over their hands. Thus they participated in the sealing ceremony, a marriage for time and all eternity. Charlotte, having lost a baby to the dark humors of Mexico, felt she was watching her nightmare unfold as her husband pressed ahead with his purpose. The wedding party returned to Dublan through beautiful country, a huge gold moon guiding them across the San Juan Ranch; yet an indelible sadness hovered over them.

The next day, Harvey took Charlotte to the mountains of Pacheco. During the week-long holiday, Evelyn tended the seven children, a peculiar way for a bride to spend a honeymoon even by polygamous standards. Charlotte enjoyed the journey to the mountains, but as soon as they returned to the squalor of the adobe on homesteaded land, she again drifted over the edge of sanity, accusing Harvey of killing her baby, blaming Evelyn for bringing them all to this godforsaken land, and hating herself for being weak.

Harvey had been feverish the night he married Evelyn, and soon he was in bed with typhoid fever. Subsequently addicted to the morphine given him to relieve pain, he would pitifully beg his caretakers for stronger, more frequent doses which conscience would not permit them to give. At one point, as loved ones gathered to pray for him, he had a kind of vision, seeing four angels in armor at the four corners of his bed, and hearing a voice announce: "These angels go to contend for you." The fever broke, and Harvey began to recover. But then the oldest of his sons, Ezra, came down with typhoid. As the disease reached crisis, priesthood leaders were called to give the boy a blessing. Both patriarchs—including Anthony W. Ivins, the mission president who had married Harvey to Evelyn—promised that Ezra would live, and gave him certain blessings indicative of a long life. Even so, the boy died and Harvey, weak from disease and drug addiction, lost his faith altogether. Everything he had believed crumbled—all the sacrifice in the name of God and family—none of it fit together. His days became loose-linked and mindless. He no longer wanted to live, and relapsed into his sickness.

After Ezra's death, Charlotte drifted through the adobe like a sleepwalker unless someone interrupted her; then she would ruff like a badger. Evelyn again took refuge in "Aunt" Helen's home, near the center of Colonia Dublan. Evelyn suspected that she was with child, and longed for her mother's advice, but Mary Catrina had opted to stay in Wyoming, where she still worked as a midwife. As her father's first wife and a kindly woman, Aunt Helen was the next thing to a mother, holding Evelyn's head during bouts of morning sickness, administering weak teas to calm the nausea, and telling stories of earlier times. In Aunt Helen's care, Evelyn felt grateful for "another mother" and she found wisdom in the Principle of Plural Marriage.

Helen, in turn, drank of Evelyn's freshness and breathed the hint of home, for the older woman's refined spirit had begun to wilt in the hot desert. For as much as a year, she had been the only person in the colonies with any medical knowledge, what she'd gained in helping her husband, Arthur, when Mary Catrina wasn't available. But day after day she confronted deprivation and disease until she could scarcely remember what it was like to be healthy. Then her young daughters developed a strangled cough. It was not the first time since entering Mexico that Helen had worried about her red-haired girls.

She had seen bandits hanging around the town well eyeing her daughters, but this was something more serious. Both young women were diagnosed with diphtheria, and within days, Sylvia was failing and Libby struggling. Helen sent for Evelyn's mother, Mary Catrina, but it was hopeless, with her sister-wife still in Wyoming.

What secret patterns traced the sky visiting such sparse rains and wicked illnesses on Colonias Dublan and Juarez? Was it punishment for those given to procreative pride? Was Helen bitter about the loss of her daughters even as she said Thy will, oh Lord, be done? If there is rhyme and reason to all things and not a sparrow falls that God does not see, why did Helen stand before the stove that day, nursing her broken heart and stirring the stew to feed the remaining family? Why did the lightning strike Helen's stovepipe when there were other high places—the silo, the lightning rod, the steeple of the new chapel? And why did the lightning come bursting out of the hot plate and jump to the spoon and from there to Helen's hand and arm, burning her so badly she was permanently disfigured? It hurt so that she could not sleep, and the constant burning did nothing to detract from the pain of her broken heart. Only Evelyn could take the heat away, poulticing Helen's arm with splayed leaves of aloe and bandaging her soul with talk of the hereafter where she would be reunited with her daughters.

After Helen's summons, it took Mary Catrina almost a year to reach Mexico. Nonetheless, Helen greeted her with gratitude and relief in much the same way as my mother and her twin would later greet their sister-wives. They looked out for each other. No sexual jealousy could make them forget that they shared a family. No petty rivalry could keep them from loving each other. Nothing could convince them that disconnection was preferable to connection.

By the time Mary Catrina arrived in Mexico in 1905, Evelyn had given birth to her first baby, named Louis, who died of pneumonia when he was two months old. Mary Catrina, trying to comfort her daughter, found herself saying the things she always said to young mothers who lost their babies—that the child had gone straight back

to Heavenly Father, having been taken before the age of accountability, and promising that God would bless her with other children as
well as the opportunity to raise this lost one in eternity, but Mary Catrina's words seemed discordant with what went on inside her, a knowledge of loss she never wanted to bring so close. Overall, the settlement
of saints welcomed Mary Catrina; she could be bossy, but she always
knew what to do—what herb to use so that the burn on Helen's hand
wouldn't become cancerous, and when Charlotte came down with
dropsy, Mary Catrina put millipedes in capsules, then insisted that
Charlotte take one a day. Charlotte thought the prescription bizarre,
but she followed orders and the swelling went down.

Despite its wild beauty, Mexico became a kind of Mormon hell.
Criminals mingled with polygamists in the settlements, buying up the
land and goods with their stolen wealth, and then reselling it to the
Mormons for ten times the price. Byron Harvey Allred Sr. had nearly
starved to death on more than one occasion. He abandoned the
notion of opening a general store in the colonies, since the saints were
trying to live the United Order, giving all they had to the bishop to be
divided up according to need. But somehow that didn't work, and the
Allred family struggled to get by on scraps from the church bakery.
Byron found work for his wives in the church store and in the school,
but after a lifetime of ranching and retail sales, he had a hard time
finding a job for himself. He was reduced to doing whatever was necessary to put food in his family's mouths: building fences, running cattle, and logging. The weather matched the mean-spirited land, hot
winds blowing seeds from the dust before a crop could take root, light-
ning-struck fires burning young crops, revolutionaries lighting barns
and sheds and houses to drive the gringo settlers off the land.

～

Arthur B. Clark fared not much better. When the Brethren had called
him to come to Mexico, Arthur Clark had been reluctant, and soon he
knew why. Born in the wet coastal weather of England, he quickly

despaired of dry farming in Chihuahua's high winds, lightning storms, and flash floods. The only people who rode horses were bandits or revolutionaries. Oxen were used for plowing and hauling. Arthur's spirit felt the drought more acutely than his crops. After a spell near Dublan, he decided in 1907 to trade ranches with a man who owned a house and property near the coast in Morales, Sonora. The man swore that the ranches were similar in all ways, save the balmier climate of the Sonora ranch.

And so Mary Catrina packed her few transportable belongings and her children into a wagon, and left all furnishings and goods behind. Indeed, the climate of Sonora was milder but the ranch house was a sty with no furnishings at all. The rainfall could take away a crop faster than the fierce sun could burn it up. Mary Catrina, known for her bravery in the face of terrible illness and want, sat down and cried.

Arthur had borne up under the constant threat of drought and revolution even though he missed his mountain ranch in Wyoming. He would not have disobeyed the Brethren for his own sake, but he couldn't bear to see his wives so miserable. Pancho Villa's revolutionaries had routed the Mexican Army in the southeast and as the revolution moved into Chihuahua, Arthur urged Helen to return to the states. As the legal wife, she could return home without recrimination from the church or the government. But Mary Catrina was the first to return, moving to Blackfoot, Idaho. Arthur soon followed. In 1910, with a heavy heart, Helen said good-bye at the graves of her two daughters and returned to the states. With the help of her son, Orson, she acquired a small house near the Logan Temple in Utah and began doing temple work for the dead. She spent many of her last days on earth there, acting as proxy, making covenants for baptism, receiving endowments, and vowing eternal marriage on behalf of women who had already died.

Even after the other Clarks returned to the states, Arthur's youngest wife, Ethel Adolphia—known to the children and grandchildren as Aunt Dolphie—stayed on in the abandoned town of Oaxaca. She seemed pleased to be the only one with enough grit to stay in the flooded settlement when the rest of the family had given up. She excused Arthur's leave-taking, saying he had to find work, and there was none in the ghost town of Oaxaca. She lived in a little shack with no door. One night, wild creatures growled and howled around her door and thinking they were rabid coyotes, Dolphie sat in the doorway all night, holding ready her husband's rifle, "armed for the kill." The next morning she learned that it was "only a pack of wild dogs" and she reprimanded herself for being so fearful. Later she discovered that those wild dogs had ravaged groups of soldiers and gunslingers, and she packed her few possessions and her children on the last wagon to leave the area. She and four young children reached El Paso with barely enough goods to trade for train fare home. She returned to the states nearly a year after the rest of the Clark family, a fact that brought her a good deal of self-satisfaction. But it was a precious year, since time with Arthur was scarce. Having lost everything in the colonies, he had to start all over again in the states.

Prior to this, in 1907, Harvey had taken stock of his family's situation in Mexico, and began to talk about returning to the states. Both wives had given birth in Mexico, Evelyn twice (to Louis, the baby who died of diptheria, and to my father, Rulon) and Charlotte once (to Rhea, who would be regarded as my father's "twin" since they were so close in age), but they feared bringing more children into an environment that produced new and horrible pestilence each year. In the Mormon colonies, where outlaw and saint seemed to merge character, Harvey had been duped out of money and land, and his small herd of cattle and sheep was stripped thanks to coyotes and banditos. He and his wives prayed about whether to leave, and decided that it was better to take their chances as polygamists with the authorities and Pinkerton detectives than to hazard another year in the badlands that had claimed three of their children, their own health, and their family assets.

Byron Harvey Sr., whose affluence had long since been lost to the dust of Mexico, pleaded with his son not to go. Harvey grieved that he had the mission president's blessing, but not his father's:

. . . dear Father went so far as to say the curse of God would rest on me. I felt he was very over-exercised and was not speaking by the proper spirit, and although it hurt me very much, I did not feel in the least that I was doing anything contrary to the will of God.

Byron then tried to persuade his son to wait just a little longer before abandoning Mexico. He showed Harvey a letter he'd been keeping to himself, notification from England that he was due a large fortune through his paternal grandmother, Mary Calvert, whose father was Lord Calvert. Harvey had heard about the family's royal links for years but such claims had not yielded anything. So he packed his family up and left on December 30, 1907, his mother's tears and his father's curse weighing on his heart.

Within the next few years Byron Sr. witnessed two murders of Mormon friends by angry Mexicans, indications that the revolution had arrived in the Mormon colonies. Byron was scheduled to testify and feared for his life, but the killers were never brought to trial. Still, the revolution drew nearer each day, on the streets of Guadalupe and on the ranch lands surrounding Dublan. Many nights, Byron gathered his families into two small rooms where he could keep watch, rifle in hand. One morning, awakening to what they thought was hail pelting the tin roof, they discovered that they were caught in a crossfire of cannon shot and bullets. The next day orders came from the Mexican government expelling the gringo Mormons from Mexico under threat of execution. Byron's three wives and sixteen children packed what they could—only two trunks and a bedroll would be allowed—but the crowd at the train station was so dense they were immediately informed that they must leave their bedrolls behind. As branch president of the Guadalupe region, Byron was in charge of assigning seats and making sure all saints could ride the train. His family waited for hours before he got to them. Eliza, the youngest wife, had been crying

nonstop. Matilda was preoccupied with organizing the few possessions she'd been able to bring. Only "Auntie" Irene had anything
cheerful to say. She had clustered the younger children around her
and was playing an alphabet game called "Crossing the Plains."

Byron seemed very tired, and Irene expressed her concern, but his
priesthood responsibilities as branch president would not allow him to
rest. At last the train was fully boarded, and the refugee Mormons
looked out on a station littered with trunks and grips, with dolls and
musical instruments and portable secretaries that the train could not
accommodate. The saints had begun their departure early that morning but the sun was beginning to sink westward as the engine chugged
out of the Dublan station. The loaded train arrived in El Paso well
after dark. From there, they were directed to a nearby lumberyard
known as "The Stables." Byron wrote this entry in his journal:

> Tongue cannot tell the gratitude of the refugees to the People of
> El Paso for kindnesses shown us when the trains would arrive. Auto-
> mobiles and buggies were at the depot to convey the Company to
> rooms where provisions were brought to feed about one thousand
> and two or three hundred. The Government as well as the Church
> appropriated well over $100,000 to cover the expenses of the fleeing
> women and children, but thanks be to God, not one life was lost in
> the flight for life.

An outbreak of typhoid fever at The Stables prompted them to
move to a house on a plateau overlooking the Rio Grande; here the
diseases of the river could not reach them. Several families shared
quarters, and once they were installed, Byron announced that he must
continue his duties as branch president. Eliza complained that they
needed him, why did he always have to be off doing good for some
other family? Things were so hard, especially since Irene had gone to
stay with Harvey in Idaho. When Byron inquired what it was Eliza
needed of him, she wept that the children were filthy, she could get

nothing clean, would Byron please bring her a washtub and wash-board? He promised to bring them as soon as everyone from Guadalupe was settled.

On an August evening, 1912, he carried these items up the hill. The families had gathered on the porch to play games, but he did not ban-ter with them as he usually did, nor did he join in. He entered the liv-ing room, the washtub and washboard fell from his hands, and he dropped dead. He was perhaps the only casualty in the "flight for life" made by the Mormon colonists from the revolutionary, Pancho Villa.

In his journal, Harvey observed that Byron's curse had come to pass. Soon after their return to the United States, Charlotte conceived twins; she and the babies died. Then Harvey lost his father to exhaus-tion after moving the endangered saints. Then he lost his only full sis-ter, Myra, to dysentery she had contracted in Mexico. After the deaths of his father and sister, his mother's life ebbed away in sorrow, and he lost her, too.

The desert kept its hold in other ways as well—in the malaria that plagued Harvey until his death and in a sense of lost citizenship that continues to shadow my family. But most of all, Mexico left its mark because it was the birthplace of my father. At the age of twenty-four my Grandmother Evelyn became mother to nine children, seven of Charlotte's and two of her own. Harvey's paternal family was com-pletely gone, leaving him to care for the families born of his father's plural wives, some of whom he scarcely knew.

Return to God's Country

 IN 1909, GRANDFATHER HARVEY fell into a deep, brooding silence. His journals from that time are a cryptic quotidian, save for a few uncharacteristic outbursts of sorrow and outrage. Pregnant with twins, Charlotte had been sick and in excruciating pain for days before she went into labor. She requested help, and Harvey sent for the doctor who was the superintendent of the State Insane Asylum. He soon discovered that Dr. Hoover had become addicted to liquor. In his journal he reports,

> It was partly at her request and by my consent that the Dr. administered an anesthetic by hypodermic. This, of course deadened her sense of the intense suffering, and as the labor advanced the doctor said the child was improperly presented and he would have to turn it. My heart seemed in my mouth, for I feared the result of his handling her in his condition. As he proceeded I noticed to my great horror that he was . . . very harsh. . . . He succeeded in turning the babe and taking it. But immediately on its delivery . . . he proceeded to take the second little one without waiting for nature to perform its part. I was almost wild with fear, and as I witnessed his rough act

115

my dear wife gasped and suddenly breathed her last in this mortal life. I quickly turned to him and said, "[Doctor] my wife is dead and you have killed her."

Only peripherally does he seem to acknowledge any part in Charlotte's demise.

Oh, I can never in my life forget her last shudder of pain as she lay there a martyr to the duty of motherhood and abuse of a drunken doctor. May the Lord forgive me if I accuse him wrongfully.

After burying Charlotte and the twins, Harvey legally married Evelyn in a Pocatello, Idaho, civil court, then moved her to Blackfoot, Idaho, where she took charge of the household, mothering Charlotte's children as well as her own. Evelyn's mother and father returned from Mexico and settled nearby, bringing some comfort during this time of loss. Arthur Clark had resumed the practice of dentistry, and he worked hard at it, meanwhile making plans to regain his beautiful ranch near Freedom, Wyoming. But in 1912 an epidemic of smallpox struck the community. Evelyn had given birth to their fifth child, a boy, and she had exhausted herself caring for the eleven children; the newborn, the sickest child, required her attention day and night. In her weakened condition, the disease hit hard, paralyzing Evelyn's upper torso so that she could not speak or raise her arms or nod her head. Mary Catrina, having exhausted her healing remedies, turned to Harvey. "The disease is internalized. Unless the rash breaks out on her skin, it will destroy her organs. You'd better send for the Elders," she told him.

The stake president and the bishop, along with a young elder who had recently completed a mission placed their hands on Evelyn's head and administered a blessing. Soon after, the rash appeared on her back and legs in huge, running sores. Most of her thick blonde hair fell out.

Evelyn's oldest living child, Rulon, was not spared the pox and throughout his life my father bore a scar on his right cheek, a reminder that he had survived the terrible disease. He had been inseparable from his half-sister Rhea (Charlotte's youngest surviving child). People called Rulon and Rhea "the twins" because they were born three months apart and both were blond, although Rulon's eyes were blue while Rhea had her mother's dark eyes. When Rulon contracted smallpox, Rhea was quarantined in the attic, where she wept with loneliness.

Gradually the household began to recover; Mary Catrina scoured the walls and washed the bedding. Rhea, now allowed to join the family, discovered that "Auntie Evelyn" had lost her hair. When the family decided to attend church to give thanks for the lives spared, Evelyn protested that she could not go in such a state. Rhea cut her own long blonde braid with the kitchen shears and offered it to "Auntie Evelyn." Later Rhea wrote in her book, *Voices of Women Approbating Celestial Marriage*,

> . . . a merciful providence overruled that a tender-headed tearful little girl named Rhea was relieved of her long hair, and it was used to make a switch for Mother Evelyn who had lost much hair with the dread disease of smallpox. How proud I was then that my hair . . . just matched Mother Evelyn's. At that time she was 28 years old or thereabouts. There were twelve people in our family then. What a burden for her young shoulders.

~

Arthur Clark, having resumed his dentistry practice and settled in Blackfoot, often invited Rulon, the oldest of his daughter Evelyn's children, to accompany him on his rounds. From the age of seven or eight, Rulon looked forward to these trips with his grandfather. Besides being a personable traveling companion, the boy was quite helpful, willing to hand his grandfather the dental instruments, time the vulcanizing procedures, and clean up. Then one morning, as Grandfather Clark prepared his monthly itinerary, he announced that Rhea would accompany him on his next trip. Rhea, still recovering from the death of her mother, had been privately troubled by a sense of not really belonging to the sprawling Clark family. If Rulon was hurt by Arthur Clark's choice, he didn't show it, but simply looked on as Rhea was scrubbed and dressed in her Sunday clothes. At the first stop, Arthur introduced Rhea by saying, "This is my granddaughter, Rhea Allred." And so it went until someone who knew Harvey and Evelyn asked, "I thought Evelyn's daughter was named Mary, after your wife Mary Catrina."

"Charlotte was Rhea's mother," Grandfather Clark explained. "Surely you remember Lottie."

"Oh, yes . . . so sad that she died after giving birth to twins—and they died too, didn't they?"

"Yes, yes." Grandfather Clark said. "But now she is my granddaughter too, and a fine little girl at that."

Once Rhea was assured of her place in the family, Grandfather Clark resumed his habit of taking Rulon on his rounds, teaching the boy to assist with clamps and swabs and the vulcanizing procedures, and as Rulon grew older, taking a larger part in the practice of dentistry. My father would look back fondly on those early years and he would one day adopt his grandfather's practice of taking young family members with him as he made house calls and traveled from state to state to see family and patients.

In the summer of 1917, Grandfather Clark gave up his horse and buggy for a "horseless carriage." Then, in July, on his dentistry rounds in southeastern Idaho, northern Utah, and southwestern Wyoming, he traveled alone to Logan, Utah, to visit his first wife, Helen. After that he stopped to gather a huge bouquet of wildflowers before visiting his youngest wife, Dolphie, in nearby Hyde's Park, Utah. On both occasions, he declined to spend the night—such risks were no longer tolerated by the members of the church, who would be as likely to turn Arthur over to the law as would any "gentile," or non-Mormon.

When Arthur reached Freedom, Wyoming, site of his beloved (and long since reclaimed) ranch, he asked his sons to assist him with his car, which had developed mechanical problems. The next day, with the car ostensibly repaired, he started for Blackfoot. Thirty-five miles out of Freedom, as he climbed out of Cunard Valley, the car lost power and rolled backward into a gully of chokecherry brush. A family along the same route heard moans and carried Arthur to a nearby ranch house, where the rancher, who knew Mary Catrina, called her to come at once from Blackfoot. After attempting every intervention she knew, Mary Catrina sat by Arthur's side and relied on prayer for her husband, who had suffered severe internal damage.

For nine days Mary Catrina remained at the rancher's house. When Arthur could speak, he begged to go home and Mary Catrina sent for her sons; with a stretcher and a wagon the group set out for Blackfoot. Unfortunately, Arthur died as his sons carried him along the sidewalk leading to his front door.

Arthur's fifth wife, Dolphie, learned of Arthur's accident when the stake president in Star Valley, Wyoming, called to ask if she knew where he was. She was alarmed that they would blatantly refer to him as her "husband," knowing that such reference could lead to his arrest. Then an anonymous postcard from Star Valley arrived with the news that her husband was gravely injured. From then on, Dolphie waited for one of "Mary's boys" to come for her, running to the door each time she heard the sound of a car or buggy on the street. Instead, the telephone brought the news of her husband's death.

Arthur Clark's sisters, Zina and Marion, said that it was a pity such a good man had been taken when he was alone, without a single member of his family to care for him or protect him from danger. Dolphie wrote in her journal, "The first thought that came to me was that was the only way he could have been taken." Dolphie was convinced that his life had already been prolonged to accommodate their marriage, for he was twenty-two years her senior, and he had fathered her seven

children. She was further convinced that if Helen and she had combined their prayers with Mary Catrina's caretaking, their faith would
have kept Arthur alive. But instead of blaming Mary Catrina for
neglecting to call her to her husband's side, as she might have, Dolphie
accepted Arthur's death as God's will.

Questions linger: Did my great-grandmother Mary Catrina sell out
her sister-wives so she could hoard Arthur's last hours on earth? Did
Mary Catrina act as I had seen some of my father's wives act—posses-
sive, conniving to get more than their share? Whatever her motives,
after Arthur's funeral, Mary Catrina withdrew from the other Clark
women and remained in Blackfoot, attending to her garden, her midwifery, and raising from infancy a child from outside the family who
had come into her care through a local doctor. In her later years, Mary
Catrina openly expressed her disillusionment with the Principle of
Plural Marriage and warned her children and grandchildren against its
practice.

Although her ability to diagnose and cure an illness seemed to have
failed her with Arthur, Mary Catrina continued to exercise her gift.
Her son, Nephi, brought his son, Dewain, to Mary Catrina after doctors had failed to help him. The boy was weak and sickly, and even
though he was three years old, his bones were so soft he had not
learned how to walk. Following an inspiration, Mary Catrina packed
soil from her garden into a tin washtub, telling the child's father,
"There is strength in the earth." She put the child in the tub and
insisted that he play while sitting in the dirt. Day by day the child
grew stronger. His legs, so floppy and weak, took shape. Soon Dewain
could crawl and before the summer was over, he could walk. Perhaps
minerals in the soil and daily doses of sunshine gave strength to his
bones. Whatever the scientific explanation, Mary Catrina's intervention seems to have worked.

My father inherited the gift for intuitive healing. When my baby
brother was born clubfooted, my father molded the soft little bones so
that the foot and leg were straight. My father's methods of healing

included naturopathy, osteopathy, chiropractic, and medicine. But he was also a shaman and a folk healer. The medicine men of the Blackfoot tribe and the brujos of Chihuahua had taught him their secrets, just as the Indians shared their cures with Mary Catrina. Before reading the family journals, I believed that the gift of healing came from my great-great-grandfather, William Moore Allred, via the Prophet Joseph Smith, a gift straight from heaven and sent through the paternal bloodlines. Perhaps, in part it did. But how exciting to find that the practical example of patient care came from Arthur and Mary Catrina Clark, through the bloodline of the mother!

Within five years after his return to the United States, Grandfather Harvey found that his political star was on the rise again, promising an auspicious change in his fortune. Since marrying Evelyn in a civil court, he was a monogamist once more, a definite advantage for a politician. In his journal, Harvey gratefully notes that Evelyn did her part to stabilize his grief-stricken household:

> Immediately after Lottie's death Evelyn came to our home and like a noble soul assumed the duties incident to care and motherhood of not only her own children, but of Lottie's too. A task in which very few are ever successful and one that is in a great measure a thankless one.

But once he was elected state senator and public service necessitated more time in Boise, Harvey felt the tug of Blackfoot. The tiny graves on either side of his first wife's grave seemed to strengthen his bond with Charlotte's children, and his aspiration to be a successful rancher made him want to stay close to the land. Traveling back and forth between the two communities, Harvey stoically endured the growing fragmentation of his family and religious life.

After serving two terms as a state senator, he was appointed Idaho's

Director of Farm Markets, which required a move to Boise for the better part of every year with a return to Blackfoot for the months of harvest. Meantime Charlotte's older girls had bobbed their hair, taken to short skirts, and squealing, "That's the cat's meow!" Though worried, Harvey seemed powerless to change their minds when the girls decided to move to an apartment in Boise, persuading Rhea to join them. The division of the family broke Evelyn's heart, and Harvey's too. His hope, then, was that he would reunite his family in the proud manse of a statesman.

In 1918, he was the favored Democrat to run for the U.S. Congress, when there was no formidable Republican candidate. Harvey, sure that he would win the nomination, resigned as Director of Farm Markets and telegraphed relatives in Washington, D.C., to find a house large enough for his family. Unfortunately, counting unhatched chickens yielded what it so often does. The night before Harvey was to accept the nomination at the state's Democratic Convention, he received a telegram from the regional representative of the Church asking him to withdraw from the race because of "certain facts" regarding his "past family relations" which "might ruin you and revive an issue affecting our people that otherwise would remain buried." The telegram was followed by a letter from Stake President Duckworth and his counselors.

> The facts referred to in the foregoing telegram are well known to you, to us, and to others who are neither friendly to our people [n]or to you. Should you be elected, the advantage offered by a disclosure of the facts above referred to would . . . be too great for our enemies to pass by. Suppose the facts alluded to were disclosed to the public, you can well imagine the result. The favorable conditions regarding our people in Idaho . . . would be materially changed for the worse and the odium (in the public eye) would affect all of our people everywhere. . . . Without doubt, the cause that is so dear to all of us would be in jeopardy.

The Church was keen to keep its polygamous skeletons closeted so as not to deter potential members from the growing church. The regional officials who wrote the letter left no room for misunderstanding: Harvey was being ordered in the name of the priesthood to withdraw from the senatorial race. Harvey responded with umbrage:

> I cannot make myself believe that every man whose name is signed to this letter and telegram gave their contents the careful consideration such a matter demanded. I understand these "facts" to mean my "past family relations" which were polygamous. If so, I ask: Has that *knowledge* become an "odium" to men? If so, what class of men? . . . [M]y life has been an open book to all men and those claiming no Church membership who have closely scanned its pages have striven hardest to show me honor.
>
> I have long noticed, with deep concern, that those who are most affected by the "odium" of my "past family relations" are those who claim Church membership and style themselves brethren, ever ready to soothe the people's sensitive social taste if there were a chance of my becoming too conspicuous in either Church or political matters.

Although Harvey obeyed his priesthood leaders, he chafed at the implication that he'd entered polygamy as a renegade rather than as an obedient servant of God. He gave up his political aspirations and hoped that his sacrifice would be pleasing to the Lord. But insult became injury when, having given up his state appointment and having moved his family from the state capitol to Blackfoot, he found that one of his brethren in the Blackfoot stake had violated an agreement. To aid Harvey in his stated purpose to make a living as a rancher, a bishop in the area had offered to lease some land with an option to buy. The understanding was that Harvey would make improvements on the property and as soon as he had gathered the funds, he would buy it. Harvey kept his end of the bargain, but the landowner, seeing that the value of the land had increased due to the improvements, reneged. Harvey sought recourse from the stake president and the regional representative—the same men who had ordered him to withdraw from the Idaho congressional race—but they refused to get involved, calling it a "personal matter." In a religion that invokes a Law of Consecration, where the devout offer all they attain to God by making it available to the bishop (the "father" or pastor of the ward), Harvey was deeply affronted to be treated so cavalierly by one of the men entrusted with his flock's earthly and spiritual wellbeing.

Within two years, with his dreams of worldly success largely dashed, Harvey's health deteriorated. Still, he harbored the fantasy of being a gentleman farmer in the style of his Calvert ancestors, just as he continued to envision a church observant of the Law of Consecration, each member dedicating everything to the Lord so that, as described in the *Book of Mormon*, "there were no poor among them." Correspondence with his polygamous cousins in Canada painted a glowing picture of Latter-day Saints who were engaged in something similar to the United Order as lived in the early days of the church, pooling resources and sharing all they had. It wasn't long before Harvey pulled up stakes and took Evelyn and her children to Canada.

~

I can only imagine this further hardship for my Grandmother Evelyn, but at age 15, my father did not mind leaving his childhood home. Always more idealistic and religious than his classmates, he had no more difficulty migrating than did the Canada geese. His closest friends were his brothers and sisters. He had always enjoyed the company of adults—his grandfather and grandmother, his mother and father. He was zealous in his church activities, happy to be ordained a deacon at the age of twelve, delighted to become a teacher at the age of fourteen, generally glad to be of service. His classmates called him "Elijah" and he carried the nickname to Canada.

My father loved telling stories of the indelible lessons learned in

Canada. His yearning for purity found an answer in the pristine wilderness of Saskatchewan. When he told us about Canada, he described how Grandfather Harvey acquired a quartershare of heavily forested land, and told how they piled the timber high in fields cleared for planting in the spring. He told of the first winter they spent there, how it froze so deep that great limbs of fir and pine cracked and plummeted at a mere footfall in the forest. When he warmed to the pivotal story, "the wolf story," the one he always told when he spoke of Canada, my father grew more animated. His voice showed alarm when he described how they discovered late one day that the woodpile beside the dugout was so depleted there wasn't enough wood to last the night. Harvey was away from the ranch, "home teaching," fulfilling a church commitment to teach the Gospel and offer service to a family in the area. My father, left in charge, put on his overshoes and flannel cap, two coats and elkskin gloves while the younger children and Grandmother Evelyn watched. Rulon was oldest now that Charlotte's sons had married, and they were fearful for him, and for themselves as well.

My father took up the leather thong—a rectangle of deer-hide with two handles for carrying a load of wood, then stepped out the door and struggled up the icy earthen stairs into the dim afternoon. It was a mile across the near field, and another mile through the forest of Douglas fir to the untouched woodpile in the clearing. He knew that wolf packs had been bold this winter. Brother Vance had announced at their last ward meeting that he wouldn't take his family to Sunday school till the cold snap was over; their horse-drawn sled had been attacked by wolves while making the twenty-mile trip home the week before.

If anything, the cold had grown deeper since the wolf-talk in the foyer of the clapboard meeting house. With all prey driven deeper into hibernation, the wolves would be bolder. This explained Harvey's plan to stay over at the Vance home, returning when it was light. But how to explain that Harvey had neglected to haul a load of wood in the sleigh before leaving? Now both horses and sleigh were gone, the wood supply was exhausted, and the sun was about to set. As my father entered the cold, dank shadows of the forest, fear urged him to race back to the dugout.

Although there is no reliable record of a man being killed by a wolf in the woods of Canada, my father truly believed that timber wolves would kill a person. Along with the usual fairy tales, wolf legends pervaded the Great Northwest, white man and Indian alike filled with respect as they spoke of the pack or even the lone wolf. Terror escalated by word of mouth, with stories about this trapper and that hunter, stories told on church steps and over lamplit suppers all through the great white land. The wolf howls alone were enough to stop the blood in a man's veins. The Mormons had their own horror stories of the long trek across the Great Plains when men buried wives and babies in shallow graves piled with rocks, and returned in the spring to find that prairie wolves had dug up the bodies and scattered the bones where they would lie until the Resurrection. All the stories coalesced into terror when my father stepped out of the woods and saw the sun resting briefly on the hillside. And silhouetted against the golden light, the wolves.

He worked quickly but deliberately as he would in later years when faced with an emergency as a doctor. While he gathered the wood, he glanced now and then at the shadowy figures against the half-gone sun. Then, balancing the thong, he turned back. It seemed to him then that the wolves moved and the sun slipped out of sight, as though turning his back had set everything in motion.

As he hurried through the trees, snow pelted his cap and coat. He grappled with the thong using both hands and didn't dare stop to clear his vision, but through the flakes he thought he could see them bounding across the clearing—four, five, maybe six of them. And he began to run, the wood thumping against his legs as if to make them churn faster until he burst into the field, his lungs burning. He set himself toward the long low mound of the dugout. He ran looking back at the camouflage of forest shadows, sure that the wolves were gaining.

Then a stump brought him down. Through shock, he sensed the wolves closing in, thought he heard a low growl, felt they were about to pounce. His face was bleeding, scraped deep from one of the logs that had splayed when he fell. He remembered that blood attracts predators and through his numbness, he had grabbed a stick of wood and struck out blindly. Seizing the lightened wood-carrier, he ran pell-mell. He thought he heard the wolves snarl as he slid down the icy dugout steps and fell through the door into the firelit room.

His mother did not seem surprised to see him. She rose from her rocker, peered out at the dark, and calmly closed the door behind him. The children cheered as he pulled off his coat and gloves—he had lost the cap—stopped to stoke the fire with a stick, announcing in a shaky voice that at least he'd brought enough wood to get them through the night. He sat at the plank table, breathing hard. His mother put his supper before him. He did not want to eat, his face growing hot as flames licked the hearth. She treated the scrape on his face with iodine, then bent and whispered something in his ear. He nodded and ate voraciously. And then the children listened, openmouthed, wide-eyed, as he told them, just as he later told us, his children, the story of how the wolves had chased him and of how he had barely escaped, and of how he had learned not to let fear rule him.

First Love

ONCE AGAIN, GRANDFATHER HARVEY ALLRED lost nearly everything. Between his failed ranching and business ventures, the Canadian winters and the ravages of influenza and measles, he had little choice but to return to the United States, which he did in 1924, settling in Boise, Idaho. The Allred clan was impoverished, the patriarch in broken health, but they held their heads high and attended the meetings of their Boise ward, which were held, oddly enough, in a synagogue. There Rulon met a young woman, Katherine Handy. Katherine, writing of her first encounter with my father, described "a wonderfully tall, blond boy who looked at me when he thought I wasn't watching him." He walked her home and often invited her to join his family for dinner at the Allred's "very poor but clean home, and their meals consisted of the plainest food possible. . . . The mother was sweet and kind, but when B. Harvey Allred spoke, everyone jumped to do his bidding."

Raised in the monogamous affluence of a doctor's home, Katherine was startled by many aspects of life in the Allred family:

> At the dinner table one Sunday afternoon . . . conversation brought out that Rhea and Rulon were both eighteen years of age.

When I remarked that I hadn't known they were twins, Rulon said they weren't twins, that his father had had two wives. I was shocked, to say the least. My whole soul rebelled against the thought of such a thing in this day and age.

My father explained that his family's polygamy was a thing of the past. His father had not been a polygamist for seventeen years, he declared (a small lie or an oversight?) and Katherine accepted his explanation. Rulon vowed that she was his kitten, his "dream girl," and the first woman, other than a relative, whom he had kissed. She declared that he was everything she'd dreamed of, too.

I don't know how to tell the rest of my story. If it is possible to feel joy and pain so intermingled that you can't draw the line between the two, that describes my feelings when I think of the hours of pure bliss that I spent with Rulon. He was two years older than I, and so sweet and thoughtful. He never called me anything but Kitty, and I was his girl, to the envy of every other girl in the Ward. Every other boy ceased to exist for me; I had found what I had waited all my life for. . . . We almost knew what the other was thinking, we were so in harmony.

My father spent that summer in the woods of Oregon, where he had taken a summer job in a logging camp. He worked to buy Katherine a diamond ring, and sent away through the Sears Roebuck catalog so that he could present her with it during her visit at the end of the summer.

They borrowed a boat and rowed toward the center of Crater Lake, the two of them caught in a shimmering bowl of stars. The moment was perfect. He fumbled for the velvet-covered box, had to stand to reach the depths of his logging pants-pocket, and nearly upset the boat. She grabbed both sides, sending slivers into her hands. He took the oars and swung the boat back to the center of the lake, trying to find another perfect moment. He looked around at the volcanic rim, and it seemed that the fire and brimstone that had formed the crater were not so far beneath the surface. The wind stirred the water and ruffled Katherine's hair; with the moon behind her she might have seemed some creature from one of Shakespeare's fantasies. My father wrote, in his handwritten autobiography, of that night,

> We rowed over the crater to the central portion of Crater Lake. . . . All the time I was trying to muster up sufficient courage to propose. However, night and ten o'clock came before I finally asked my little sweetheart if she would marry me. We both had tears in our eyes and the moment she hesitated left me wondering again just how much she loved me.

"Will we go to the Temple?" she asked.
"Of course, Kitty. I wouldn't have it any other way. I want you for eternity."

> I told her I would never marry her any other place, and our future was outlined. For a long time we sat on the brink of the huge crater, some 2000 feet above the lake, watching the deep blue water dance and move below us, reflecting the light of the moon, before we strolled back into camp.

They were married "for time and all eternity" in the Salt Lake Temple on June 9, 1926, then set off on their honeymoon, ultimately destined for Los Angeles, California, where they planned to make their home, near Katherine's family.

> We ate hastily, made our beds and retired without pitching our tent. When we awoke it was glaring daylight. We were very con-spicuous. Attached to our car were numerous old shoes and chalked

inscriptions: "Just Married"; "On Our Honeymoon"; "California or Bust". Scampering into our clothes, we cranked our war-horse and were off without breakfast. We did not forget to say our prayers.

The next day they crossed Idaho into Oregon and followed the Pacific Coast Highway until the moonless night became too dark for safety with their headlights dim and the fog rolling off the sea. When they reached Astoria, Oregon, they threw down their bedroll, so exhausted from the long day that they slept like stones. Upon awakening in the grey light of dawn, they found that they had slept at the edge of a two-hundred-foot cliff. Had they made love or even rolled over in the pitch-black, they'd have died the first week of their marriage.

Further adventures awaited them. The car broke down, and Rulon had to send it back to Blackfoot. He bought a bus ticket for Katherine, then caught a freight train under the tutelage of a hobo named Slim. When at last Rulon and Katherine found each other in Los Angeles, they spent an evening reveling in fresh fruit and big-city lights. The next day Rulon found that he had to upgrade his high school diploma in order to enter the Los Angeles Osteopathic College, so he enrolled in the Los Angeles Coaching School. Soon he was admitted to the Los Angeles College of Chiropractic, and he and Katherine both found jobs—he as hod carrier, she as secretary. "God was blessing us abundantly," my father wrote.

They seemed so happy, the newlyweds in their apartment working to build a better life. Katherine's brother George lived nearby and attended the Chiropractic College with Rulon. In the evenings the young couples double-dated, attending the latest movies. Katherine's parents moved to Los Angeles and they gathered on Sundays at the Handy home where the chiropractic students shared their learning with Dr. Handy.

Now I feel a sharp nip at my heart as I compare two records: the first, my father's autobiography in his hand, and the second a typed version of the same, with additions by Katherine in red ink. My father's account:

> We were living at these [the Noelle] apartments when we lost our baby daughter at the Monte Sano Hospital. She was born June 3 and died June 4, 1927. We thought we could never recover from her loss, but time heals great wounds, and we know she is always ours. My little wife did not quit work at the college until the third month before our baby was born. I gave our daughter a blessing and a name and sealed her against the power of the destroyer to come forth in the morning of the resurrection. At first, the attendant at the hospital gave me the wrong baby and I gave it the same blessing before learning of my mistake.

Katherine's account, appended to Rulon's journal:

> On the evening of June 2 . . . all the family had come from Long Beach and we were all together in our apartment. The boys [Rulon and George] were enthused of course, with all they were learning at the Chiropractic College and my father was showing them certain spinal adjustments, etc. Rulon, wishing to demonstrate something he had learned that day, said, "Kitty, sit here. I want to show Doctor something." He told me to clasp my hands behind my neck, then proceeded to make an adjustment that hurt me. My father said at the time, "Oh Rulon, you shouldn't have done that to her." Sure enough, next day my labor pains started, resulting in the loss of our darling baby girl. True, I was working too hard, even having to carry a typewriter from one section of the college to another. Our grief was tremendous at the loss of our baby. Dr. Curtis Brigham, who had ushered me into the world, was my doctor and he assured us he had done everything possible to save our baby but she just wasn't strong enough to keep breathing. She weighed four pounds.

And elsewhere, beneath a photograph of their three children standing at the graveside of the baby girl ten years after her burial, Katherine wrote:

> When our Darling was sinking fast, my father and Rulon asked for the baby that they might give her a blessing. After asking the Lord to care for her and let her be ours for eternity, they found out they had been given the wrong baby who was also near death. They then blessed our own darling, but Rulon was so sure that both babies would be ours forever.

A disturbing ellipsis, my father's omission of these events surrounding his first child's death. When I was growing up I saw him as incapable of error, as did most of my family. We knew of their first baby's death, and added it to our lists of sorrow, another loss he had to bear, so stoic in his grief, bolstered only by his faith. The year before he died, my father told me about the tragic death of his first child, how in his enthusiasm to demonstrate what he was learning, he had performed a chiropractic correction on his wife, and how his father-in-law had taken him aside afterward and warned him that he may have done damage to his wife or his baby, and sure enough she'd gone into premature labor, and the baby died. My father told me that remorse had never left him, not up to that moment when he was seventy years old. Many years afterward, when I came upon these disparate versions of the baby's death, his confession preserved my trust in him. Yet I cannot help but wonder how many of his other journal entries are suspect, information carefully applied to smooth appearances.

The death of his firstborn surely yielded a hard and important lesson. My father sustained an eagerness to prove himself, yet kept his ego in check and gave credit for every healing to God. Through discipline he sharpened the clairvoyance that allowed him to diagnose without X-rays or blood tests in the days when these methods were not available, and he whetted a hunger that led him to midwives and medicine men and university medical centers to find cures and treatments. From childhood, when he accompanied his grandfather, Dr. Arthur B. Clark, on his rounds, Rulon had known his purpose as a healer; it was a relief to fulfill it.

Curiously, his healer's art became a source of discord in his marriage, even though Katherine, as a doctor's daughter, had lifelong experience with the demands on a physician's family. By this time they had a son, Sherwood, who was often sick with croup and other respiratory problems. During Sherwood's harrowing bout with whooping cough, Rulon stood vigil over the boy for ten nights straight, yet Katherine begrudged Rulon the daytime hours he spent establishing his practice. In 1930, as the Depression swept the country, Katherine's father, Dr. George Handy, died and she felt the loss keenly, demanding her husband's comfort and reassurance. Despite their financial pressures, she complained that he was always busy with his patients or with his church work. The year their daughter, Patrica, was born Katherine often came to Rulon's chiropractic office, sometimes hovering near him as he worked. Gradually Rulon noticed that Katherine stood sentry if a woman was listed on his appointment book. Realizing that she must be desperately jealous of his women patients, he worked up the courage to ask her about it. She nodded miserably. He reassured her of his love, but she confessed her fear that he would one day leave her to raise the children alone.

In keeping with the LDS tenet of eternal progression, Rulon believed strongly that church members can ensure the progress of loved ones and ancestors who have passed to the "Other Side" through "work for the dead" which entails conducting genealogical research, and then completing their sacred ordinances by proxy. He organized several bus-trips across the Mojave Desert to the Mesa, Arizona, temple where people from his stake participated in baptisms and received endowments for their dead ancestors. Everywhere he went, on the beach, in the desert, or in the mountains, he found opportunities to treat the afflicted and to preach the Gospel of Jesus Christ. Katherine complained about his absences, but he justified himself by saying that he was doing the will of the Lord. Sometimes he was so absorbed in what he called "my continual church work" that he neglected to attend to his patients, and Katherine would track him down to remind him of his appointments. She objected whenever he went to a fireside or a priesthood meeting, perhaps fearing that his spiritual zeal would take him away from her.

On March 10, 1933, Rulon was sitting down to the dinner Katherine had prepared when he realized that "all nature seemed to be holding its breath." The uneasy barking of dogs ceased and insects stopped humming. When the earth began to shake, Katherine clung to him, saying, "Oh Rulon, is the world coming to an end?" Rulon reassured her that they had God's protection. Sherwood was thrown to the floor. Katherine snatched the baby, Patrica, from her chair as a piece of statuary struck her, opening a gash on her head. At first my father was awed by the might of God, then bolstered that at least he would know what to do. The house shook off its foundation at one corner, and a front porch pillar crumbled. At each quake, the earth bucked beneath them. For a few moments, then, all was quiet, after which came a low rumble and the aftershocks, one wave following another as if the ocean were moving the land. When at last the earth stopped heaving, my father attended to the baby's cut, reassured his family, then set out to help the neighbors. Lacerations, broken bones, shock—he moved through the city giving relief and assistance. He arrested heart failure by administering a tincture of foxglove. He helped a woman in shock by putting cold packs on her feet and heat on her upper torso. He pulled on a man's hand while pressing against his chest, and the loud pop confirmed that he had corrected a dislocated shoulder. As he approached each injured person, he seemed to know what was needed before actual confirmation. And he seemed to know what to do, as though "an angel on his shoulder" whispered specific instructions for each situation.

In 1932, Grandfather Allred announced to his children that he was completing his book, called *A Leaf in Review*. In the book, Harvey argued that the Church of Jesus Christ of Latter-day Saints, having abandoned the Principle of Plural Marriage, the United Order, and the actual practice of the Law of Consecration, was "out of order." Harvey's children and brethren must have wondered, after a life of devoted membership, why he would turn against his church. Perhaps Harvey harbored bitterness about a political career deflected by the Church's effort to bury its polygamous past; then there was the wound inflicted when he lost the farm he thought he had earned and his ecclesiastical leaders' refusal to stand up for him. As Harvey struggled with poor health and poverty, he echoed his father Byron's dismay that some saints were shamefully affluent while their brethren suffered from abject need even though the Doctrine and Covenants promised that "there shall be no poor among them." Acrimony seeped through Harvey's careful reasoning and logical arguments. Perhaps advancing age motivated him to speak out, as well as a strong desire to serve his fellow man:

> If some honest souls can, by my compilations and writing, be moved to think for themselves, to watch and to pray, and if some truth be found, make it their own, my humble purpose shall be well served.

He states his purpose in the book's preface:

> . . . its purpose is to prove to the honest searcher for truth . . . that the Church . . . as an organization, and its leaders have apostatized from many of its divine truths.

Harvey describes his internal struggle to get words on the page:

For seven long years I have tried to reason against my better sense of duty in this matter. I have searched in vain for an acceptable excuse for leaving this thing to more worthy and capable minds. Several times I have gathered courage to make a beginning, but my overwhelming fear of facing worldly consequences of a publication of my convictions has driven me to desist and destroy much of that I had written.

But commitment to speak his mind prevailed.

I have at last arrived at a milestone in my journey of life where . . . [I] fear . . . facing the known consequences of a violated conscience through continued silence far more . . . than the displeasure and abuse of mortal man.

Rulon's half-brother, Elwood, wrote to his younger sibling in Long Beach, urging him to talk their father out of publishing the book. My father's response is recorded in his journal on July 18, 1932:

Received a letter from Elwood telling me that Father was openly opposing the church authorities, advocating doctrines out of harmony with present doctrine and was claiming the church was corrupt. One of the most sorrowful days of my life. I would much rather have my loving father dead than have him fall away into apostasy or be excommunicated. We drove one hundred and fifty-three miles to pick peaches to give to our poor. I told Brother Steed about Father and cried.

Rulon felt torn between loyalty to his father and loyalty to his church and he was dismayed to discover that his sisters, Rhea and Olive, defended their father. Rulon talked with Katherine and corresponded with his older brothers, then wrote a long epistle meant to divert Harvey from apostasy, supporting his argument with quotes from scripture and church doctrine: "That man who rises up to condemn others, finding fault with the Church, saying that they are out of the way while he himself is righteous, then know assuredly that man is on the high road to apostasy, and if he does not repent, will apostatize as God lives." He accused his father of "kicking against the pricks" of prescribed authority. When Harvey's course did not waver, Rulon contacted Anthony W. Ivins, the mission president who had married his father to his mother, Evelyn, in Mexico and who was now second counselor to Church President Heber J. Grant. Rulon suggested that perhaps his father's excommunication would be required, for he feared that Harvey's apostasy would lead others astray:

> Maybe only immediate excommunication can be followed. Perhaps your influence will bring about repentance. . . .

When his attempts to reason with Harvey failed, Rulon began fasting, studying scripture, and praying fervently for help in dissuading his father from a heretical path. At first he looked up the scriptural notations in Harvey's letter to him, and then searched deeper into church and biblical history, writing to his father with questions and postulations that Harvey answered passionately. My father wrote that his own bishop and stake president warned him against scriptural study regarding the topic of plural marriage, and tried to dissuade him from making his impassioned inquiries of God about who and what was right, but he only intensified his religious quest. If he couldn't use the main vehicle of his religion, prayer, if he was being told that he could not do what Joseph Smith had done, following the Biblical counsel in James 1:5, "If any of ye lack wisdom, let him ask of God," if he could not trust in prayer, then something was amiss in the church, just as his father had said.

Katherine tried to dissuade her husband from delving into his father's contention with the church. In 1933, she wrote in her journal,

> Rulon is neglecting his practice terribly. He spends all available
> time reading up on polygamy—in order to dissuade his father, he says.

What's undeniable is that Rulon disappeared for long hours, saying
that he would be in the Los Angeles Library, researching church history and exploring genealogical records. When Katherine protested
that she and the children required more of his time, he reminded her
that time spent in church-related activities promised spiritual progression and blessings for the whole family. Katherine's journals indi-
cate that during those difficult months, Rulon was gone nearly every
evening to priesthood meetings or to speak at firesides, leaving her to
care for the children. Often he did not come home until long after the
meetings were over. Filled with suspicion, Katherine lost all tolerance,
and initiated bitter quarrels. The more she railed at him, the more he
stayed away from home. His correspondence with his father escalated.
He no longer seemed to care about providing for his family. Katherine
didn't know what had taken hold of him; she feared it was Satan.

> Rulon won't listen to my pleading anymore. Everything he says is
> in favor of polygamy. He acts like some demon possesses him.

Katherine expressed her fears to her mother, Julia Handy Hawkins,
who quickly arrived on the scene. Katherine's mother had remarried a
scant two months after the death of George Handy, Katherine's
father. She had lived in Idaho briefly, and now returned to California
where she was close enough to monitor her children's marriages. First
she accused Rulon of immoral behavior (a mother-in-law's accusation
that he had failed as a breadwinner and that he had been with other
women which she did not support with evidence or instances). According to my father's account, she then ordered him to abort Katherine's
baby—their fourth in eight years—claiming that her daughter was too
frail to keep bearing children for a man who wouldn't provide for
them. Rulon refused to allow the sin of abortion, stating that his pro-

fessional and spiritual commitment was to life, not death. Katherine's mother then spread a rumor that Rulon had tried to abort the baby. At this point, he broke off all contact with his mother-in-law, believing her to be the adversary of his marriage and his family's solidarity. Grace was born in November of 1933, just as Rulon was beginning to surrender, through the long correspondence with his father, to the Principle of Plural Marriage.

Two years after Rulon had charged his father with apostasy, a member of the High Council that governed the Long Beach, California, Stake levied the same accusation at Rulon. By 1935, Harvey had convinced Rulon—who was, after all, the oldest living son of his plural wife— that in adopting the Manifesto, the Church had allowed the laws of men to prevail over the laws of God. Harvey did not encourage Rulon to live the Principle; he seemed more concerned with being accorded his criticisms of church leaders. The more he corresponded with his father, the more Rulon fasted and prayed and studied scripture, the more Katherine worried. Rulon took note of her concern:

> My sweetheart constantly fears I am overzealous to attain eternal life, saying that I neglect this life with its obligations and pleasures; and she fears spiritual progression draws me nearer to living Celestial Plural Marriage. She thinks, "I would rather die than live plural marriage; I would rather inherit an inferior glory." And so she has often stated.

Even as his attitude in favor of plural marriage emerged, my father had continued to fulfill his church callings as president of the Stake Genealogical Society and as leader of stake temple excursions. Because of his leadership role and his dynamic delivery, he had been invited to speak at many cottage meetings throughout the region, and gradually, subtly, his text shifted from genealogy to plural marriage, from temple work to what he came to call "the Most Holy Principle." No one can say why he decided to shift his loyalty from the citadel of the official church to become, as the scriptures say, "a law unto himself." My father was an intelligent man, capable of seeing the rigor as well as the dark underside of living an outlawed Law. Perhaps he felt that in turning against plural marriage, he would betray the religious underpinnings of his existence. Perhaps he saw the tide of opportunity come in, and caught the wave that would take him to greater power and leadership. Perhaps he had a revelation from God (as he implies in his writings) that it was his responsibility to "keep the Principle alive." The waters of belief heated steadily, coming to a slow boil until there was no turning back, for in 1935 Rulon told Katherine point-blank that he knew that the Principle was true and that he had been called to live it. Each fought ferociously, she for monogamy and he for polygamy. In his journal, he refers to one incident that shows the desperate turn his marriage took:

> During this time my wife was persistently opposing my continual church work and on many occasions I was obliged to leave against her will. One night I left her in tears and attended my officer's meeting. Upon my return home, I felt the terrible appalling spirit of the devil in my home as soon as I entered the door. I cried, "Katherine, what is the matter?" Her answer was like a scream for help. "Oh Rulon, come quick, I am possessed of a devil. He keeps telling me to kill the baby." I found my wife with the scissors in her hand and in the act of destroying our child. I rebuked the devil in the name of Jesus Christ and by the authority of the holy priesthood. I felt his presence depart through the window and a spirit of peace and undeniable joy came and abode in our home. For hours during the beauty of that night, I taught my dear wife the things of God.

No mention appears in Katherine's *Book of Remembrance* to corroborate my father's autobiographical account of her brief conversion to the Principle. The baby, Grace, was not harmed. But Katherine's jealousy intensified, and as the drama unfolded the stakes escalated with each new episode. Rulon continued to study and pray. He continued to spend long hours in research and Katherine would have to bring him from the Los Angeles library to treat patients. Their resources dwindled as his interest focused more acutely on spiritual matters.

Soon Katherine's mother brought formal accusations against her son-in-law, calling him to account before the stake president. On March 11, 1935, my father wrote in his journal:

> The rift between my wife and [me] has continually grown because of my belief in the necessity of plural marriage and because of my church work. I believe plural marriage is an essential of the gospel ordinances . . . and should be lived by the worthy saints, that it is now in force and has never ceased being a law of the priesthood and must be abided by those who hope to become like God.
>
> On four occasions I have been called before President Muir [his stake president] because my beliefs are still unaltered. On each instance I have expressed my views clearly. The second time I was called before President Muir I was threatened with excommunication if I maintained my beliefs.
>
> Sister Julia Curtis Handy Hawkins [Katherine's mother] has run everywhere spreading stories of my misconduct, my beliefs, my father's family and their apostasy. She has called me immoral, reported my father is crazy and that three of my sisters are married to one man. She states I have deserted my family, refuse to provide for them, etc., etc. All of which is untrue.

What Katherine did not know, and perhaps never knew, was that two days before my father wrote this journal entry, he took a second wife, marrying Aunt LaVerne in a spiritual ceremony. They had met when he spoke at a cottage meeting in the Hollywood Ward and twenty-five-year-old LaVerne made it clear that she was available. (Later she would admit, "I always knew I would marry a man who was already married.") Brother Joseph Musser, a leading theologian among the fundamentalists, performed the plural marriage, citing his authority as a former "seventy"—one of seventy people set apart to witness for Christ and to preside over missionary efforts and other ways of building up the Church of Jesus Christ of Latter-day Saints. Brother Musser charged LaVerne with responsibility to "give Rulon all the wives he has coming to him" and she took this instruction to heart. The day after my father made the journal entry above, he married Rose. Their marriage had been pending for several months, arranged by John Y. Barlow, head of the Short Creek fundamentalists. Rulon himself had postponed it, explaining that his wife was opposed to plural marriage and besides, he wanted the fifteen-year-old Rose to mature a little before marrying. But now that LaVerne had preempted Rose, it seemed necessary that he marry the young woman in order to keep good will among the fundamentalist patriarchs. This marriage was also performed by Brother Musser.

On his twenty-ninth birthday, March 29, 1935, Rulon told Katherine he was going to help a friend proofread the galleys of a book, but he didn't return until 11 P.M. Katherine, who had planned a birthday dinner, was so angry that she took the three children and went to her mother's house. The next day she moved her belongings, and Rulon moved as well, probably into Aunt LaVerne's apartment. There's little question about where he spent the evening of his twenty-ninth birthday—with his two newlywed wives, among other people who believed as he did. Perhaps by then he longed for separation, and that's why he did nothing to bring Katherine back to the home they had shared.

Imagine the two of them: Katherine, horrified as her marriage capsized, trying to bring it to shore, calling for help in every direction— her relatives, her church advisers, her friends. The harder she tried, the worse it became and her passion more destructive. Rulon, driven by deity or devil, determined to fulfill his purpose, felt that either he or his wife must be wrong. Adjured by brethren in the official church, both Rulon and Katherine returned to their house and tried once again to live together in peace. But, he wrote, "trouble was inevitable as long as my belief remained unaltered."

At another point during the summer of 1935, Katherine and the children went to live in a little flat, alone. She wrote,

> Today I am taking my sweet babies and leaving the husband I love. I will continually pray that Rulon will not let us stay there alone, that he will yet come to his senses. The Lord has always answered my prayers.

Then, three weeks later:

> The miracle happened! Rulon came to the flat last night and started to cry. He said since I had left he had tried to look at *both* sides, and had spent many hours out in the hills in prayer. He knelt . . . and asked me to forgive him, saying that he knew that his father was wrong, that he would never again go against the church's teachings. We both felt the sweet spirit that was with us. My heart is so full of thanksgiving today. I can never thank my Heavenly Father enough.

And then, after two weeks,

> It is the end. Rulon told me that Satan had made him shed tears and be weak, and tell me he knew his father is wrong. He says he will enter polygamy as soon as he can. I feel as though I'm losing my mind.

All the time Katherine was casting about for a way to change Rulon's orientation, he had been praying that Katherine would receive a testimony of the Principle. He wrote that at one point she did have a burning knowledge of the beauty of it, but that a devil came and threatened her life, and that she dared not run for help. His interpretation contradicts Katherine's record that she thrust his beliefs away, then summoned her mother, who assisted her in freeing herself from Rulon.

> After living for a month alone except for my babies . . . I was so desperate and blue that it seemed as though I must try hard to understand Rulon's teachings and go his way with him. So I asked him to help me understand, that I'd try. In answer to my request, he brought me literature and pamphlets late at night so I'd peruse them quietly and undisturbed. . . . After Rulon left, I started to seriously study his doctrines. No sooner did I start, than I felt such an evil spirit in the room and trying to take possession of me that I was almost frightened out of my wits, and I grabbed his documents and ran the 10 blocks to his office . . . on Anaheim Street, and put them inside the screen door. It was about 10:00 P.M. I went home and was troubled no more with the evil spirit.
>
> Rulon's response to this the next day was, "Satan won again, didn't he? He kept you from reading the truth."

A week later, Katherine loaded some things for the children and prepared to leave for Yellowstone. There she would meet an old friend, and after vacationing with the children, she would return to Boise, Idaho, where her mother lived. She wrote of this departure:

> I don't believe I could believe Rulon again if he told me he had changed, so I will never be back, I'm sure. I'm not big enough to take this thing any longer. I asked Rulon before I left him this morning if he'd be satisfied with just one other woman, maybe I could take that, but he said I had no right to limit the Lord's commandments, he'd take all the women he could. President Muir put

Rulon on the High Council last month, in order to be near him. It only impressed Rulon with his own importance and made things worse than ever, if possible. On the day they put him in [the High Council] he came home and told me that [his appointment to the High Council] proved that he was all right, and that from then on, he was running the home or there wouldn't be any home.

Katherine left a letter for Rulon, telling him that she was going to visit a friend near Yellowstone and that she did not want to see him and would not permit him to see the children until he gave up the ridiculous notion of living the Principle. She hoped that he would follow her, for the children's sake if not for hers. Despite her keen awareness, she had not counted on the divisive force of religious pride. Rulon had read Christ's admonition to the disciples: if he would give up flocks and houses and children for His sake, the Lord would bestow flocks and houses and children in abundance. When Katherine realized that Rulon was not going to follow her, she bypassed Stake President Muir (who had not been able to stop her husband from being led into polygamy) and she wrote directly to the president of the Church of Jesus Christ of Latter-day Saints, Heber J. Grant. She told him the long, sad story of Rulon's apostasy. President Grant, once a polygamist himself, sided wholly with Katherine. In his letter to her, he states,

> I tell you, Sister Allred, as the president of the Church of Jesus Christ of Latter-day Saints entitled to the inspiration of the Lord to guide me, that your husband is in sin and that he will never be saved and you can never have him in the life to come unless he repents.

When Katherine shared this correspondence with my father, he wrote President Grant and his counselors a thirteen-page letter, explaining the foundation for his convictions. President Grant did not respond to my father but wrote to Katherine instead:

I certainly have neither the time nor the disposition to read a thirteen-page letter from a man who is in sin, who is practically commit-
ting adultery, and any inspiration he has comes from the wrong source.

It was not the only time President Grant had called those who practiced plural marriage adulterers and apostates. In 1935 he had issued
such a statement in support of local, state, and federal authorities in
rounding up polygamists and sending them to prison. Now President
Grant urged Katherine to remain in the official church, and reassured
her that any woman who would marry my father was no better than a
woman of the streets.

The man who did respond to my father's discourse was Anthony W.
Ivins, the one-time mission president who had sealed the plural marriage of Rulon's parents. Anthony Ivins had corresponded with my
father when he agonized over Harvey Allred's apostate book. As counselor to President Heber J. Grant, Ivins responded to Katherine's
questions about the supposed revelations of Church President John
Taylor. President Ivins carefully refuted the notion that President
Taylor had recorded and signed two revelations sustaining the Principle of Plural Marriage. He was careful to acknowledge all possible
instances when something might have been written or recorded that
might have been mistaken for a revelation. He called the handwritten
paragraph and other missives "purported revelations" which the
Church did not recognize and had never recognized as revelations.

In his own journal, my father revised Ivins's statement enough to
become evidence supporting the cause of plural marriage:

> He acknowledged the presence of the 1886 revelation, saying it was
> "in President Taylor's handwriting, but was only a paragraph and
> had no standing in the Church."

The fact that President Ivins never acknowledged that the paragraph was a revelation, seems to have slipped past my father. When

my father traveled to Boise to visit his children, Katherine refused to let him see them, refused the birthday presents he brought, and once she ascertained that he was still on an undeviating course, she refused to talk to him. Her parting words predicted that he would never find another woman to marry him. (She did not know that he had already been married twice, with his marriage to Aunt Emma pending.) Within five years he had five wives. Within ten years, he had seven. Twelve years and twenty-three children after their divorce was final, I was born, his twenty-eighth child.

In October of 1935, when Katherine first filed for divorce, she learned that it would take a year to finalize. Meanwhile, she prayed for reconciliation, asking for help from church leaders, friends, and relatives. Somewhere along the line the divorce proceedings were interrupted by custody matters, and she took this as a sign that her differences with Rulon could be resolved. Rulon had written to her of his undying love, and had asked her to come back to him and bring the children. Still, he had not changed his belief in plural marriage, and Katherine heard rumors that he actually practiced the Principle. The delay in divorce extended to an additional year since my father was out of the state in October of 1936, and Katherine took this as a hopeful sign that perhaps the marriage would survive. On their eleventh wedding anniversary, June 9, 1937, Katherine saw a notation of my father's civil marriage to LaVerne in *The Salt Lake Tribune*. That same day she received a card from Rulon commemorating their anniversary, with a letter beginning, "My Darling Wife." Adding insult to injury, when Katherine wrote to express her bitterness about this happenstance, Rulon wrote back, inviting Katherine to join him and LaVerne in Salt Lake City. This pushed her over the edge to finalize the divorce. After a long courtship, she agreed to marry Kenneth State on April 10, 1941, a man who, as it happened, had been baptized into the official Church of Jesus Christ of Latter-day Saints by my father. This man

had consistently comforted Katherine during the painful years of separation and divorce. As they discussed the marriage, she warned him
that she would need "extra understanding" to make their marriage
work, given her broken heart.

~

Over the years, Katherine continued to write to President Grant, and
eventually she learned about plans to excommunicate her former husband from the official church. However, in the correspondence of
1937, the issue of temple divorce was raised, and she asked for a post-
ponement, to give her husband the opportunity to repent. By then the
process known as excommunication had been initiated, presumably a
process of repentance and redemption, but in my father's case, a
process meant to condemn his way of life. On May 8, 1940, my father
was officially cut off from the church, the witnesses against him being
his former stake president, Leo J. Muir, and his former mother-in-law,
Julia Handy Hawkins. The letter informing him that he had been
excommunicated read:

> You are hereby advised, that in accordance with notice and sum-
> mons given you, the High Council . . . met on Wednesday, May 8,
> 1940. . . . At this meeting, documents written by you were pre-
> sented, as well as affidavits submitted by President Leo J. Muir and
> Mrs. Julia S. Handy Hawkins. The evidence contained was . . . suffi-
> cient to establish your guilt as accused . . . and you are officially
> excommunicated from the Church with loss of your Priesthood and
> blessings.

When Bishop Edward Sorenson wrote to Katherine to announce
the excommunication, he apologized for a delay of over a month,
explaining that he had been very ill. Nonetheless, he asked her permission to hold onto the letters Katherine had provided as evidence
against my father's church membership so that they could be used in

the excommunication proceedings of his plural wives. A year and three months later, LaVerne, Ella, Emma, Sally, and Adah were also excommunicated. (Rose, it seems, never had been baptized into the official church.) Soon after the plural wives were excommunicated, in December of 1941, Katherine wrote to President Heber J. Grant asking if she could still be sealed to Rulon. President Grant urged her to request a cancellation of that temple sealing and asked, "Are you quite sure you are being fair to your present husband if you still hold in your heart a love for your first husband?" At this prompting, Katherine requested a temple divorce, which was readily granted.

Katherine continued to fast and pray, hoping against hope that Rulon would somehow change his mind. But one thing she resolved, which is clearly communicated in her journal: so long as Rulon lived polygamy, Katherine would not let him see the children. If she did, she believed, they would love him as much as she did and they would want to be with him, would succumb to his way of life, and then her sacrifice would mean nothing. So the years passed and his letters, cards, and birthday gifts to them were returned, unopened.

~

When Katherine took a job with the Atomic Energy Commission and moved to the Nevada Test Site in Mercury, Nevada, my father threw a fit such as I'd never seen before. It was insane, he said, Katherine's moving into an atomic zone and risking her health and the children's (he was not stopping to think that by now they were grown and living their own lives). It was as insane as the fact of her leaving him and marrying a man she didn't love, he said, when God and she both knew that it was he, Rulon Clark Allred, she really loved, and to whom she was promised for time and all eternity. No Devil could break their bond for they were sealed by the holy priesthood.

In my father's mind, their marriage was never dissolved. Long after their divorce, he continued to write to her with the salutations, "My Darling Wife" and "My Eternal Companion." He frequently reminded his plural wives of God's promise that if he remained faithful in his covenants, Katherine would be returned to him, if not in this life then in the next, when she would spring forth from the grave to embrace him. Even though Katherine's rancor seemed to fuel the forces that sent him to prison, he continued to cherish her memory. But I was fifty years old before I came upon the journals and learned how we lost the brother and sisters we had never met. Then I could taste the tears my father shed each time he sang, "I'll Take You Home Again, Kathleen."

TWO

The Raids

No one openly blamed Katherine for our family's constant terror of being torn apart, although my father and the mothers may have secretly wondered if she was the source of our trouble. In fact, a number of factors influenced the "polygamous roundups" that would affect our lives so thoroughly, including her many missives to an LDS Church Presidency no longer tolerant of its embarrassing and contrary polygamous remnant. Our parents' main concern was to protect us from any and all realities that might unravel family bonds, including those with our father's ghostly first family. We knew nothing of Katherine's lengthy correspondence with President Heber J. Grant and the ripple effect of her struggle to change our father's mind. And we were not told that Aunt Sally's father, in his fury that his devout daughter had become the fifth wife of a polygamist, had raised a ruckus at church headquarters. Later, we would find that an ambitious U.S. District Attorney named John S. Boyden had been gathering information about fundamentalists for years, and he collaborated with Utah Attorney General Brigham H. Roberts (the grandson of LDS historian and polygamist B. H. Roberts) to draft a plan for getting rid of the Church's polygamy problem once and for all. Boyden's plan included state and local authorities from Utah, Arizona, and Idaho, as well as federal agents and U.S. marshals. The hounds loosed by Boyden pursued us for years to come, yet we had to learn about them by eavesdropping and doing our own research, for no one—not my father, not the mothers, not our many aunts and uncles—came out and told us the whole truth.

During my early childhood, my father's wives often gathered in the white-house kitchen to quilt or to bottle fruit. Even though they had established themselves in their own apartments on the compound, they still seemed to crave companionship, sharing the household and the labor as they had in the beginning. One morning in 1954, the mothers worked together to can a bumper cherry crop, and believing that all the children were outside (except for me, hiding beneath the kitchen table where their garmented knees shone like fourteen white moons) they spoke openly, confiding their fears, their thoughts, and the latest gossip. Their voices fell when they told secrets, and on this particular day the secret had to do with Aunt LaVerne being suspended from her secretarial job at the law office. Her income helped make ends meet, and the sudden change made everyone nervous. Aunt LaVerne suspected that the trouble at work arose because someone recognized her from the family pictures in *Life* magazine. Someone else said, no, that was so long ago, there must be a new conspiracy afoot. Maybe another raid.

In a strangled voice, Aunt Melissa asked how on earth we would survive, and someone mentioned the time we had borrowed money from my father's wealthy patients. Aunt Emma said we could not go to that well again; they were regular patients and we would lose them altogether if we imposed on their kindness. Someone else said, don't worry, God will provide. Aunt Melissa suggested that we gather windfall from the neighbor's orchard, and Aunt Sally said we hadn't done that since the days when they had to visit Rulon through the prison fence.

"You don't talk about prison in front of the children, do you?" Aunt Adah asked in alarm.

"Of course not." It was my mother's voice. "I always call it 'when Daddy went away to college.'"

"Well, I don't see how you can lie to them," Aunt Melissa said. "They need to know that we're being persecuted."

"You could tell them he was in World War II," Aunt Rose said. "That's when it happened."

"But he wasn't in the war. He was in prison. I ought to remember." Aunt Melissa's voice was full of heat and conviction. "I married him the day before he went to prison and I had to wait nearly a year before I could spend the night with him."

"You were only fifteen, Melissa. It didn't hurt you to grow up a little," Aunt LaVerne said.

"The way we live," Aunt Sally said, "we can't afford to split hairs about what's a lie and what isn't. I think it's ingenious of Ella to say 'when he went away to college.'"

Then Aunt Emma said, "If Rulon goes to prison again, his practice will collapse. Another raid means the family will have to live in separate houses—think what it would cost! Make no mistake . . . the wolf is always at the door."

I heard Aunt LaVerne offer some common sense, telling Melissa and Emma to stop worrying about what they couldn't help. Aunt LaVerne said that the older children could go to work for our Japanese neighbors, harvesting spinach, and whether they earned money or a portion of the crop, it would improve our situation. Everyone settled down then, and the mothers shared tips learned during harder years: how to make a child's dress out of a man's worn-out shirt; how to make shoes last with an innersole of cardboard; how to make cookies and cakes using wild honeycomb.

At the time, I wasn't sure what was worse: learning that my mother had lied to me or realizing that we children could be put in foster homes and our parents sent to prison. What I learned that day never left me altogether. When the air took on an autumn chill, or when the milk was thin and blue, I shivered. Soon the wolves would prowl and with them, the cold ache of not enough—not safe enough, not pre-pared enough, not strong enough.

When I raged at my mother for lying to me about my father's days in prison and the dangers around us, she soothed me with stories of how the family had grappled with polygamous roundups and poverty before I was born. She told these stories while kneading bread or darning socks or making jam. She let my questions regulate the flow of information, and by the time I was six I knew many details about the raids conducted by the FBI near the end of World War II.

I never asked my father about that painful time, although I saw him every day when we gathered for prayers and when he came to kiss us good-bye before he took Aunt Emma with him to work. It was from my mother that I learned how the FBI banged on the front door of the white house at 6:00 on the morning of March 7, 1944, and when my father answered, they pushed past him and began searching the house for "evidence." LaVerne rushed upstairs to awaken sleeping sister-wives and gathered them into her bedroom, where they prayed for deliverance. FBI agents continued their search throughout the house, yanking drawers open, tearing beds apart, and ripping up floor-boards, so that the children screamed in terror and the women cried. The agents confiscated diaries, birth records, and issues of the religious journal called *Truth*, to which my father frequently contributed. As it turned out, my mother said with a smile, they couldn't use any of the items they confiscated in actual court cases because they'd taken them without a search warrant.

Although all the mothers lived with my father in the white house, the agents had singled out my mother and Aunt Emma, "the doctor's twins" for arrest. As the matron ushered them out the front door of the white house, my father was still sitting on the sofa between two detectives. He told my mother and Aunt Emma to be calm, not to be afraid, and they gratefully drank in his words. When they arrived at the police station, my mother was charged with playing the piano at our religious meetings, and Aunt Emma with teaching Sunday school.

Fingerprints and mugshots were taken as the twins blushed bright with shame. Newspaper reporters from *The Salt Lake Tribune* and *The Deseret News* photographed them just before they were interned.

In the county jail they were served a stew seasoned with so much pepper that my mother could not choke it down, not with morning sickness and fear curdling her stomach. They overheard two newscasts about mass arrests of polygamists from Pocatello, Idaho, to Short Creek, Arizona. During the disruption of our household, similar scenes had played out in households of friends and loved ones who also lived the Principle. From their cell window, the twins could see the street, and noted the arrival of Aunt Adah's brother, along with Joseph Musser's son, Guy. More polygamous patriarchs and their wives arrived, including my father's half-sister, Aunt Rhea, and her husband, Morris Kunz. When Rhea came in, the twins welcomed her, saying, "We're the reception committee. Join the club." Soon they caught sight of Aunt Rose's father, John Y. Barlow, who was the head of the Short Creek fundamentalist group. His fat wrists were bleeding where the tight handcuffs bit into his flesh. Then Brother Joseph Musser himself arrived, his dapper figure upright and dignified. Soon after that, my father came, smiling and waving at the press as though he was receiving a medal for valor. My father and the other patriarchs were charged with violating the Mann Act (which prohibits the transportation across state lines of minors for immoral purposes), the Lindbergh Act, with sending obscene literature through the mail, with bigamy, and with unlawful cohabitation. Everyone who was arrested held a center of power in fundamentalist circles; clearly the raid had been concentrated on the leaders of polygamy.

At one point, one of the jailers brought blankets into the women's cell, and he said, "Don't you twins remember me?" He then reminded them that he had been a member of the Cannon Ward bishopric that had excommunicated them from the Church in 1941. Aunt Emma said sharply, "Well, you must be proud of yourself. First excommunicating and now imprisoning us." The man had the grace to blush and hang his head.

As more women arrived, they buoyed each other's spirits. Someone started them singing, "For the Strength of the Hills we bless thee, Our God, Our Fathers' God." Then they sang "Rock of Ages." The matron told them to hush, they were disturbing other prisoners.

The night went by slowly. The women were hungry, but refused to eat the peppery food which looked to have been prepared under less-than-sanitary conditions. My mother and Aunt Emma had been locked up long enough to miss their husband and to worry about their children (my mother's Saul and Jake, and Aunt Emma's Ramie and Isaac), although the little ones were safe in the care of their sister-wives. Intermittently the matron invited the women to "send a message to your husband." The wives quickly recognized the scheme to incriminate them and their spouses should they provide the matron with evidence that could lead to charges of bigamy, and they ignored her invitations, although she persisted throughout the night.

When morning came, their arraignment was delayed while the patriarchs were taken to Federal Court. At 2:00 P.M., the women became community entertainment. Crowds of friends, newspaper reporters, and curiosity seekers had gathered to watch the polygamous patriarchs and their plural wives arraigned. Friends and loved ones brought sandwiches, casseroles, cookies, and cakes. At some point that afternoon, Aunt LaVerne, Aunt Adah, and Aunt Sally were also booked, although none of the other polygamous clans had to offer up more of their women. One woman, Rula Broadbent, who was secretly married to my father's oldest brother, Lothair, put up her property as bail so that "the girls" would not have to spend another night in jail. They returned to their cells with light hearts and full stomachs, and only a few hours passed before they were released pending trial. The women in our religious group who had not been arrested had prepared for their homecoming. They cleaned the house. They gathered eggs and milked the cow and baked gingerbread. They bathed the babies and dressed them for bed and tucked them in. When my mother walked through the door of the white house, the sight of her children bathed and lullabied and sleeping soundly combined with the heavenly fragrance of hot gingerbread to assure her that even though the serpent had stung, something of Eden had been preserved.

Aunt Emma dreaded returning to work at my father's office, since photographs of the twins had been plastered on the front page of both newspapers, but she found that most of my father's patients were sympathetic and supportive. Soon photos of our family dominated double pages of *Life* magazine, an article called "Utah Polygamy Trials" presenting a small photo of my father standing before the white house, and a page-and-a-half spread of the mothers and their children smiling. Then on *Movietone News*, my father pitched the ball as Saul hit it during a family picnic and baseball game.

When the media reached Los Angeles, one of the brethren in Katherine's LDS ward remarked on the "beautiful clan" featured in *Life* and said, in Katherine's hearing, "If this is the kind of family bred by polygamy, let's have more of it." The nation ate up news of the "polygamous roundup" glad to be distracted from unpleasant reports of Japanese internment camps in the United States and casualties on the Pacific and European fronts. My family's crimes were easier to contemplate than that of their cell-mate, a Japanese woman driven to kill her eight-month-old baby because "his crying annoyed me."

The women were not present when a blanket trial for "conspiracy to commit a felony" was held for all thirty-one defendants—twenty men and eleven women—with a blanket conviction of "guilty" rendered by an eight-man jury. But the attorneys appealed the conviction to the Utah State Supreme Court, so my mother and Aunt Emma and the others remained free on bail. They turned their attention to planting and harvesting and shoring up the family stores for no one knew how long they would be free. The days for my father's trial loomed, then overshadowed the family. It was clear from the start that District Attorney Boyden had set things up carefully. Judge Ray Van Cott Jr. became both jury and judge, convicting fifteen patriarchs of illegal cohabitation. The Church had extended fullest cooperation. Newspaper articles shouted this fact, and an article in the March 20 edition of *Time* declared, "Last week's polygamy crackdown was prompted by an appeal by Mormon leaders." The frustrations of defense attorneys were summed up in *The Salt Lake Telegram* article of November 10, 1944, after they had petitioned for a new trial.

> . . . defense attorneys J. H. McKnight and Knox Patterson said that two witnesses for the state were commissioned by the LDS Church to stamp out polygamy and claimed that the jury had not been thoroughly examined for church affiliation.
>
> Included in defense arguments was a letter written by Mark E. Peterson of the LDS Council of Twelve Apostles to Murray Moller of the United Press asking that the wire service set forth the LDS Church opposition to the fundamentalists and stating that the witnesses for prosecution were men who have been appointed by the church to search out cultists, turning over such information they obtained for use by the prosecution.

The Utah Supreme Court broadened the definition of legal cohabitation in December of 1944, and refused the fundamentalist petition for retrial in 1945. In April, when my father was sentenced to five years in prison for illegal cohabitation, the apple trees still bloomed, the cows gave cream, the babies grew fat. When all efforts to get a new trial were denied, my father went to prison on May 15, 1945. At first he was placed in the cell once occupied by President Lorenzo Snow, who also had been imprisoned for living polygamy, and my father preened over that. Then he was transported with the first prisoners interred in the newly constructed Utah State Prison. Now his wives could bring the children to wave at him through the chainlink fence. His younger brothers were still soldiering in Europe and the South Pacific, which left the wives and children and Grandmother Evelyn without income or protection.

The authorities (the prison warden, the director of state social services, the leaders of the official church) assumed no responsibility for the "plygie kids." Perhaps they felt they had already spent enough prosecuting our family, for the cost of the investigations, arrests, trials, and subsequent incarceration was mounting and would one day reach half a million dollars. No one attended to the children's well-being except the mothers, who would go to any length to feed their children (short of signing up for welfare, which could give the state grounds to take us away). Still, without my father's income, the family resources dwindled. The mothers had applied for work, but by now their faces were well-known and most people didn't dare hire them. Soon the situation was desperate.

Often my mother took my brother Saul, who was six, and Jake, who was three, to Cottonwood Creek. Together they rigged a green willow pole with kite string and a safety pin. While the boys fished, she lugged the new baby and browsed for pigweed to steam as a vegetable. Saul discovered that if he put a crust of bread inside a bottle, then anchored it downstream, he would snare a trout for dinner. Jake waded along the banks and picked watercress for salad. My mother cut a green willow and showed Saul how to fashion a whistle by moving the slippery bark and notching the stick here, and the little boys laughed at the high, sweet sound. As they wandered home, the afternoon sun waning behind the tall poplars, they gathered wild raspberries. The days of bare subsistence taught my brothers about the profusion of the earth and whetted an appetite for invention that would last a lifetime.

The mothers kept believing that God would provide, but with so many mouths to feed, hunger loomed larger than the war. When it was announced that the atomic bomb had been dropped on Hiroshima, the mothers fell to their knees in horror. Someone declared that the last days had come. But even as they knelt, their empty stomachs distracted them from their prayers for the people of Japan.

My father was haunted by his children in need, and often awakened in his prison cell with their faces vaporizing before him. He wrote poems and letters to them and he prayed for each of them. But ultimately he knew that words don't fill bellies and he longed to be free to provide for them. A man named Dayer LeBaron wrote to him, offering refuge in Mexico. Dayer LeBaron had seen the publicity, and he believed that an evil was being perpetrated against my father. Dayer claimed to be a prophet and a seer on the grounds that his maternal grandfather, Benjamin Johnson, was purported to be a personal friend of the Prophet Joseph Smith. Dayer claimed to have inherited the "mantle of Joseph" including the right to ordain plural marriages. He had two wives himself, he said, and the Mormons had driven him out of Colonia Juarez—so many of them born into plural marriage had now become detractors of the Principle. "A prophet is not known in his own land," Dayer quoted, although he had been born in Arizona, not Mexico.

My father did not know what to make of such claims to greatness, but decided that anyone who would offer his home to a stranger in need must be either a saint or an outlaw. He wrote back, thanking LeBaron for his hospitality and expressing his trust that the Lord would soon release him to his home and his family. In December of 1945, having served seven months of his five-year sentence, my father was offered early release in return for a written promise not to practice the Principle of Plural Marriage in the United States.

For almost a year Rulon lived exclusively with Aunt LaVerne, and when he went to visit the children of his other wives, a parole officer attended him. He was reduced to having his wives visit the office as patients, sneaking an hour with them in one of the examining areas with only a drape to afford them privacy. However, the visits were effective. After twelve frustrated years, Aunt LaVerne proved fertile, perhaps as a result of consecutive nights with her husband. As they rejoiced that at last LaVerne would be "a mother in Israel," Aunt Adah and Aunt Rose also conceived. Then Aunt Melissa, who married my father the night before he went to prison but waited until his release to consummate their marriage, announced that she, too, was pregnant. Soon four of his wives would display the results of his promise to abstain from polygamy, and he worried that he would be arrested again, this time for the full sentence of five years, plus the time that would most certainly be added for breaking his promise and his parole.

～

In 1947, after more than a year of sporadic, sparse, and secret encounters with his plural wives, my father announced that his family would move to Chihuahua, Mexico, to live on a ranch owned by this LeBaron whose letters promised "a land of milk and honey" where my father and his family could "embrace freedom" and join "the cause of right." My father told his wives and children the story of Moses from Exodus 16 as he did whenever we were about to take flight, describing how Pharaoh had finally agreed to let the people of Israel go, just as the state of Utah had let him go, and now they must gather their things and venture into the wilderness. The Lord had provided for the chosen ones in the days of old, sending manna to sustain them until they arrived in the land of milk and honey. He would do the same for his people in this day, the last dispensation in the fullness of times.

My father went to Mexico first, to make things ready. Only Aunt LaVerne planned to stay in Utah, working at her job as legal secretary and "holding down the fort" at our compound. The women and children came two weeks later, six of the seven wives and fourteen children stuffed into two cars, plus the drivers. The trip to the border took several days, and they stopped at night, sleeping on pavement, in parks, wherever they could. At the border, Rulon Jeffs, the driver of one of the cars, announced that he had to return to Salt Lake City. The dispersed group stood in the dusty heat of the border town, wondering what to do next. Fortunately, some acquaintances on their way to the Mormon colonies stopped to say hello and invited them to climb aboard. They piled into the foul-smelling bed of a truck with their few possessions. For three days, they traveled along highways of the Southwest, the mothers and children wedged between suitcases and bedrolls in the rear of a panel truck that was stifling during the day and freezing at night. They traveled mud-rutted roads that caused the truck to lurch and throw them like rag dolls. The women, focused on protecting the children, rode stoically, singing songs and telling stories until it came their turn to ride in the car where they let their heads fall back, mouths open, drinking sleep. For much of the journey, my mother sat in the back seat of the car, her lap a pillow for the three youngest boys. The pregnant wives feared early labor as they were thrown from side to side and soon they took a permanent place in the car. That left my mother, Aunt Emma, and Aunt Sally to endure the ride in the rear of the panel truck. Instead of complaining, they counted jolts, competed in a bruise-count, and invented ridiculous games while sliding from one end of the truck to the other. The gasoline can slopped and the fumes added to their giddiness. Forty hours later, the truck stopped before a horse trough in Las Parceles and they washed the dust and grime from their faces before asking directions to the LeBaron ranch, which was about five miles away.

Melissa, my father's youngest wife, cried out. "I've been counting my contractions and they're fifteen minutes apart. Please, let's hurry! I don't want to have this baby without Rulon." The older mothers reminded Melissa that she had hours, maybe even days to go—this was her first, and first babies always take a long time. "It's probably nothing but 'lightning,' " Aunt Emma said with the voice of experience, and the drama of the moment faded.

Reassured that the journey was almost over, they continued. After another half hour on the worst roads they'd encountered yet, the truck stopped. When the dust settled, they stepped, one by one into a bright expanse of sand. The "LeBaron ranch" consisted of an adobe hut, a few animal pens and a huge tent bucking in the desert wind. My father stood in the center of the tent, his straw panama tilted rakishly, a shovel in his hand.

"Welcome home!" he said, throwing an arm wide, as though he was standing on the veranda of a mansion.

Aunt Emma burst into tears.

"I want to go home," my mother said.

Later, Aunt Melissa labored in earnest, with my father in attendance, just as she wished. But his presence didn't keep dust from blowing through the flap and beneath the tent. A large brown tarantula crept from its hole and made a slow path to the pallet; Aunt Melissa, straining for breath, couldn't even scream a warning. A fierce wind shook the tent and snapped a corner beam. As the tent tilted, the flap ripped away on one side, revealing a girl of about twelve chained among goats in the corral. The girl was curled in fetal position around the post to which she was tethered and never looked up when Aunt Melissa finally let out a cry that keened along the wind and frightened the little children playing at the well. The older children, working in the garden or in the corral, knew that a birth was taking place and from embarrassment and training, they pretended not to notice. Without a hint of apology, my father did what needed to be done, propping up the tent and restoring a little order. He kept smiling and talking to Melissa, nonplused by the natural drama surrounding him. Comparing this with my experience of laboring on sterile sheets in softly lit birthing rooms in a hospital of personnel trained to meet a mother's every request, I can hardly believe Aunt Melissa or her baby survived such a primitive advent.

Aunt Melissa's firstborn was not the last Allred baby to arrive on the sands of Chihuahua. And the tarantula was not the worst of the predators that lived among them. Instead of the land of milk and honey promised by Dayer LeBaron, my father had brought his wives and children to a land of saguaro cactus and scorpions and rattlesnakes. Instead of men engaged in "the cause of right," my father found men obsessed with a will to power. And nothing to feed the wives and children but yams, yams, and more yams.

They learned that the girl in the goat pen was named Lucinda, and that her brothers chained her whenever she had one of her "spells." The LeBarons were Old Testament, eye-for-an-eye people, and they preferred being "the One Mighty and Strong" to being "Brothers in Christ," as the men in our group called one another. During Sunday sacrament meetings, during Wednesday-night priesthood meetings, and even when there was no meeting, my family endured the LeBaron's doctrinal ranting. My father listened as long as he could, tonguing the grit of the desert, biting the inside of his lip until he was snared into discussions that quickly became arguments. Everyone could see it, even Saul who was only eight years old at the time: Dayer LeBaron was challenging our father's authority; indeed, the LeBarons were challenging anyone's authority other than theirs.

One day, LeBaron and his sons captured a wild horse and named her Diamond. The mare quickly earned a reputation, and the LeBaron boys challenged each other to take turns trying to break her. Each of them claimed some outstanding prowess, some saying they were greater than Moses or Abraham. The bronco riding was a spiritual test: one must stay on the mare's back a certain number of seconds, the LeBaron boys said, or that boy was a withered branch, ready to be lopped off by the Almighty. My father and his sons stood by, watching the brutal game. My father warned that someone would get hurt, but Dayer laughed and said boys would be boys. This sport continued for a few days before my father and the older LeBaron, driven by a craving for meat, packed up their rifles and rode toward the Santa Catarina mountains to hunt deer.

The LeBaron sons were twice the age and size of Saul, whose personality was too unpretentious and honest to lay claim to territories in heaven. Some of the LeBarons, on the other hand, having been objects of ridicule in Arizona when they were young, had become, as my father said, "a law unto themselves." As one of the oldest and certainly the strongest-willed of my father's sons, Saul stood firm when the LeBaron sons gathered around to taunt him. When they demanded that Saul ride Diamond to prove his manhood, he straight-ened his back and took the challenge. He wasn't experienced with horses, but he was brave and tough, and he mounted the mare without hesitation. It took Diamond about two seconds to throw Saul, then two more seconds of flailing hooves to crack his jaw, dislocate his shoulder, and give him a concussion.

For two days Saul lay unconscious while my father hunted deer in the Sierra Santa Catarina. My mother sat beside her oldest son, aware of other first-born sons who had died in Mexico, all the time praying and pressing a cold cloth to his forehead. Aunt Emma's six-year-old daughter, Ramie, knelt at the end of the pallet, her hands clasped as she prayed fervently that Saul—the brother who stood up for girls— would get well. At last my father returned, dragging a two-point buck on a litter of mesquite. He went directly to Saul and even before he examined his wounds, my father gave him a priesthood blessing, pouring a small coin of consecrated olive oil on the crown of his head and promising Saul that he would be healed. He listened to Saul's heart and administered medicines from his meager supply. At last, with a deep breath, he adjusted Saul's shoulder and put the arm in a sling. Satisfied that he'd done everything he could, my father went outside to skin and butcher the deer.

The smell of venison broiling over an open pit brought Saul fully awake. "I'm hungry," he said. My mother wanted to feed him broth, but Saul wanted venison. My mother worried that he would throw up the meat and aggravate the concussion. My father turned from the fire with a slice of rare meat and said, "The boy knows what he needs. Let him have this."

Saul ate the venison. With each bite, Ramie clapped her hands, and Saul smiled at her through his broken teeth. Saul sent her to ask my father for more venison, and he ate that as well. The next morning Saul got out of bed and went out to ride Diamond. When the LeBaron boys saw Saul heading for the corral, they moved off and watched as he mounted one-handed, edging around his injured shoulder. For a moment, everyone stood still, including Diamond. Then my mother exploded from the door of the tent. "Get down!" she shouted. "Right now!"

Saul looked up, surprised. He'd never seen my mother so angry and he complied without question. As he climbed down, Diamond snorted, then crowhopped away. My mother shook an angry finger at the LeBaron brothers. "What's wrong with you? You'd let him ride this mean horse again, after it almost killed him? What's gotten into you?"

The LeBarons turned away, not used to being upbraided by women. My mother's questions gave them nothing to fight.

～

As my family realized that the LeBarons were a threat to our well-being, the wide sky felt too small to hold Allreds and LeBarons, too. But in taking his families to Mexico, my father had broken parole and if he returned, he could be put away for a long time. My mother tried to be grateful for Saul's narrow escape, tried to count the blessings of her husband's freedom, but she would look at Lucinda chained in the goat pen, and she felt dark and empty.

Saul's injuries healed as the desert heat gave way to the strong winds of wintertime. But then dysentery set in, and the members of my family, always thin, became gaunt. Maud LeBaron cooked up a concoction of olive oil and mustard, instructing the mothers to feed it to their dehydrated children. My father went hunting again, and once again the venison rescued Saul from hunger and sickness. But some of the children did not recover, and they lingered on the edge of death. Then Aunt LaVerne left her job in Utah and crossed the border to spend Christmas with the family. She announced that she was staying until everyone could go home together. She brought a lace handkerchief for each of her sister-wives, a wooden top for each of the children, and best of all, she brought cornflakes and oranges which even the sickest children wolfed down with delight.

"Cornflakes and oranges," my mother recalled in a voice thick with gratitude. "Manna in the desert."

Manna in the Desert

I HAD NOT YET BEEN BORN when the family celebrated that Christmas with cornflakes and oranges. They
endured nine months in the Chihuahua desert before my
father brought his family home to Utah. He paid for the homecoming,
spending thirty days on Death Row as the penalty for breaking parole.
My mother told me this story and other stories of deprivation while
ironing the shirts she took in to supplement the grocery allowance my
father gave her. My mother earned a dollar a basket, and every basket
contained a dozen shirts. It made me tired to watch her arms sweep
back and forth, up and down, move it along, shake it out, hang it up. It
made my stomach rumble to hear of the family subsisting on pigweed
and yams. But oh, the stories that rippled out before that iron! I could
not consider myself hungry, not with such stories spilling out before
me. Besides, I was full of milk with cream rising each morning in the
pans on the back porch, full of tomatoes that ripened along with a
dozen other vegetables in the garden, full of peaches and pears and
burgundy cherries that glistened first in our orchards and then in shining jars to be stored on fruit cellar shelves. I was full of ideas and questions. What would happen, I asked my mother, if everyone shared

everything everywhere? She responded that this was the United Order, and it was beautiful—when people chose to live it, which they rarely did. It had been lived by the Utah pioneers under the direction of Brigham Young, and that was how they survived the crickets and the drought, giving all they had to the bishop who redivided it according to need. The United Order was God's plan and not to be confused with communism, she said, which was Satan's counterfeit of the divine order. She explained that the communist government controlled everybody; people weren't allowed to exercise their free agency as we did in democracy.

I wondered why, if people in America could live as they choose, were we always afraid of being arrested or split up? But I didn't want to make my mother worry or break the spell of her story; so instead, I asked if we should go hungry again, what would we do? She replied that the Lord would provide, just as He had always done for his children, and she reminded me of Moses who led the children of Israel through the desert to the Promised Land, with nothing to eat but manna. It seemed to me that manna would be something like great puddles of tapioca pudding, and I imagined people clear and bright as sunshine talking with the Lord over dinner. What would happen, I asked my mother, if we were made of glass, if we could see through one another? And she whispered that life can be this way, transparent and fragile, and that is why we must be very careful of one another. When she went through her breakdowns, she said, she felt as though she had been dropped and broken, and this was why she didn't judge people who couldn't do as much. This was how she learned to treat children like "little people," which is what they were. She listened carefully as I spoke, her eyes on mine. She did not try to contain my feelings or redirect my thoughts. She did not withhold her love so that I would say what she wanted to hear. From the straw of poverty my mother spun gold.

"There is beauty all around," we sang at home evening, "when there's love at home." It was 1953. The Korean conflict was over, and the soldiers were coming home. A whole year had passed since the last raid. As our world became kinder and more abundant, we learned that if we kept faith, there would always be enough. If we ran out of something, we just had to open a spigot elsewhere in order to increase the flow. If one woman was barren, another would share her babies. If one cupboard was bare, another would overflow. And when we were short on food and goods, we grew long in creativity and ingenuity. We learned to tend gardens and cultivate orchards; we invented games and created our own toys; we found treasures in the land and in each other.

On Saturday nights we attended the group dances at a rented dance hall, and my mother brushed up on old waltzes and polkas and learned to play folk tunes the saints had danced to around campfires when they crossed the plains. Men lined up across from women and their heels clattered on the wooden floor as they moved together, then danced away as Uncle Rosy played his fiddle, sky-bright eyes twinkling above a dark beard as he stomped a foot to the beat of the piano. My father danced with each of his wives and with some of his daughters, and my uncles and older brothers cut in to make each of us feel beautiful. Young men not yet married or with only one or two wives danced with the young girls approaching adolescence, as if to remind them that one day they would be someone's sweetheart. Everyone danced, even the little children, and we all went home smiling, feeling adored. Life was full of promise, for we believed that our poverty was temporary and that God would not let us go hungry. And when my father had the door to his heart and the door to his doctor's office open, we had more than enough—enough for ourselves and plenty left over of both love and goods to give to others.

One autumn Sunday we sat around the dinner table in our Salt Lake County home—my mother and Aunt Emma and their children. Through some miracle, my father was eating with us that day and he asked the blessing on the food. Because it was a Sunday, we got to have meat for dinner—venison steaks cooked Swiss style, dusted with flour and browned in oil, then simmered a long time with tomatoes and onions and green peppers. Our mouths watered as my father prayed until we peered through our eyelashes at the source of aromas that spoke of wilderness and strength. My oldest brother, Saul, was almost fifteen at the time and growing so tall so fast he needed the protein more than any of us. His eyes said as much.

It was the custom, when our father ate with us, to pass our plates to him so he could "dish up." We squirmed as we waited our turns and received our portions. (Sometimes my father spooned up too little of something wonderful and always too many turnips or beets, given that we must stay at the table until everything was gone.) Then we set to eating the Swiss steak. Each tender spicy bite sent the message to our cells—be reborn! The faint wildness of the deer set up an echoing wildness within that would render the power to get through another week of mockery at school. When the other children teased, "Plygie, plygie" we wouldn't mind so much, knowing we had the flesh of the deer to make us quicker, to make us stronger, to make us more beautiful.

I devoured my meat, then contended with the peas, the boiled potatoes, the carrot-raisin salad. Across from me, my half-sister, Ramie, took quick, delicate bites, nervous as a coyote pup watching for mountain lions to move in. Beside me, Saul ate calmly. He exhibited a maddening self-restraint; a psychologist would have predicted that his impulse-control destined him for success. Long after everyone else had devoured his or her venison steak, Saul lingered over his plate, the red of the tomatoes, the green of the peppers, the rich brown gravy reminding each of us that life is abundant and that we were blessed. We anticipated Saul's feast with the contemplative joy we had failed to bestow on our own.

A knock at the back door made us freeze like animals caught in headlights. Any knock could signal another raid or a polygamous roundup, could be an FBI agent with a search order to tear up floorboards and mattresses in order to find journals, birth certificates, and any other papers that would prove our relationship. But it turned out to be one of my father's followers, a corpulent man with wrists so fat he couldn't button his cuffs.

"Sit down, Brother Joe!" Relief spread in a grin across my father's face. "Bring him a plate," he ordered my mother. Then, reaching across with his fork, my father speared Saul's venison steak and plopped it onto the clean plate. "Here, Brother Joe," my father said. "You need your strength. Besides," he said, and looked meaningfully at Saul, "you are our guest."

Aunt Emma's daughter, Ramie, stared at Saul, whose eyes smoldered with fierce pain. Her lips trembled. She bent her head, and tears dripped onto her plate.

Aunt Emma looked up. "What, Ramie?"

Ramie hid her face in her hands. Brother Joe went on eating.

"Daughter!" My father spoke firmly. "For heaven's sake, what's wrong?"

Ramie sobbed softly. We waited, the scrape of Brother Joe's knife and fork sharp on our teeth and in our ears. He finished his meal. No one told jokes or made the usual after-dinner talk. Chairs slid back and the mothers began clearing the dishes. My father invited Brother Joe into the living room. Ramie went on crying.

"It isn't fair," she said. "Daddy shouldn't have done that to you."

Saul swallowed hard. "It's all right. I wasn't that hungry."

Saul does not remember being deprived of his venison steak that day. But Saul and I agree that we were expected to give the best of our lives to the men on the priesthood council. And eventually Saul decided that there would never be enough—whether of venison or of love and respect. Ramie could not do enough for Saul. She made cookies for him. She darned his socks and sewed buttons on his two school shirts. She sat by and watched as he tied flies for fishing, trying to make everything right again. Perhaps she suspected that we were losing Saul. Often the two of them sat beneath the willow, talking long into the night.

Ramie began hoarding things that autumn. In a plastic soapbox, she collected the small toys that came from penny-vendors. In a cigar box she collected silk scarves. In a shoebox she hid a variety of pom-poms she had made or received. She kept all these things in a trunk in the bedroom she shared with Aunt Emma.

Aunt Emma had predicted that the threat of a raid would gather force and as usual, she was right. In 1953 and 1954, the McCarthy investigations and the tensions of the Cold War aggravated the climate of paranoia in the country and in our group. Rampant conservatives mirrored our fundamentalist stance, sending messages of criticism and judgement, the conviction of being in the right, the horrifying possibility of being in the wrong. Our fear grew with every newspaper article that spread dark rumors and half-truths about polygamy. Unmarked cars lurked outside our compound, and spies took down license plate numbers at our religious gatherings. At about the time my brothers and sisters were going through their first nuclear attack drill at school, a friendly policeman was phoning my father, warning that a polygamous roundup was pending. My father called us together and again he told the story of Moses leading his people out of Egypt.

"They knew not where they were going, nor where they would eat or sleep. But they went into the desert, relying entirely on the Lord," he recited, referring again to Exodus 16 where the story is told of how Israelite faith was rewarded, manna raining down in the morning and quail flying to them in the evening.

When he said, in an admonishing tone, "Each took only what he needed." I searched my mother's face for an explanation. My mother whispered that Daddy had been pushing us to live the United Order again. He wanted to establish a system that would help us survive even if he could not provide for us.

Now he reminded us that "the Lord helps those who help themselves." With the world threatening our solidarity, we must close out neighbors and friends who did not believe as we did. We must act from greater faith, reduce our commerce with the larger community, and keep to ourselves. If we were not extremely careful, the state would intervene and place us children in foster homes, or put us up for adoption by strangers. Thus we reworked clothing, furniture, whatever we could. We grew streetwise and self-reliant, resolving never to depend on our enemies, never to descend into debt, never to bear the tattoo of the Beast. We had no idea that millions of hungry, frightened people lived in the world outside our group who might be able to identify with our constrained lives.

The more we were persecuted from the outside, the more the group patriarchs expected of us. "Will you survive the refiner's fire?" the priesthood council would say, or "The Lord demands an unblemished lamb as a fitting sacrifice." They punished any hint of rebellion, including a point of view that didn't agree with theirs. They invoked the choice posed by LDS Church President John Taylor during the persecutions of the 1880s: "Are you for us or against us?" When people refused to swallow the brethren's oblique doctrines, or when reflective souls such as Saul silently sat through the invitation to "bear testimony to the Principle," the patriarchs accused, "If you are not for us, then you are against us."

After another warning in July of 1955, my father went into hiding. Thus began "the scattered years," the mothers escaping with their children to take up anonymous lives, individual families living furtively in towns across the west. My father traveled from state to state to visit his families; without his leadership, the power structure inside our family and inside the religious group shifted. Men stood and declared their authority while others vowed to fight them. The secrecy maintained to protect the group had created pockets of darkness that now spawned subversion. In our closed system, any polygamous patriarch with a spark of personal power could commandeer our lonely souls, ignite our fear, and fuel his own ambition. The conviction of "one right way, one true church," burned hot in our fundamentalist world, especially among those of us who did not want to live the hodgepodge of ideals called the Principle.

As with most exiles we had little trust in each other during the sea-
sons of fear. Intuition sent the alarm: there is no safety, the message
said, there is not enough. You may have to fight your brother, your sister, your sister-wife for food or living space or love. We felt the
shadow of Esau cheated of his birthright; we remembered Joseph,
whose many-colored coat caused him to be sold by his jealous
brethren; we understood why the children of Israel worshiped the
golden calf. The walls between us only reinforced our insularity from
the larger world, holding at bay much that was good, holding in much
that was not, interrupting the flow of good will so that there was never
enough to go around. Some sons were blessed and others disowned.
Some daughters were greeted with a kiss, others with a reprimand.
Without daily access to our beloved Daddy, someone was always
scheming to get more love, more attention, more praise.

When my mother and Aunt Emma moved to Nevada, somehow we
survived, eating my mother's homemade bread with Utah honey, and
peaches and pears from the fruit-cellar shelves back home. Even so far
from home, we continued to be rich in most of the things that really
matter—in health, in intelligence, in the love of one another. But as we
grew older, it became necessary to prove our worth to the outside world.
We strove to be top students, star athletes, conscientious citizens. Saul
was elected student-body president; Ramie grew into a beautiful young
woman with more dates than she had free evenings. Still, we did not feel
we were good enough. In our own minds, we were on the run, afraid
that others would find out who we really were, and if they did, our real
selves would be inadequate. So we told ourselves we needed something,
wanted something. This is how we became susceptible to worldly
temptation, the serpent appearing to Ramie and me as a stack of cast-
off *Seventeen* magazines. We sniffed the magazine's perfume samplers,
overnight addicts to sensory pleasure. We pored over the slick pictures
of frothy prom dresses and tuxedoed young men and thus we became
devotees of the material dream. When we had worn the magazines out,
we begged for a subscription and Ramie got one for her birthday. Aunt

Emma overlooked the fact that the ads and articles didn't foster the staples of polygamous life: the United Order, which prevented people from accumulating wealth while others suffered in poverty, and the Law of Chastity, which prevented people from having sex for any reason than to have babies. Ramie soaked up the pages and shared them with me at bedtime as the radio played softly; in the dreams that happen just before sleeping, we'd dress ourselves up and take ourselves out. Before Ramie turned out the light, regular as scripture-reading, she'd gaze at the Lane cedar chests and choose the Art-Carved diamond she liked best and she would say that she wouldn't mind being a plural wife so long as she got a diamond ring and a hope chest. Oh, Ramie added quietly, her eyes dreamy with white lace and diamonds, it would be very nice to be the first wife.

~

In 1961, the Bay of Pigs focused the nation's attention on Fidel Castro and people seemed to lose interest in persecuting the polygamist remnant. After years hiding out, traveling from state to state, family to family, my father had returned to the compound in Salt Lake City and reestablished his doctor's office. He had created an agreement for more education so that the state medical board would allow him to practice, and an unofficial agreement with authorities of church and state that would allow him to live unmolested in Utah. Now he summoned his families home. We moved from Nevada, Aunt LaVerne loaded her heavy furniture and came from Idaho, while Aunt Sally gave up a housekeeping job in Montana to take another one in Salt Lake. Most of us lived on the compound in Salt Lake County, where the orchards still bore good fruit, where the garden burgeoned with vegetables. But we brought back some things we had not taken with us: a hunger for material goods, walls that kept us separate from one another, and secular tastes acquired in exile that now tainted the sweetness of being together.

My father had brought us home, but he was distracted by the dream of gathering all his people to a haven in the mountains. Soon he acquired one hundred and sixty acres of ranch land at the foot of the Bitterroot Mountains in Montana where he planned to build a new polygamous settlement. We felt his distraction. Even after he brought us home and we were all together again, he still did not have enough time and attention for Ramie or for me.

A short-circuiting of the energy that perpetuates life, whatever its form—love, food, money—leads to scarcity. As survival instincts take over, people usually abandon arbors of integrity and faith for waste-lands of greed and judgement. If I had stopped to pay attention, I might have realized that we were squandering something precious the day I stole a tube of mascara from the corner market. The owners had been our neighbors before the raids, and it was almost like stealing from family. I put the black stuff on my eyes and the next time I saw Ramie, I fluttered my eyelashes.

"You look pretty," she said. She didn't ask where I'd gotten money for mascara. She didn't say the obvious, that I was too young to wear makeup. It was as though we agreed, without speaking, not to face what was hap-pening. No female in my family charged me not to sell my birthright for the pottage of the secular world. Perhaps that was because no female in my family was very clear on what, exactly, our birthright was.

Over the years, Ramie worked on pillow cases in pastel embroidery, crocheted lace along the edges of a dozen white sheets, and helped our maternal grandmother feather-stitch a black satin quilt for her trousseau. She placed these between layers of tissue in the Lane cedar chest Aunt Emma had given her for Christmas. She was being courted by a young man in the group who drove down from the group's settle-ment in Montana once a month to pay homage to one of my father's princesses. We noticed—with some amusement—that Ramie was cau-tious. Would the young man continue to cherish her after she took his name, bore his children? she wondered aloud. Perhaps she had seen the longing on Aunt Emma's face those nights my father went to my mother's room.

For awhile, Ramie ignored her suitor and dated Saul's old pal, Roy. But Roy was a leather-jacketed, ducktailed bad boy too good-looking and too hot-blooded for our quiet revolution. He wasn't interested in Art-Carved diamonds or marriage. After a struggle with her heart (that was as much about loyalty to Saul as it was about her attraction to Roy), Ramie gave up the boyfriend and took a more spiritual approach to her future: She underwent punishing fasts, pre-sunrise prayers, and solitary walks to help her make her decision.

In the end, she saw in the young man from the religious group what she wanted to see: the promise of abundant love. She saw that my father had offered rich supplies of tenderness to his wives, and caught in idealism about the Principle, Ramie chose. The young man had come up with the requisite Art-Carved diamond ring. The Lane cedar chest was full, waiting to be plundered. She would be the first wife. They would live in a little clapboard house at the southwest end of the Salt Lake Valley. These were the signs Ramie wanted, and she accepted the young man's proposal.

Within the next three years, Ramie's husband took another wife, a woman as different from Ramie as night is different from day. Ramie did her best to keep a generous spirit: So what if her husband didn't seem to have enough love to go around? So what if the second wife didn't iron her sheets or discipline her children properly? She was Ramie's sister-wife, and Ramie must love her. But it wasn't easy; especially when they shared a house, and Ramie was so particular, so careful with her possessions, while the second wife was always saying, "No big deal. They're only things."

I'm not sure what God had in mind, given a divine hand in what happened next: perhaps a lesson in mutual respect, or a reminder to lay up treasures in heaven. I've pieced things together, drawing on details I've heard from Ramie and others, here and there. There's much that I don't know, that I'm left to imagine. I do know that soon after her husband took his second wife, Ramie's Lane cedar chest, stocked with the linens meant to last a lifetime, was ruined when

Utah's version of the Jordan River overflowed. A year or two later, the toddler of Ramie's sister-wife tossed my sister's Art-Carved ring into the same river. As if a spell had been cast, Ramie lost her ambition, wore her clothes to shreds, suppressed any desire to go out and work. She defended the homefront as if it was her last reserve, yet there never seemed to be enough of anything. Her little boys were too thin, too hungry. Ramie and her children took to creeping down the dirt road at midnight, crossing the highway and raiding the garbage bins behind Safeway. There they found abandoned wealth: whole heads of lettuce with only a touch of rust on the outside leaves; lambchops and chicken breasts with only a little freezer burn; cookies and potato chips with the faintest aftertaste of stale.

Knowing how my family responded to our poverty, always keeping themselves a rung above the rest of the world, Ramie probably rationalized that it was a moral act to salvage good food. Perhaps she drew on our religious ideals to justify her behavior, identified with Ruth gleaning in the fields of Boaz, and Elijah fed by ravens. Ramie fluctuated between the sweet sacrifice of martyrdom and the stealth of a revolutionary, an oscillating energy that lifted her depression. She began to rise at the crack of dawn to scour her sparsely stocked refrigerator with harsh cleansers that scraped softness from her flesh. Her cupboards sparkled, white and bare as bones. As night fell, she flushed with excitement as she boosted her little boys into the big dumpster, instructing them what to throw back. It was, I suppose, a form of fishing—but since it was done in the dark it took on the shame of poaching. Thus Ramie relived the sieges of our childhood.

Now the boys knew where to go for a snack. Sometimes, when the oldest had finished kindergarten for the day, they told their mother they were going down to the Jordan River to spear catfish, or over to the neighbors to play tug-of-war when, in fact, they darted across the highway to raid the garbage bins behind Safeway. They had learned that the bakery tossed its day-old stuff in the afternoon. If they could get there before the big truck came to empty the dumpster they would be rolling in doughnuts and banana bread. Once in awhile they'd get an entire two-layer cake.

One afternoon the boys told their mother one of the usual stories, although no one could remember later what it was they said they were going to do—were they going to the river to fish, or to the neighbors to play? Traffic had been diverted off the freeway while a ramp was under construction and the stream of vehicles was relentless. Driven by hunger, the boys darted in a lapse between cars. So did a motorist who had been waiting for his break. The car struck both little boys. Fractured skulls, broken bones, ruptured spleens.

Ramie knew when she heard the screech of tires on the highway that her boys had been hurt. Still she waited until a neighbor called. "Ramie! Get over to Safeway's! It's your boys." Ramie ran along the lane, pulling up her housedress so that her long thin legs stretched out as she prayed with every footfall, "Dear God, don't let it be. Dear God, I promise: I'll never steal again." She knew as she darted between cars that the small lumps covered with army blankets were her boys. No prayers could change what had happened.

She had always been discouraged from making her own decisions. Now, as the paramedics spoke urgently, Ramie was gripped with an impulse to turn and run the other way. But her boys were bleeding, unconscious. The paramedics moved them to stretchers, preparing them for transport to the nearest emergency room, but Ramie balked at signing the release form. Authorities were everywhere—policemen, paramedics, an attorney who thrust his card in her face, all promising to save her injured boys. All her life she had been coached to listen only to the patriarchs of the group. She begged the attendants to wait until her father arrived. "He's a doctor," she pleaded. "He'll know what to do." The police and paramedics reasoned that the little boys could die if they didn't get help at once. Ramie wrung her hands and worried. What would happen when they put themselves at the mercy of the authorities? Would the police and social workers find out about the other wives, about the trips to the dumpster? If her boys survived, would she be declared an unfit mother?

The paramedics said damn the paperwork and ordered Ramie to get into the ambulance or be left behind. Ramie jumped in but couldn't think with the siren screaming and the boys so silent, their ribs showing through thin sheets, chests barely moving. When they arrived at the emergency room and the boys had been whisked away by hospital attendants, she worked up the courage to borrow coins to call her husband from the public phone. When he arrived, Ramie sagged gratefully against him. But when she begged him to act, please do something, he reminded her that the Utah Legislature had just passed a measure clarifying that women could be prosecuted for polygamy, with the same consequences as the men. They hovered in the emergency-room foyer until a hospital social worker sat them down, took their hands in hers and gave them a full report: The children would be transported across town to the children's hospital. Would they like to ride in the ambulance or could she drive them?

Perhaps the social worker's sharp blue eyes reminded Ramie of Grandmother Evelyn, and she surrendered control to this kindly woman who promised that everything would be all right—not to worry about money or anything else, just focus on what was best for the boys.

Later, as family members gathered in the lobby of the children's hospital, Ramie stared at a bronze caduceus on the hospital wall. She got to thinking about the Book of Exodus, remembering that Aaron had thrown his rod down in front of Pharaoh, and it became a serpent that swallowed up the rods of Pharaoh's sorcerers. Moses had used his rod to call forth water from rock and he used a wooden rod to heal the bitter waters. Later he made a serpent of brass so that the children of Israel who were bitten by the fiery serpents might look on the brass serpent and live. The serpent and the rod, the symbol of medicine. Our father had been a healer and a leader, like Moses. He had a caduceus hanging on the wall of his office. If only he would come now, and save her.

She thought of the war in Vietnam and the hippies who shouted make love not war. How could they arrest her for plural marriage when cowards dodged the draft, when women slept with women, when men lived openly with their mistresses, when actresses didn't marry the fathers of their babies—all of them wrong, so wrong! Then the old feeling of not being good enough took hold, and she shifted from being the righteous one persecuted by the wicked world, to the axis of shame for the misbegotten. Why had God singled her out for the refiner's fire? Her mind spun, hopping from one gyre to the other, until she was not the shy, terrified polygamist wife, but the center of the universe, animated, laughing, garrulous.

Seeing her flushed face and bright eyes, the pediatrician may have assumed she was in shock. But he remembered the social worker's briefing, the warning that this family was different. He was kind and careful as he approached them, but the father of the boys recoiled. A group of women huddled to one side like chickens in the rain. Noting the number of men versus women, the pediatrician also saw the long dresses and old-fashioned hairstyles, and suddenly understood. His wife's great-grandfather had served time for polygamy before Utah was granted statehood. The doctor knew about "polygamist roundups" and he had treated more than one "plygie kid" off the record. He must have realized that there would be no insurance to cover medical costs, not in a subterranean society that spurned hospitals and other institutions. He asked a few gentle, probing questions. Ramie's husband was tight-lipped as ever, but Ramie saw in the doctor the same healing light that radiated from her father. She became charming, entrancing, the beauty queen revisited. She quickly volunteered all the information he asked for.

When our father showed up, the pediatrician already knew who he was, had identified him through his reputation. After making a promise of professional courtesy, the pediatrician spoke with the hospital administration to insure that the boys would get the necessary treatment. He dealt with police officers and set up meetings with the social worker so that any issues could be addressed within the family.

Meanwhile, in the tradition of our faith, we fasted and we prayed. My father placed his hands on the little boys' heads and gave them each a blessing. The men formed a prayer circle and prayed again. And when the men had gone, the women gathered around the little boys' beds and said their prayers. When the boys were pronounced out of danger, the fast was broken and everyone thanked God. How blessed to be sent a pediatrician of good will, and surgeons who knew what to do. How blessed that the social worker was kind enough to offer help instead of beginning a witch-hunt, and that the authorities hadn't split up Ramie's family. How blessed that the power of God provided what human hands could not. Ramie seemed to reclaim her primal knowledge about abundance then. She found some tolerance for outsiders, and more trust in life.

The boys are still skinny, even today—tall and rawboned, the hungry look that goes with sagebrush and horses, with fishing poles and rabbit pelts. Ramie moved them from the city to the ranch property in Montana where the odds of life were more predictable. She has rebuilt some of the walls that came down that day at the hospital. She has forgotten some of the lessons learned there about how big the family of man really is, that it extends beyond fundamentalist borders and religious boundaries. She has blamed many of our tragedies, including the accident, on there never being enough. I agree with her that hunger drove us to the edge of tragedy. But I doubt that it was the hunger for food. What drove us, what drives us all, is an omnipresent longing to be part of the human family, to feed and be fed, to love and be loved.

Crossing the Border

BETWEEN THE INTERMITTENT THREATS OF "polygamous roundup" and sporadic visits from strange people—some of them informers for the Church, some of them from the ferocious LeBaron family—we began to feel like fugitives. The children did not shout in the yard, the parents spoke in low whispers, and every time a car rumbled down the lane to our compound, we ran into the house and peered from behind curtains.

How ironic, my father said, that we lived in a democracy formed to honor religious freedom while our freedom was threatened because of our religion. "The prophets say that in the last days, the Constitution will hang by a thread. Each of us will have to face the difficult choice— will we stand for our freedom? Will we stand for Christ? Or will we succumb to the ways of the world and the buffeting of evil?" My father often posed such questions.

I didn't know what he meant, or why he was always so concerned. Eventually I would understand that we stood outside the law because of our religion, and that this fact had made us susceptible to outlaws and fanatics, people who committed crimes and people who climbed the mountains to watch for space visitors. I also came to understand that a step into lawlessness is also a step into paranoia. But at the time I didn't know what my father meant about facing difficult choices. Many difficult choices had already been made, such as his decision to live plural marriage, and it seemed to me we'd already lost a good deal of our freedom.

They say that each man carries the seeds of his own destruction. I know that my father attracted the LeBarons to us, but it never occurred to me to connect my father with death. For us, he was the one who delivered babies, who set broken arms, who stitched up cuts. He fixed things; he did not destroy. So how was it that he brought the Destroyer to our home?

The day I met the LeBarons, my brothers were slaughtering chickens in the back yard, hunched over a wooden table set up beside the tack shed. Jake held the chicken's head in one hand, the body beneath the other. Saul wielded the cleaver, brought it down with a thump between Jake's hands and the hot tang of blood filled the air. The headless chicken ran in widening circles, round and round, until the body thudded on the graveled drive. My brothers laughed. Saul picked up the chicken and with another thump of the cleaver, he ripped out the feet and the tendons. Danny rigged them to his fingers and was making the claw move when a truck rattled down the lane and Danny yelled, "Holy Cow! It's the LeBarons!" The truck screeched to a stop and the LeBarons jumped out. By then everyone knew that the older one, Ben, was crazy. He had blocked traffic by doing push-ups in the middle of Main Street at South Temple, and had challenged the police to arrest him. Ervil, who was younger and handsomer, seemed sane enough, yet he was there to support his crazy brother. They had come to make their point, that the LeBarons had a corner on religious truth.

Aunt LaVerne came out the front door of the white house and let the screen door bang loud as a rifle shot. She said hello, and nodded first at one LeBaron and then the other. "Ben, Ervil, how are you boys?" They didn't look like boys but like the cold, cruel men in gangster movies. Neither of them spoke. The one she called Ben growled low in his throat, and the one called Ervil looked at the ground.

"Rulon isn't here," Aunt LaVerne said, her voice lifting. "But I'll call him. He'll be here right away."

She went back inside. The LeBarons looked over at Saul and Jake, who stared back at them. Ben flopped down on the drive and began doing one-handed push-ups on the gravel. After he'd done several he sat against the truck's tailgate and began spitting rocks in the direction of the tack shed. Ervil watched him, then sauntered toward Saul and Jake.

"We'll kill them chickens," he said. It was an order, not an offer.

"That's all right," Saul said. "We're done, anyway." Saul wiped the cleaver with a rag and hung it in the tack-shed beside the handsaw and the ax. Then he closed the door and snapped the padlock in place. He sat beside Jake who was bent over a bucket stripping feathers from a chicken.

Danny and I huddled against the cold cement step. It wasn't the first time I had to huddle against cold cement and be absolutely quiet, for we hid in the basement whenever a raid was threatened. Danny whispered that the LeBarons were dangerous, that they had once been Mormons, but then they claimed to be the leaders of the church, so they were excommunicated.

When I asked if they believed as we did, in Christ and in the Principle, Danny snorted. "They say they do. But they're always trying to pick fights."

Ervil said he could do twice as many push-ups as Ben and flopped down, counting each push-up so loudly his voice echoed off the barn. Then he jumped to his feet and slapped dust from his hands. "I told you—*I'm* the One Mighty and Strong!"

Just then my father's car rattled down the lane, and he jumped out of the car before it fully stopped. He had his hand stretched out, his voice rising with good will halfway before he reached the LeBarons. "Brother Ben! Brother Ervil! Good to see you! What can I do for you today?"

That's what he said to everybody. Whether it was a patient, or a member of the group, or one of his wives or children, my father was always asking what he could do for them, as if there was no other reason for anybody to come to him. As if no one would want to give something to him, or just want to see him for the sake of loving him.

My father invited the LeBarons to stay for supper, saying LaVerne was making her famous dumplings. But then the men started talking loud and hard about the priesthood, and Danny whispered that the LeBarons thought they had the *all* the keys to the priesthood, a loony bunch like them. They actually thought they were in charge of the Lord's church. They were the reason Saul's teeth were crooked, Danny said, from that time with the mare in Mexico.

My mother came to get me, and didn't seem to care that the LeBarons saw us, and she even said hello to them, but they didn't say hello back because, my mother told me later, the LeBaron men usually didn't talk to women. On the way to our house, she said that she met Ben the first time the family had gone to Mexico, when my father broke parole. She had made some mild greeting, and Ben had roared at her; when my father objected to this treatment of his wives, Ervil explained that Ben was the Lion of Judah. "Have you ever heard of anything so ridiculous?" my mother murmured, and I realized that she wasn't talking to me, she was wondering to herself. She made me get into my nightgown even though it was still daylight, and then we had bread and honey and bottled pears for supper—a cold supper on a weeknight, which was unheard of in our family. After that she put me to bed way too early. There I was, my eyes wide open, with nothing to do but listen to the peacocks crying across the road.

Looking back, I can see the picture within the picture—a design imprinted when I was four years old. The LeBarons. The cleaver. The killing of chickens. My father. The peacocks crying. The beginning of the end.

The night we fled from the United States, I was five. Saul woke me
from a sound sleep and carried me beneath cold stars and installed me
in the big back seat of the green Hudson. (We had not one, but two of
these humpbacked monsters: the green one that Aunt Emma drove,
and the maroon one driven by my father.) I snuggled in to find some
comfort, so surrounded by other children that I felt like one of a litter
of kittens. My mother climbed into the car, holding the baby and
weeping, and Aunt Emma sat in the driver's seat and slammed the
door hard. Aunt Sally covered us with a soft blue blanket, kissed us
good-bye, and gave each of us a peppermint to make us stop crying.
We drove away, followed by my father who drove Aunt Rose and Aunt
Melissa and their young children. We left the compound in shadow,
and most of my brothers and sisters stayed behind.

When I asked why we had to leave, my mother dried her eyes and
said that my father could get in trouble if we stayed. When I asked
why Saul and Jake and Ramie and Isaac weren't with us, Aunt Emma
spoke up. "Ramie and Isaac and the older ones were born before your
father went to prison. If the authorities found out about you, he'd
have to go back."

How can I describe the nausea that crept through me then, the confirmation of what I'd feared, that my being alive could send my father
to prison?

That night we traveled toward the moon, which waxed to fullness,
and which refused to disappear in the daylight. For three days we
drove through deserts pocked with Joshua trees and yucca, then
slipped past sentries of saguaro and barrel cactus. Everything threatened—the air too hot to breathe, the water bag marked "Deseret" that
leaked and left us with parched lips and raw throats, the sweaty bodies
sticking to the back seat, the sharp elbows and knees that left bruises
everywhere. At night we kept traveling, the moon growing larger,
rounder, softer as we neared the border. By the time our caravan
reached El Paso, everyone was too tired to go on. The babies were
sick, and the mothers ruined. My father booked a hotel room and

lined us up on the floor, fourteen small bodies swathed in sheets. The mothers and my father lay crosswise on the twin beds, feet dangling, mouths open, drinking sleep.

The next morning Aunt Emma called us together and stood with her arms folded as though we were about to get one of her Sunday school lessons. She warned us that we must not say anything to the border guards. "Just keep your mouths shut!" she said, as though we'd already committed the sin of blurting something out.

I understood that our crossing into Mexico without getting arrested depended on the good will of the border guards. I knew something about creating good will, and I ached to be of some help. The border guard was dark and handsome, and he spoke in a soft, melodious voice. He asked if we had anything to declare, and my mother confessed that we had a sack of oranges in the trunk. She had purchased them in Albuquerque, remembering a time in Mexico when all they had to eat was yams. Aunt Emma gave her a withering look as she turned off the engine, got out of the car, and opened the trunk. A line of cars had formed behind us. The guard picked up the sack of oranges, examined them, and shook his head.

"You cannot have these," he said to Aunt Emma. She set her mouth and got in the car.

"I am sorry, senora," he said to my mother. "We cannot allow oranges from the United States into Mexico. The vermin, you know."

"We didn't mean to do anything wrong," I said for my mother. "We just like to eat oranges."

The guard smiled at me. His teeth were bright white. He handed me one of the oranges. "For you, little one."

For three days we drove, sometimes on highways, sometimes on dirt roads. We passed through miles of what seemed to be a great mudwash, with no evidence of life but a few scattered bones. We drove through stands of mesquite, past miserable shacks of corrugated tin or adobe without doors or windows. Naked children sat in the dusty light staring vacantly as we rolled slowly past them.

At last we arrived in Monterrey, a beautiful city with wide streets. Palm and banana and orange trees lined sidewalks. Flowers bloomed everywhere. We pulled up before what seemed to be a mansion, and got out. My father helped us lug our bedding and sacks of clothing into the big house. Then he kissed us good-bye and he and Aunt Emma began the long drive back to Salt Lake City. Marble floors and staircases, a fountain in the front hall and another on the back patio convinced me that we had entered the forbidden realms of vast wealth. But my mother explained that this was the way of life in Mexico: people were either rich or poor.

My mother said that some friends—patients of my father—had invited us to stay here until the raid was over in Utah. We had to be well-behaved, she said, and very quiet.

I was lonely. Most of the children were younger than I, and they clung to their mothers or stayed to themselves. Everyone seemed to sleep a lot. Looking back, I can see that most of us were coming down with various ailments. I, alone, seemed to have retained most of my energy, and I was bored and peevish during the hot afternoons while others slept.

The garden behind the hacienda adjoined the neighbor's patio. I discovered that I was not the only child bored with siesta. A dozen beautiful dark-skinned children played beneath the orange and lemon trees while a white-haired grandmother watched over them. She saw my wistful watching and beckoned. She spoke a melodious language— Spanish, I knew it was, a language my father could speak. I did not know the words, but I looked into the grandmother's eyes and I knew exactly what she was saying. She asked me if I was alone. She asked me if I had moved here to stay. She admired my blonde curls. She invited me to sit with them and have cookies and punch; afterward I could play with the other children. After this encounter I was not so afraid, not so homesick. At least not until I heard that the LeBarons were in the area.

I don't know whether they were actually in Monterrey. I have a vague memory of seeing them all together, the puzzle of telling them apart. Did that happen at the border or in Monterrey? I don't remember. Joel and Verlan seemed kind. Ervil seemed strange, spitting pine-nut shells as he leaned against the truck. Somehow we learned that Ben had been locked up in the state asylum in Arizona, and the family seemed relieved to know that Ben wouldn't be coming around.

One night soon after I learned that the LeBarons were in Mexico, my mother told me that she and Aunt Melissa and the woman who owned the hacienda were going to the movies. She told me she needed to get out of the house, everyone said so, even Aunt Rose who would be staying with the children because she was too sick with dysentery to go out. I must stay upstairs, she told me, and listen for my baby brother, who was asleep in the crib in the next room. Aunt Rose was in bed downstairs, and I mustn't wake her unless the house was on fire. Then, in an unfamiliar cloud of perfume my mother left. I sat in the bedroom, listening to my baby brother, imagining that my mother had gone someplace dark and dangerous where the LeBarons taunted and challenged.

An enormous sun slid into the flat horizon and I heard clattering in the distance, and the faint pop of fireworks or pistols. Down the street a line of people snaked along the wide boulevard. As they grew closer, I could hear people crying and screaming, pushing each other along as they beat themselves with what looked like clusters of whips. I wondered if the LeBarons could be behind this. I thought of Saul, challenged by the LeBaron brother to ride a dangerous horse. I thought of Lucinda, the LeBaron girl chained in the goat pen, and wondered if Ben or Ervil had pushed her to hurt herself. Then I wondered if Ervil and Joel and the others could make my mother hurt herself. The noise on the street grew louder and I stayed absolutely still. Finally the noise faded and the sky went dark and the night was still. My mother came home sometime later, and asked why I was still awake. Her voice was brighter, lighter than it had been since we came to Mexico. She said that she hadn't understood a word of the movie, but it had been good to get dressed up and get out for awhile. When I asked her if she had seen the LeBarons, she seemed puzzled, and told me it was time for me to get some sleep.

I don't know how long we were in Mexico, but when my father finally came for us I had changed. I knew that there was something wrong in the world, something that worked against life. I knew that it was deep and forceful enough to penetrate our insular world. I had found it in Mexico, though I could not say exactly what it was. I only know that by the time my father got word that Monterrey had run out of water, we were all desperately sick. The babies nearly died of dehydration, and the dysentery had hit me so hard I felt like a baby myself. But in spite of the fever and the aching in my stomach, happiness swelled in my heart as my father drove us toward the border. "Vaya con Dios, my darling," he harmonized with my mother. "Vaya con Dios, my love."

After that time in Mexico, we were always looking over our shoulders, waiting for the phone to ring with warning of a raid. That spring of 1955, we watched the lane for strange cars to rumble along the gravel, bearing spies. We were coached by the mothers about what to say if anyone asked about our father. They warned us that the wrong answer could cause trouble, could mean that we would have to move, or that we would end up in the houses of strangers. I felt restless and uneasy, and wondered if there was any place on earth I belonged. When I looked at my brothers and sisters and mothers, I saw my own fears reflected there.

Every summer our group of fundamentalist Mormons went into the mountains to worship. We took to the road filled with the determination our Mormon forebears must have felt as they fled persecution in Ohio, Missouri, and Illinois. Like our pioneer ancestors, we had no place to call home, and their courage gave us hope for they had found refuge in the west and built a city that bloomed like a rose in the Great

Salt Desert. The parallel ended there, for we were already in the west, cast out by our own people. Questions began gnawing at me when I was very young, and in time I learned to articulate them: If I was not at home in Zion, was there any place I belonged? If we lived in a country that guaranteed religious freedom, why were my parents in trouble for practicing what they believed? If even Latter-day Saints would not keep the commandment to love one another, how could ordinary people be expected to tolerate our throwback way of life?

Our yearly pilgrimage into the mountains salvaged our dignity and restored our sense of belonging. On any other Sunday our ragtag little clan would be whispering hymns and taking the sacrament in my uncle's garage. In the mountains we didn't worry that my father had been imprisoned for illegal cohabitation. In the mountains it didn't matter that I was illegitimate, born into a spiritual marriage without civil license. In the mountains, where Russian thistle and Lord's candles stood sentry to the order of life, our patched clothing and worn shoes mattered not at all.

We waited until the snow melted and the first wildflowers bloomed. The summer Sunday I remember best, we were newly home from Mexico, the babies just pulling out of their sickness. I had started kindergarten and my fear of the larger world felt exactly like the nausea of dysentery. I was both anxious and eager to leave the city with its police cars and FBI agents and church spies far below as we caravanned along the narrow canyon, my father leading the way in his maroon Hudson. In the voluminous back seat, we were tossed by switchbacks and hairpin turns until one of the boys got carsick. I covered my mouth with one hand and with the other held white-knuckled to the door. Although I trusted my father more than anyone, I could not keep myself from gazing at a thin ribbon of river, imagining a dive over the edge, the heavy car crashing, our bodies exploding. At last we arrived at a high meadow surrounded by quaking aspen and pine trees. We children spilled from the car and stretched in the open and ran the kinks out of our legs. Here and there, bluebells nodded and open-faced Alpine daisies let us know that somewhere on this earth we were welcome. As more of our people arrived, we gathered in a clearing to shout our praises in song:

> *O ye mountains high,*
> *where the clear blue sky*
> *Arches over the vale of the free,*
> *Where the pure breezes blow*
> *and the clear streamlets flow*
> *How I've longed to your bosom to flee!*

At the time, I was beginning to understand freedom and its relationship to democracy, having just celebrated the Fourth of July. I knew about having the right to vote, but I didn't know if our vote mattered. I didn't know if we belonged in this world. Not with people spying on us and threatening to take us from our parents, like they'd done with Sister Black, putting all her kids in foster homes because she was a polygamist wife and wouldn't testify against her husband. Not with people driving us away from our homes to places like far-off Mexico where we had to do without water and the babies nearly died of dysentery. What good were these mountains with their wildflowers and their clear streams if they were not ours?

> *Oh Zion! dear Zion!*
> *land of the free,*
> *Now my own mountain home,*
> *unto thee I have come,*
> *All my fond hopes are centered in thee.*

Still, something happened in the mountains. Something I call soul or spirit triumphed over the dialectics of the ego—though of course I did not think this way back then. What I observed as a child was that the mountains were bigger than our biggest voices. The sheer cliffs echoed our choir to the sky and the call went on and on. The heart of the sunflower opened like a small replica of the sun. Perhaps a macrocosm above reflected the microcosm below, suggesting that my father's belief in the Celestial Order of Marriage and Eternal Family was really possible.

This larger view brought my own way of seeing into sharper focus, yet I can't remember a single Sunday school lesson from those wilderness meetings. My favorite Bible stories—Esther Saving Her People, Daniel in the Lion's Den, Mary and the Angel—were learned in the city. In the city we could not ignore the forces that had colluded to put my father in prison and the mothers in jail. We could not forget that we divulged a past most Utahns wanted to erase. But each time we met in the mountains I discovered something vital, something you could call the spirit of God. The warm white energy vibrating from tree to rock to flower and from one person to another initiated my first moments of true worship: a reverence for life and a personal experience of the Divine that helped me grasp the roots of our religion.

I remember the shadows thrown onto my father's face as he stood beneath the aspens, speaking to our congregation about raising a righteous seed unto the Lord. He spoke of Abraham and Sarah, and her handmaid Hagar, and he said that plural marriage was the Most Holy Principle. But his words were drowned by the whistle of birds, the rush of river over rock. I breathed deeply and the damp sweet air awakened a prickle of pine needles at my neck and the itch of nettle at my ankles. When I sat down, a jagged edge of slate sent a charge of pain from my tailbone to my head. I was learning about the mountains—how they can break the shell of an idea and yield secrets of flesh and bone and blood, a process that gave me great relief, for even when I was young I knew some disappointing things about myself. I knew, for instance, that I could never be as good as Mary or my own devout mother; that unlike young Joseph Smith or my zealous father, I was not worthy to receive personal visits from the Lord. My faith was weak, for my mind insisted that if I met one of Daniel's lions in the mountains, it would tear me to pieces.

My father was going on about how the church had surrendered to political pressure and signed the Manifesto ending plural marriages. Now Utah's state constitution forever forbade polygamy. He talked about the war in Heaven and Satan's plan to oppose the will of God, giving no choice to the children of men. He talked about the righteous souls who followed Christ, and how they had come to earth to live the Gospel. The talk was familiar and I didn't pay much attention. I followed the darting of a dragonfly; I saw a fish kiss rocks at the riverbank; I watched the faces of the people I had known all my life. Our religious group was made up of stubborn people; I sensed, though I could not have articulated it then, that many of the patriarchs were so convinced of their righteousness that they were swollen with self-importance. I was especially glad to notice that the overhanging cliffs seemed to cut the priesthood council down to size.

That day, I could see that in the mountains everything was different. Aunt LaVerne got impatient and interrupted my father's sermon to lead us in the closing hymn. Before the benediction, my uncle challenged the brethren to a round of mumblety-peg. My brothers and sisters took this as permission to throw off their starched shirts and petticoats to wade in the stream. Even my father ran wild on mountain Sundays. When meeting was over, he played horseshoes with such fervor that he forgot himself and swore. He got caught snitching the first slice of a double-layer cake from Aunt Adah's tent and Aunt Adah wouldn't talk to him until after our picnic, although she was his sixth wife and in no position to be uppity. That day when the sandwiches were eaten, and the corn cobs gnawed clean, when the last of the cake crumbs had been lifted on the tip of a finger and the afternoon sunlight touched the river, my brother Jake took me by the hand and we walked to the start of a rocky trail. "You want to see the Eagle's Perch?" Jake smiled and pointed up at the flesh-colored promontory of rock.

Generally speaking, Jake was happier than the rest of us, the only one of my brothers who didn't seem trapped in his own mind. When he was little, he had tried to fly from the top of the silo. Somehow he wasn't injured, but the other boys said he was an idiot before Jake could explain that he'd dreamed about it, he knew he could fly—he just needed practice. In school, Jake didn't work for grades as though his life depended on it, as did most of my father's children. Everyone but my mother worried about his "lackadaisical attitude." My father lectured that we needed to prove that we were solid citizens and the other mothers said if Jake didn't keep up his grades, the district would send someone to investigate his home life, and then the whole family would be in hot water. But Jake knew how to turn down the school part of his brain and listen to the trees until he knew their true names, the ones Adam had called them in the Garden. Jake's eyes were like a lake that lets you see to the bottom. He already seemed to know himself and not to mind what he knew.

That Sunday the boys had challenged each other to dart out of the path of boulders set in motion from above. I think now that the game was a fitting activity for fundamentalist Mormon boys who must evade the big, thumping realities that roll down mountains in life. Jake and I stood watching them. "Go on, Jake," I urged. He smiled shyly and shook his head. "Let's go up."

We made our way over loose shale until we came to a clearing. I looked up, remembering a story my mother had told of a family who left their toddler in a clearing safe from the creek. The mother heard a rushing noise, and turned but the child was gone. No footprints, no sign of the kidnapper. The sheriff concluded that a large bird of prey, probably an eagle, had taken the child. Once I saw an eagle grasp a ground squirrel in its talons and tear it apart with pitiless precision, piling bones and skin in a tidy heap as it consumed every shred of flesh. These thoughts made me scramble after Jake; I found him standing before the promontory of stone. Jake walked out on it as if it were the route he took to school every day.

"Jake! Don't!"

"Come on, sis. It feels like flying." He reached a hand toward me. His eyes were the same color as the afternoon sky. I shook my head. "Don't you trust me?" he asked.

A whirring filled my ears. I did trust Jake, and I wanted to feel what he felt. What would it be like to have big wings to carry me over the valley? I took a step toward Jake's outstretched hand.

At the second step, my foot slipped and I threw myself backward. Jake turned with the slow grace of an acrobat and came to help me up. He brushed the gravel off my butt, then stood back.

"Go on. It's easier to do it by yourself."

"No."

"Don't you believe me?" he asked.

I nodded, then shook my head.

"Then believe in yourself," he said. "Or believe in that." He pointed at the valley spreading like a giant palm with long, curving fingers of canyon. Without knowing what he meant I stepped out, heel to toe, heel to toe, as though walking a fence line. I reached the knuckle of the great pointing finger and stood there until my heart stilled. The stone wasn't as slender as it had seemed. I held my balance, then flapped my arms once. For the briefest instant I wanted to jump and I wobbled. I got down on my knees and crawled back to Jake. I thought of the scripture about rising up with wings of eagles, the one my father said was about us, the children of the Millennium. But I couldn't fly. I couldn't even walk. Jake sat down and put his arm around me and we looked out at the valley for awhile.

We started down without talking. As we neared camp, we could hear my brothers and sisters hooting as another boulder rumbled past. Only Jake knew that I had been on the Eagle's Perch. I made my way through the baskets and blankets to where my mother sat crocheting and talking with the other women. I put my head in her lap.

Perhaps I dozed, I don't know. But the next thing I knew, my mother was pushing my head off her lap, her voice shrill. She was running toward the rocky trail, toward the shriek of children. "Jake! Jake's been hurt!"

I ran after her to where he lay at the base of the trail, a pool of vomit beside his mouth; a rivulet of blood from his temple stained the collar of his white shirt. My mother knelt in the dirt beside him, and then my father was lifting her up, bending over Jake.

He was our doctor and our spiritual leader and we believed he always knew what to do. He gathered Jake in his arms and carried him to the Hudson. My mother sat me on her lap while my father stretched Jake out in the back seat. "He's still unconscious," my father said. Just then Jake threw up again but didn't open his eyes. I'd never seen anyone throw up in his sleep; it scared me.

My father took the S-curves so fast I got carsick myself, what with the smell of Jake and the smell of fear. I added my part to that sour ride, and my mother patted the front of my dress with her lace handkerchief. We arrived home as the sun was slipping toward the Oquirrih Mountains. I had never seen the white house so silent, so hollow. It was like glimpsing a tunnel that I wasn't supposed to know about, but there it was, whirling into tomorrow.

My father carried Jake into the quiet house and put him on the living room sofa. I sat on the floor beside him. I watched his eyeballs roll under blue-veined lids. I watched his lips lose their color. I watched the sun slip low. If he doesn't wake before the sun sets, I thought, he will never wake up again. I saw the tunnel again, a dark spiral in the corner of my eye.

Jake stirred at a sharp knock on the door. I heard Uncle Anthus and Uncle Lawrence in the hallway. I could hear them telling my father that Short Creek had been raided—all the men put in prison and the women under guard in some trailer camp, their babies and children parceled out to foster homes. Now the authorities were threatening to do the same to us. What if they came after us, what should we do? And then my father's voice, strangled and scared, saying, "I don't know."

My father stood with his hands pressed against his temples. I knew that Jake had heard everything, but he wanted to slip into a dream and fly away. I didn't want to lose him. "Open your eyes," I whispered. "You have to stay with me." I poked him until his eyelids fluttered open; I saw the endless blue, the ground too far for anyone to reach. Jake was barely there, a thin cloud you can see through. I had the sense of being lifted, of looking down at my father, my mother, our home from a great height. Once aloft, I wondered if I would ever find a place to land.

The next day Jake was well enough to attend home evening, although he had to be still and lie flat. But my father told the wolf story that night, and we could feel fear looming up dark and fierce.

Perhaps it was the next morning or a morning a day or two later when I awakened to the roar of the hay-truck at my mother's back door, and the voices of Uncle Anthus and Uncle Lawrence shouting orders. They were moving the sofa onto the truck, then the kitchen table. Across the yard, the white house door hung open and the mahogany furniture from the parlor and the dining room was being loaded onto Uncle Renfield's manure truck. My mother stood in the empty kitchen, her eyes wide, her voice tight, explaining that we'd received a threat of another raid. This time, my mother said, we must move for good. Today. The authorities are coming. We have only a little time. Fear was a palpable presence, a shadow that raced to and from the truck as I carried bottles of fruit, my favorite books, my clothes stuffed in a pillow case. Pain wrote a message on my father's face as he kissed me good-bye.

"I'm sorry, princess." The pound of his heart as he pressed my head to his chest, the rasp of his breath as he said good-bye, told me that the wolves were very near.

On the Run

 MY MOTHER AND AUNT EMMA, along with their children, moved into an abandoned miner's shack near the ranch town of Mountain City, Nevada. Nine of us lived in a single room with no running water or bathrooms. We bathed in a corrugated washtub, and visited an outhouse overgrown with belladonna and inhabited by field mice and black widow spiders. Next door, Aunt Sally lived in a two-room bunkhouse that had been built for ranchhands. Sometimes we gathered to play pinochle and rummy or to sing songs at Aunt Sally's, and she would serve caramel-pecan rolls and homemade root beer. Mostly, we spent the balmy August nights in the tin shack, sprawled across beds made on the floor, listening as Aunt Emma read to us from the scriptures. After awhile even Aunt Emma grew weary of the scriptures and our dusty, boring lives, and she read other things for our entertainment: Reader's Digest Condensed versions of *Little Britches* and *Old Yeller* or anecdotes from the tattered *Dog Stories*, including my favorite, "Old Troll and the Wolves." When I closed my eyes, picture-plates of the long-toothed pack were imprinted there.

Animals cried in voices that made us shiver although the air of the tin shack was so stifling we kept the door open. We burrowed into our beds on the floor to watch as moths and June bugs crashed into the kerosene lamp, while Aunt Emma droned on. Sometimes weasels would slink up to the back door and peer inside, curious passersby with eyes suddenly blinded by the light.

My brothers took me walking through the sagebrush hills and we would climb the lichen-stained rocks, watchful of rattlesnakes shedding their skins, for they would strike at anything. When we came back my mother sat us down in front of the tin shack and with the sun shining on our scalps fine-combed our hair for ticks, leaving each of us with the sensation of having been meticulously loved. Sometimes we made the three-mile walk to town which was a cluster of weathered wooden buildings, including a saloon with the best strawberry ice cream I've ever tasted, a general store, and a two-room schoolhouse.

In September, we enrolled in school, swelling the ranks so that the two-member school board talked about building an addition. We were close-knit, the older children teaching the younger ones how to read, how to add and subtract, how to hold back the truth without actually lying. We thought we had safety in numbers, but our numbers evidentally gave us away, and one evening, during a rainstorm, Utah authorities appeared at the door of the mining shack and asked for our father. We could hardly hear them speak through the din of raindrops on the tin roof, but truthfully told them that we had no idea where our father might be.

One thing we did know: it was time to move again, and this time we scattered across the west: My mother and Aunt Emma rented a duplex in Elko, Nevada, a gambling town rimmed in sagebrush. Aunt Sally left us to visit her sister in Oregon before taking a job in Montana. Aunt Rose was with Aunt Melissa in Rock Springs, but soon Rose's children would be hidden away in the Mission Mountains of Montana where they couldn't tell the neighbors about our family. Aunt LaVerne and Aunt Adah had taken new surnames and they had good jobs in Idaho.

Now none of my brothers or sisters attended my school. After Aunt Sally took her children to Oregon, only my mother's and Aunt Emma's children remained, and everyone except me was in the upper school. I had never been so alone. Sometimes I longed desperately for Jake's companionship or even Danny's teasing. Coyotes roamed the outskirts of town, hunting prairie dogs and jackrabbits, occasionally venturing onto the Indian reservation to steal scraps of jerky from the hogans and log huts. Danny told me that coyotes live in family groups, while wolves run in packs, usually of about eight, a quorum, like the priesthood council in my father's religious group. All of them had remained in Utah, their homes and families unmolested, and I wondered why they had been safe, but we had been persecuted. I called their faces to mind, those powerful men on the priesthood council: Brother Joe with his fat hands always trying to pet my bare legs above the white anklets. Brother Orson with his slick dark hair. My Uncles Anthus and Lawrence smiling with their kind blue eyes. The others— the short one with the moustache, the two who were bald. I couldn't think of them without thinking of my father, and his memory swelled like a splinter in my heart.

I had begun to dream of my father's wolves chasing me home from school. I woke with my heart in my throat. I lay awake in the dark, palms wet, eyes stung dry. I watched the shadows creep forward, then ebb, then creep forward. I refused to cry out or tell my mother about the nightmares. Most nights she had to get up to tend to my youngest brother, whose teeth were ruined by the dysentery that took hold in Mexico. Eyes wide in the dark, he screamed at terrors we could only guess about, and I wondered if he, also, dreamed of wolves lurking at the border of our world.

In the darkness I counted my fears: that my lies would be discovered and announced in class; that my classmate, whose father, the district attorney responsible for the sheriff coming to ask my mother questions, would tell everyone at school that my father had seven wives; that I had been lying, not only the lies to protect the family, but also little fibs that made me cringe inside. Each time a breath of wind rushed through the furnace vent, the pilot light flared and I could see a fierce presence watching, planning to attack somewhere on the trail ahead.

When did I decide that life inside church was not as real as the world outside, and that the world beyond Sunday school was far more challenging and therefore a better test of God's love? All that year in Nevada I had tagged along with my mother as she went from one church to another playing the piano at the Church of the Nazarene, the organ at the Baptist Chapel, the pipe organ of the Episcopal Diocese, even the ancient instrument in the Presbyterian Church. And in spite of all the talk about God and Jesus, they seemed to slip farther away from me. The air inside those churches seemed gray, while outside the sun shone hot, the rain dashed wet, and flowers left color imprinted on my brain.

The notion that God manifests in myriad ways outside of churches might have started the day I went with my brother Jake on his paper route. In Nevada we had no garden, no animals, no stream, and for the first time in my life, I understood what it meant to depend on money—in many cases, money others had gambled away. With my father in hiding and unable to see his patients, we had no way to buy food. Aunt Emma got a job waitressing and her wages paid the rent and her tips paid for lights and heat. But food was another matter. When the powdered milk can held only a dusty coat, when the peanut butter jar had been scraped, when all that remained was some whole wheat flour and our bottled peaches from back home—only then did the mothers let us venture out into the world to find work.

Jake took the job of delivering *The Salt Lake Tribune* to earn grocery money and so that he could buy books and clothes to start school; he was in eighth grade and the girls had started to notice his curly blond hair and transparent blue eyes. He usually rode his bike on the newspaper rounds. One evening, he coaxed me to come along, for the company, I suppose, and because he was so shy. We did just fine, collecting fees at one warmly lit home after another until we crossed the tracks and stopped at a house opposite the Silver Dollar saloon. When a redheaded woman flung open the door, we stared at her great crown of hair—flaming and glorious like a Viking queen's. It was as though the morning sun radiated in that doorway even though the time was early evening. And Jake's mouth dropped open as his eyes traveled from her face to the pink chiffon of her robe. Her naked body, burnished by tiny brown freckles, shone through the thin pink film. She might as well have worn nothing, which I am now sure she appreciated since she smiled at Jake and placed her long, red-nailed fingers on one hip and jutted it toward him. "What do you want, young man?"

Jake couldn't speak. Young as I was, I knew the answer, so I said, "He came for your money."

The woman's laugh rang like the bells of St. Mary's Cathedral up the street. She peered down from her majestic height and gave me a little smile. "Now there's a switch." Then she flushed and bit her lip, as if she had disappointed herself. She looked carefully at Jake. "You're the paper boy aren't you? Step inside."

We didn't dare go into the parlor where she said we should sit, but waited on the Oriental rug just inside the door while she clicked across the wooden floor and up the stairs on her high, high heels. We looked over the fringed lampshades and up at the sparkling chandelier in the middle of the parlor ceiling. A round wooden card table and a brown velvet loveseat faced a settee of red satin. Heavy maroon drapes with gold piping hung at the windows. The glass gleamed with the gathering night beneath pink curtains in the same filmy hue as the redhead's robe.

"Why isn't she dressed?"

Jake shook his head and blushed. But he didn't try to shush me up so I continued, "Do you suppose she has any kids?"

We heard the click, click of her heels on the stairs, and the slide of her hand on the wooden bannister, and we tried not to watch. She had put on another robe—this one of frothy blue, a fabric you could almost but not quite see through. She gave him a white envelope. Inside were ten wilted dollar bills, three more than the monthly fee of seven dollars—"your tip" she said, smiling at Jake. "Every hard worker deserves a tip here and there." Then she held up a shiny silver dollar. "You're a working girl already, aren't you honey?" I nodded. "You're a good sport to help out your brother." She winked as she slipped the heavy coin into my pocket. "Always remember to take care of your menfolk."

Jake hurried me down the steps and we climbed on the bike. He took off so fast I almost fell off, and scraped the inside of my thigh as I struggled to stay on the fender. We could have been robbing a bank for the way my heart thrilled to the wobbling back and forth, the gravel spitting as we flew. But before we had lost sight of the red light that shone from the woman's doorway, Jake ran over an old horse-shoe with the rusty spikes sticking up. The back tire wheezed and we had to walk the bike home. A harvest moon shone upon casino lights and sagebrush, over the dim fires of the Owahee Indian village beyond town and the Humboldt River rolling alongside the railroad tracks. As we moved away from the town, the stars seemed to brush the hills and I had a glimpse, so quick, of God's great hand sprinkling light down on us. I waited for Jake to speak, to start into one of our deep warm talks, but he was silent, panting as though the bike was heavy.

That winter, as the air grew crisp and the snow fell in wispy layers that blew away before they could melt, Jake gave up his paper route and took work at the service station repairing automobile tires. He'd come home with grease under his fingernails and his knuckles scraped raw, and after he ate the plate of supper my mother kept warm in the oven for him, he'd do his homework, and sometimes I would sit with him and draw pictures or practice multiplication, waiting for him to talk with me and remind me that we were people capable of amazing things, of standing on the perch, of spreading our wings, of flying above this sad little town.

~

A year later, my father was still in hiding, his doctor's office closed, his patients turned over to colleagues. Aunt Sally had moved from Oregon to help him with a new job as caretaker of a large estate on Flathead Lake, Montana, at a place called Wolf Point. I believed that if my father would come to us, he could stop my little brother's nightmares—give him herbs or lay hands on his head and banish the bad dreams with his priesthood power. Aunt Sally and her children would be safe inside the big warm house in Montana playing checkers and chess and carom with my father, while we were still in Nevada with nightmares and coyotes, with casinos and whorehouses and my mother playing the piano at a different church every week. Aunt Sally and her children were the luckiest people in the world, and I was sure that God had forgotten all about us in Nevada. For the first time in my life, I knew the bitter taste of envy. Lying still in the dark, I called to mind the photographs Aunt Sally had sent, of my father standing beside a glittering body of water. I imagined my father diving into Flathead Lake and swimming to Wolf Point, unafraid to pull himself out of the water and walk the wilderness, and then I could go back to sleep.

Once every three or four months, my father visited us in Nevada, slinking up the back stairs at night, swinging his black medical grip with one hand, shouldering a sack of flour or powdered milk with the other. He would set down his burdens and put a finger to his lips while my mother switched off the light and closed the drapes. He embraced us one by one, his smile flashing in the dark as he whispered, "I love you."

Sometimes when we expected him, he did not come at all. A baby case or bad weather or the demands of his new job would keep him away. The flour in the sack dwindled, the potatoes were almost gone, and my mother would have to spend the money she earned giving piano lessons to buy groceries. During these times, we hurried through the days looking over our shoulders or down at the ground. We picked up pennies and hoped to find quarters or silver dollars. We counted the days till my father's next visit, hardly daring to hope that this time he would really come.

I had just turned eight when my father came for me. Since I had reached the age of accountability, it was time for me to be baptized. We left for Montana in my father's new Fairlane Ford, and a feeling that I would one day call portentous loomed as we traveled north through Idaho, across lava-rock and sagebrush and into the great evergreens of the Sawtooth Mountains. I reflected, as we spun beneath green-black shadows, that when I was baptized, the name of Christ would be upon me, and I would be one of the lambs of His flock. I wondered if I should tell my father about the nightmares, ask him if they would stop when I was baptized. I wondered if I should tell him that I had been thinking thoughts that made me quake inside, that I didn't want to be a second or third wife or even a first wife. That I didn't like him living with Aunt Sally all the time. That I wanted a different kind of life, one where my father could be home when I woke up and went to sleep, a life like Polly had, her father sitting at the breakfast table every morning.

But now my mother sat beside my father in the car, and the two of them harmonized love songs, one after another, "Indian Love Call," "Some Enchanted Evening," and "Let Me Call You Sweetheart." I was so filled with a wild, volatile joy at our being together, just my father and my mother and me that I could not bear to spoil it with confessions. My little brother slept soundly, his head on my mother's lap, his arms thrown wide. Everything seemed to be starting over, brand-new. When we ventured across the river gorge at American Falls, I was cocooned in the hope that somehow there would be enough safety, enough love, enough to eat. Soon I would be baptized, born again. My father drove without blinking, clenching the steering wheel and his teeth until we got to the other side.

Tenderness overwhelms me as I remember my father's hands tight on the wheel. For an instant I glimpsed something hunted or haunted in my father, and I wondered if what he once told us about overcoming fear was really true, or if it lurked forever on the edge of the wilderness. But I was too happy for questions at the time, so they never got asked.

As we made our way north through the Bitterroot Mountains, my father told me about Flathead Lake, that it had always been a sacred place for Indians and once I was baptized in it, it would become a sacred place for me. He explained about his priesthood, about his authority to seal me to Christ in the waters of baptism. When we reached the large estate, Aunt Sally came out and seemed glad we were there even though Aunt Emma hadn't come along, and my mother had become the shadow of a person. I worried because we did not bring white clothes for me to be baptized in. My mother berated herself: "How could I forget something so important?" she said, her eyes dark with shame. I begged her not to worry, Aunt Sally would let me borrow a white blouse from my half-sister, Corrine, and a pair of long johns from my half-brother, Tanner. The water froze my feet, my knees, my waist in icy clarity, as if each step was a photograph, my body framed forever in this moment. My father smiled at me, but his eyes were serious. The water made him shudder. He dipped me under, and I came up gasping from the cold.

"Now you're on your own," he said to me.

~

For awhile I was strong in the face of adversity. I survived strep throat, a broken arm, a kidney infection. I was a good student, popular with my classmates. I was almost happy: if only my father could take me to the Girl Scouts Daddy-Daughter Dance; if only we could visit the ocean like Aunt Sally's children; if only we could be together again.

One weekend, my father visited us in Nevada to take me and my three older brothers fishing. "The boys," as my mother called them, didn't usually invite me to go with them on their fishing trips. Week by week, year by year, they had drawn farther and farther away from the family, forming a tight little circle that excluded me. Although their grades were good and they were star athletes, my mother suspected them of drinking beer, maybe even smoking. That may be why my father had made special arrangements to take them fishing on the Jarbidge River up near Mountain City. My father was the one who invited me to come along, reminding my brothers that I needed his influence as much as they did.

Driving into the Jarbidge Mountains, my father recounted again why he had chosen to live the Principle of Plural Marriage: he reminded us that we owed our lives, our excellence, our eternity to the Principle. He reminded us about eugenic breeding, how a few God-fearing, obedient men had been chosen to bring forth a righteous seed, giving every good woman her chance to be a mother in Israel. He talked about the fullness of the Gospel and our responsibility to live it, since we had been born into it. He told my brothers that they should be willing to follow in his footsteps. "Where much is given much is required," he quoted from the *Doctrine and Covenants*. My brothers listened in silence.

I, too, was silent. I could feel my brothers' resentment burning under my own skin. My father was always telling us that we were chosen and we had worked hard to prove him right, vying to get the best grades in our class, suffering when we didn't. We were careful never to laugh at the wrong things, never to slip up and let on about the family. I watched my classmates from a distance and wondered how they could be so careless—so carefree.

I worried what my father would do if he found out that I didn't want to live polygamy. That if I had it my way, our mother would be the only mother, even Aunt Emma out of the way. Such thoughts about my brothers and sisters, the other mothers, people I loved, sent shame licking up my neck, across my cheeks, along my hairline.

My brothers, who frequently fished the northern mountains near the Idaho-Nevada border, knew every bend of the river, every acre of the surrounding hills and mountains. One way they had kept me from begging to go with them on their fishing trips was to tell the Indian legend of Chi-ho-bidge, the hairy, bigfooted monster that lived in the canyon. Smiling grimly at my fear, they insisted that even the Indians refused to enter the canyon, much less a young girl who didn't know how to fish.

When I told my father about Chi-ho-bidge, he talked about the Prophet Joseph Smith, who said he met a bigfoot in the woods of Illinois, that he stood as tall as a horse, and that he was Cain. I wanted to ask my father how he knew, and if so, what about Cain's mark, and how did he live so long? But my brothers were grinning and my father had fallen into offended silence.

My father and I were intruders. It wasn't just that the three brothers fished together so frequently. My oldest brother, Saul, had been questioning our parents' belief for five years, since the age of fifteen when he accepted my father's challenge to go into the woods, as Joseph Smith had done, and "if . . . ye lack wisdom, . . . ask of God." Saul had received no answer at all, and decided that there was no truth in how we lived, and perhaps not in the official church, either. He even began to question the existence of God. The other boys had followed Saul in his skepticism. Now the three boys held themselves apart, standing like a barricade across the river so that my father and I had to go downstream to catch anything. One by one the trout were layered between grass in a creel.

"More than enough for Sunday dinner!" His hurt feelings forgotten, my father's exuberance filled the car as we drove home through starlit clumps of cedar and juniper. Suddenly a shadow darted across the road. "Look!" my father cried, pointing. "A timber wolf!"

No one said anything. Saul smiled to himself. Jake looked out the window and said nothing, but I could see his teeth glinting in the reflection. Danny snickered behind his hand. I looked at them wide-eyed. I had never seen anyone laugh at my father, ever. Not even the

LeBarons. When we arrived at the duplex, Saul went straight to the back yard to clean the fish. I followed him out, watched him slit the white belly and slide out the insides with his thumb, digging his nail along the spine to clear away the ridge of blood that, he explained, give fish a muddy taste.

"Why did you laugh?" I asked him.

"When?" he said. He concentrated on the knife-tip as it punctured the belly of another fish.

"You know."

After a pause, he said. "There haven't been any timber wolves in this part of the country for twenty, thirty years."

"It was big. It looked like a wolf."

"It was a coyote. A big one—but a coyote, for sure."

"Then why did Daddy say it was a timber wolf? Daddy knows. He was chased by wolves."

"Maybe." Saul gutted the last fish. Then he shrugged. "Maybe he just wanted to believe it was a timber wolf." I felt something cold and unforgiving in the air, the first inkling that a bond had broken between my father and my older brothers. The battle to be right was just beginning, and before it was over, my mother's heart would be broken, and none of us would fully escape the pain. Home was not a place we would ever fully return to, and my family would never be the same again.

THREE

Versions of Love

OF THE EIGHT WOMEN WHO married my father, my mother was the only one to say "No." Unfortunately, I was not aware of this in those teenaged years when I most needed to know when to say "No" and when to say "Yes." But even when I was getting too many curves too fast, I knew something about the versions of love that produced our sprawling family. Through sheer audacity—I was always a shameless eavesdropper and asker of questions—I had gleaned a few details of my mother's romance, and I had gathered bits and pieces of information about the other mothers' marriages as well. Everything centered around my father, a fact that seemed to be taken for granted by everyone but me. No one else seemed capable of imagining my mother or her twin sister, or even my father's first wife, Katherine, in the arms of another man—even though, after my father and she divorced, Katherine married another man and divorced him too. Everyone believed, although it was never verbalized, that without my father, there would be no love story at all.

So how did my mother come to tell him "No"? She was a loving and compliant woman, not the obstinate type. When I heard the story of her refusal, I pondered it, knowing that my life and the lives of my brothers had hung in the balance of her "No." So I asked her straight out, "Mama, what were you thinking?"

She seemed surprised by the question, and then puzzled by her own motives. I continued to puzzle over her motives myself, wondering if my mother's "no" revealed a reluctance to marry him or if it was a way to prove that my father really wanted her and that he had the capacity to "behold" her for her own sake, as she really was. It took years for me to learn that my mother had subjected him to a test of love.

As a teenager, I knew very little about the commitment required to really see someone through. And I didn't consider the ripple effect of "no" until I had said it myself and experienced the consequences.

The romantic dreams of my teen years did not mirror the versions of love that surrounded me; rather, they inflamed the mothers' disapproval. According to them I was already too opinionated, too provocative, too worldly, and they suspected I harbored a selfish dream of being the only wife. Aunt LaVerne reminded me that nice girls don't wear short skirts and Aunt Emma cautioned that nice boys don't stare at girls' breasts. Aunt Sally warned me about the dangers of lying out in the sun in my bathing suit, and Aunt Melissa told me point-blank that only cheap girls walk "that way," adding that wolf whistles proved that the devil was involved. But as I undulated along sunlit sidewalks, I thought of myself as a river, and something deep inside stirred and flashed when horns honked or when a deep voice shouted "Hello there!"

Given that my parents met in Hollywood, how fitting that I would be initiated into love by a movie. On my last night as a thirteen-year-old, I had made a rare request of my father. More than anything in the world, I had wanted him to take me to see this movie that everyone was talking about, the widely advertised "West Side Story." But my father said, "No." He declared the movie risque, and wondered what this country was coming to. Then he kissed my mother good-bye and went off to be with Aunt Emma since it was her anniversary. I burned with jealousy and disappointment. I fumed at Aunt Emma's audacity in being married the day before my birthday (overlooking the fact that she had been married long before I came along). Leaning against the railing of the front porch, I watched my father speed away in his grey sedan and my chest tightened. The sun sank in a red haze, and I sat there hating my life, half-convinced that I had been adopted away from parents who lived in monogamous simplicity.

Ordinarily I would have been in my room, reading. Books had long been my refuge from the constant anxiety of living as we did. Books had become my best friends during the years when my mother and Aunt Emma shared a house and I did not dare bring friends home; any sort of book—romance, mystery, adventure—could distract me from loneliness and the fear of being taunted as a "plygie kid." But now we had the blessed anonymity of this arboreal red-brick neighborhood—in Utah, of all places.

We left Nevada because my mother was pregnant. Everyone rejoiced over our new baby brother, but not everyone had wanted to move. Jake and Danny had stayed behind to finish school and to work. When we first returned to Utah, my mother stayed with Aunt Emma in the basement apartment of the grey house where Aunt Adah had once lived. During the previous year, Aunt Adah had left my father, taking the children with her to join her brother's group. My father's attempt to reassemble his family at the old compound only pointed up the losses and irrevocable changes. The place had fallen into disrepair, and my father felt skittish about his families living together, knowing that the Utah legislature had recently passed a law stipulating that women who lived polygamy should be actively prosecuted, along with the men.

So my mother moved her family—what was left of us—to the red-brick cottage with lilacs blooming at the window and long fingers of birch stroking the lawn, where no one would guess the truth about us. My mother was the only wife in this household, and I could have sleepovers and phone calls and parties in the basement like other girls my age. I worked hard to create an illusion of normalcy, using books as my guide to life in the monogamous world. None of the books contained a hint of my family archetype: the perfect harmonizing of man and woman raising a righteous seed unto the Lord. And man and woman number two. And man and woman number three. Most people did not know that Adam could claim a wife for every rib.

On the contrary, most novels traced the experience of an individual. Literary versions of love suggested that romance was monogamous by nature, for genuine intimacy allowed only two participants at one time—otherwise, violence or dissolution would result. The more novels I read, the more I hungered for singularity and equality, believing that a typical monogamous relationship would include literary order, epiphany, and resolution as a matter of course. It wasn't easy to find female heroes, but I knew from my early literary escapades that they could be found, smart young women like Nancy Drew, or Jo in *Little Women*. Such female role models didn't exist in our polygamous world, where the women were proud homemakers and wise midwives who knew how to treat thrush and milkleg, and who knew how to put up three bushels of peaches in one day and make the bread rise in half the time.

The union of wives might counterbalance one man's voice, but priesthood authority gave the man ultimate command. For instance, all my father's wives agreed that my mother should be permitted to earn money playing the piano in nightclubs; she needed to make a living now that she was in her own house, and she couldn't give lessons during the day—not while she was nursing the baby. For awhile, my father tried to be compliant. But he distrusted the men who dropped dollar bills in a shot glass and leaned across the grand piano to praise my mother's talent. He didn't like her coming home late, the smell of cigarettes and bourbon clinging to her clothes. He never did admit his jealousy, but if he happened to be at our house on the nights she played, he spent the evening at the kitchen table, playing solitaire at a furious pace until she came home, whereupon he punished her with curt responses and long silences until she gave up her nightclub dates and succumbed to the tedium of after-school piano lessons in our living room while we older children took care of our baby brother. Her reward was a happy husband on that one night a week when we were graced with his presence.

Between my father's visits, we lived in pleasant expectation. I lived in my fantasies, building a Prince Charming made of fact and fiction. I wanted someone monogamous, but my father was the prime example of excellence in my life. I knew that he had been chased by wolves when he was a boy, that he had rescued a child from drowning before he graduated from high school, that he had helped dozens of people during the Los Angeles earthquake. Since then he had delivered thousands of babies, mended hundreds of broken hearts, and saved lives through the potent blend of priesthood blessings and scientific knowledge. He was the hero in many lives.

My mother knew how to love a hero. When my father failed to come home for lunch as he promised, she reasoned that someone must have given birth or broken an arm—someone who needed him more than she did. When he didn't give her the money pledged for school clothes, she surmised that God was testing our faith, and waited patiently for Him to provide. On the nights when my father didn't meet with our little family as planned, she took the confusion on herself, and reasoned that it must be someone else's turn. Love meant making excuses for the beloved, and the sacrifice of one's selfish desires. If jealousy should strike, then love required an hour on your knees, praying alone, asking for forgiveness and the resurrection of love's promise.

I regularly witnessed the phenomenon of resurrected love. Six nights a week my mother slept alone, or with my baby brother tucked against her breast. The first night alone, she yearned silently, sometimes weeping, sometimes playing reveries on the piano. Then she waxed strong, spending an hour each day pounding out vigorous scales on the piano, shining the windows, scrubbing the laundry on the old washboard until my white socks had holes where stains had been. And

so it went until the seventh night, when my father appeared. By then
my mother had erased any lapses and the celebration began—a string
of moments given the pearly shine of "yes!" to anything and everything my father could possibly want. We had meat for supper, and
potatoes and gravy, and fruit or vegetables and fresh homemade bread.
And dessert—bread pudding with lemon sauce or baked apples with
cream. They would wash the dishes together, my father up to his
elbows in suds, my mother drying. Then my mother would sit beside
him, the two of them holding hands, or she would sit at the piano and
play while my father sang love songs or hymns. And when Saul helped
us to acquire a television, my father would sit at my mother's feet and
she would brush his silvery hair with a natural-bristle brush, and he
would watch *Perry Mason* and *The Fugitive*—to which he strongly
related. Neither of them liked the repartee of *The Honeymooners*. It
was beyond their experience. What they knew best was how to protect
each other, how to preserve the ideal regardless of intrusions from the
outside world.

My parents loved each other, just as they loved their children and
wanted the best for us. I know they prayed for my eternal happiness as
I entered my fourteenth year; but I was just beginning to discover
what made me happy, and it wasn't what they wanted for me. From
their romance, I had come to be. Now I wanted my own romance, a
fitting birthday present for someone about to turn fourteen. Juliet had
been younger, and love had come to her. The hunger for love swelled
like a seed inside me. I had watched couples kissing in the park, had
read between the lines of my books, and had eavesdropped on my
older brothers who whispered about forbidden things in their cement
room in the basement. I wanted to be someone's one and only love. A
great urgency attended my yearning, for I believed that if it did not
happen quickly, the window would close.

My time in the red-brick cottage was running out. Soon I would
lose this chance at normalcy, along with these old trees and mature
rose bushes, and the group of friends who admitted me to their

monogamous world. Aunt Emma wanted my mother to live next door to her, where she could leave her young daughter without any fuss, and my father wanted his nurse/receptionist, Emma, conveniently close to his office, to make things easier for him. No one seemed to care a whit about me—about the friends I would be giving up and the precious anonymity I would lose. Soon we would be back in the neighborhood where I had been born, where everyone knew all about us—back to peculiarity and notoriety. We would go to the same schools and I would be a "plygie" once more. We would not be returning to the family compound, to the dignity of towering poplars and weeping willows, for the land and houses had been sold to strangers. Instead, we'd be living in a boxed-up, ticky-tack version of our former paradise, with only a brown, dusty plot around the small duplex my mother would share with Aunt Emma. Gone, all my girlfriends and the chance for a boyfriend who would be exclusively mine. I would be would be thrown to the religious group where old men ogled young women, selecting their next crop of wives.

I was sitting on the front porch of the red-brick house nursing these injustices when a boy from up the street, Matt James, came whistling through pools of streetlight, throwing his head back to look at the stars. I knew, even before he reached our red-brick cottage, that my life would never be the same. It was not such a surprise that a hero would arrive, given my legacy. My grandfather and great-grandfather had followed the heroic blueprint of King Arthur, Martin Luther, and Joseph Smith, battling evil through faith and good works. I had been fed faith-promoting stories all my life, and I had witnessed miracles; in this mystic context it was quite normal to expect deliverance. Matt, I decided, must be my deliverer.

A June of hot, dry days gave way to soft nights where flowers bestowed their fragrance in the dark. Later I wondered if it was fate or the weather that made me stay outside, drawing imaginary lines

between the stars, drafting my own constellations. The boy named
Matt sauntered up the walk and onto the porch, raised his hand to
knock, then peered into the shadow of primroses. Seeing me, he broke
into a grin. "Hello," he said.

He was a grade ahead of me, almost two years older, and I was surprised he knew me. I told him that if he was looking for my brothers,
they had already gone to the gym to play basketball. He shuffled a little before confessing that he had come to ask if I would go for a walk.

I said, "Of course."

Matt was earnest, blue-eyed, with a dash of pirate smile. He lightly
held my elbow as if to keep me from falling as we descended the steps.
We strolled through moonshadows to the school at the end of the
street, and shuffled across newly mown lawn. We sat between a pair of
saplings, their trunks small enough to circle with my hands. I stared at
the ground, searching in the dark for four-leaf clovers or something to
say.

He asked if I had seen "West Side Story" and I flushed when I said
no. There were so many things I had not heard, seen, worn that my
schoolmates enjoyed: Mantovani in concert, Malibu Beach, madras
shorts. I decided to tell the truth, a novel idea: "My father won't let
me."

Matt shook his head in sympathy and proceeded to tell the story in
careful detail, speaking kindly and slowly as if I were a child who could
not readily understand.

"There were these great dances," he said, stretching out, propping
his blond head against one hand. "And these great-lookin' chicks go to
the dance. And these tough guys, dressed in black suits and colored
shirts—purple and pink and green." He described how the tough guys
protected the great-lookin' chicks from the other gang, and then this
couple fell in love across gang boundaries, and I thought of this boy
who lived up the street from us, with his powerful mother and quiet
father so different from mine—and I believed I understood something
about the bright edge of forbidden love. I knew, for instance, that if

my father caught me here on the lawn with a boy he might ground me, slap me, or send me away to the ranch in Montana.

But Matt's voice cast a spell, and as the tale wore on I relaxed and stretched out too. I imagined the shriek of sirens and the ringing of chainlink fences in New York City. The perfect harmony of male and female bodies dancing at the gym. The bright silk swirl of dresses. And then he stopped talking. He looked down the length of bare leg beneath my cut-off jeans and his look was like a touch.

"They were bitchin' chicks," he said. I could feel the heat of his look. There was a shine in his eyes that seemed unreal—as though he was seeing what he wanted to see, not what was really there. Like my brothers when they talked about the girls they dated. Or the men of the religious group who wanted to marry as many baby factories as possible. None of them seemed to see who I really was. All seemed to hold an idea of me that connected only vaguely with reality. So what was real? The curve of the earth under my hip, that was real. The rustle of new leaves, that was real. The sweet smell of the grass, the light wind, these were real.

But I wanted to believe that what Matt was telling me was real, and I had learned from my mother how to bridge gaps and fill in spaces. It was my parents' legacy, second nature for me to make excuses in the name of love. And so when Matt stopped mid-sentence, without telling me the end of the movie, I let him kiss me, let him slip his hands under my brother's shirt and trace the lines where my back met the earth, let his fingers gradually move toward the front before I pushed him away. He shoved me flat and kissed me hard.

"Let me touch them." he gasped. "I've . . . I've seen them. It's all I think about."

"What?" My head ached a little from being pressed against the earth by the force of his kiss. He smelled vaguely of sweat—a sharp, silty smell.

"I . . . I looked in your window." He closed his eyes. "I watched you. You . . . I felt . . . when I watched you undress . . . it was like watching a dream. Like you were in a movie and I was supposed to be in it."

A splash of feeling like cold water. But then the slow heat of flattery spread through me. He had been thinking about me, dreaming about me. And when he moved his hand again, I let him touch my breasts through the covering of my brother's shirt But when his hands traveled to the crotch of my jeans, I moved them away. "No." I was surprised that I was breathing hard, as if I'd been running, as if I was in great danger.

"Tell me the rest of the story," I said, trying to move out from under him. "What happens after the dance?"

"Come on," he pleaded. He sounded too much like my younger brother wheedling more cookies from my mother. I had the peculiar sensation of watching us from a place high above the saplings, above the school building. Nothing my father or mother taught me had prepared me for this. The prickle of grass against my neck, Matt's hot breath against my ear, the weight of him on top of me. Again I tried to push him away, tried to get up. But his hips jerked against me, pressing so hard that metal buttons bit into my flesh. Groaning, he threw himself onto his back.

My clothes and hair were damp from the lawn. Was this romance? No. It was more like one of the bad novels I'd read last year, running on and on, the events loosely connected. Like too much of my life. If he would hold me, I thought, just hold me. Make it real.

"What's the end of the story?" I asked.

He turned his head, his voice surly. "What story?"

"You know, the movie."

He grunted and stood slowly. "Let's go," he said, stretching. He didn't reach out to help me up, but squinted overhead at the moon.

My knees shook as I stood. A horizon of houses on the mountain-side glowed in the moonlight, a thousand other lives beckoning. Matt started out and I followed along, feeling left-behind and insignificant as I often did with my brothers. But as we walked, I thought of myself saying "no" so clearly, so definitely. I felt stronger, connected to the earth in a way I had not ever felt before, as though my legs had just discovered gravity.

We walked toward the red brick house. I felt his anger breaking up, drifting away. He draped an arm over my shoulders. I said something about my brothers being home by now, and he let his arm drop.

"Do you feel bad about this?" he asked.

"No," I said. "I don't feel bad. I just want to know how it ends."

He cleared his throat. "Tomorrow I'll be going to Boy Scout camp for three days. I'll call when I get back."

"I'm moving. In a week."

He looked at me, then looked away. We walked a dozen or more steps in silence.

"Do you think—would you ever—do it?"

I knew exactly what he meant. "No," I said, my parents' favorite word. "Not until I'm married."

"Huh," he said.

"Maybe we can talk—before I move."

His kiss was soft and fleeting as moth wings on my cheek, then he disappeared into the dark.

My birthday passed in a haze. My mother made a yellow cake; the frosting had orange zest in it. I received a diary from my oldest brother, Saul. That night I decided to write about Matt on the fresh white pages of the diary; after all, it had a lock and key.

The next two days were spent preparing to move. My mother was busy, exasperated, close to tears. The heat plus the sharp dry edges of the packing boxes parched my hands and face and throat. I wanted to go swimming, to lie out in the sun, then swim again. I thought of Matt with the scouts in the Uintah Mountains, sweating, swimming in the lakes and streams, letting all that nature seep into him. I wanted to be there with him. I wanted to stop time and stay forever in this red-brick house where my dreams had bloomed, wanted the green yard and old-fashioned garden. And so I went out back, leaving a box half-full of linen and my mother's question, "Where are you going?" hovering in the air behind me, and I settled in a metal lawn chair where I could see the lilacs and my bedroom window. I imagined Matt crouched here, watching me undress. The sprinkler whirred and sprayed as I replayed the thirty or so minutes at the elementary school, rehearsing his touch, refining each moment, adjusting the light, finding new words for him to say. The remembered sensations played nicely into the scene I constructed. The tentative stroke, the awkward rubbing, the frantic pushing, even the metal biting into my skin, these I improved and integrated. I relived the sharp ache in my chest, the bruising of my pubic bone, and found sense even in the pain.

I rewrote the moments until they suited me. In my revision, Matt was taller, more muscular, more articulate. He wore aftershave like Saul, instead of smelling like a baseball uniform. He knew more about what he was doing, what to say, how to really take someone in hand. And there was meaning; he was teaching me about the outside world, teaching me that boys and girls were equals on this planet—with a basic respect as they stood toe-to-toe, face-to-face. I memorized the vision, held it fast in my mind. Now I had something to go on, something locked in place, something more satisfying than the moment as it happened. Later, I would weave in the scent of lilacs and the moonlight streaming through my bedroom window. Part of a movie I could play in the heat of the afternoon, with the sprinkler hissing. I could saunter to the elementary school and lie on the damp lawn and listen to the chain clink against the flagpole and relive the experience. One part fantasy, one part reality—my mother's recipe for married life. The little mixture couldn't possibly hurt.

The three days spun out and I waited for Matt to call. I looked up his phone number, let the phone ring once, twice. His little sister answered. I hung up without speaking. The next day I called again. I had only a little time—three more nights—to renew my romance. I watched up and down the street. I sat on the porch after dark. Matt did not come by. He did not call. I decided he was not such a hero after all.

Now something familiar surfaced when I closed my eyes. The feeling was shame with the sting of rejection. There was a reason he did not call. Did he have another girlfriend, someone who said "yes" to him? Had someone told him the truth about my family? Had I been too dull in my world of white nightgowns and homespun morals? Did I need a twin sister to plead for me? Sometimes I was sorry I had told him "no."

The day we moved, the girl who lived across the street came over to say good-bye. She was a heavyset, deep-voiced girl of fifteen named Memory. She invited me to spend the night with her if I ever got homesick for the old neighborhood. I had never paid much attention to her before, but I asked if she knew Matt, and she said yes, their parents had been friends for years. I agreed to visit the next week. I asked her to tell Matt that I was coming. She gave me a cat-like grin as she wiggled her fingers good-bye.

The new house had no lawn, no bushes, and hence no sprinkler to sit beside. I locked the door, filled the tub with cool water, closed my eyes. I ran my hand over the curves and hollows of my bare body. I imagined the old neighborhood, the elementary school in the moonlight, Matt and I carving our initials, his Boy Scout knife breaking the tender skin of the sapling.

Memory called that weekend, saying everything was set. In my diary I anticipated what would happen, my mind lilting over the possibilities. A week later I arrived at Memory's, shouldering my brother's brown sleeping bag with elk printed on the red-flannel lining. I looked at the empty red-brick cottage across the street, then quickly looked away. I reached into my pocket and fingered the envelope with Matt's name on it; it contained an index card with my phone number neatly written below my new address. I had decided to go to Matt's house and give it to him. But before I could muster my courage, Memory made an announcement.

"Matt said he can't come."

My eyes stung. I was glad it was dark and that we had rolled out our sleeping bags on the lawn. Just then, Memory slipped her hand up my shirt and started scratching my back. I froze. Then I turned over, pinning her hand beneath me.

"You shouldn't use safety pins to mend your bra straps," she said comfortably. "You're better than that." I thought of the way my mother's sister-wives watched out for each other, how they had taken care of my mother when she was recovering from giving birth or her nervous breakdowns. But Memory's attention didn't feel like that kind of convivial concern. I wriggled away from her hand.

"What did Matt do to you?" Memory asked. Her voice cloying.

"Nothing.

"He did. I know he did. Did he do this?"

She rolled on top of me and kissed me.

She was heavy and pressed me into the earth. I felt disgust. A little amusement. But no anger.

I turned my face away, grinning in spite of myself. "You're heavy. Please get off me."

After a few seconds, she did. "You could pretend I'm Matt. I could make you feel better."

"No thank you," I said primly.

In the dark, I was still smiling. But I also felt shame; I knew what pity was, had felt the supercilious sweetness of people when they found out about my family. Here I had stumbled into yet another kind of romance. This one fit like a clown costume, and I thought of my mother's opera record, of the clown who made people laugh to keep himself from crying. I could see the Matt episode in a new perspective—in black chinos and a purple shirt, snapping his fingers in time to the music. Ridiculous and sad and dear as Memory was, in her way. Another version of love.

So I told her the story of Matt, spinning it into the fine romance of my fantasies with an open window, a soft light, the scent of lilac, and an edge of suspense—the danger of being discovered narrowly averted. When I was finished, she sighed. "I wish I had a boyfriend."

I held out the envelope with my new address and phone number inside. "Make sure Matt gets this, ok? It's important." She nodded, her eyes round.

My brother Saul called the next morning and ordered me to roll up my sleeping bag; he would pick me up in a few minutes. He didn't say who had found the key to my diary, who read it, who decided I should be grounded for a week, and not go anywhere with boys until I was sixteen. It was a joint decision—my father and my mother, and perhaps Saul was in on it, too. I was alternately contrite and furious, penitent and rebellious. But through the days of sequestering, I began to see my punishment as still another version of love.

My mother watched soap operas on television while she ironed shirts for my father's wealthy patients. I went to Saul's basement bedroom and sneaked his books out of the cinderblock bookcase by his bed, books that tasted brackish as blood: *The Diary of Anne Frank, The Miracle Worker, The Agony and the Ecstasy*. I stopped writing in my diary. I decided to live my life instead of imagining it. I would take responsibility for making my life story something substantial—real, like the characters in the books I was reading, who catalyzed events instead of living someone else's script, who were fully engaged in love instead of waiting for a few fragile moments of romance as my father's wives did. I would no longer leave my love life up to the likes of Memory and Matt.

Following these early versions of love, I was, as they say at the racetrack, "hot out of the box." I didn't make time with anyone like Memory, who was much harder to convince that I wished to keep my body to myself than any boy I met for some time to come. But once I found that romance is a means of exchanging power, I became quite good at the game of using before being used, and I enjoyed myself until I lost track of what I really wanted.

I was a typical teenager, in the throes of unidentified hunger. My father watched me from the corner of his eye, his gaze skittering over my short hair and short skirts. I could hear the unspoken condemnations for breaking the pattern of women in our religious group whose uncut tresses were "their crowning glory" and whose modest clothing spoke of chastity and loyalty. He winced when my voice keened above my mother's quiet reminders to please, please remember who you are. He didn't seem to know what to do with me. Occasionally I wondered if my father was afraid of me. The thought crossed my heart with a thrill, first of terror then of joy.

Innocence disappears in increments, rather than vanishing overnight, but usually there is one point of despair when we know that the world is irrevocably darker. Everyone remembers where they were when John F. Kennedy was assassinated. I was at the door of the junior high school cafeteria trying to bum a quarter off a young man who would be killed six years later by an AK-47 bullet in the jungles of Vietnam. Another ninth-grade boy announced the president's death, his blue eyes wide with horror; he would one day be my husband and he, too, would go to Vietnam. We would not realize for many years how many dreams died with John F. Kennedy, how many would lose their lives, or how many futures were thwarted by what he had set in motion.

Life in Zion

 CURIOUSLY, THE LEBARON BROTHERS were among those suspected in the assassination of John F. Kennedy. In 1951, three years after our family left the LeBaron ranch in Mexico, Dayer LeBaron had died, leaving his sons at loose ends. For awhile my father's association with each of the LeBaron brothers was one of physician to patient and ecclesiastical leader to acolyte. Then came a religious debate with Ben and Ervil and a verbal joust with Joel over doctrine. The fundamentalist council paid the LeBaron brothers a visit, and the LeBarons swore their loyalty to the Allred group but they failed to ask for guidance. My father saw them only when they called him to attend a baby case, or when he was asked to treat Ervil's recurring bouts with malaria. While they did not ask him to officiate in plural marriages or request spiritual advice, things seemed peaceful. But the year before we moved from Utah, Joel had proclaimed himself "the Lord's appointed" prophet. In 1955, the first of those "scattered years" when my father was in hiding and our family lived in five different states, Joel delivered an open challenge to my father's priesthood authority by serving up a "revelation," which ordered my father to move to Mexico onto the LeBaron ranch which Joel now called "the Land of Zion." According to this "revelation" my father was ordered to become Joel's "counselor" and bring his followers to participate in the new "Church of the First-born in the Fullness of Time." The "revelation" detailed what would happen if Rulon Allred did not follow its dictates: he would be "turned over to the buffetings of Satan and shall be cut off from among my people . . . and left to the destruction of the wicked and ungodly."

At first my father gave only passing notice to this threat in the form of revelation. He put himself above the fray, behaving as though Joel's words didn't deserve comment. But the furor escalated as the LeBarons began to proselytize among Allred group members. At that point my father penned a response, pointing out the main discrepancy: that the words of Joel's "revelation" contradicted the gospel restored by the Prophet Joseph Smith. My father clearly stated his belief that the LeBarons had formed "a church founded by false prophets upon false doctrines."

Then in 1956, my father took another step, sending his longtime friend and follower John Butchreit to set the LeBarons straight. But instead of straightening them out, John Butchreit converted to the Church of the First Born and became a missionary for the LeBarons, calling on his former brethren in Utah to "repent, come to the waters of baptism and be cleansed [or] they are in open rebellion against God's legitimate authority." He said that those who did not heed the warning were "playing with fire."

When people in our group asked questions about Brother Butchreit's affiliation with the Church of the First Born, my father warned them to stay away from the LeBarons. By then, Ben LeBaron had "lost his mind" (in his mother, Maud's, words) and would spend his remaining years in the Arizona State Mental Hospital. Joel had seemed kindly and peace-loving until the reversal of his commitment to the Allred group and the decision that he was God's representative on earth. Overnight he began spouting commandments and judgements, talking about the Civil Law of God and the death penalty for those who broke it.

As the patriarch of the newly formed Church of the First Born, Ervil added one of the religious notions he and Ben concocted, a frightening interpretation of the Blood Atonement doctrine which provided for people to kill in the name of God combined with the belief that the Law of Consecration meant turning over all one's goods to the LeBaron family church. According to Ervil, there were three kinds of people in the world: First and best were those who would do whatever God wanted them to do, including kill others. Second were those who followed along and supported those who did whatever God wanted them to do. Third were those who pulled in the other direction, doing the will of Satan. According to Ervil, my father and his council belonged to the third category. Ervil, of course, belonged to the first.

Ervil began proselytizing, urging saints all over the earth to build up Zion in Mexico. In his view, Mexico was "Book of Mormon country," the homeland of the Nephites and Lamanites, the site of ancient battles and sermons as described in the *Book of Mormon*, the most likely place on earth for God to gather his Chosen Ones under the leadership of "the One Mighty and Strong." In his role as patriarch, Ervil made various prophecies and he drew up a list of people "condemned to die" for breaking "the Civil Law of God"; among them were President John F. Kennedy, Prime Minister of Israel Ben-Gurion (and later, Moshe Dayan), and President of the Church of Jesus Christ of Latter-day Saints, Harold B. Lee. The list targeted those who stood for freedom, those with political clout, and many who had ecclesiastical power. We would not learn of the list for many years, not until we discovered that my father's name was also on it.

In 1963, the year of President Kennedy's death, Joel and Ervil sent my father a treatise which specifically upbraided the Allred group for "character assassination" of "the Lord's appointed." Invoking "the Civil Law of God as practiced in the days of Moses," the men pronounced death as the penalty for refusing to follow the dictates of "the Lord's appointed." They also declared that the purpose of the

LeBaron family church was enforcement of the Ten Commandments. Other writings such as Ervil's *Priesthood Expounded* had been used to convert people in Utah, Arizona, and Mexico, as well as a group of Mormon missionaries in France to the LeBaron's Church of the First Born. Ervil's passionate diatribe and charismatic personality had catalyzed rapid growth of the family sect, but his brother Joel, the "president and prophet," insisted that they adhere to Christlike practices despite their strong words about God's Civil Law. Joel discouraged Ervil's doctrinal justifications of theft and murder to improve the economic condition and power base of the family church. Brothers Alma, Floren, and Verlan LeBaron sided with Joel, which outraged Ervil.

The growing division among Church of the First Born leadership may have led my father to disregard Ervil's menacing diatribe. Or perhaps my father was disarmed by his own humble situation, the sense that he had nothing anyone else would want. In any case, Rulon Allred was glad to muster troops to serve God, but he was a poor field marshal when cries for a real battle sounded. His attempts at peace talks had resulted in the defection of one of his trusted brethren, and he was unwilling to squander more of his following or his time on an enterprise so unsuited to his character. Unlike his ongoing dialogue with the official Church of Jesus Christ of Latter-day Saints, my father despaired of agreement from Ervil LeBaron, who refused to be fettered by reason or restrained by generally accepted moral codes. The LeBarons had become, as my father said, quoting scripture, "a law unto themselves." Yet the LeBarons were such a pathetic, thrown-away group of people, most observers did not think them capable of waging any sort of revolution, let alone a war staged between heaven and hell.

Evidence of this dismissive attitude showed up when, in 1963, the FBI launched an investigation of Church of the First Born members who had issued what amounted to terrorist threats, vowing to disrupt civil authority, destroy communication and public utilities, and engage in undercover operations that would overthrow secular power structures all over the world. The FBI probe focused on the LeBaron brothers' dual citizenship and their unwillingness to serve in the United States armed forces. Ervil had actually lost his U.S. citizenship for remaining outside the country during the Korean War, ostensibly to avoid the draft. The LeBaron presence in Texas along with their conspiracy to bring down the government made them brief suspects in JFK's assassination. The FBI investigation ended in 1964, when agents concluded that First Born leaders were incapable of carrying out the threats they made.

One afternoon in October of 1966, I came home from school to change clothes for my waitressing job just as my father rushed through the front door. He wore his grey felt panama and held his medical grip in one hand and his car keys in the other. He followed me into the front room, then began speaking about his longtime friend and follower John Butchreit. It struck me as peculiar to be standing there in our coats while he spoke of someone I had not seen since early childhood. Then he told me that Brother John had been shot dead. With a pang, I remembered the bald, bespectacled "Uncle" John from when I was five and we fled to Mexico. We had followed him in the light of a huge, orange moon across the Saguaro Desert, and he stopped often so that we children could relieve our bladders and stretch our legs.

"I warned him not to stay down there," my father said, and his voice cracked. "I told him that the LeBarons had fallen to Satan, that they were doing his dirty work." My father gazed at me in silence, then kissed my forehead. "I have to go to Mexico," he said. "The authorities have asked me to pick up his body."

I did not find out until later that it was my father who sent Brother John to "straighten out" the LeBarons. Several years later I would find out that Brother Butchreit had criticized Joel and Ervil for sloppy accounting of First Born tithes and offerings. Later, a pair of young

men asked to borrow his car, and it seems he'd been shot for refusing
their request. That day, all I knew was that my father carried deep sorrow in addition to his other responsibilities. I sat on the sofa, still
wearing my coat and wondering why he made sure I always knew
about the strange goings-on in Mexico.

My mother came into the living room. "Where are you running off
to now?"

"Did Daddy tell you he's on his way to Mexico to pick up Brother
Butchreit's body?"

She looked up, startled. "I knew he was going to Mexico. I didn't
know he was going to pick up Brother Butchreit's body. How did
Brother John die?"

I told her what my father had said, that he'd been shot, a pistol
emptied into his body. She covered her face with her hands, as though
trying not to see the image my words evoked. "He was always so kind
to us," she said into her hands. Then she went to her room to pray. I
thought of the round I'd sung in childhood, *"Frere Jacques, Frere
Jacques, Dormez vous? Dormez vous?"* always imagining the Brother
John in the song as the bald-headed, mustachioed Brother John who
bought us root beer in El Paso. Now he slept in a deep freeze on the
other side of the border, Ciudad Juarez.

I wondered again why my father always told me about the activities
of the LeBarons. Did he fear that I would fall into the wrong crowd, as
Brother John had done? Did he intend to curb my rebellious spirit and
scare me into obedience? Or did he speak from a need to unburden
himself? That particular afternoon, my father may have feared for his
own safety and perhaps bestowed these facts as a way of preparing me
for what might happen to him. Perhaps he knew, in that way we have
of knowing naturally what could be, that one day I might write about
our family, and he wanted me to know how he felt about making the
long, lonely drive to Mexico to claim the body of a friend he had sent
into harm's way.

Later that year, my father was sitting in my mother's kitchen when I came home from school. It wasn't his usual Thursday afternoon off, and I was surprised that he would wait for my mother to finish her piano lessons. He invited me to sit at the kitchen table and play a hand or two of rummy. Given our recent arguments about my choice of friends and my reluctance to attend meetings of our religious group, he was surprisingly voluble. After counting up the number of grand-children he'd delivered and describing the garden he had designed behind Aunt Melissa's house in Montana, he said, "Ervil Morrel LeBaron has gone against his brother, Joel."

I thought of my father's most recent lecture about the boys I was seeing. He'd said, 'You must be careful of the company you keep. When I served time at the prison, I was on Death Row. The worst sort of men you can imagine. Rapists. Murderers. Is this what you want in your life?" Now a sarcastic little voice rattled in my brain, asking if my father had been careful of the company he had kept and did he want people like Ervil LeBaron in his life?

My father shuffled the cards and dealt another hand. As he arranged the cards, he complained that he had tried to get help in the office in case something happened to him, but no one was stepping up to share the growing responsibility of his patients. He confessed that he was tired and unwell, and he wanted more time with his wives and chil-dren. I wanted to hug and reassure him, the way I might have done when I was little. But too much had come between us.

What had him so worried? The murder of John Butchreit had rocked him, there was no doubt about that. Certainly he was worried about making payments on one hundred and sixty acres of forested hills in the Bitterroot Mountains, the site he had selected for gather-ing his people. The forested property reminded him of the pristine wilderness of Canada, and he set about populating the ranch even before the papers were signed. There, where the air buzzed with hon-eybees and clean sunshine, he could make real his father's and his grandfather's dream of a wilderness refuge, a bulwark against the com-ing storm. But the new promise held new challenges.

Certainly my father worried about his children. My brother Saul had written an epistle to him, thirty-odd pages rationally renouncing polygamy. My father retaliated in sermons and in passing commentary, but failed to engage in a one-on-one encounter with Saul. Since Saul ultimately wanted our father's respect and attention but did not get it, their relationship continued to deteriorate. Meanwhile my father worried about his daughters, several of them approaching marriageable age, all of them a worry, especially those who attracted boys from school instead of from the religious group.

My big quarrel with my father had happened one night when he took me for a drive to insist that I attend the meetings of our religious group. If I was going to "date," he said, I must go with boys and men who lived the way we did. He told me these restrictions were for my own good. I came right back at him, told him that he had no right to tell me what to do—I am a free agent, I said. I accused him of neglecting my feelings and of ignoring my mother's needs. I accused him of making things up as he went along. It was to be the only time he would ever strike me, and he did it quickly, sharply as an incision. I wanted to cower, whimper. Instead I held my head high, the print of his hand burning on my cheek, too proud to cry.

At school I was seen as a "nice girl"—the model of a well-adjusted teenager. No one knew about the shadows, the shame and fury buried so deep I could almost pretend that I was not a child of polygamy. And yet I was rebellious even by the standards of my maverick family. Banished from the banished. Psychologists have long recognized the phenomenon of the "acting-out" teenager who exemplifies the family dysfunction so that society may be aware of what has been included—wittingly or unwittingly—in the cultural stew. Something in me rebelled at having my hard-won identity judged by the people who claimed to love me most, my family.

It was the sixties. Free love in San Francisco. The first protests against the war in Vietnam. The Beatles had long since staged their coup, staking a place in hearts longing for personal meaning. My father's group burgeoned with seekers after a better way of life. Besides the ranch in Montana and the gathering of followers in south Salt Lake County, the group established communities in Delta and Cedar City, Utah. But his longtime followers, those men of the priesthood council under my father's guidance, had grown more insular and rigid, more impoverished and more peculiar over time. One man (whose dapper appearance belied the fact that his wives lived in squalor, their children hungry, their rent overdue) denied that he needed assistance when my father offered medical care and financial help. Two of his wives were my half-sisters, and the hungry children, my father's grandchildren. My father must have seen the bare rooms and crumbling foundation of their rented home, and when he treated them for strep throat or measles, he must have suspected that they weren't eating enough. But he couldn't seem to interrupt their pathetic way of life no matter how often he offered help.

Another man, also on the priesthood council, refused to admit that he had a problem but my father must have seen disturbing evidence: emotional and physical scars that showed up when this man's grown daughters gave birth. As a doctor, my father must have known that terror of vaginal exposure can be ascribed to sexual abuse during early childhood. This council member often opposed my father's wishes when decisions regarding group tithing funds were pending. Was this pressure the reason my father did not call the Salt Lake County Sheriff's Office, or was he afraid to act on what he must have known, that incest and sexual abuse of minors had taken place and could still be taking place within his religious order? Was my father afraid that an investigation into this man's behavior would jeopardize him and the other patriarchs in the group, that they would be imprisoned for child abuse as well as polygamy? Or did he simply stay in his idealistic groove, refusing to see that the men who made up his priesthood council were capable of such flagrant behavior.

Since our return to Utah my father's status had grown along with his religious following. All along, women had tried to worm their way into our family, drawn by my father's charisma and his religious standing as well as his compassionate heart and native wisdom. Years before, the day we fled to Nevada, "Aunt" Hattie had asked to come into the family and my father had refused her, saying that he could scarcely care for the wives he had, let alone take on new responsibilities. But in the late sixties and early seventies, as his practice thrived and his religious power expanded, "Aunt" Hattie was asking again, and this time my father didn't know how to put her off. The men on his priesthood council were urging him to take more wives since protocol did not permit them to have more wives than he did. Citing the life and behavior of the Prophet Joseph Smith, they made a case for Rulon to take on widows and divorcees and even the wives of unrighteous men who still lived.

I couldn't get my mind around it. "Aunt" Hattie was old enough to be my father's mother. Her husband had left her many years ago, yet now she needed my father as a husband? Another woman, married to a man deemed "unworthy" of the Principle, the mother of my childhood friend, was a shrewish presence who had made her children's and her husband's lives a hell on earth. I had never liked her and as a child had been particularly grateful that she was not my mother. I couldn't imagine being sealed to her for all eternity. How could my father endure the thought? I asked my mother. "I don't know what your daddy is thinking," she agreed.

As lifestyles fluctuated all over the country—people experimenting with communes, open marriage, and live-in relationships—more and more people joined our fundamentalist way of life, and more and more women voiced a desire to marry the spiritual leader of the group and thus become part of our family.

My father met with his wives (minus Aunt Adah, who had left him to join her brother's group, and Aunt Rose, who had died of a heart attack in 1963). They refused the proposals, all but Aunt LaVerne who had been charged with the responsibility of making sure Rulon had all the wives he had coming. The question was, how many wives *did* he have coming? Aunt Sally and Aunt Emma said he had enough. My mother said he had more than enough, perhaps thinking of Saul's complaints. Aunt Melissa said she'd go along with the majority. The plural wives identified all the women who would flood into our lives once the gates were opened. There were women who disliked their husbands, especially when comparing them to my father with his sweet nature. There were women who had left their husbands, declaring that these men were not worthy of them. There were women who lost their husbands to automobile accidents and heart attacks, who argued that a loving Heavenly Father would not want them to grow old alone. There were women abandoned by their husbands who demanded that their children receive the guidance of a kindly father— my father. Rulon asked, wasn't it his responsibility, as leader of the religious group, to fulfill their needs?

No, the mothers said. You have enough responsibility. You can't keep up with what you've got. You're not as healthy as you used to be. Besides, you promised us you would marry only virgins. And my father fell to musing over his scriptures, a signal to leave him alone. When the potential wives called asking to meet with him, he blushed like a schoolboy. I wondered how he could give his time and attention to women he hardly knew when my mother was fading for lack of his attention. How could he think of bringing more strangers into his life when he had not met the needs of his own children?

I knew only the crust of his troubles, absorbed as I was in teenaged narcissism, already consigned to a shadowy life of secrets I had sworn to keep and family secrets I sensed but wanted to know nothing about, such as what Aunt Rose's Malcolm had done to get himself kicked out of the house. I had lost my appetite for covert knowledge about my family; I no longer rifled through Aunt Emma's drawers or searched my father's pockets. I was embarrassed by the fanatics of our religious group who scanned the skies for flying saucers bearing the translated citizens of the City of Enoch who, it was said by certain priesthood leaders, had been lifted up and now lived in the solar system of the

North Star. I didn't want to be associated with the zealots who rose in sacrament meeting to speak in tongues or to predict Second Comings that didn't transpire.

After my confrontation with my father, I met a boy—a man, really, though he was seventeen or eighteen. I heard from a neighbor that I should stay away from him: he had a reputation, had made a girl pregnant, had hurt people in ways that would last a lifetime. I could not have met him at my high school, the neighbor said, because he had been in reform school. I had heard from schoolmates that he was so cruel that he had put someone's eye out during a fight at the drive-in. But I knew how it felt to be maligned and misunderstood. I also knew, firsthand, how effectively people can lie. I wasn't willing to listen to anything that smacked of rumor.

On the first date he came to the door, bringing me a bunch of daisies. He didn't try to kiss me. On the second date, I let down my guard. I didn't protest when he took me to a drive-in movie, even though it was against Saul's advice. Afterward, he refused to take me home. He drove down a lane and parked in a grove of trees across the highway from the house where I was born, empty and up for sale. He kissed me once, twice, then tore away any clothing that wouldn't snap off. He dug deep grooves in my back. He clamped my wrists together and lashed them over my head with his belt. I cried no, then he covered my face with his hands and I couldn't breathe. He made me bleed. I was filled with the dark knowledge that I had been headed for this, in fact that I had been waiting for this attack for most of my life.

As he drove me to the duplex, I told him that I would turn him in to the police. He said he would deny what happened. He said his friends would testify that they'd had me too. He said I'd wanted it all along. I wept. You can't get away with this, I said. Oh no? he said. I have before. Your word against mine, baby.

I would not learn for many years about my Grandmother Evelyn, about the man who attacked her when she was only a little older than I was then, on her way to marry my grandfather in Mexico. She was committed to keeping herself virginal for him—such an important thing for my people. But I was already cast off in some indefinable way—too rebellious, too outspoken, too something to have a place in our religious group. Perhaps I did not know that I could call on the power of Jesus Christ, as my grandmother had done. Perhaps it didn't seem important enough, my virginity not worth much to anyone. Certainly I had no reason to believe that law enforcement officers would help.

In the days afterward, I awakened in my own room, and for the first instant wondered who and where I was. Then I remembered: I was part of my father's family, in my father's house. My father would arrive soon, would sit at my mother's table and eat his breakfast of shredded wheat and bananas, would tell my mother about a baby case or an automobile accident that had required his attendance during the night. If I didn't leave my room, didn't look him in the eye, he would not notice, would not know what had happened, would not cast me out.

The boy was brazen, even after I told him to go away. He prowled the alley behind my parents' house and sometimes I could feel him peering in my window. He waited in the bleachers at the high school and watched me march with the pep club. He parked in front of the restaurant where I worked and followed me home through moonlit streets, his car rumbling as my heels clattered on the pavement. My blood burned in a profusion of fear and desire. I wondered how long before he would pounce on me again. If I began to run, would he give chase? And then . . . and then what? A constant terror heated my insides. I had begun to dream about war, launching grenades, hiding behind sandbags, throwing myself into trenches. Battle sharpened my tongue and blazed in my eyes.

That year, 1966, the war in Vietnam escalated. Alongside announcements of who was going and who had died, a local newspaper carried an unusual obituary: at a zoo in Oregon, a wolf pack singled out the runt of the litter, a female with a deformed paw who could run as fast on three legs as the others did on four. The pack wouldn't let her eat; they crowded her against the electric fence; they slashed her with fangs and claws. From one attack to the next, she grew weaker until despair overcame her. She stopped trying to eat, stopped drinking. She was buried, along with her deformity.

I was no longer a virgin, no longer acceptable in my father's group. I had not been formally cast out, but an aura of shame and rage surrounded me. The boys and men in my father's group retreated, perhaps sensing an alien wisdom in me. My father no longer reported to me how this man or that asked for one of his lovely daughters. They no longer spoke to my father about the possibility of having my hand in marriage. Some members of the group, including members of my own family, stopped speaking to me altogether. I no longer attended our religious meetings or our family home evenings. I came home when the house was dark and silent. I curled on my bed, made myself small, pretended that I was not there at all.

During the years of hiding in the cellar, holding my breath so that the investigators would not find us, I had learned to hold my fear inside. I had learned that the daughter who causes no trouble would be highly valued. My father maintained an even keel; he and I colluded to "make no waves" by being carefully polite or mildly affectionate whenever he saw me.

One day the young man who raped me came to the place where I worked as a waitress after school. He sat at the counter. I didn't let him see my hand shaking as I drew a coke and set it before him. But all I could think about was his hand over my mouth, his weight pressing the breath out of me, and I knew that this much fear must be tamed or put to sleep.

I let him believe he had a chance with me. We had a few exchanges, but I was wiser than before. I kept my distance, practiced parry and thrust. I would coax him out onto some promontory of the heart and make him jump. But it was a dangerous game I played. One night we drove toward Wendover, a gambling town across the Salt Flats on the Utah-Nevada border. He talked about the boy from my school who killed his prom-date. He had hit her on the back of the head with a hammer and buried her in the salt dunes.

"Why would he kill her?" I asked. "It's such a waste."

"She wouldn't shut up," he said.

"What a reason to kill someone!"

"She was a mouthy bitch," he said. "He told me about it when we were roommates at the reform school." He gave me an exaggerated smile, showing teeth and tongue. "We knew each other's secrets. We had a lot in common."

Did I hold my breath, as it seems, for the rest of that night? We drove through the sad little town of Wendover, the Stateline Casino Cowboy waving his metal arm. We parked beneath its sawing groan and I went inside and called my brother Jake, who lived in Elko and worked at the Nevada State Reform School. But even if I confessed my fears, could Jake do anything to stop it? The phone rang and rang. Jake didn't answer.

"I called my brother who lives nearby, right here in Nevada. He offered to take me back to Salt Lake," I said, sliding into the car. "I told him you would, instead."

He looked me over, sucked his teeth. "Guess we better get started."

I did not speak on the long, tense drive back across the Salt Flats. I was almost surprised to arrive home alive.

During this time I had been dating a friend from my high school crowd, the same one who had announced JFK's death and held me as I wept for our president and our country. His name was Jess and he must have heard the rumors about my family, yet he seemed to accept me as I was. In some ways his background was a negative print of mine, coming from serial polygamy, his mother a matriarch now married to her third husband. The first had died of melanoma, and most of the family idealized his memory. The second (Jess's father) turned out to be a philanderer and she drove him out of the house. The third husband, who came to her stunted by poverty, war, and alcoholism, married her for refuge. Jess said that if his mother had been a man, she'd be the bishop of his ward; she already ran the Relief Society, and often told the bishop what to do. When the bishop urged her to go to the temple and have her children sealed to her, she said the only way she'd do that was if she could be sealed in marriage to her first husband who was dead and have her third husband sealed to her as one of her children. The bishop did not approve her plan.

Jess and I shared a taste for beat writers and gunslinger stories, for funny movies and rock-and-roll. Jess had a reputation for intervening when the weak and the meek were bullied. But when I was with him, he was proprietary and challenged my other boyfriends. At school, he followed me with his eyes, somehow knew my every move. But he escorted me to restaurants where we talked about romance and friendship, about individuality and belonging; we talked about the Holocaust and the founding of modern Israel; we discussed the difference between spirituality and religion. Jess gave me books and wrote me poems and read aloud to me. He invited me to settle down, relax a little, let him take care of me. In Jess, all possibilities seemed present. But I refused to be tied down. I even lied to Jess, withholding the truth about my family and telling him I was sick in bed when I was out playing the dating game.

Later that year my father's ulcers began to bleed, hemorrhaging as they had during the days of the raids. Sick and weak, he was confined to my mother's bed, unable to go to work or attend his religious meetings. Aunt Emma took care of things at the office. My mother took care of him at home. His patients would call for help, but he was too weak to come to the phone. People in the group called for advice, but he could not share his wisdom. Members of the priesthood council came to pray over him, but the bleeding did not abate and they left with tears in their eyes, most of them frightened or sad. In the faces of two or three members of his council, I saw an avarice that turned my stomach. It was terrible to see him wasting away, his strength sapped a little more each day as his spirit struggled to free itself of a body in rebellion. My mother and Aunt Emma stood in the kitchen and debated what to do. He had consistently refused to receive treatment except from his wives in his home. Finally the mothers decided he had to be hospitalized and when my brother Danny came home from school that day, the mothers whispered instructions. Danny picked him up, my father light as a child, pounding feebly on Danny's broad shoulder and crying, "No! Put me down!" as Danny settled him in the back seat of his car. I watched as I often watched, helpless and grateful. I prayed for another chance to let my father know I loved him. After the surgery, I drove my mother to see him at the hospital. His spirit had returned to his body. One by one we bent and kissed him. My eyes met his, and instantly filled with tears. I told him that I loved him, and reminded him that we needed him to stay with us for awhile longer, and he nodded, yes, and then he said, but not that much longer. I hurried from the room, unable to confront what he suggested.

During my senior year of high school I was attending a football game when I ran into Matt James, from the neighborhood of the red-brick house. I was dressed in my Pep Club uniform and Matt wore an alumni letter-jacket. I gave him a brilliant smile; Matt couldn't have guessed his part in my introduction to yearning and loneliness, to jealousy and loss. He couldn't have guessed that I had been taken by a cruel boy who wouldn't take no for an answer—a version of love whose path is revenge. He couldn't have guessed that I was so lost to myself that I could not accept real love when it was offered.

"Hey." Matt had finally figured out who I was. "You don't know how many times I've thought of you." His voice was much deeper.

"Well, I could say the same thing."

"You want to do something after the game?"

"Uh . . . I have plans." I had a date with Jess and I had been thinking that tonight I might tell him the truth. Confess that I was used goods, and a plygie, to boot. What did I have to lose? I was tired of pretending to be something I wasn't, of trying to get cast in someone else's movie as the bitchin' chick.

Matt showed me the scar from the time he dove off a forty-foot cliff at that long-ago Boy Scout camp—a concussion and a broken collarbone had kept him in the hospital for three days, he said. Thirteen stitches. My first thought was straight out of my father's world, that God gave him what he deserved.

"I waited for you to call me," I said, surprised that my voice trembled. "You never did."

"I tried to call you once I could think straight. But you had moved. And no one knew your new phone number or address."

"Memory? That girl across the street from where I lived? She said she gave it to you."

He shrugged. "She didn't. But look . . . you're great. I knew you'd turn out to be this fine."

"A bitchin' chick?"

He blushed. "Yeah. Well . . . since we found each other again . . . don't you . . . do you think you'd want to go out sometime?"

I took a deep breath. "No," I said. I walked away without explanation.

I was years away from real forgiveness. It took another window, and the boy named Jess to teach me about grace and the clemency of life. Jess paid a big price to prove that I was his one and only love—put up with other boyfriends and flirting and lies. And still I tested him. On graduation night I said "No" when Jess proposed marriage. "Wait until we're through with college," I said. "Ask me in three or four years." He shook his head, pressed his lips together. But he kept asking me out, bought me pearls for my birthday and told me I was his true love.

A month after graduating from high school, I came home from a date with the shadow-man on whom I was still plotting to avenge my lost honor to find Jess waiting for me. I tried to make a joke, and when Jess called for a fight, I tried to shame him, told him he was acting like an animal. I stood between them, offered myself to whoever would refuse to fight. As Jess walked away, the other one started his car, muffler growling, tires squealing as he roared off. I stood alone, shivering, even though it was summer with starlight everywhere.

The next day I learned that Jess had joined the Marine Corps. I met him in a restaurant, a place where the dark and cool atmosphere soothed my swollen eyes. "I'm so sorry. I'd do anything to take it back," I said. "Can't you get out of this Marine Corps thing?"

He shook his head. "Nope. I'm in the good ole USMC now—one of 'Uncle Sam's Misguided Children.' "

"I'm afraid you'll end up in Vietnam."

"You've got that right. I'm told there's only two kinds of Marines: those that have been and those that are going."

"Jess, I don't want you to go to war. I never wanted that."

"There's no taking it back, babe. I'll be in boot camp one month from today."

The night he flew to San Diego to begin basic training, I dreamed that he stepped on a land mine and was blown into fragments that rained red on my face and hands. I woke my mother with my screams.

"What is it, darling?" She patted my cheeks until I opened my eyes. I sobbed out that I'd do anything, anything he asked. Marry him right this minute if it would bring him back alive.

"What are you talking about?" my mother asked. She stroked my forehead as if I were delirious with fever.

"I told Jess 'No' when he asked me to marry him. That's one reason he joined the Marines. I don't know why I said 'No.' I meant 'Yes, but not right now.' But I told him 'No.' And if he dies over there, it's my fault—it's all my fault." I burst into fresh tears.

My mother gave me one of my father's big white handkerchiefs. I wondered why she had my father's handkerchief but I blew my nose and wiped my wet face anyway.

"I told your father 'No.' " Her voice was soft.

"You told Daddy 'No'? When?" I was skeptical, even in my distress.

"After he asked me to marry him."

"You didn't . . . !"

"Yes she did." My father was at my bedroom door in his long white undergarments, my mother's blue-striped bathrobe drawn tight around him. I'd forgotten it was her night with him.

"Really? She told you 'No'?"

"That's right. And you were born anyway. If you survived 'no' once, I suppose you can survive it again. And so can your young man." My father had the clipped, dry tone he'd used when he set my broken arm eight years before.

"You really did." I looked at my mother and then at my father and back at her. "You refused him."

My father slipped an arm around her shoulders. "The only one of my girls to tell me 'No.' " He kissed her cheek. "Spunky wife."

A mix of anger and relief surged through me. And then a deep peacefulness. "I guess I'll write to him. Tell him 'Yes' before it's too late." I looked at my father and choked on the next words. "If it's all right with you."

"Well . . . it would be appropriate if your young man asked me for your hand."

"Daddy! He's in boot camp!"

He closed his eyes to gather patience. "I know, I know."

"Do we have your blessing?"

He smiled. "How can I say no?"

❧

Unlike my father, Jess's mother did say no. Adamantly. She said we could marry when he returned from Vietnam. Period. Since Jess was only eighteen, he could not marry without parental consent. I was eighteen, too, but I was female in the state of Utah where girls of four- teen could marry without parental approval. It seemed so ironic that my father had agreed to something I wanted although I didn't need his permission, yet Jess, who never agreed with his mother, could not marry me without her consent. The ultimate irony was that Jess was old enough to go to war, old enough to kill, but he was not old enough to vote or get married without his mother's permission. On his first furlough, Jess made the trip home to plead with his mother. She refused again, but Jess formalized the proposal with a diamond engagement ring. We were seized with a wild urgency, a sense that if we didn't marry before he shipped out, Jess would never return from Vietnam.

Finally my father lent me the money to fly to Camp Pendleton, California, so that Jess and I could cross into Mexico where we could be married without his mother's consent. The day we drove to the dirty border town of Tijuana, I was dressed in slacks and a turtleneck, Jess in his standard issue uniform of green. I thought of Grandmother Evelyn who had been about the same age when she crossed the border into Mexico, the only way she could legally marry my grandfather. My wedding, like hers and my mother's, would be a sad affair, without my parents or other loved ones attending. I soon learned that Mexico marriages were no more binding in the eyes of the United States Marine Corps than my parents' spiritual ceremony. Here I was, repeating history despite my strong desire to take my life in another direction.

War without Honor

 BY THE TIME JESS SHIPPED OUT TO Vietnam, I was pregnant. We had debated taking refuge in Canada, and I was all for it, but Jess said that would make him a deserter. I reminded him of my family history and the polygamous relatives who had gone north and south of the border after the Manifesto in order to live as they believed. Though I begged Jess to come away and avoid the war altogether, after a period of painful introspection, he said, "I made a commitment. I have to keep my word or I won't be able to live with myself in Canada or anywhere else."

As I watched Jess's plane disappear I thought of my mother so alone while my father was in prison, not knowing whether he would be away the six-month minimum or the five-year maximum of his sentence. The government had a knack for providing these long, lonely absences.

The government delayed my marriage allotment and I was too plagued by morning sickness to work, so I returned to my mother's house and my old room. I continued my studies at the University of Utah, knowing that if I succumbed to the daily bouts of nausea, I would lose my scholarship. Over the months my belly grew until I could barely slide in and out of the desk chairs. But at last classes were over and I settled into the summer. My military allotment still had not come through, and I had no money to buy baby clothes or furniture. Knowing my parents had no extra funds—they never did—I didn't ask, instead calling on my own meager skills as a seamstress. I recognized the patterns of poverty and scarcity from my childhood and realized again that what I had tried so hard to avoid had materialized anyway.

After the morning sickness diminished, I signed up for part-time work as a waitress at a nearby café, but I felt embarrassed, big as a house with all those truck drivers and construction workers looking at me, thinking how I got that way. Finally I called the American Red Cross and asked if they could facilitate my marriage allotment. A woman with white marcelled hair like my Grandmother Evelyn's predicted that I'd start receiving checks in two months. In the meantime, did I have a layette for the baby? She presented me with a box of white flannel clothing trimmed in pink: nightgowns, diapers, receiving blankets and a tiny hat, the simple things the mothers had made for their babies—no frills, only usefulness and purity.

I had made a clear decision not to have my father deliver the baby, although he had done so for most of my sisters and all his wives. "I've delivered about five thousand babies so far," my father bragged one night over supper. "I hope to deliver at least a thousand more before I'm done." Was he hinting that I should ask him to deliver my baby? I didn't know and didn't want to think about it. He had delivered me into the world, his the first touch on my newborn skin. Perhaps I loved him too much to share more of such intimacy.

My government-appointed obstetrician was himself a Marine, a man who had served his tour of duty in Vietnam. He agreed that I could deliver naturally and that I would be allowed to breast-feed, according to the customs of my family. He was kind and sympathetic, but when the labor pains began, he was attending a birth at another hospital. By the time he arrived, I had been drugged with Demerol and examined by eleven different interns. At midnight, when our daughter, Erica, was born, he crowed, "She's too pretty to be a Marine!" The Red Cross sent a telegram to Jess announcing the birth of his daughter. I fell asleep toward dawn with an enormous sense of accomplishment, truly happy. Now Jess would have a reason to come home; he would live and our little family would thrive.

I wrote to Jess every day, but each letter took two weeks to be delivered and another two weeks for his response to reach me. At times we seemed to be connected through dreams. For instance, when Erica was about three months old, I dreamed that Jess called me and I panicked, for I'd heard from wives and mothers of Marines that the only time they got a phone call was when their men were wounded. In the dream Jess reassured me that he was not wounded, that he'd called to arrange a meeting in Hawaii. Just as the dream ended, the telephone rang. I staggered to the wall phone in the kitchen and glanced at the clock: 2:30 A.M. It must be a baby case for my father, I thought, and then I realized he was visiting Aunt Melissa and his followers in Montana. The phone rang again and I grabbed it. The crackle of long, long distance. The voice, barely audible.

"Hi Baby," I thought I heard him say.

"Jess! Are you all right?"

"I'm fine." Did he say that, or did I just want to believe that he said that?

"What?"

Crackle, hiss, crackle.

"What?"

A stranger's voice interrupted the crackling to tell me that he was a ham radio operator in Hawaii relaying the telephone call.

". . . meet me, ok? I have R and R." Jess's voice came through again.

"What's R and R? Meet you where?"

Even through the static, I could hear his frustration. "Rest and Recuperation. I need to see you. In Hawaii."

The line was full of static and the ham radio operator broke in "We have to say good-bye, now, Ma'am. Do you want to say anything else?"

"Be careful! Be safe!" I yelled.

Crackle. Crackle.

"What?"

"I said—" crackle, hiss, pop!

"What? I can't hear you. Jess?"

"He says he loves you, lady. Good-bye."

The line went dead. As I stood looking at the phone, elation spread through me. But then I realized that I had no idea *when* I was to meet him. I knew that if he had gone to the trouble of calling me, it must be urgent. In the dream I had met him just after the presidential election. Tomorrow was Halloween. That meant I would have to be in Hawaii in a week. I had no money. I had no idea whether I should take the baby.

The American Red Cross intervened once again. This time they sent a telegram to Jess's commanding officer who confirmed that Jess's R and R would begin in Hawaii on November 8, the day after the presidential election. They also suggested that I leave the baby with a relative since young infants didn't tolerate long flights well, and could contract illnesses from fathers stationed on foreign soil.

Once again my father helped, cosigning a bank loan to fund my airline ticket and a room at the Ilikai Hotel in Honolulu for seven days and nights. I was secretly surprised that my father trusted me to repay the loan, and that he cared enough for my happiness to take the risk in my behalf.

How to explain what it was like waiting for Jess, so frightened that he would not get off the plane in Honolulu? And when he did, those blue eyes singling him out among the uniforms, what had changed about him—more handsome than ever, a stronger presence, but something missing, too. After clearing customs, the soldiers would be transported on a bus to Hickam Air Force Base for R and R orientation. I was prepared to take a taxi and wait for him at our hotel, but

Jess insisted that I ride on the bus with him, that we not miss a minute together. No other wives or sweethearts were on the bus. The officer in charge frowned, then glanced at Jess and said nothing as I preceded him onto the bus. There was no seat for me, but no one seemed to question my presence. I perched on his lap, embarrassed and out of place, feeling safe only because of Jess, trying to be proper in a bus full of love-starved young men. Jess and I were the only people who spoke during the trip along the rim of Oahu toward Pearl Harbor, eager whispers at the back of the bus.

During that week we did not get out of the hotel much, our days lovely and filled with pain. As each hour passed, we tried to extend our time together by being very quiet, very deliberate. Jess told me that this was how he moved through the jungle, like a shadow of himself. He confessed that he had killed Viet Cong and NVA and that they wore the faces of boys I'd been with. But he also said that it took him only a little while to discover that revenge doesn't alleviate pain. And only a little longer to discover that the United States had no real right to be in Vietnam. The Vietnamese people didn't want our capitalistic way of life. They had always lived communally, in villages that functioned something like the United Order, where everyone brought their crops to the community storehouse, and then all was divided according to need.

"Their systems are communes, but they are no more 'communist' than your family is. The people in the villages are free to do what they want—at least they were until we came along. Powerful nations like the United States, France, Russia, and China confuse everything with their interference." He shook his head. "There's got to be a better way."

Jess had made a decision early in his tour of duty. More often than not, he was a squad leader, charged to carry out orders and make decisions that would result in lives saved or lost. Once Jess was convinced that he was fighting a war without honor, he decided he would keep as many people alive as possible—on both sides. In any event, he was committed to bringing his own men back alive. He got very good at leading them home from each mission and got the nickname "Moses." But his priorities made him a loose cannon in the military hierarchy.

"The 'brass'—the officers—they don't know what to do with me," he said. "They'll assign me to missions. I go and we bring everybody back. Most of the time. When it doesn't work out, I have to live with it."

The silence stretched between us. "Sometimes I refuse to accept missions," he said. "It's called insubordination."

I caught my breath. "Jess . . ."

"I have to be true to myself. I can't take men out on a mission that has no purpose and no chance in hell of succeeding. Not if I value their lives."

His commanders either loved or hated him, although all of them seemed to rely on him. They kept sending him back to "the bush" where he had been busted and promoted four times. In the jungle, something was always happening—ambushes, booby traps, unexpected encounters with Vietnamese of every stripe.

The more I heard, the more frightened I was for him. When I dropped him at the international terminal to board a military flight to Vietnam, the taxi driver tried to comfort me, but I was beyond consolation. At my own terminal, I checked with the gate attendant and found that my flight would not leave for two hours. I went to the restroom and cried, then soothed my burning eyes with wet paper towels. In one of the stalls I prayed for Jess's safety and when I came out, I was still fighting tears. As I stood at the mirror combing my hair and repairing my makeup, a young woman came in, also crying. I went to her and put a hand on her shoulder. "I know—it's so hard to see them go."

"He never arrived. He was supposed to be here a week ago, and they don't know where he is. Now my money's gone and I have to fly home. We have a baby he's never seen, maybe he'll never see."

My self-pity disappeared. I'd had seven glorious days with Jess. No matter what happened, I'd always have that.

From mid-February through March of 1969, I did not receive letters from Jess, and I worried that he was dead or wounded or taken prisoner. At last I received letters from a hospital ship in the South China Sea, where Jess was recovering from shrapnel wounds. There he'd met a North Vietnamese officer who had lost most of his right leg. Jess shared his pain medication with the officer, and the two men talked about the war. The NVA officer had been educated in Paris and spoke French and English. He said to Jess, "You will not win this war. It is our country, and we have no choice but to win our fight for unity. The North and the South belong together, just as your North and South belong together. If your President Lincoln were alive, he would tell you that you are wrong to make war in a country that is not yours. You should go home."

After he returned to the DMZ (Demilitarized Zone), Jess's letters reeked of cynicism about the war, about the United States government, about the Marine Corps. He seemed to have more respect for the people he was fighting than he did for Americans. Once he wrote that a buddy from Salt Lake City had been killed; Jess himself had loaded the body onto the chopper. He asked that I call the man's mother to express our condolences. When I phoned, I discovered that the young man's mother didn't know her son was dead. When I wrote my outrage that the government would withhold vital information, Jess responded with the equivalent of a verbal groan. "I know about the games they play, changing the body count to manipulate public attitude toward the war. I'm just sorry I asked you to call. Sorry you had to break the news to his mother."

Jess was slated to come home in June of 1969, on my birthday. In April, he wrote that the Marine Corps had offered him ten thousand dollars to reenlist. "No!" I wrote back. "Come home!" But two weeks later, I received a letter from him, now three weeks old, saying that he had been detained. "The bastards set me up!" he wrote. He went on to explain that he'd been returned to a rear area, as was the custom with "short-timers"—people who had less than a month left of their tour of duty. He had gone to the showers, took off his combat-filthy fatigues and gave them to the laundry in exchange for a fresh set. He had showered, put on the clean uniform and started back to his quarters when a Military Police jeep sped by. A group of six Marines, all in the same squad, strolled along, sharing a joint, and when the MP jeep passed, they threw six "party packs" which flew out like a deck of cards along the side of the road. Jess explained that a "party pack" contains ten marijuana cigarettes, rolled and packaged by Vietnamese dealers. The MPs rounded up the party packs and the group of six Marines, and for good measure they took Jess.

Inside headquarters, the MPs conducted a shake-down and found nothing on Jess. No money or identification, other than his dogtags. As a matter of routine, the MPs called headquarters, after which they searched Jess again and mysteriously found a "roach"—a half-smoked marijuana cigarette in the pocket of his clean fatigues. They released the group of six Marines and held Jess.

"It wasn't that I couldn't have had it on me," he said. "You know that." In Hawaii, he had confessed that he "smoked dope" to get through the really hard times. It gave him perspective, calmed him down, kept him from going crazy. "But I didn't have it on me then. And now I'm charged with possession. As if everybody—including the MPs—didn't use weed. The bastards set me up, probably because I wouldn't re-up. They're hanging onto me, and they're making it impossible for me to stay in the rear. So they're getting what they want. I'm headed back to the bush."

His letter, written nearly a month before, sent me into a panic. He'd been in the jungle, probably near the DMZ, for at least two weeks. Was he even alive?

The next letter came to me with slashes of black marker through some of the sentences and even an entire paragraph. What "Black Ops" was he part of now, what undercover campaign had he put his life on the line for today? I began a campaign of my own, to bring Jess home. First I went to the Marine Corps Recruiting Depot in downtown Salt Lake City, where a gunnery sergeant listened to my story, nodded sympathetically, and promised he would help. Each day when I phoned, "the Gunny," as he asked me to call him, promised something that didn't materialize. After three weeks had passed with no developments, he invited me to come down to the recruiting depot and "talk strategy." When I arrived, he suggested we get a bite to eat, and took me to a bar where other recruiters hung around, sucking the heads off their beer and watching us. "So what shall we do?" I asked.

"Give this old gunny just one dance," he said, gesturing toward the small wooden floor.

I hesitated, not wanting to lose his support. "You know I'm married."

"Just one dance. Then we talk."

I stopped in the middle of the dance floor. "I'm not here for this. Let's sit down and come up with a strategy to get my husband home."

He followed me back to the table.

"So what do we do?"

"Well . . . there's a number of things," he drawled. "Sure you wouldn't like a beer? Or one of those mai-tai's?"

I shook my head. "I don't drink. Besides, I'm not old enough."

He laughed. "You're such a fine looking woman . . . I keep forgetting you're still a teenager."

This struck me. I was a teenager for four more days. My husband was barely twenty and he could die any minute. "What *can* you do? Really?"

"Well, there's his CO. You could call him."

"Ok. Let's go back and you give me his number."

"I'm not allowed to do that."

"Well what are you allowed to do?"

"Well, miss . . ."

"Mrs. Mrs. Solomon."

"Mrs. . . . Solomon. About all I can do is tell you that he's broke the law, doing drugs and all, and now they get to do what they want with him. That's the sad news."

"Why didn't you tell me this over the phone? Why didn't you say so in the first place? You've just wasted my time. And his. My husband could die while you're playing these . . . games!"

He raised his shoulders slightly.

I grabbed my purse. "Thanks for nothing."

I called Wives and Mothers of Marines, a local organization of women who had banded together in support of their men, but none of them had encountered a situation like mine. I called *Public Pulse*, a radio program designed to help citizens get assistance with their problems, and *Troubleshooters*, the television equivalent of *Public Pulse*. After some research, they told me to contact my senator and congressman. I did so, and wrote Jess to do the same. The days crawled by. Jess's letters arrived smudged with what looked like red mud. Each one held more despair.

"They've rotated my attorney," he wrote. "Now he's in the states and I don't have a legal representative. When I ask about it, they tell me that's tough luck."

The next week he wrote, "They've appointed a new prosecutor. He doesn't know anything about how they fixed it so they could keep me. The last prosecutor kept saying that once it went to trial, everything irregular would show up and they'd drop charges. Headquarters says I have a defending attorney, but I've never talked to him. I'm still in the bush, near the DMZ. I don't know what will happen."

In another letter, he wrote, "I'm the only one in this mess who cares what happens. I don't know if I'll ever get home. I don't know if I deserve to come home." I wrote back that he must not give up. He had to come home. He had a child to raise, a wife who loved him. I urged him to write to Utah Senator Frank Moss, as I was doing. Jess wrote daily and received regular responses until he and the senator were on a first-name basis. The senator suggested that I write to the Oval Office, directly to President Nixon. Nixon wrote back that there was nothing he could do. The day I opened that letter was also the day that our daughter turned a year old. I wondered if she would ever get to meet her father.

Then Jess wrote that the six Marines, his witnesses, had disappeared; they'd been rotated or they had been killed in combat. The arresting MPs had also been rotated. Now he was the only person involved in the "trial" who had actually been present when the arrests were made. Still the Marine Corps would not release him. Never had I felt so helpless. Everything human and decent seemed powerless against the forces that held Jess in Vietnam.

Early in September, I dreamed that Jess died. I awakened with my heart pounding in my ears, feeling once again that it was my fault that he had gone to Vietnam, and my fault that he had died. Our daughter slept softly, her breath deep and trusting. What had happened to my ability to trust life so completely? The answer came immediately. I had violated trust, therefore I did not trust.

What was there to trust? Earlier that year, President Nixon, defending himself before world censure, had sworn that there were no U.S. troops in Laos. A week later I had received a letter from Jess saying that he had just returned from Laos, on a mission called "Operation Phoenix." Ultimately no one seemed in charge when it came to Vietnam—not even the Commander-in-Chief, President Nixon, who confessed that he had no power to bring my husband home.

So who, then, could I trust? Not myself, certainly. I was the one who had lied to Jess and betrayed him, who broke his heart and set him up to be at war in the first place. Who, then? It struck me that God, the giver of life, was the only being to trust now. Only God could look at the big picture, see what was salvageable, and spare a life.

I spent the night on my knees, crying, praying, sleeping very little. At daybreak my father came to my room and opened the door. He had never done that before, opened my bedroom door without knocking. He raised me to my feet. "Tell me daughter, what's wrong?"

I blurted out the whole story, wondering why he had not asked before, why I had not sought his help. I told him the truth about the marijuana, explaining that Jess did smoke pot but he hadn't this time, they had framed him, and President Nixon couldn't do anything, no one could do anything and Jess was going to die over there.

He hugged me until I stopped shaking. Then he held my face in his hands and with his thumbs wiped away my tears. "Don't worry, darling. With the help of the Lord, we'll bring your young man home."

The next morning I went to see a colleague of my father, who examined me and said that I was on the verge of a nervous breakdown. "This is Satan's war. We're losing the cream of our youth over there, and it's all for nothing. We have a responsibility to those young men." He telephoned the American Red Cross and told them that I had to see my husband immediately or I would suffer a complete emotional collapse.

A third time, the American Red Cross came through for me. They dispatched a telegram to Jess's Commanding Officer the next day. That same morning, Jess had been awakened by gunfire and grenades exploding. The concertina wire protecting their perimeter had been cut. Sappers had crawled inside the lines, killed the sentries and made off with their ammunition stores. Now they were using it against the Marines, most of them green FNGs, Jess called them, Fuckin' New Guys. Jess held one young man as his life bled out, promising to write his mother and girlfriend, promising that he wouldn't let the VC or NVA carve up his remains. Jess worked with the radio man, calling for air strikes on the sappers and organizing triage. He was calling in helicopters to evacuate the wounded to a hospital in DaNang when the radio man received a command to med-evac Sierra 7891.

"But that's me!" Jess said. "I'm not hurt."

"They say to get on the next chopper," the radio man said.

"But who's taking over? I've got a full-blown firefight and nothing but FNGs here."

The radio man handed him the headset. "You talk to them."

"Get on the next chopper," headquarters repeated. The chopper settled down. Jess pushed the body bag on board, grabbed an enemy SK instead of his own shotgun, and climbed inside the bird. It lifted him up above the canopy; he looked down at the tracers and smoke signals of the firefight and thought of all those FNGs with only the radioman to tell them what to do. The chopper bore him to DaNang and within hours he was on a plane bound for Okinawa. When he called me from Okinawa, we could speak only long enough for reassurance that no one in our family had died. Then he caught another plane. He got off the airplane at San Francisco International Airport in blood-stained fatigues, carrying an SK rifle. The protestors at the airport shouted: Motherfucker. Babykiller. Warmonger. Jess walked past them, pretending that this was better than no homecoming at all. In Hawaii he had told me that there are things worse than fear, worse than death. What? I had asked. Dishonor, he replied.

I waited at Salt Lake City International Airport, holding Erica in my arms, all my nerves coiled tight as the plane emptied. Jess did not get off. I began to tremble. Was this yet another cruel cosmic joke? At last the flight attendant came down the ramp, dragging her overnight case. "He's coming. Just be patient." She gave me a sad smile.

Later I would learn that after Jess changed his clothes in the airplane lavatory, he wouldn't open the lavatory door. He and the flight attendant talked through the door about his feeling that he had no right to be alive, not when all his men had died, much less home and alive, and that he didn't know how to be a husband or a father, he'd never had a father, not really, so how could he be someone else's father, and at last she convinced him that everything would be all right. As he stood at the top of the jetway, he put on a brave front then sauntered toward me. He looked at his daughter and smiled, but his eyes were haunted with memories that would never entirely leave him. "Well, hello," he said. "There's a whole bunch of little Vietnamese kids over there who look just like you!" His idea of a joke.

Something had broken, perhaps it was ice; more likely it was the first fissure of heartbreak. What was born at that moment was the beginning of doubt and despair beyond anything I had ever known, and a counterculture life that made my father's seem mild by comparison.

The charge for holding marijuana vanished, and before the month was through, Jess received an honorable discharge from the Marine Corps. When one of his medals came through, he refused to attend the ceremony and so they brought it to him, presenting the Navy Achievement Medal in our tiny apartment. He worked in a bank until I graduated from the university and accepted my first teaching position. The day I began working full-time, he quit; I found this out from his secretary when I called at lunchtime.

Jess grew out his hair. He enrolled in college under the GI Bill, but often skipped his classes and had to pay for those he failed. Sometimes, instead of going to his part-time job, he hung out in front of the Marine Corps Recruiting Depot, where he'd waylay young men who thought of enlisting, and tell them all the reasons they shouldn't sign up. He'd read the newspapers, listen to the news on television. "There has to be a better way to run a world," he'd say. When I worried about paying the bills on time, when I recited my father's admonitions to stay out of debt, he'd remind me to "Seize the day!" He'd seen young men stash their money, their drugs, and their feelings and then die in a heartbeat, never having spent them. He didn't want to miss his second chance at life. He'd take car-struck dogs and cats to a veterinarian, and pay the bill before bringing the animal home. He'd sit on our porch, see a young woman walking home alone and he'd leave me sitting in the dark, wondering at his explanation, "She needs to be protected." He'd pick up hitchhikers high on heroin and cocaine, invite them to spend the night, and as they passed the mirror around the dining room table, I'd feel like a stranger in my own life. I need protecting, too, a tiny voice pleaded within.

The war had left Jess prone to midnight prowls. I would awaken as the front door opened, allowing a dark wind to enter, and I smelled

death in the house. I used the rebukes I learned as a child: "Get thee
hence, Satan," I said in my mind. I was not rebuking my husband, of
course. I wanted to conquer the darkness, wanted to wash the blood
away. Though I had never told her ghost stories, our daughter, Erica,
spoke of the spirits in our house as if they had names and a place in the
family. She seemed preternaturally spiritual. Since we had moved
from my mother's house, she often asked for her grandfather, and
when she played, she liked to don a large white shirt and spectacles to
play doctor.

We led lonely lives, pacing the periphery of separate spheres. I
stopped trying to connect with my family; told my father "Happy
Birthday" over the telephone. Jess and I couldn't run with the crowd
from high school; we didn't fit. Unspoken truths hung like wet sheets
between us, and blocked us from the world outside.

In 1973, experts predicted we would be out of Southeast Asia before
the year was through. But I knew that the war raged on in my young
husband, and in his foxhole-buddy, Stan, who had come to stay with
us. They looked remarkably alike, these two, as though some force of
nature had shaped all Marines at birth, made them broad-shouldered
and Roman-nosed, waiting for the years to overtake their ancient
hearts and haunted eyes.

I couldn't get over the feeling that we had left part of ourselves in
Vietnam, along with the POWs and MIAs. I sensed a change in our
national character, from hero to bully, a failure to combine the imper-
atives of democracy: responsibility with freedom. I longed to reclaim
our innocence, or to justify things by acknowledging accountability—
mine, Jess's, everybody's.

"We need to go back before it's all over," I said. "Or we'll pay into
the next century."

The men laughed. "Go back?" my husband said. "What for?
There's nothing left."

"Nothing but flies and bald mountains," Stan said.

"We bombed them into the dark ages," Jess said.

"That's about where they were when we started," Stan said. They shook their heads with that look of regret that seemed to be one of their features, like the drooping moustache or the long hair.

"Whatever happened to the Eagle, Globe, and Anchor?" Stan blew smoke at my rosebush.

It was a while before Jess responded. "Even an eagle can't carry the weight of a lie."

"What lie?" I asked.

Stan grimaced. "A lot of people died so your neighbor could have two cars and an RV."

"It was a war. People die in wars." I said.

Stan lit one cigarette with the butt of another, pulling the smoke deep in his lungs and holding it there. His eyes burned as he looked at me, sending the message of the smoke, closing out all other possibilities. "Tell me about it since you know so much. Tell me about the war."

Jess narrowed his eyes. "Cool it."

Stan sucked his teeth. "She doesn't know the first thing."

As if to educate me, Jess explained, "They sprayed this stuff called Agent Orange all over the jungles and the rice fields. It'll be twenty-five years before they can grow anything in some places."

Stan gave me a hollow-eyed grin. "See—the war isn't over."

Panic hit me, then guilt, two hard punches in the stomach. "How will the people survive?"

The men shook their heads in unison. "The worst of it is, they didn't want us there. We had nothing to stand on."

Stan nodded. "No place to stand."

"Now nobody has a place to stand." My husband chuckled, but he wasn't laughing.

I busied myself sweeping the porch so they wouldn't see the blood rising in my face. In our strict Mormon neighborhood, once again my family was the anomaly: Mormons who drank beer, smoked cigarettes and "weed," and who swore in earshot of the bishop. I took my daughter to the official church but I did not attend myself. The persecutions of my childhood ached like a once-broken bone as I realized that if they knew the truth about me, I would be considered an apostate even though I had left the fundamentalist group. I couldn't have felt more marked if I'd been wearing a scarlet letter.

Still, the habits of my childhood urged me to gather with others in the name of God. Maybe I could forgive the persecutions, erase the scars of paranoia, balm the searing guilt of the war. I asked my husband, "If I went to church, would you come with me?" I must have known what he would say even before he spoke. "Do you know what I was ordered to do in the name of loyalty and obedience?"

I thought of the rumors that our soldiers had killed women and children in Vietnam. "What were you ordered to do?" I asked softly.

He fumbled in his pants pocket for a wooden match. "I'd die before I'd promise obedience to another institution. Their walls are reinforced with bodies."

Stan nodded agreement. The two of them sat on the front porch smoking "squares"—as they called cigarettes made with tobacco instead of marijuana—while I walked my daughter down the street to the ward-house and waved good-bye at the double doors.

The two men were still lazing on the front porch when I returned. Stan, who had grown up in the hills of San Bernardino, was amazed at our craggy mountains and wanted to spend the Fourth of July "up there."

"Independence Day," he said. "I'm ready to declare my independence." Jess and I looked at each other. Like many Vietnam veterans, Stan was utterly alone. We worried that he might climb a cliff and jump, just to end the angst. The next day we packed hot dogs and potato salad and watermelon; we dropped Erica off so she could go to see fireworks with her grandmother; then we traveled up the canyon and stopped at a campsite near the Eagle's Perch. I told Stan that my family had often camped in the mountains when I was a child. Stan said he lived by the beach as a child. "We had a picket fence," he said.

"The waves took it. The waves took everything." Then he reached into his backpack and passed around little brown buttons shaved from a cactus in the Mojave Desert.

Jess lit a fire, but as the peyote moved through my blood, my senses heightened and provoked a need to move. On the trail, I was enthralled by one thing, then another. Who knows how long I sniffed the primrose before I recognized the sweet and piercing fragrance of love? A doe stepped onto the trail, bent her head and nibbled. I took a sharp breath and she bounded away.

I climbed the face of the rock and looked down at the fire. I closed my eyes and saw huts burning, children with missing limbs, animals exploding above the trees. I imagined that my own house was on fire. The wind came up and the higher I climbed, the harder it blew. A black cloud blotted the last red lip of sun. Darkness blended rock and bush and shale until I stopped and hunkered on a ledge, trembling. In the valley below, fireworks and lightning shot across the sky. Heat emanated from the clouds, and then I saw an eagle, wings locked, flying into the storm. The eagle disappeared, then reappeared above the black cloud. A few heavy drops splashed on my bare arms. Far below my husband motioned me to come sit beside him. Stan was out in the night trying to find something he'd lost. I climbed down, feeling sad for all of us, scarred by the war and our own foolishness.

"Let's have a baby," Jess said. I looked up, thinking he was mocking me, but he meant it. He was ready to claim his life again. The only way out of the pain was to push through it. I nodded slowly. We would have another child, an affirmation of the life we shared despite the legacy of war.

Blood Atonement

 I HAD BEEN MARRIED FOUR YEARS when the LeBarons entered our lives again. At my mother's house, my father announced that he'd received a warning from a patient who was a member of the Church of the First Born: Ervil LeBaron planned to kill his brother Joel.

"Joel excommunicated Ervil from the Church of the First Born for his disobedient and violent attitude," my father explained. "Then Ervil started his own church, the Church of the Lamb of God, where they justify all manner of sin, including the shedding of innocent blood." My father added that Ervil had threatened the president of the Church of Jesus Christ of Latter-day Saints, and other religious and government leaders as well.

When asked if Ervil planned to kill my father, too, he sighed. "Who knows? He's under the influence of Satan."

Two weeks later, on August 20, 1972, Joel was lured to the home of one of Ervil's Mexican followers, where two men beat him, then shot him through the head. I found out about it on a Saturday afternoon. My father had just completed his day at the office, and I was visiting my mother again. "Ervil didn't do the wicked deed himself; I guess he didn't want to get his hands bloody. He had his henchmen do it for him." My father paused. "I told the police what I know and they've been asking us questions, watching us like hawks ever since. Even the FBI are involved because of the threats on President Lee's life."

My father explained that the justice system in Mexico was not like ours in the United States, although both had their share of corruption. In Mexico, an investigation didn't go forward and criminals weren't arrested unless money changed hands.

"But how could Ervil kill his own brother?" I asked.

"How could Cain kill Abel? It's a matter of trading a birthright for a mess of pottage. Ervil wanted Joel dead so that he could take over his following," my father said. He stared at the kitchen wall as though he were reading something there. "It's tragic how these brethren let Lucifer lead them astray. All because they want glory for themselves."

I suspected that some people, such as my father's first wife and other members of the official church, said the same thing about my father with his strange band of followers. As if he could hear my thoughts, my father spoke. "The Lord's church was restored by Joseph Smith in 1830 and no other can take its place. Some of the brethren in our group have suggested that we form another church, but I've made it very clear that it would be wrong."

In September, an anonymous friend of Joel's put up a reward of $25,000 for the apprehension of Ervil LeBaron, but Ervil kept moving and no one tracked him down. In December, Ervil walked into an Ensenada police station and dashed everyone's hopes of collecting the reward money by turning himself in and demanding the reward money for himself, and insisting that charges against him be dropped. The police arrested him on the spot. Joel's followers found a Mexico prosecutor willing to take the case, but when the First Borners arrived in Ensenada for the hearing, the prosecutor was off celebrating an election victory. The Church of the First Born had to pay fines in order to reinstate the charges against Ervil.

During the summer of 1973, while Ervil was awaiting trial, my father told us, "Ervil's right-hand man came to me and demanded money to bribe the Mexican judges so that Ervil could get out of prison. I told him, 'Absolutely not!' He argued that I owed Ervil a favor because the LeBarons had offered me a place in Mexico when the authorities wouldn't let me live with my wives and children. This man tried to convince me that Ervil was in the same boat I was in back in 1946, when Dayer LeBaron invited me to come to his ranch. I told him there was a big difference—the freedom to live our religion doesn't give us the right to commit murder.

"But these so-called 'Lambs of God' say that we should be willing to do anything in the name of God—including kill," my father went on. "He pointed out that Nephi killed his brothers because the Lord told him to. He talked about the Oath of Vengeance sworn by the Danites in the Early Days. Ervil and his people justify this whole mess through the doctrine of Blood Atonement."

Blood Atonement was one of the most controversial doctrines of our religion. I had heard of bloody deeds carried out by Orrin Porter Rockwell, who had been bodyguard to the Prophet Joseph Smith and to Church President Brigham Young. The Danites were also famous for their Old Testament way of visiting "God's vengeance" on any who harassed Latter-day Saints. Too many grisly events in the Church's early history had been justified through Blood Atonement. Now fanatics like Ervil LeBaron were using it to justify murder. I asked my father how he reconciled the doctrine of Blood Atonement with Christlike love.

"Blood Atonement has nothing to do with murder. It has nothing to do with taking the lives of our fellow beings."

"I thought the doctrine of Blood Atonement was about making people pay for their sins with their own blood. Like it says in Deuteronomy: 'Life shall go for life, eye for eye, tooth for tooth.'"

"Blood Atonement refers to the sacrifice made by our Savior, who died on the cross to atone for our sins so that we can return to God's presence. Our Father in Heaven sent His Only Begotten Son to be resurrected into eternal life so that we, too, might live. Once that sacrifice was made, there was no need for more sacrifice, and no reason to kill."

My father shuffled the cards and slapped them down for a game of solitaire. "In any case, if I was rolling in money and had a gun at my head, I wouldn't put up a single cent to get a killer like Ervil out of prison."

He sighed again. "We are living in the last dispensation in the fullness of times. Satan is doing his utmost to thwart the elect before the Savior comes to call them home."

A few months later, soon after our second child, Maya, was born, my father made a house call down the street, then came to my front door. Soon he was sitting at my dining room table, bouncing the baby on his arm while telling me that Ervil LeBaron had been released from prison after serving only one day of his twelve-year sentence. Eighty thousand dollars had been "raised" from the wealthy Kingstons, who knew how to get and hold on to money better than the other polygamous clans. The Kingstons had formed cooperatives and businesses, and sent a few of their people through law school to protect their business and personal interests. At the same time, the Kingston group put their children to work at an early age and sometimes urged their plural wives to collect welfare (something my father would not allow us to even think about doing). My father had often remarked about the hard bargains the Kingstons drove. Now he explained that when the Kingston leaders' lives were threatened, Ortel Kingston had readily forked over cash to Ervil's henchmen. My father dealt out this information in much the same way he dealt cards for rummy—his tone was direct, his manner brusque, yet I sensed bitterness beneath his words.

From my mother I found out about the pamphlets, letters, and phone calls threatening my father's life, sent anonymously although everyone suspected that Ervil LeBaron's people were the source. As with earlier LeBaron diatribes, my father was exhorted to repent and acknowledge the true leaders of God's kingdom on earth. My mother explained that Ervil had served only one day of his twelve-year sentence before it was overturned; the court reasoned that the actual murderers had not been arrested, so no one could prove that Ervil had directed them to commit murder. But everyone, including their mother, Maud LeBaron, was certain that Ervil had instigated Joel's murder.

~

I was lost in the design, seeing only the backside of the tapestry, everything knotted and tangled haphazardly. All I knew for sure was that the connections meant something, and they formed a kind of pattern. Writing narratives helped me make sense of things, but my own conclusions terrified me. In one of the early stories I wrote, I took on the challenge of capturing the polar opposites of polygamy. This fictional piece was not all that fictional. For the main character, I drew on my father. Although I had chosen not to follow in his footsteps, he had provided the best example of our way of life. Another character I based on Ervil LeBaron, the example of polygamy at its most exploitive and rapacious. In expanding my story, I created a wife for the LeBaron character, a woman with auburn hair and the character flaw of vanity and a name I'd never heard—Rena. I was enrolled in a creative writing class at the University of Utah at the time, and each student was to provide a piece of writing for the workshop. I hadn't completed the story when it came my turn to present it for the other graduate students to critique.

"I don't know how to finish it," I admitted.

"Well . . . the ending is obvious. The bad guy and his wife are going to kill the good guy, the narrator's father."

"I can't write that!" A rush of emotion made my voice shake.

"Why not? It's here in the story. All the foreshadowing. Everything. Your story has dictated its own terms." This from the professor.

"I can't write that ending." The class eyed me and waited. "My father is the good guy."

The students fell silent then, and I knew I had said too much. In the shock of exposure, I put what might have served me as a warning out of mind.

As time went on, there were other warnings, but as a family we were half-blind, unable to distinguish true danger from the paranoia that tinged our lives. And we didn't know how to address the general disregard by law enforcement personnel, who diminished the threats on my father's life even though the name of Rulon Allred appeared on a LeBaron hit list known to the FBI, the same hit list that named presidents and prime ministers.

Ervil LeBaron had conducted doctrinal tirades in print, notably a booklet called "Hour of Crisis: Day of Vengeance," which proclaimed that the anointed one would soon take over the world. All fundamentalist groups—the Allred order, the Kingston clan, the Colorado City group, and the LeBaron family's Church of the First Born—were ordered to acknowledge the Church of the Lamb of God as the true church, orders underscored with religious rhetoric in the form of "revelation." Ervil demanded that my father, Merlin and Ortel Kingston, Rulon Jeffs, and his own brother Verlan LeBaron as well as LDS Church President Spencer Kimball surrender their authority and obey "the true prophet of God." He challenged them to show their fealty by rendering the tithes of their congregations and the deeds to their land to Ervil LeBaron, patriarch and president of the Church of the Lamb of God. The names of religious leaders and heads of state appeared alongside names of Mexican peasants who had somehow offended Ervil. Anyone who defied Ervil, even those who inadvertently disagreed with him had their names added to his list of "criminals" sentenced to death for disobeying "God's Civil Law," which was basically whatever Ervil said it was. He drew a few of his notions from scripture, but mostly "God's Civil Law" was made up of manipulations to increase Ervil's power, figments of his imagination, and distorted reasoning of a mind that had become "a law unto itself."

That Ervil LeBaron's church held up the Lamb, a symbol of sacrifice, as its main icon should have been warning enough. In December of 1974, dark figures had conducted a firebombing raid on Los Molinos, a small community of First Born members in Baja, Mexico. As the huts flamed, and people fled, snipers picked them off with rifles. This action was attributed to Ervil's Lambs of God. Soon after the raid on Los Molinos, Merlin Kingston personally warned my father (who had delivered a good many of the Kingston children) about Ervil's order that Rulon Allred had better start obeying "God's Civil Law" or he would suffer the death penalty.

Apparently threats on a polygamist were not important enough for law enforcement officials to provide my father with protection. So we steeped like the proverbial frog in the pot of water slowly heating to a boil, unable to tell when our fear took on immediate and dangerous implications. An apocalyptic state of mind attends all forms of fundamentalism. When you have already decided that you are living in the last days, and you have preselected your team of good guys (you are on the good guys' team, of course) and when you fully believe you know who the bad guys are (anybody who doesn't agree that you are the good guys), then you're up against the entire world. This pressure makes it easier to overlook "little problems" like rent and utility bills and death threats because the earth could be destroyed at any moment. In terror and righteousness, you hope to be translated (taken to heaven without tasting death) or lifted up in the Rapture, so what you focus on is prayer and scripture study, all the while cringing, waiting for reality to hit.

"Us against the world" whets an enormous hunger to be right that does little to satisfy physical or spiritual or emotional appetites. All our prophecies indicated that the Second Coming of Christ would coincide with the new millennium, and the patriarchs warned that there was only a little time to set our lives in order. The earth must be redeemed; prophecy indicated it would die and be resurrected, so we must prepare for the worst. As the end of the twentieth century approached, some fundamentalists initiated stints of fasting and prayer that left the women anemic and the men too tired to work. In my father's congregation, there were as many people competing to sustain the most stringent liquid diet as there were men competing for the most wives. In other fundamentalist communities, the patriarchs urged parents to marry their thirteen- and fourteen-year-old daughters to much older men so they would be lifted up in the Last Day. (According to fundamentalist doctrine, only those women who are married can aspire to the celestial kingdom.) The brethren urged their wives to have more and more children until the women were too overwhelmed and depleted to take care of their sizable broods. Though it seems extreme, if you live with the expectation of apocalypse all your life, the end of the world must come.

Perhaps these reminders of his own mortality provoked the next crisis, for my father's troubles increased with his responsibilities. Women were asking to come into his family and his brethren urged him to take more wives. It would not do for them to have more wives than their "priesthood head" and the leader of their group. Under protest from his long time wives (all but Aunt LaVerne, who felt it her duty to make sure he married as many women as possible—women she, of course, would manage), he proceeded to marry two women. One was a white-haired widow whose husband had been a doctor; she made it clear that she would be pleased to share her small fortune with my father. In truth, he dreamed of replacing our long-lost white house with a new version, a fourplex large enough to hold the entire family in case of emergency. My mother and Aunt Emma speculated about his motives in choosing to marry again despite their reservations. Was it the widow's sweet spirit or her money that drew my father? And what did this new trend portend for his long-time wives and family? For my part, I reread John Cheever's "Torch Song" and wondered if these were portents, my father inviting a widow of such significance into his life.

The other wife was also new to the group, tall and handsome with clear blue eyes and a profile that resembled my father's. A native of

South America, she insisted that she was destined to be my father's wife. His wives of long standing objected because she was divorced. They reminded Rulon that he had promised never to marry a divorcee, who would bring her confusion into our demanding way of life. When he refused the South American woman on this basis, she told him that since he had introduced her to the Principle of Plural Marriage, he was now responsible for her soul. If he rejected her, she would not live the Principle and her damnation would be on his head. He spent the night alone, in his doctor's office, weighing the situation. Sometime during the night he made up his mind. The South American woman claimed he'd been visited by an angel who ordered him to marry her, although I found no reference to this angelic visit in his journals.

My mother could not bear to speak of those plural marriages, although certainly she was present at the ceremony, her right hand beneath Sally's and Melissa's, and resting atop Emma's whose hand rested on LaVerne's whose hand rested on the hand of each new wife as the long-time wives "gave" her to Rulon. However reluctantly, they spoke the holy words in chorus and rendered covenants under duress.

The new wives turned out to be outspoken and generally insensitive to the ways of the family. Accustomed to the indulgences of monogamous life, they often manipulated their way into my father's time and attention. After so many years of practicing harmony through self-restraint and respect for each other, the long-time wives were devastated. Both my father and the new wives ignored their wishes. They murmured among themselves, so this is what it is like to suffer an affair or a divorce, their eyes cast down with disappointment.

I was furious with my father. As I watched my mother trace and retrace the steps taken to protect family boundaries, identifying how this perimeter and that had been breached, I could see her nerves sizzle, her thoughts spark as though passed through frayed wire. How could my father abandon those who had given the greater part of their lives to him and turn his "golden years" over to these interlopers? I

was not jealous for my own sake, since any hope of holding his attention on me had long since been submerged, but I did have dreams for
my mother. I had been plotting a little anniversary getaway for the
two of them, a trip to Twin Falls to stay at the Rogerson Hotel where
they had spent their honeymoon. Now my little plan was out of reach.
In addition to the four other wives, we would contend for time with
these newcomers.

What infuriated me most of all was my father's vaulting ego, and
the way his people supported it. Their frequent comparisons to Joseph
Smith. Taking upon himself the salvation of the woman from South
America. Who did they think he was, the Savior Himself? Or was it
simple male vanity, an aging man pleased to still be attractive to
women of substance, the same phenomenon that made professors at
the university flirt with me? When I thought of it, a flash of imagination revealed my father approaching the Pearly Gates, a lengthy caravan of people stuck to him like the Boy with the Golden Goose. I
imagined I could hear Peter say, "That's some camel you've got there,
Brother Rulon."

One day in 1975, my father showed up at my doorstep and urged
me to come with him: he wanted to show me his new house, his new
wives. Vile, the thought of seeing the house funded by the widow in
exchange for my father's precious time. But Aunt Emma sat in the
front seat of my father's Oldsmobile, her profile disapproving as ever,
while my mother waited in the back seat, having made room for me,
and I didn't want to disappoint her. Besides, my father had asked little
of me. In a flash I remembered his help bringing Jess home from Vietnam. I swallowed my anger and hurried out to the car with the baby in
my arms.

He showed off the house and the new women and after I shook
their hands, he showed me their talents of embroidery and pottery-
making. Gradually I realized that he was at once flaunting his new
acquisitions and asking for my approval. What was his statement,
exactly? That I had made a mistake, leaving our polygamous way of

life to devote myself to a monogamous marriage? An admission that he had broken a promise to my mother combined with a protest that the breach of faith was justified? I must admit that for all my anger and skepticism, I was grateful, as my mother and Aunt Emma were grateful, to have a little slice of his life, a little piece of his time.

Soon there were other women, widows who had been "sealed" to their husbands requesting now to be "sealed" to my father whom they felt was more worthy of them than their departed spouses. Some of the women who pushed their way into our family were obviously motivated by my father's status as patriarch of the group. Others truly longed for companionship and for my father's kind leadership with their children. My father seemed to enjoy the strident attention of these women and he was by nature magnanimous, willing to serve whenever he was asked to do so. Yet he worried about "robbing the dead." Again, his priesthood council urged him to marry the widows and again cited Joseph Smith who had sealed to himself the wives of living men. It had been a test of their loyalty to the Prophet, to the Church, and to God. Perhaps the dead had to be subjected to such tests on the Other Side. After all, the men of the priesthood council reminded him, how could they take more wives if their "priesthood head" was unwilling to take on more responsibility? Following much debate, my father considered the response to his two new women, and apparently felt that a few more wives would not do much more damage. By the time the marital flurry was over, my father had a total of sixteen wives. These additional marriages created enormous unhappiness throughout the family and sent my mother spiraling into another nervous breakdown, one that lasted for the rest of my father's days.

The children of these newly acquired wives called him "father" and brought their problems to him. Many asked to be "adopted" into my father's family and sealed to him for time and all eternity. All drew upon his financial resources. Everyone wanted a piece of his time. My father did his best to meet their needs and fulfill their wants. Gradually it dawned on me that his motives were not lustful nor even prideful, but the inclination of a magnanimous soul. If they wanted something he had the power to give them, he would give it.

My father still moved briskly under the burden of his daily responsibilities, despite the increase in his burdens. But at some point, he decided to spend more time with me. For all of one evening he talked with me about my writing and about his early life, including his first marriage. He told me that Katherine had recently come back into his orbit because of events relating to their fiftieth anniversary. Their son, Sherwood, now a doctor, had gone to visit his mother in her retirement home only to find her sobbing uncontrollably for her "lost love." During the forty years my father and she had been separated she maintained she had never loved another man. Sherwood, enraged by his mother's condition, jumped into his car and drove across the Mojave Desert, then north along I-15 in Utah to confront his father. Dr. Rulon was with patients, but Sherwood waited and then his father was standing there with his arms open. Sherwood had been prepared to deliver harsh words, but his rage dissolved in a wave of love. He did not say what he came to say; instead the two men shared a mild conversation full of soft explanations and kind words. Bold honesty came later in a long, private letter. But this first interaction led to a flurry of letters between my father and Katherine. She upbraided him for failing to pay child support during the time when he was in hiding from the law, and he managed to send the money he owed her. Throughout their correspondence, Katherine's letters were written from the persona of her Guardian Angel, who described the torments of life without her beloved.

> Well, Dr. Allred, at last we meet! . . . Say, whatever happened to that sweet little daughter of Dr. Handy's that you married? . . . Do you remember how she worked at your Chiropractic College all day and then accepted the night shift too, in her very simple mind knowing she was doing what was necessary for you to be in a position to sup-

port the beautiful babies you both dreamed of? And then you killed her baby girl, and she loved you so much she couldn't even tell you she knew.

My father's responses—explanations and apologies, for the most part—were written to that Angel.

> Dear Guardian Angel of my Beloved Katherine . . . How grateful am I to receive your missive . . . How glad am I that at last we meet! . . . Yes, whatever happened to that sweet little daughter of my most honored father and friend, Dr. Handy? I have never ceased thanking my Heavenly Father that I married her. . . . Yes, I remember how gladly she worked at the Chiropractic College and even how her worthless husband worked, as she did, by day and night . . . so that I might one day be better qualified to support all the beautiful children we both dreamed of . . . Yes, I remember, how can I ever forget, what happened to our baby girl . . . ? My suffering for what happened never ceased.

The artifice kept their dialogue in the realm of "what was" and "what might have been" with an occasional eternal perspective, "what might yet be." "What is" was not addressed. They still did not communicate directly to each other, still required "divine intervention." But at last some kind of peace grew between them. Perhaps Katherine would yet "leap joyful from the grave" into his arms as he had predicted in a poem he wrote to her during the first year of their separation. I knew, from the way his eyes misted when he spoke of these things, that he loved her still—even after all those years and all the heartache.

My father's troubles continued to escalate. The ranch in Montana that my father had purchased for the religious group in 1961 had grown into a town called Pinesdale, and its polygamous residents were sustaining a benign, if not friendly relationship with the nearby communities of Hamilton and Missoula, Montana. But the seventies brought about sweeping changes of lifestyle across the nation, and Pinesdale attracted experimenters and charlatans. Among them was Alex Joseph, who had come to my father's group soon after converting to the official Church of Jesus Christ of Latter-day Saints. Alex seemed to abandon the official church as easily as he had entered it, having been on the lookout for a stronger patriarchal form and a chance to create his own following. On the Montana ranch, with my father gone most of the time, Alex found his opening. He soon tired of the hierarchy and flaunted the authority of the priesthood council. He decided to place himself in a position of authority and did so by marrying, as a plural wife, a coed from the University of Montana. He allegedly encouraged her to recruit her friends and roommates to be his wives. These young women had been raised in good Protestant homes and as they disappeared into the "polygamous cult" their parents were outraged; their recriminations fell on my father, leader of the Allred group. According to my father's journal, when he called Alex to account for marrying without permission from his "priesthood head," Alex said, "You did it, Rulon, and now I'm following your example." My father asked him to leave the group before he caused more trouble, and Alex Joseph took his wives and settled in a place called Bigwater near the Glen Canyon Dam. Meanwhile others tried to wrest power, tried to gather community assets and claim authority for their own purposes.

Repeated throughout my father's journals is the plaintive note, "What shall I do?" Even as I commiserate with him, reading these journal entries, I remember Katherine and her children, abandoned by my father to his great spiritual ambitions. I remember Aunt Rose and her children living off fifty pounds of carrots for an entire month during the cold Montana winter. I remember my mother, her eyes streaming as she recounted my father's promise, now broken, to marry only virgins. And always in the background, the dark cloud of the LeBarons.

The danger to my father's life became palpable. In 1975, the instances of threat multiplied, and they were more than attempts at extortion or doctrinal mutterings—they were unmistakable death threats. Ervil LeBaron demanded that my father acknowledge him as the true head of the priesthood and patriarch of God's church. Strange phone calls to my father's homes and his doctor's office, the veiled voices issuing ultimatums, underscored the sense that Allred homes were being watched. Cars prowled past my mother's house, circled the block and crawled past again. One night a rock wrapped in a threatening note was thrown through my half-brother's window. He was caretaker of the newly constructed RCA (Rulon Clark Allred) building where members of his group held fundamentalist meetings, cultural events, and school for their children. The leaflets on my father's car window and on the automobiles of his parishioners were warning enough, all of them petitioning polygamists to join the Church of the Lamb of God, and stipulating capital punishment for any who ignored the summons. My father turned these over to the local police, who said that there was nothing they could do until a crime was committed.

At the LDS General Conference in October, 1976, LDS Church President Spencer Kimball issued a warning to the Mormon congregation about polygamist and other apostate groups. "They come to you in sheep's clothing," he said in a voice trembling with age, "but within they are ravening wolves." He warned the flock, cautioning them to stay in the church, stay close to home. I wanted to tell President Kimball that polygamous or not, we all have fears that prey on us, hungers that warp us as we struggle for survival. I wanted him to meet my father, who could usually transcend his own appetites long enough to shepherd others to safety.

But Spencer Woolley Kimball knew more about the LeBarons than I realized. Years before, in 1943, he was asked to support his childhood friend, Maud LeBaron, in her efforts to be reinstated into the official Church. Her sons Joel, Ervil, and Ben interrupted the meeting and treated their mother roughly. When they found that she wanted to regain her membership in the official church, they mocked her and made fun of the Church. Apostle Kimball noted in his private journal, "Never before have I come into such close contact with Lucifer and his devils."

～

Winter came early in 1976. At Thanksgiving my father's wives (including the new ones) gathered with his children and their children in the great family room of the new house he'd built in Taylorsville, Utah, thanks to the funds of the wealthy widow. A brand-new baby, my father's first great-grandchild, and the progeny of Aunt Rose, cried in her mother's arms. My father said that he had delivered her grandmother and her mother, and that he had delivered the baby, his face proud as he claimed three generations of obstetrical success. My father balanced a toddler on each knee and sang "A Frog He Went A-Courtin" and he recited "The Cremation of Sam McGee" just as he did when I was a child. After several requests, he began to tell the story of when he was chased by the wolves. But by the time he reached the point in the tale where he falls and cuts his cheek, he had grown weary of the tale. He had forgotten the moral altogether.

"I can't remember how I got home," he said simply. "The Lord must have protected me." And then he began the other story, of how a rattlesnake scared his little horse, and how it threw him from the saddle and dragged him until his spirit left his body and how he looked down on the racing pony and his own body, his head bouncing over sagebrush and rocks. "That was when I discovered that I would not die when my body does," he said, and he looked at each of us, his eyes glinting strangely. "I love my darlings," he said. And then he got up, spilling toddlers this way and that, kissing and hugging his way out of a room that suddenly seemed much too small to contain him.

Later, I asked my father what the LeBarons wanted from him. He shrugged. "Power. Peace of mind. Things I can't give them." My

father had once treated Ervil for malaria in Mexico. Now Ervil
LeBaron had put out yet another pamphlet threatening death by the
hand of the Destroying Angel for all who did not accept Ervil's claim
of ultimate priesthood authority. The power lines to the RCA building were cut, and a phone-caller coldly asked, "Do you think you're
really secure?" Notes were left on the dashboard of my father's car and
a brick shattered the plate-glass window of his doctor's office. The
night my mother came home and found footprints in the snow
spelling out "We'll be back!" signaled an even bolder threat. That
night men sat in trucks parked outside her house, their deer rifles
loaded.

The next morning my father's followers organized themselves in
shifts, sitting in his waiting room with their hunting rifles. "We want
to protect you, Brother Rulon," they said.

He shook his head, noting the contradiction presented by their
rifles in a place of healing. "You men go back to your families and your
work. I'll be all right. I'll go when the Lord wants me. Not one minute
sooner—or later. Nothing you men can do will keep that from happening."

~

I spent the morning of May 10, 1977, with an architecture student
who was researching the structures of polygamous homes. I took her
to the compound of homes where I was born. That day, a deep hole
yawned in the front lawn, dark and disconcerting as a grave waiting to
be filled. My three-year old daughter, Maya, whispered that ghosts
were around us, and as I backed out of the compound, I thought I saw
my father's mother, Grandmother Evelyn, rapping furiously on the
car window as she had once rapped on my mother's bedroom window
with her cane. I drove west across the valley to the huge fourplex my
father had built to house his wives and any of his children who might
need a place to live. The architecture student peered into the vast stor-
age areas, the expansive family room, the high, wide bedrooms, each

of them large enough to shelter an entire family in case of emergency. Three times that day I traveled past my father's office. Each time I had the impulse to stop, but remembered that I had an appointment with him later that day. My father was always so busy, and I had no valid reason to demand his attention.

While I was driving back and forth, two women were purchasing disguises at Deseret Industries on the corner of 45th South and State Street. They bought a blonde wig and a brunette wig and a couple of parkas. At about 4:40 P.M. they entered his office on 48th South, just east of State Street. The waiting room was crowded with patients. Aunt Emma nodded at the one in the curly blonde wig and asked if she could help. When the woman asked to see Dr. Allred, Aunt Emma said that he was examining a patient, but that he would be with her in a few minutes. Soon my father needed to run a blood test; he walked down the hall and glanced into the crowded waiting area, perhaps reflecting that there never seemed to be enough of him to go around, always more responsibility than he could fulfill. He went to the hematocrit machine and the woman in the blue parka and blonde wig followed him.

"Doctor?"

He turned and she emptied the .25 magnum handgun into his neck and chest. She couldn't seem to hit his face, even when he was on the floor, the blood running out, his hands vibrating—the hands that had delivered so many babies and given so many blessings, the last part of him to give up life. The shooter followed the other woman out and grabbed her cohort's loaded pistol. Back inside, she fired directly at the doctor's face, but missed again. The bullets ricocheted off the floor into the walls and ceiling. One of the male patients, perhaps thinking he could save the doctor's life or bring the woman to justice, wrestled for the gun. She turned it on him. "Don't," he begged. "I have a family." He ran for the restroom and she fired after him. Then she left.

At first, the office was still. Then Aunt Emma fell on my father, crying, "Rulon! Darling! Speak to me!" But he was gone, even his hands limp, fallen on his chest. She couldn't rouse him, couldn't get him to respond to CPR or mouth-to-mouth. She kept dialing 411, the number for information and couldn't remember the emergency number, Aunt Emma with her memory for entire accounts, for full pages of scripture, so capable until that moment. Pray as she might, give of her healing touch as she did, she could not bring him back.

I had scheduled an appointment with my father at his office that afternoon: the 4:45 slot was mine. My appointment is on the books, witness to my remedial character. If I had kept the appointment, I might have been there to stop the bullets. But my brother's wife had pressed Jess and me to make a foursome at golf. When I had called at 2:00 to cancel, Aunt Emma said it would be just as well. The doctor's day had been even busier than usual, all sorts of unexpected events and emergencies.

And then all I had was the news. The phone call to my mother. "Someone shot him," she said. Her voice so perplexed, so sad. "He isn't . . . is he dead?" My brother Danny was across the street ordering hamburgers and cokes for all of us. The clouds gathering over the Great Salt Lake seemed congested around my heart. Jess, so familiar with death and its effect on the living, stopped me as I entered the fast food restaurant. "What is it? Is it one of the kids?" I shook my head. "My dad—he's been killed. Someone shot him." I searched his eyes. He was there, really there for me. "You have to tell your brother," he said.

Danny, always looking for the joke, said, "You're kidding." Then his smile faded.

While we were driving the children to my mother-in-law's house, the radio reported that two women had killed my father. Behind the pain, I felt the shame of being misunderstood yet another time, of knowing what the world would think—that he'd been killed by a woman he had wronged, one of his "harem," someone in the throes of jealousy or bitterness.

Then the video footage of my father's body on a stretcher, his face covered, his black oxfords tipped out, the soles worn thin. My half-brother's face as they put the body in the ambulance, a grown man weeping like a little boy, a scene that pierced me every time I saw it— and I saw it repeatedly in the years to come.

As with Job, what my father feared, what we all had feared, had happened. The wolves had taken him down at last. But he had died quickly though violently, perhaps even mercifully, as Aunt Sally said, "the way he wanted to die." As a martyr to what he believed was true.

The year following my father's death, my brothers and sisters met along with my father's wives in the family room of the big white house to celebrate our father's birthday. Each of us contributed a story. Our stories were mostly idealistic and impossible or sad and sentimental; often they were unconscionably censored. Usually our stories included a reminiscence of our father. Aunt Sally's youngest, Miranda, was the first to retell our father's wolf story. In her version, our father does not fall, but turns with a stick of wood and drives off the wolves. They snarl, they snap, but they back off. The following year, it was Eileen's turn. In her version, he stands as a protector at the door of the dugout and orders the wolves away. The stick, like Moses' rod, is a scepter to bring life from death, good from evil. The wolves whimper, scampering into the forest like scared puppies. I found myself wishing my father could have heard these versions, wondering about his reaction. What would he say about this evolved nightmare that we share with him? Did he know how much work he left us to do? Would he be delighted or amused or dismayed to realize that we have made him into an icon? How would he respond to this irony, that in his evangelical majesty he stood between many of us and a direct relationship with God and with life?

Certainly the wolf story reflected what our group of fundamentalists wanted to believe: that evil exists outside the perimeters of the human soul, that Satan can be defied, controlled, crushed. But I think somewhere along the way, my father recognized his role as a creator, with the propensity to make his dreams and his nightmares real. All this time we had missed the point of the wolf story. Dealing with fear is not simply a matter of control or dominion—of "schooling our feelings" as the brethren would have said. It is not simply a matter of seeing, through the story, our personal affinity for the animal or monster within. Perhaps my father wanted his children to know that whatever we do not claim will ultimately claim us. Perhaps he wanted us to know that there is no escape from the shadow but love.

The Trial

TWO YEARS TO THE DAY BEFORE he died, my father wrote in his journal: "May 10, 1975. I have two years to put my affairs in order." He died on May 10, 1977. About a year later, I found the notation in his elegant script—remarkably legible for a doctor—in one of the looseleaf binders where he kept his journals, and I marveled that he knew his death was impending, knew it to the very day. He'd wanted to die as a martyr, as did his heroes, Jesus Christ and Joseph Smith. Perhaps God *had* fulfilled his desire, had sent a Destroying Angel in answer to his prayers.

Some of the facts surrounding his murder came out when Ramona Marston, who was allegedly the number two gunwoman in my father's murder, and three others were arrested after an extensive investigation yielded eleven warrants and a roundup conducted by police in Denver and in Dallas. Some "lambs of God" turned state's evidence, and others (including Ramona Marston) jumped the paltry bail set by the Utah court. Then, on Halloween night in 1978, Mexico *federales* conducted a commando-style raid on two houses. They arrested Ervil's sidekick, Dan Jordan, believing him to be Ervil LeBaron. They also arrested Rena Chenowyth, whom they suspected of being the shooter.

The police found Ervil in one of the houses, and questioned him, too, but they were convinced that the infamous LeBaron was handcuffed in the police van, so they released the real Ervil. Rena and Dan were transported to Mexico City, where Dan was held for the murder of Joel, while Rena was expelled from Mexico and apprehended at the border by FBI agents. Rena Chenowyth, the alleged gunwoman, was charged with first-degree murder. More information hit the press when the first trial was held in the spring of 1979, *Salt Lake County vs. Rena Chenowyth* for first-degree murder, and *Salt Lake County vs. Mark Chenowyth, Victor Chenowyth, and Eddie Marston* for conspiracy to commit murder. The prosecutor displayed photographs of my father's body, pointing out to the jury the wounds in his neck and chest. I went home that night and curled in a fetal position, unable to purge my mind of the photographs of my father, his chest and neck riddled with bullet holes. Even the circle of Jess's arms could not banish those pictures from my mind.

In the course of the week's testimony, we learned that the waiting room had been full of witnesses—seven people saw the doctor killed. But when she was arrested and brought to trial, the defendant, Rena Chenowyth, was eight months pregnant. She weighed considerably more than the woman who shot the doctor, and her face was round and soft, without the hard planes of the shooter. Anyone would feel sorry for a pregnant woman locked in a jail cell. Her mousy brown hair was straight and stringy—nothing like the curly blonde wig worn by the alleged assassin. None of the witnesses, including Aunt Emma, could positively identify Rena Chenowyth as the shooter. They seemed to remember the accomplice better, the woman named Ramona Marston who jumped bail after being arrested.

When Rena sat on the witness stand, she licked her lips and said no when asked if she had killed my father. Prosecutor David Yocom paused long and studied his notes between questions, playing it safe. Rena kept looking at her attorney, who gave thumbs up or winked and smiled with each response. Prosecutor Yocom didn't seem to notice this interaction. He seemed less disturbed by the possibility that Rena had actually killed my father than by the possibility that she was lying, now that he had displayed more than a hundred pieces of physical evidence (the parka, wig, and pistol had been found in a nearby dumpster). It was a trial where personalities, rather than truths prevailed. David Yocom worried about how the press spelled his name, while Chenowyth's attorney, an ambitious young man who seemed to regard Rena with affection, displayed confidence in his ability to win.

By the time Rena and the others were brought to trial, investigations yielded the possibility that the "lambs of God" had been involved in more than a dozen murders. Although each of the jurors had been questioned about the influence of the media, no one had asked questions about the influence of fear on their equanimity. After the first days of trial, one of the eight jurors told the bailiff that he was spooked because his wife had reported a car with dark figures inside, watching their house. Yocom upbraided the bailiff for not reporting this to the judge, and then raised the issue himself, but the juror was not removed. Instead this juror became foreman of the jury. Except for the police and the prosecution team, the people in the room—representatives of the press and people from the legal sector—seemed more interested in the trial's conclusion than with justice being done. The jury, too, seemed anxious to be done with it, meeting only four hours. Perhaps they felt that if they returned with a verdict of "not guilty" Ervil LeBaron was unlikely to send anyone looking for them. The eight jurors acquitted Rena Chenowyth, Victor Chenowyth, Mark Chenowyth, and Eddie Marston on all four counts. Years later, other jurors would admit that in one way or another all had been "spooked" or threatened in some way during the course of the trial.

As I walked back to my car that night after Rena Chenowyth and her companions were acquitted, I felt that I was suffocating. It seemed to me that she had behaved like a liar, licking her lips, asking for water when the big question was asked, "Did you kill Dr. Rulon Allred?" But how could I know for sure, when my own sense of truth was warped from telling lies to protect the family?

Rena had said that she had never met the doctor, and knew him only by reputation. He had delivered lots of babies, including the children of some members of the LeBaron group and even some of the Chenowyths back in the days when her father and mother were looking for a group that would accommodate them. Rena's mother, Thelma Chenowyth, had gradually usurped her husband's patriarchal stance to make her family a matriarchy. Such female forcefulness had no place in the Allred group, but Ervil, when he was patriarch of the Church of the First Born had formed a coalition of women called United Women of Zion, whose first rule was secrecy. Through these women he was able to affect their husbands and their children and create his own church, the Church of the Lamb of God. Thelma had lobbied for her daughters to marry Ervil, whom she considered to be the greatest man she'd ever met. Lorna married him when she was eighteen, becoming his fifth wife. Rena, the youngest of the Chenowyth daughters, became Ervil's thirteenth wife.

From Ervil's son Isaac, and from Lamb of God defectors Lloyd and Don Sullivan, investigators learned that in selecting the women who would kill my father, Ervil appealed to their vanity. "It's because you're the most beautiful women among the lambs of God," he told them. He "set them apart"—bestowed religious authority on them— to act in behalf of the Destroying Angel. Ervil had told them to destroy my father's face, drawing on an obscure doctrine. "That will be proof that he is a false prophet."

Ervil was counting on the Utah mind-set, believing that citizens would not prosecute a woman as readily as they would a man. I had to admire his ingenious madness, knowing that a society harboring sexual discrimination would try to compensate in a court of law. He also may have known about the tendency to dismiss any real concern about polygamists, be they man, woman, or child. I had encountered such prejudice when I appeared on a radio talk show to discuss my early writing about polygamy, a woman called to express her reaction to my father's murder. "He was breaking the law, wasn't he? Seven wives!" she said with disgust. "He deserved to die." Ervil was right in his prediction that Utahns would not hold a woman accountable for the murder of a polygamous patriarch. Too many Bluebeard nightmares in our Latter-day subconscious.

As a result of the investigation surrounding my father's death, Ervil was now suspected of instigating the murder of at least five people: his brother Joel, his daughter Rebecca, a man named Robert Simon (whose beautiful wife and daughter Ervil had coveted), my father, and a man named Dean Vest, in San Diego. Ervil was also suspected of having catalyzed the Los Molinos raid. The number of violent deaths attributed to Ervil's direction induced the FBI to take renewed interest in the LeBaron clan, revisiting other murders, since many of these names were included in Ervil's list of those "sentenced to death" by God's Destroying Angel. Public fascination with JFK conspiracy theories promoted reawakened questions about the part the LeBaron clan might have played in the Kennedy assassinations.

On the last day of May 1979, Mexican authorities apprehended Ervil LeBaron after he had ordered the kidnaping of a Mexican woman. The *federales* forced him across the border at Laredo where he was taken into custody by FBI agents on June 1. Utah investigators interrogated him in the Laredo County Jail before arranging for his extradition to Salt Lake City. Ervil was voluble, adopting stentorian tones as he claimed authorship of the pamphlets defining the "Law of Liberty" and outlined his strong beliefs that God's judgements would not wait until the hereafter. The Church of the Lamb of God could not afford to hire a private attorney, so Ervil had to settle for attorneys from the Legal Defenders Association. I still wasn't sure who had actually pulled the trigger, but I was certain that Ervil had engineered my father's death. David Yocom was again appointed the prosecuting attorney, bringing his extensive experience and knowledge to the case, as well as the strong relationships formed with Murray Police investigators during the Rena Chenowyth trial. Yocom had gone into private practice, yet the Salt Lake County District Attorney's office asked him to take the case because of his familiarity with it. I decided to sit behind him throughout the trial and I was prepared to help him this time, if necessary. Still haunted that I had canceled my appointment to see my father at the moment he died, I determined not to miss any more opportunities. I wasn't leaving anything up to hope or chance.

On the first day, I waited outside the courtroom for the doors to open, my heart pounding. Beside me sat a cousin who also had grown up in a polygamous family and who had left the fundamentalist group of our childhood for the wider world. He is a brilliant attorney, but suffered greatly as a child from what he called "a fractured personality," the result of growing up in a small town that persecuted him as a polygamist child and pitted him against his people in a subculture where the gifted are considered dangerous. Now, as we waited for the doors of the courtroom to open, I asked my cousin how he felt about fundamentalism.

"Don't you ever worry that the polygamous patriarchs are right and we're wrong?" I asked. "What if they really are headed for glory in the celestial kingdom, while we're earthbound in our monogamous state, locked forever in the terrestrial sphere? What if we wake up on the Other Side in the low-class cabins, unable to visit the first-class berths of loved ones who kept all the commandments?"

He gave me a sad smile and shook his head. His hound-dog eyes told me he wished he'd never heard of fundamentalism. "If there is an afterlife, I think the patriarchs will keep on doing just what they've been doing all these years—having their School of the Prophets and their Sunday meetings and their home evenings with a dozen different families and their soft moments with a different wife and children every night. They'll go on being right for all eternity, and nothing will change; they'll always be tired, and always be overworked. And they still won't accept you and me because they don't see any other way to live righteously."

We went inside the courtroom and sat down.

"Do you think they'll get Ervil this time—that justice will be done?"

"I don't know what justice is, anymore. I thought the issues would be clearer once I got outside the polygamous group. But it's always a roll of the dice. Anything can happen."

The moment Ervil walked into the courtroom he found my face in the crowd. I stared back, refusing to give in to fear. He crossed the room to the defendant's table, craning his neck over his shoulder to glare at me.

I wrote notes to David Yocom throughout the trial, and sometimes he incorporated my suggestions. In the summation, he referred to the Jonestown suicide/massacre as a measure of the evil Ervil LeBaron could perpetrate. But it was the testimony of Ervil's son Isaac that really made the difference. He had been present for the "military training" to "do battle" with Ervil's own brother Verlan as well as other fundamentalists. He'd been there when Ervil outlined the conspiracy to kill my father, when he appointed the shooters, and when he explained his motives for wanting my father dead. Isaac's testimony revealed that Ervil's reasons for killing my father were manifold: to kill what he deemed "a false prophet"; to assimilate my father's followers, collect their tithes and assume their property; to perpetuate what had become an addiction to murder, now that Ervil had ordered the killing of dozens of people, among them his daughter Rebecca, who had spoken against her father's violent ways and so got "the death penalty." Isaac revealed that Ervil's primary purpose was to initiate a funeral where he could kill his brother Verlan, head of the LeBaron family Church of the First Born. Since as a doctor, my father had treated Verlan, Ervil predicted that Verlan would attend, and in fact, he did. My father's funeral at Bingham High School went on record as the largest private funeral Salt Lake City had ever seen. More than three thousand people came to mourn or to witness the spectacle, including a cadre of police and media representatives from around the nation. The press and police coverage prevented the three men parked at the ward-house across the street from barging into the funeral and firing subautomatic machine guns that held two banana clips taped together capable of spewing sixty rounds into the crowd in a matter of seconds.

Many people testified against Ervil, but it was probably the testimony of seventeen-year-old Isaac with his liquid brown eyes that affected the jury most. As he sat on the witness stand, he knew his father would give the order to have him killed. Isaac had seen Rebecca murdered, and he knew that his father's orders would be carried out if at all possible—even if Ervil was confined to prison. But Isaac told the truth anyway. When he stepped down from the witness stand, no one in the courtroom had a doubt: Ervil LeBaron would be convicted. Except, possibly, Ervil himself, detached as he was from reality, continuing to move with haughty assurance, as if he believed that God would intervene to save him.

We expected the jury to meet overnight at least, but they returned in three hours. After the verdict was read, I met one of the detectives, Dick Forbes, on the front steps. He grabbed me and whirled me around. "We got 'im!" he yelled. "We got the dirty son of a bitch!"

Two years later, guards found Ervil LeBaron dead in his prison cell; the coroner diagnosed the cause of death as a massive heart attack. By then Ervil had cultivated a following at the Utah State prison and he had expanded his hit list to include all those participants in the conspiracy who had failed to complete the mission, which was ultimately to kill Verlan LeBaron. Verlan himself died in an automobile accident two days after Ervil's body was discovered in his prison cell, thus resolving the central struggle for power that precipitated my father's murder.

After Ervil's death in prison, I hoped to be through with polygamy and its lunatic fringe. I thought my life would change and, to some degree, it did. I thought of my father and mourned him, but, true to my fundamentalist roots, I took comfort in believing that evil was buried in a vault below the ground somewhere in Mexico.

For a handful of years I was relatively happy. My husband and I had married in the temple and our children thrived in our new commitment. I loved the little ranch house where we lived beside White Pine Creek, with the full mile of field between the house and Quarry Mountain where deer and porcupine and goldfinch visited our yard. Satisfaction striated our days, and for once in my life I did not seek change.

In the spring of 1990, the wet weather that usually accompanies the biannual Conference of the Church of Jesus Christ of Latter-day Saints had given way to sunshine. It was April Fool's Day, and we had tuned the television to hear the preaching of church leaders in two-hour sessions. It had been a glorious spring day, the willow budding gold, the grasses radiating a neon brilliance, the sun shining benevolently after the long, deep winter.

My father had been dead for almost thirteen years and I reflected, as I listened to the conference talks, that time does heal all wounds. But I could not watch the brethren speaking without thinking of my father. He had been first for me in so many ways—the first preacher, the first doctor, the first human being to touch me.

Gordon B. Hickey was speaking. As second counselor to an ill and aged president, it was up to him to close the conference. He spoke of our troubled time and the heartache of mankind. He urged us to create a kinder, gentler world. His words swelled like seeds in my heart, promising to bear sweet blossoms and delicious fruit. Someone gave the closing prayer. Then the Tabernacle Choir sang the closing song, "Come, Come Ye Saints."

The Salt Lake City Temple appeared on the screen, the place my husband and I had been married and our children sealed to us for eternity, the place my father and Katherine, his first wife had been married sixty-five years before. The Tabernacle Choir swelled to the last line of the song, "All is well, all is well."

I stretched and smiled in the late afternoon sun, the huge picture window of field and mountain behind me, and before me the image of the temple surrounded by flowers of every hue, the sun bright, the tabernacle organ with its technicolor chords, the temple fading to resolve on a new image, of the woman Rena, who had been tried for the murder of my father. She wasn't pregnant, and she'd dyed her mousy hair a vibrant auburn. Carefully made up, she looked very pretty as she spoke with a reporter. He was asking her how it felt to pull the trigger when she killed the doctor. Rena smiled and said something savvy, something like, "If you want to know, you'll have to buy the book." Despite speculations, this was the first I knew for sure that she'd killed my father. That Rena had worked with a ghostwriter to turn out a book exploiting the murder she had committed yet been acquitted of, made me physically ill. I couldn't comprehend how words, which had always been a way to enhance and expand life, could be used to diminish my father's life, how a book could make a mockery of his death. But here it was, in living color.

The television station showed footage of my father on a stretcher outside his office, his shoes tipped out. A weight as heavy as the television sat on my chest. I reached for the phone and called the reporter. "What are you doing? Don't you realize that you're helping the woman who killed my father? She was acquitted because she lied on the witness stand! Yet you're helping her sell a book focused on the murder she got away with!" He said something about news being news and would I like to come on the air and tell my side of it.

"My side of it? This isn't a disagreement! This isn't a political debate! My father was murdered!"

"Well . . . wasn't he breaking the law, too?"

It was like losing my father all over again. My mother grieved harder about this violation than his actual death, and a profound sense of victimization took hold of me, a deeper sense of injustice than when my father died—perhaps because it brought up all the issues of denied citizenship, our history as untouchables, and the violation of our civil liberties by state and federal governments.

Each night I awoke at 2 A.M. with my father's hands before my face. Those hands, long-fingered, clean, radiating healing power, waving away sleep. I sat at the kitchen table and wrote and wrote. The flow of words did not wash away the hurt, and I found no healing in the process that had once preserved my sanity.

I went to see David Yocom, who had used the Ervil LeBaron conviction in his campaign ads for Salt Lake County Attorney. After so many years of posing as something I was not, I had no more patience for maintaining a front. I got right to the issue. "So what are the chances of bringing Rena Chenowyth back to trial for murdering my father?"

"Nil. Zilch." He spoke emphatically.

"What do you mean? She confessed on television!"

"She has already been tried. She can't be tried again for the same capital crime. That's double jeopardy."

When I insisted that confession was new evidence, and asked didn't that mean she could be tried again, he said, "The people of Utah don't want that." He reminded me that vast amounts of money were spent on the investigation and trials for my father's murder. "They put a man behind bars. Now they're sick of it and sick of polygamy. It's an embarrassment to Utah—surely you know that."

"Ervil said she was chosen for her beauty and it was a privilege to be called by God to kill him. She didn't even know my father!"

"I know. I'm sorry." He opened his hands to show he had given me all he could.

I asked if she could be charged with perjury since she had lied on the witness stand.

"The statute of limitations won't allow that. She lied nine years ago."

I had done a little homework. "The clock won't start ticking until her book comes out. We have two years from then."

"The County will not bring a nuisance suit against Rena," he said. "It won't do any good, anyway. It won't bring your father back." Then he added, "We already got the murderer. Ervil LeBaron killed your father."

There it was again, the elaborate social rationalization designed to overlook the power and significance of women. I fought for self-control. "A trial could hold this woman accountable for the ways she supported a system that works against life. And a trial could make up for some of the injustices done to my family by the state of Utah. It could send the message that my father's life was worth something—that he was a good man and he didn't deserve to be killed."

David Yocom shook his head. "I'm sorry."

Three weeks later, my Uncle Matthew called. He is my father's youngest brother, active in the official Church of Jesus Christ of Latter-day Saints, the only one of my grandfather's sons by Grandmother Evelyn who had chosen not to live plural marriage. As a young man he'd served in the Marine Corps, surviving wounds incurred in the Pacific War, and he always had a favored place in my heart. I sometimes wondered if I had unconsciously chosen to marry a Marine because of Uncle Matthew.

"We've got to do something about this woman Rena," he said. "She is misrepresenting the Allred family. She's going to go on the Oprah Winfrey Show and she's already been on other talk shows making it seem that dear Rulon was in cahoots with Ervil LeBaron. Can you come meet with us and we'll plan to do something?"

That night I dreamed what had become a recurrent dream, that my father was following me through my house, trying to talk to me, and I was moving away from the sound of his voice, even putting my hands over my ears, attempting to avoid what he was saying. In this night's version of the dream, he cornered me in my youngest child's bedroom. He took me by the shoulders and turned me around, then took my face in his hands and looked into my eyes. 'What I'm asking you to do isn't for you. It isn't for the family. It isn't even for me. It's for Rena," he said. I woke up, my face wet. I wondered when I'd ever get a good night's sleep.

The next morning, as I drove down the mountain to teach a writing workshop at a Salt Lake City high school, a local radio station interviewed Rena promoting her book. She blithely announced that the book would be released on the thirteenth anniversary of my father's death—May 10, 1990. I was so incensed I almost rear-ended a car before I realized I had punched the gas-pedal to the floor.

I kept imagining Rena standing before a judge. Later that day, a colleague made the mistake of asking how I was. When I was through ranting about Rena Chenowyth, my colleague called her husband, an attorney. Doors flew open. Within an hour, I signed a complaint charging Rena Chenowyth with the wrongful death of my father. But how would we find Rena to serve her with a summons to appear in court? According to the interview I'd heard earlier that day, she had gone underground because the "lambs of God" were carrying out Ervil's orders to kill anyone who talked. Now the attorney indicated that we'd have to commit ten thousand dollars for a private investigator to find and serve her. In my family, ten thousand dollars might as well be a million. Words spoken on impulse came back to me, that I'd like to meet her on one of those talk shows and slap her with a lawsuit. The attorney loved the idea. I called Jess with the concept, and he began to work his magic as a communication trainer, yielding powerful results. By the time I arrived home that evening, I had an attorney, a lawsuit, and thanks to Jess, a date to confront Rena Chenowyth on the *Donahue Show* in two weeks—the last show of the season. Justice seemed so close I could smell its clean scent, something like fresh lime.

My attorney had a keen sense of the social issues pertaining to polygamous families in Utah. So relieved was I to have an advocate for my family that I slept deeply, eight hours a night for the rest of the week. The following week, the attorney called; he'd been given notice by his firm that he was attracting unwanted publicity, and he'd have to drop the case or lose his job. Would he help me find someone else? I asked. Yes, he would.

As it happened, Nelson Mandela was released from prison the next day. The free world celebrated. The following day, Winnie Mandela announced she was coming to America and the *Donahue* producers called to say I'd been bumped to make way for her appearance. Since this would be the last show of the season, I'd have to wait through the summer to confront Rena Chenowyth.

I knew I could not endure an entire summer without some kind of resolution. Seeing my face, Jess picked up the telephone. A few minutes later, he asked how I would feel about going on the *Sally Jesse Raphael Show*. Ten minutes after that, my original attorney called and said he'd found a replacement.

God himself could not have found a better attorney to represent my family than Jim McConkie. Jim agreed to go to New York City to stand by me and to present the legal issues on the show. The Sunday before we were scheduled to appear, he was appointed the bishop— the ecclesiastical leader of his local church or ward—so in many ways he also represented the Mormon people.

Jess and I had promised to take our children to the Shakespeare festival in Cedar City, Utah, that summer, and the trip to New York meant giving up our vacation time. Since his recovery from the war, Jess has become adamant about family time and we decided to bring the children. They would have a semblance of a family getaway and support me as I confronted the woman who had killed my father. I did not sleep on the plane to New York, nor did I sleep the night before the show. I spent the night on my knees, praying that I would know what to do and say, that I would accomplish what I was there to accomplish, and that I wouldn't bring more shame on my family.

Jim McConkie met us at the broadcast studio the next morning. Our two younger children, Brett and Clarissa, slept off jet lag in the greenroom, the picture of trusting innocence as the producers prepared me to go on the air. Jess and my older daughter, Maya, saw me through the hard questions about my relationship with my father, his death, and the circumstances that had brought me here. We watched in dismay as Rena stated her case to the television audience. She made it seem that she had no choice when she killed my father—that it was kill or be killed, and that she was in danger now. The audience asked why she would write a book that would put her in greater jeopardy. I had ploughed through every muddy sentence of the book and I knew that Ervil LeBaron had promised her she would not be punished. So far he'd been right. She'd gotten away with everything.

When it was time for us to go on the air, the producers ushered me onto the stage and seated me beside Rena. She put her hand on my arm and gazed at me with simpering sweetness, counting on me, I suppose, to adopt the fundamentalist aspect of Christ-like love. I stared down at her hand until she took it away. Then I met her eyes, where I saw the beginnings of fear. Although I hate to admit it, her trembling gave me a sweet jolt of vindication.

The time on the air passed quickly. After I emphasized that Rena had taken the life of a father, a healer, a kind man, Jim McConkie spoke about the turpitude of someone who would exploit a murder she had committed by lying on the witness stand, being acquitted, and then confessing in a book designed to make money. Rena's new husband and her cousin Tony were then introduced. Tony wore a panama hat and a fake moustache and sunglasses to protect him. (Although Rena's life was supposedly in danger also, she wore no disguise as she had when she first entered our lives.) After a set of go-nowhere questions directed at Tony and the husband, the audience redirected their attention to Rena. Delivering far more pointed questions than I could have posed, one person asked Rena why she had never asked forgiveness or said she was sorry. Another accused her of wanting to be the center of attention. And still another asked if she shouldn't be locked behind bars.

Then came the moment for which everything had been orchestrated. In my mind, this appearance was not about confronting my father's murderer on television. It was about holding her accountable in a court of justice. Two minutes before the show ended, a slender man in a tan uniform appeared from the audience. Hired by Jim McConkie, he was the constable there to serve Rena Chenowyth with a summons to answer civil charges that she had caused the wrongful death of Dr. Rulon Clark Allred. Clearly, Sally Jesse Raphael had no idea what was happening. She was openmouthed as Rena received the summons. Rena stared at the papers, then at me, then at the constable. Then the show was over, and Rena's husband guided her out the door. My children ran to me, and hugged my waist. My husband lifted me and swung me around. The producers urged us to move toward the dressing rooms, to safety. We could see Rena down the hall and hear her loud sobbing. At the end of the hall, she collapsed. I felt a stab of guilt.

Then we burst out the studio doors onto the streets of New York. My body ached everywhere; my brain pounded; my soul felt bruised. It felt very strange to have asked for justice for my father and accountability from the person who murdered him. After all my religious training in Christian charity and forgiveness, I wondered if I had done the wrong thing. My breath came in short, dizzying spurts and my heart skipped, stopped, then skipped again. As we walked to our hotel, a small man who looked to be from India stopped us. "God bless your family, sir," he said to my husband. That was the reassurance I needed. I took a breath and tears fell—of gratitude and relief and sorrow.

~

I believe that we often set ourselves up for life's lessons although we don't always enjoy the learning. Some media reports were sympathetic, but others suggested base motives, that we wanted money, or revenge. One news program made this assessment: "The Allred family seeks vengeance by taking their bitterness to court." As I reexamined the roots of such unwholesome media encounters, I considered my ongoing struggle with sensationalism. Although I resented the lurid light Rena's book had cast on my father and my family, I felt sullied by the brawling media, and I remembered what my father used to say: "If you lie down with pigs, you smell like them." People in Rena's group had called her "Queen of Sheba" and said she held herself above them. I had set myself up to stand out, to represent the family. I began to wonder if I had something in common with Rena. Perhaps it took being exposed on television to force me to examine my true motives in bringing Rena to trial.

As I did so, I concluded that I wasn't interested in money that would be forthcoming should our case succeed. Money would only generate disagreement among Uncle Anthus and the family members still in the group who would vote to give any settlement to the religious organization now formalized as the United Apostolic Brethren. By contrast, Saul and Jake and I would stand firm for an educational foundation for my father's grandchildren or something of that nature. I also knew that I wasn't committed to vengeance, since I had learned bitter lessons from the war in Vietnam. That moment of guilty delight when Rena collapsed after the Sally show reminded me that revenge isn't sweet enough to justify the energy it takes, and that it does not perpetuate life. While both of us had received strong doses of attention, I had in my repertoire many ways to be in the limelight that didn't require such unsavory confrontation. There had to be another reason I was pursuing this, perhaps the reason my father had expressed in my recurrent dream. If I mucked through this for Rena's sake (an idea I still found repugnant) what would come of it for me and my family? And how would such a process serve her? These questions took me to new depths, where I examined the nature of forgiveness. My participation in this trial, I decided, would allow me to forgive Rena—and forgive myself for having been more like her than I wanted to be. And perhaps when I had forgiven, she could be accountable for having taken the life of a good man.

Thus, I would not aim for any fringe benefits: not money or family unity or even the enlightenment of intolerant and ignorant people who made our lives so hard. I had to keep my motives pure, focused on the real issues—of forgiveness and accountability.

~

With the trial date set, the attorneys invited my father's heirs to participate, and about half of them chose to support the action. But I discovered the full meaning of "plaintiff" as the psychological weight of the trial rested on me. I absorbed the disapproval of those who disagreed with what we were doing. I created agreement for the attorney to interview members of the family. I helped the attorneys dredge up issues that might be useful in the actual trial.

The trial began February 2, 1992. The groundhog saw his shadow, and Utah citizens braced themselves for another six weeks of winter. After jury selection, a dozen people—most of them Mormon—sat in the box. Rena Chenowyth did not show up for the trial. She said that her life was in danger and I was grateful that she did not risk her life to answer our summons; I did not want her death on my conscience. I was also grateful that I did not have to confront her in person again. I didn't want this trial to be more difficult than it had to be.

Several of my sisters were called as witnesses, and so was my mother's twin sister, Aunt Emma, my father's nurse. She had seen him die, had knelt beside him and begged him to speak to her when it was too late. She seemed thankful for one more chance to rectify things. Pain distorted her features as she remembered watching her husband die, but peace shone from her when she closed her testimony.

The night before I was scheduled to testify, I attended a meeting of my writing group. After our workshop, I stood in the hall, answering their questions. They wanted to know what the family would be asking in the way of damages.

"Are you really asking for seven million dollars?" they asked. They seemed amazed by the most recent media speculation.

"I don't think we've set an amount," I said. "We're going to leave it up to the jury."

"But how could she ever pay seven million dollars? It's not like her book was successful. It was an awful book," someone said.

"It isn't about the money," I explained for the hundredth time. "It's about the principle—that people shouldn't be able to commit murder, lie on the witness stand, then write a book and make money from the murder they got away with. And it's about my family's citizenship—we want to see that no one else has to go through the torment we've experienced."

I felt anxious, eager to get home from the writing workshop before the scrim of snow became a blizzard. I hoped to get a good night's sleep so I would be clear and effective the next day. Suddenly I realized I had left my purse behind and started down the hall to retrieve it.

But it wasn't the hall. It was a flight of stairs. As I fell I remembered the degenerating disks in my neck, the part of my body, my doctor told me, most likely to be injured in an accident. I was falling sideways, sure to break my neck. I'm going to die, I thought. And then I thought, I can't die tonight—I have to testify tomorrow! Until that moment, I hadn't thought much about angels. But unseen hands seemed to be turning me so that I somersaulted backward, tail over teacup, down a steep flight of fourteen stairs. I came to a stop sitting upright on the cement floor, my arms and legs straight out in front of me like a doll's. "I'm okay," I sang up the stairs. I stood quickly, more embarrassed than hurt. To prove it, I hurried back up the stairs. My writer friends fussed over me. Outside, the snow came faster, heavier. "I have to go," I said.

I got into my little car and started up Parley's Canyon, headed for my house in Park City. In the funneling winds of the canyon, the snow swirled madly, reducing visibility to nothing. I couldn't even see the white lines of the highway. I had no idea where I was, or how much danger I was in. It dawned on me that in addition to the swirling snow, my vision wasn't working too well. Finally I turned around at a ranch exit and made my way back down, past the cliffs at Suicide Rock.

When at last I could see, I spied a grocery store near my mother's house. My head had cleared enough for me to realize that I had a concussion. My neck hurt something fierce. I decided to go inside and ask the pharmacist to give me something to help me sleep, then go to my mother's to spend the night.

The pharmacist, a middle-aged woman who blinked and pursed her mouth, seemed about to tell me "no."

"Please," I said, "I'm a witness in the trial of the woman who killed my father, and I have to testify tomorrow, but I have a bad neck since I rolled my car two years ago. Tonight I fell down the stairs and there's a white-out in the canyon and I can't get home. . . ."

She looked alarmed, as if she thought I might pull a gun, then phoned another drugstore for my prescription. She shook two tablets into a brown bottle. "No charge," she said.

I called my husband, Jess, and described my predicament. He offered to come down the canyon to get me. I wanted him to hold me more than anything, then I thought of the swirling snow, of waiting another hour, maybe longer, and the long ride home—if we could get home. I told him I'd spend the night at my mother's.

Her house was empty. Then I realized she was next door with Aunt Emma who had been ill. Surveying myself in the bathroom mirror, I found bruises here and there, then settled in my old bedroom. Just as I was falling asleep, I recalled a television movie about a woman who fell downstairs and lay on a backboard in an emergency room while all around her medical personnel attended to gunshot and knife wounds. As she waited to be x-rayed, she fell asleep, her head rolled to one side and the broken vertebrae transected her spinal cord, leaving her paralyzed from the neck down. My eyes popped open and I worried that the same thing could happen to me. I stood stiffly and went to the phone, dialed information and the nearest hospital emergency room. Could I have a broken neck and not know it? Yes, they said. It happens all too often. People will stand up after an accident, think they're fine, then collapse. What shall I do? I asked. Just stay there. Don't move. Keep your neck straight. We'll be there shortly. No sirens, I said. My mother is next door and she doesn't know I am here. If you come with sirens screaming, you'll give her a heart attack.

Minutes later they arrived with the lights flashing bright against the night. They hurried into the dark house, where I stood in my mother's orange polyester bathrobe, and loaded me onto a backboard.

At the hospital I lay stiff and straight for two hours waiting for an x-ray technician. I could hear the workers chatting in another room. "Hey," I shouted. "I'm freezing! I'm tired! How about getting me an x-ray technician? I have to testify tomorrow at 9:00 at the trial of the person who killed my father." They looked at me as if they heard this story every time someone was admitted to the hospital with a neck complaint.

At five-thirty, still no x-ray technician. "Look, I'm not kidding. I have to meet with the attorney at 8:00 to go over my testimony. If you don't get me out of here, I won't be able to finish this—and it's been fifteen years of grief." Finally, they wheeled me down the hall to the x-ray room. At 6:00 the technician showed up with his hair askew. The news was just coming on the television in the waiting room across the hall. The x-ray technician was grumpy, as most people are when suddenly awakened.

"So where's the fire?" he said.

I repeated the story I had told six people already.

He looked at me skeptically. "You have to testify where?"

I told him again. "Please hurry. I've been living with this for almost fifteen years."

"Sure," he said. I could tell he still didn't believe me.

Just then my face came on the television. The reporter was asking me about my family's motives in going to trial and I was telling him it was about the principle of the thing—about not allowing a murderer to exploit the crime. "Look—that's me!" I said to the technician.

He looked at the television screen, then back at me. "It *is* you!" He was astonished.

"I told you."

"Yes, you did." He hurried then, and within minutes processed my x-rays. A doctor pronounced my neck unbroken, prescribed a pain reliever for stretched ligaments and something else for mild concussion. Then I stood at the door of the hospital wearing blue paper hospital slippers, my hair sticking straight up in back from lying on the board in one position for four hours, dressed in my mother's orange robe. I had asked my brother-in-law to take me to my mother's house so that I could get my car and dress for the day. As I waited in the cold dawn, a well-groomed man in a dark suit walked past me. He stopped, turned, looked me up and down, assessed my orange robe, my straight-up hair, my blue paper slippers.

"Looks like you had one rough date last night, lady," he said with a charming smile.

❧

The trial ended before the day was through. At six P.M. the jurors— nine men and women, all of them Mormon—returned a verdict of guilty of wrongful death. To deter future abuses, they assessed 50 million dollars in punitive damages and an additional 2.5 million in personal losses. The jury watched the plaintiff's table where I sat, letting vindication wash over me like salt water, at once bracing and burning on a lifetime of wounds. I put my hand over my mouth to stifle a sob of relief. It was over. We had taken possession of our citizenship. To some degree my father's goodness had been recognized. And Rena Chenowyth had been held accountable for the crime she had committed, as well as the crime of reviving our pain.

We did not attempt to collect, not a single cent, even though Rena collaborated with Detective Dick Forbes to make a TV movie with herself as a victim of circumstance and Dick Forbes as the hero distilled from many committed lawmen who helped to bring Ervil

LeBaron to justice. My family felt that collecting anything from Rena would be accepting "blood money" and they wanted none of it. Even the attorneys were respectful of our wishes, and didn't try to collect anything, not even their contingency fees.

Years later, the Goldman family called upon our case against Rena Chenowyth as a precedent for preventing O.J. Simpson from making money through the death of their son, Ronald. This, more than anything, made me feel clean and strong and vindicated. We had proved ourselves as citizens.

I am still living with the basic question: Was my father's death the will of men or the intention of God? I have looked for a shape that renders meaning, and I must confess that nothing I see makes up for the loss of my father—that firm hug, that matter-of-fact voice, those sentient hands. I must look in my heart, because that's the only place I can find an answer. On this path called Forgiveness, I think I've reached the home stretch: the part that teaches us to let go and leave it to heaven.

FOUR

Interface

 WHEN I ENTERED A MONOGAMOUS marriage, many members of my family disowned me. Perhaps they felt I was a coward or a traitor, but I saw my leave-taking as an act of loyalty—to myself and, ultimately, to the community. I began writing about my family, and my father gave me his blessing to publish, with the admonition that I present the Allred family as "a good and saintly people." However constrained, my early writing helped me discover my voice and the responsibility of speaking out. Apparently, my coming forward invited others in the polygamous underground to contact me and I began to receive anonymous phone calls, nearly all of them from women. They seemed to be asking permission to be honest, in addition to asking for help, and the burden of their confidence weighed on me.

"I read what you wrote. You know how hard the Principle is, but every father was not as kind as yours. Every time I spoke up to my father—and sometimes when I didn't—he beat me."

"In our family the father gets the virgins before he gives them in marriage. They're his girls, after all. But it seems wrong for a man to do that with his daughters. Do you think it's wrong?"

In a voice disturbingly familiar, "My uncle molested me and now he's after my daughters. The brethren won't do anything about it. They don't listen to me."

"If I complain, my husband stops giving me money and the children go without. I can't go to the state for help like other people; the state will take the kids away."

The sound of someone calling up from a well: "I'm so discouraged I could die. No one loves me. Don't tell me to ask God for help. He got me into this in the first place."

These women and their stories haunted me. I felt like I needed to do something, but I didn't know how and what. So I did what I could see to do: I called a discreet social worker; I distributed small amounts of money from very private sources; I located refuge or hospitalization if a life was on the line. But it was too little. And I suspect it was too late for some. The women rarely divulged more than a first name, and often wouldn't give out phone numbers or addresses. Perhaps they were afraid that I would betray them to their priesthood leaders.

Closer to home, I knew of the terrible impoverishment of Aunt Rose and her children, but in my writing I had skimmed over deeper secrets and darker issues. I had allowed my father's dictum that I present the family "as a good and saintly people" to supersede the truth, unconsciously selecting facts to support my father's view of life. One of the lovely lies I had perpetuated was that our family was happy, living in a little Eden where lions lie down with lambs. In this blissful garden, persecution came from outsiders, not from members of the family. But now I had discovered another story to tell.

As more truths surfaced, my awareness grew. The choices facing me were the same I had always had: to commiserate in silence or to deepen my knowledge and expose the lies. And so I am telling these stories. I do not know if I tell them for my loved ones or for the world or for myself. But I do know that it is wrong to pretend *not* to know, for knowledge implies responsibility—the ability of the individual to respond.

Some things have changed for those whose stories I tell in these next pages. Some have died. Some have been reborn. Some brothers and sisters are freer while some are in greater bondage. Some have transcended and forgiven instances of victimization, while others remain trapped in grief and disappointment. Some have taken heroic journeys and accepted huge responsibilities for healing the polygamous subculture. A few are predators, distorting doctrines for their own purposes. I claim them all, in the blind way that the heart chooses even while the mind knows the truth. My wish for them, for all of us, is that we find a way to live together as loving members of the same family.

Clutches of the Pond

ONE OF THE FIRST LESSONS the children in my father's family learned was the danger of going near the water. My father said that it was the Devil's domain, and he refused to go swimming without his temple garments for fear of being affected by the spirit of evil. I don't know what scripture or doctrine he'd read to corroborate this attitude toward bodies of water. Perhaps he converted the mythic subversions of Neptune or Pluto to Christian terms. Or perhaps he was drawing on tragic experience, conclusions made when my half-sister Marie drowned in the pond behind our house and my father's youngest wife, Aunt Melissa, sobbed over the small wet body. My father could not call Marie back, not even with a priesthood blessing.

At roughly the same time we learned to distrust water, we also learned to distrust the world beyond our gates. As each of us acquired the ability to speak in sentences, we also learned to submerge the truth in order to protect the family. At first, keeping the family secret was like hiding a treasure, something precious to tuck away with the river rocks and barrettes beneath the underwear in the one drawer that was mine. "My father has seven wives," I would whisper to the girl reflected in the pond behind the house, and her eyes would shine with the secret.

I had to move through the reeds to see my reflection in the pond, and sometimes I would slip and get my feet wet, a mistake that could get me a green-willow switching. I knew I was not supposed to be there by myself, that I could be pulled down by the moss as Marie had been. She was only a month older than I and we had been playing together that day. Although I was only a toddler, it seemed I could remember her spirit caught in wings of sunlight, rising from the pond. The memory of her death combined with the religious taboo to make the pond mysterious, lending significance to the fish and ducks and water lilies.

Marie's absence left a hollow place in my life that made the days stretch out long and dim, even when Aunt Rose's daughter, Lorinda, sought me out and taught me new pastimes. Lorinda was three years older, and when I was three or four years old, she introduced me to the world of dress-ups and fantasy, her favorite being the game of doctor, where she usually played the role of my father, and I was her nurse; together we saved our dolls or the babies in the family from burning buildings and car wrecks, from dreadful diseases or drowning in ponds. Lorinda would put on our father's old white shirt and pull her blonde curls back with a rubber band; she did look something like my father then, her eyes a paler shade of blue, her curls giving off the same platinum sheen. Lorinda's companionship became especially important when mosquito clutches at the pond's edge began to hatch. According to my father, the mosquitoes carried deadly diseases. Since he was our doctor as well as our father and spiritual leader, he made us stay inside during the hatch even on the hottest evenings, feeling claustrophobic and frightened, just as when a raid was threatening.

Lorinda had an imagination both delightful and dreadful, full of dragons and witches, crazy people and wild monsters. She had made up outrageous lies about our family–that our father was a king who kept his children in cow stalls and fed them oats from the mangers, that Aunt Adah was a witch who fed children poisoned birthday cake, that her own mother, Aunt Rose, had been a mermaid cast onto the shores of the Great Salt Lake. But she also would boldly state forbidden facts: that she had more than thirty brothers and sisters, that her mother was the second wife, that her grandfather had headed a huge group of polygamists in Short Creek before he died. When Lorinda told someone at school about our family and the principal called my father in to explain, the mothers and my father had an emergency meeting and decided it was time to take action before the girl ruined our lives. She was sent downstairs to live with Aunt LaVerne, who was happy to teach Lorinda a thing or two. But Lorinda longed for her own mother, Aunt Rose, who by now had so many children she couldn't keep track of them.

The truth is, we children could not stop deceiving, just as my father and his seven wives could not stop conceiving. Their commitment was to raise up a Righteous Seed unto the Lord. Our commitment was similarly impossible—to keep from telling the truth without actually lying. Lies were forbidden by the religion, but a few drops of undiluted truth would give the authorities sufficient evidence to rip us away from our parents. So we mixed fact with story until we could scarcely remember what was real.

The temptation to blurt out the truth sometimes seized me like vertigo. I'd be standing before strangers, keeping my mouth shut, and suddenly I'd be overcome with a terrifying impulse to utter forbidden realities: "My dad has seven wives. I'm the twenty-eighth child in his family. He went to prison and my mother went to jail." In those days, it didn't occur to me that my yearning to tell the truth was an instinct to survive. I didn't know that lies can smother life the way moss can choke the fish and frogs and water lilies right out of a pond.

Throughout my childhood, the injunction against speaking out was so strong, I can feel it now as I search for words—my heart hitching, my blood flowing hot and fast as though I've been poisoned by something that will either kill or save me. I have heard that heartworm, a disease carried by mosquitos, can only be cured by a dose of arsenic. The arsenic must be measured carefully: too much, and the patient dies of heart failure; too little and the heartworm survives and kills the host. I think of Lorinda and of pond hatches, and I wonder how to dispense this medicine called truth, knowing that it can be a poison that will stop the heart before it cleanses the blood.

My current preoccupation with ponds has been prompted by a dream about Lorinda. In the dream I am on a crosstown bus, vaguely disturbed that I must travel with strangers. But then Lorinda touches my shoulder. She sits at my left hand, eyes enormous behind her thick glasses. Lorinda smiles in her knowing way, as though she has swallowed a slice of life that I will never taste. Then, with a chill I realize that Lorinda's mother, Aunt Rose—who died when I was sixteen—sits at my right. She emits her native odors of baking bread and river grass. As she casts her slow, dark gaze over me, I wonder why she walks the shadow world, why she isn't firmly situated beside my father, in the Celestial Kingdom. The other mothers have envied her the extra time they assume she enjoys with him on the Other Side, but I can see that she is tormented and very much alone. Her black eyes plead with me, and I know by the heaviness in my chest that what she asks of me won't be easy. Then the bus begins to fill with water and Aunt Rose keeps smiling in that sad way as the water covers our hands, our shoulders, our mouths. Suddenly I remember that Aunt Rose and her children cannot swim; I'm the only one who can save them. When I awaken gasping, Aunt Rose's bitter smile persists, piercing my heart, taking me back to that time when our family scattered to the four winds.

The family had already survived so much. We had lived through my father's time in prison, twice had fled to Mexico. The persecutions had made us grateful for our Salt Lake compound and for each other. We had been living happily together when the summer of 1955 began, but by mid-summer the high, bright dome that protected our lives was shattered by the threat of another polygamist roundup. We packed up and scattered across the Rocky Mountain states. My father and Aunt Sally became caretakers of an estate on Flathead Lake in Montana, where he posed as a monogamist. He must have worried about Aunt Rose because he moved her big family as close as he dared—onto a small farm in the Mission Mountains, seventy miles away. No one passed through the glacial canyon that connected them except, sometimes, a Flathead Indian driving a truckload of sheep to Missoula.

What was my father thinking when he moved Aunt Rose to such an isolated spot? Aunt Rose had married at fifteen with no experience keeping house or raising children. Her own mother had died giving birth to her and her twin (who also died) leaving Rose in the care of the childless first wife. Rose's father had been the head of the fundamentalist group and he may have sensed my father's destiny as the next spiritual leader, or perhaps he had some other reason to press for Rose's early marriage. The young doctor, recently separated from his first wife and newly married to Aunt LaVerne, had postponed consummation so that Rose could mature physically and emotionally before she began to bear children. But Rose had an earthy, sensual nature, and a strong desire to prove herself as a mother in Israel. At seventeen she had mastered her one domestic art of making bread like ambrosia, and then she gave birth to Malcolm; thereafter, she never really learned to keep house or anything else. She had barely survived when we all lived together, with Aunt LaVerne and the others helping her out. Now she was isolated in the cold shadows of the Mission Mountains.

Certainly one reason my father moved Aunt Rose so far from civilization had to do with her talkative children, what with the raids continuing. Even Lorinda, bright and imaginative as she was, couldn't seem to get the hang of hiding our lives from the neighbors. On the mountain overlooking the small town of Ronan there were no neighbors to tell. The house itself was a well-kept secret—tucked deep in evergreen beside a pond with no apparent bottom. The silence that hung over the farm was broken only by birds speaking an idiom of sky.

Soon after they moved in, Lorinda wrote me a letter on a Big

Nickel pad in large printing. She wrote that she'd been baptized. She had drawn the dark pond beyond the house, my father and herself as two stick figures, her hair like the reeds that fringed the pond, the picture cut through with blue lines. My father brought me Lorinda's letter when he visited us in Nevada. He seemed satisfied with himself; at last everyone was settled and he had a job. Over supper he reported that when he moved Aunt Rose to the farmhouse near Ronan, the first thing he did was order all the kids down to the pond. He gestured at the dark water and reminded them about Marie and told them again of Satan's power over water. The children nodded fearfully; no one had taught them how to swim.

And then he turned to Malcolm, who was sixteen—the oldest child of my father's plural families. Unlike my tall blond father, Malcolm was swarthy and short. He had a peculiar habit of grinning vacantly at the ground. Nonetheless, my father told him, "Malcolm, it's your responsibility to watch over your sisters and brothers. Take care of them when I'm not here." My father was idealistic; he found humility in the way Malcolm bowed his head, and didn't notice Malcolm's way of smiling into his own chin.

Before my father baptized Lorinda, he set Malcolm apart as a priest so that he had the authority to prepare and bless the sacrament and head the family in my father's absence. And then my father turned to pale, thin Ren, four years younger than Malcolm but half a foot taller—Ren, with his deep quiet energy and shy grin. My father ordained Ren a deacon with responsibility for the family's spiritual welfare, the duty of reminding everyone to pray and to study the scriptures.

Then my father baptized Lorinda. Before he left, everyone followed him into the kitchen, the only room with a stick of furniture, for it was necessary to confirm Lorinda's baptism. They dried her hair and wrapped her in a blanket, then gathered around as my father put his hands on her head and commanded her to receive the Holy Ghost. Afterward, the boys helped him move mattresses from the truck onto the wooden floor of the living room. In the only bedroom, my father set up a bed frame of cinder blocks for Aunt Rose and the babies. He dropped a fifty-pound bag of flour, another of potatoes, and another of carrots in the empty pantry. He stopped at the door and pointed out a space where they might plant a garden, and talked about the pond as a kind of hatchery where they could plant carp or trout for Sunday dinners. If they had to, he said, they could survive on what the farm produced just as his family had done when he was a boy in the remote woods of Canada.

"All it takes is a little hard work," he said. He kissed them all, including the boys, and said he would be back to see them soon. Then he drove through the twilight toward Flathead Lake where Aunt Sally was waiting.

Some time passed before my father could make the seventy-mile drive to Ronan again. Chopping wood and fixing fences for the rich owner of the Flathead estate wore him out. And for the first time in the fifteen years they'd been married, Aunt Sally had him to herself. Before long the snow flew and winter hunkered deep in the Mission Mountains. My father didn't get word from Ronan, but Aunt Rose wasn't the type to take initiative. She had no phone. She didn't write. She never did tell him that anything was wrong.

The third summer of our scattered years, Lorinda and Ren visited us in Nevada when my father made his quarterly visit. The children had slept on the sacks of flour and powdered milk he carried in the back of his station wagon and when they were awake, they rode beside him and combed his hair and asked questions on the long drive. My father parked his car a block from our house to throw off suspicion, and Lorinda darted ahead through the rain, sneaking up the back stairs and peering into the kitchen until my father and Ren came up behind her. She stood like a blurred reflection of herself, all covered with raindrops, and I could not believe my eyes.

A shadow crossed my mother's face when she saw Aunt Rose's children standing there dripping all over the linoleum. By way of apology, my father whispered that both Ren and Lorinda had been overcome with tears when he visited them on the way down, that they had clung so close he couldn't bear to leave them behind. It wasn't easy to share what little time we had with my father, but I was truly glad to see Ren and Lorinda. For one thing, Ren was my brother Danny's age; Danny would be too busy showing off for Ren to bother with teasing me. And getting some time with my favorite playmate restored a little of my lost home in Utah. Even though Lorinda was one of Aunt Rose's unkempt brood, she was smarter than ever and quick as a ferret; her delicate beauty had gone from pink to pale in the years since we left home.

My mother eyed Lorinda's wet feet, told her to take her shoes off, and gave her a pair of her own white anklets. She made Ren take off his wet shirt and put on one of Danny's. After she'd toweled my father's hair dry, she put on an apron and washed her hands. Then she whipped powdered milk into a pan full of water and set it on low heat. She cut neat slices of homemade bread, and spread a thin coating of peanut butter on each slice. She halved the sandwiches and arranged them on a blue and white platter. She mixed cocoa and sugar and water together and stirred the mixture into the heated milk, then added a teaspoon of vanilla and a dash of salt and beat it until it frothed. She opened two quart-jars of peaches and we sat down with the weary travelers to eat supper.

As soon as my father had said the blessing, Ren began wolfing his food. It shocked us, for Ren had always been the most docile of Aunt Rose's children, the one inclined to wait for permission. Back home, when Danny and the other boys were spanked for wading through the swamp in their Sunday shoes, Ren had watched, his feet dry and his eyes sad as though he could not decide which he regretted most— their punishment or his lack of participation. Of Aunt Rose's family, Ren was the one most like my father—spiritual, fastidious, nervous in the reflective way of zealots and visionaries. Now my father spoke in sharp surprise. "Where are your manners, young man?" Ren's mouth parted but no words came out. That was when I first noticed his twitch—the left eye blinking like a yellow caution light. My father asked in a gentler tone: "Don't you remember how to behave in other people's homes, son?" Ren's eye opened and shut, opened and shut, as if the effort of thinking sent a spasm through his face. The sense that Ren's eye had been unhinged from the rest of him left a sick spot in my stomach. Was this what leaving home had done to us?

"C'mon," Danny said to Ren. "Let's go downtown." And without asking permission from my father, Danny left the table. My father looked up, startled. Ren's eye blinked furiously. Danny put on his jacket, threw another to Ren and fixed him with an impatient stare. Ren blinked and fidgeted, shoved an entire half-sandwich into his mouth and pulled on the jacket. Danny threw back his shoulders in a kind of challenge, and strolled past my father, giving him plenty of opportunity to stop them. My father studied the half-empty bowl of peaches as if it were newsprint. The boys slammed the door behind them, leaving an offended silence in their wake.

At last my father spoke. "These children are getting out of hand," he said. "Along with everything else." He stared at what was left of the sandwiches. His eyes were lined in red, and we all felt what he didn't say aloud—that the family standard had slipped since we'd scattered.

My mother had flushed to her hairline, her eyes dark with humiliation as though she suspected he was speaking of her children–which he might have been. But then my father sighed and resumed eating, suddenly ravenous and talking almost as hungrily, stuffing food into one cheek while he finished his sentences. He gave a quick sketch of life with each of his other families. Sally, of course, was well. (Who wouldn't be, I thought jealously, with Daddy there all the time?) Aunt Melissa was expecting again, a real blessing considering that she'd not recovered from the loss of Marie. Aunt Adah and Aunt LaVerne both had jobs, but each had committed the minor sin of buying new furniture, instead of giving their surplus to the family's United Order. "How am I supposed to make ends meet?" he complained. "Those who live to the Most Holy Principle won't live the United Order! God's Laws are God's Laws. We don't get to pick and choose!" His spoon rattled against the bowl as he pushed his dishes away.

"I . . . I can give you the money from my piano lessons," my mother said. My heart skipped a beat. My mother's meager earnings kept the lights on, the coal bin full. How could she even think of giving away what little we had?

My father shook his head. "You're doing all you can. I just wish everyone was doing as much." He glanced at Lorinda, who ate silently, her eyes huge and round behind her thick glasses. I wondered why she couldn't see very well, since most of my father's children had perfect sight. I thought of Aunt Rose who never did get glasses or false teeth, though she needed both.

Lorinda concentrated wholly on her food, sliding each peach slice around in her mouth like a goldfish before she sucked it down. She sipped hot chocolate until it was gone, then ran her tongue over the rim. She took small bites of sandwich, carefully tasting each mouthful. When she finished her sandwich, she pressed crumbs with her fingertips and licked her fingers clean. Then she stood. Although she was only eleven-going-on-twelve, her breasts and hips curved like a woman's.

"Thank you, Aunt Ella," Lorinda said emphatically. "That was the best supper I've ever had."

My mother blushed. Perhaps her carefully hidden resentment was confounded by Lorinda's gratitude. "It was only peanut butter and hot chocolate."

"It was the best thing I've ever tasted," Lorinda insisted.

"Oh, Lorinda, don't you remember some of our grand dinners at the white house—all of us sitting down to turkey with the trimmings?"

Lorinda cocked her head. "Anything's better than carrots," she said, and stole a look at my father who thumbed through some papers he had taken out of his wallet. "All we've had for a month is carrots."

"You girls go on now," my father said without looking up. "Play some games."

My mother nodded, lowering her eyes. "It's all right. I'll do the dishes."

My father murmured as we left, "I'm afraid those kids have gone hungry. Malcolm won't fish or hunt to save his life—let alone anyone else's. And I just couldn't get down there. . . ."

We went to my mother's bedroom and curled on the white chenille spread. Unlike our younger days when we chattered so fast we ran over each other's sentences, Lorinda and I sat in stagnating silence.

"So," I said finally, with the brightness I had learned to force into my voice, "how do you like Montana?"

Lorinda blinked. "I don't."

"You—but you live so close to Daddy," I said.

"Daddy lives on the moon," Lorinda said.

"I'd trade places with you in a minute."

"Okay," she said simply. "Then you can see how things really are."

Her words routed hidden memories, little creatures running from a forest fire. I knew that I had always been special to my father, a favored child; this created a mix of delight and guilt. But when I came down with the red measles, my father didn't come to take care of me. A strange doctor looked beneath my nightgown and listened to my heart. And the next winter when I burned with fever for days on end, my father did not come with his herbs and healing hands. Others needed him, my mother said, and detailed his excuses: Aunt Sally was about to give birth, someone else had rheumatic fever, another was down with strep throat. My father had been too busy for me. Somehow, between the fever and the disappointment, my sight had dimmed; now I had to sit in the front row to see the blackboard. Someday I would wear glasses; maybe they'd be thick as Lorinda's. Was this what she meant by seeing things as they really are?

"So . . . we can trade places and Malcolm can take care of you, too." Lorinda gave me a half-lidded look.

I shook my head. I didn't understand. I didn't want to understand. "Well, I couldn't leave my mother. Neither could you."

"Yes I could," she said. Her words were sure, clipped.

"How could you do that?"

"I've lived away before. I could live with Aunt LaVerne again."

"But Aunt LaVerne's four hundred miles away. You hated living with her at the white house. Why go there now?"

She shrugged. "There's stuff I didn't know."

"I thought you wanted to live with your mother."

Her smile stretched and broke. Something about her seemed damaged beyond repair, a ruined quality that did not fit the family portrait of being strong enough to "endure to the end." It didn't fit with our belief that through Jesus and the Plan of Redemption, nothing was ever beyond repair.

"Have you told Daddy that you don't like Montana?"

She squeezed her eyes shut and put her hands over her mouth. A sound escaped.

I wanted to cry too. "You must be homesick. I know how that feels." I took a breath. "Sometimes . . . when I miss home . . . and everybody . . . I close my eyes and imagine we're playing together again. Or I talk to someone—Saul or Jake or Mama—and I feel better." I touched her on the knee.

Lorinda jumped and her eyes flew open.

"Is there anybody that helps you feel happy?" I asked.

She thought a minute. "Ren's my good brother. Sometimes we sit beside the pond and talk."

"Well," and I patted her shoulder, "that's it, then. Go with Ren. Then you won't be homesick." There, I had handled it in my father's way, with shining advice. He would be proud of me. Our talk turned to what would happen when Lorinda started junior high school in the fall.

"You're lucky," I pouted. "You don't have to go to school when it snows."

Lorinda's gave me a blurry smile. "Those are the worst days," she said.

"I love to stay home from school."

"I'll never get to be a doctor if I don't go to school. And there's nothing to eat at home."

That stopped me. I sat miserably while Lorinda bounced her knee in a syncopated rhythm and twirled a lock of her platinum hair so tight I thought it would break. Then I had an idea.

"What if your mother could earn money, like my mother does giving piano lessons? Aunt Rose makes the best bread I ever tasted. She could sell it."

Lorinda looked over her shoulder. "She doesn't even bake bread for us anymore."

In our way of life, the industrious beehive was sacred, and laziness was a sin. "Put Your Shoulder to the Wheel" was one of my father's favorite hymns. "What does she do all day?"

"Lies in bed and looks at the ceiling."

I remembered what my mother had told me about Aunt Rose and Aunt LaVerne: that my father had met and planned to marry Aunt Rose first. But Aunt LaVerne became the legal wife, marrying him three days before Rose. Something to do with Rose's youth and lack of education and how LaVerne would be able to meet the public as the doctor's wife. Perhaps something in Aunt Rose had been broken when her wedding date was changed. Or maybe she had been broken even before my father agreed to marry her. I thought of my sicknesses, and how my father had not come when I needed him. Then I thought of him moving Aunt Rose and her children so far from everyone. My head ached, and a voice inside me shouted, stop thinking!

But I wanted to help Lorinda. Malcolm was older than my brother Saul who worked at Chevron even though he was student body president and a star athlete. "Couldn't Malcolm work and give your mother the money? He could work in that little town and come home on the weekends."

Lorinda's eyes brightened. "Maybe . . . I'll bet Daddy could make him go live in town. Yes!" She clapped her hands. "He could go to work and buy me some school clothes. That's the least he could do. I hate him so much!!" She stopped suddenly, as if confused.

I stared. My mother's sons were full of vinegar, terrible teases. But wonderful, too, always making me laugh. I couldn't imagine hating them.

"Why are you so mad at Malcolm?" I asked.

She studied the bedspread. "Why? Because he's bad."

I didn't know much about bad, although I had always been certain that the authorities who tried to break up our family were bad. But since we moved to Nevada, I had run into some stuff I knew was bad: the man who tore his clothes off outside the Silver Spur and screamed about spiders crawling all over him; the new baby crying beyond the thin wall of our duplex and the man with the red moustache yelling, "Make that kid stop or I will!" and the whack and the scream and the mother crying and another whack. We chewed our nails and paced, wondering what to do, but we didn't dare call the police for fear that they'd start asking about our family. The dark pool of horror that kept me awake that night mirrored the feeling I had now about Malcolm. How could someone so small, so quiet, be bad? He had never joined in the mischief of Saul and Jake and Danny, had always stayed on the periphery, grinning vacantly. They ignored him, mostly. Made fun of him a little. What could have happened to him since we left home? Had he taken up smoking foul-smelling cigars like the red-mustached man who beat his wife and baby? Did he steal like the boy who'd been arrested in Lundberg's Drug Store last week? Did he drink like the Silver Spur man with his invisible spiders?

"What does Malcolm do that's bad?"

"He thinks he can . . . make us do stuff."

"You mean . . . he bosses you? Makes you do his chores?" I thought of my brother Danny who just last night had barricaded me in the kitchen until I washed the dishes—even though it was his turn.

Lorinda pinched the skin on her arms and giggled. "I was kidding."

"You were kidding?" Relief and disappointment all at once. In our family, bad behavior was unacceptable. With our father being the head of the group, we had to be the example, the Righteous Seed. But it was difficult, always doing our best. Another example might open an easier path.

"Don't you get tired of always working for A's?" I blurted. "I do!"

Lorinda raised her eyebrows above the rims of her glasses. The look told me she'd never get tired of working for A's. She looked at the white anklets my mother had given her. "I really need some school clothes. . . ." She looked down at the dingy white shirt. "Nothing fits me anymore. I have to wear Ren's clothes."

With this kind of permission I stared at the phenomena I had been carefully avoiding since Lorinda first arrived. She watched me watching her, a kind of smugness in her eyes, as though she had waited for this attention.

"Do you want to see them?" she asked. I didn't know what to say. My face felt hot.

She lifted the white shirt and showed me her breasts. I looked and quickly looked away. In my mother's house I was surrounded by boys, and my mother was a private woman. The sight of Lorinda's inverted white blossoms leaning into the light repulsed and thrilled me. Lorinda waited expectantly, her blouse drawn up. I didn't know what to say. I got up and left the room. I don't know if I spoke to Lorinda during the rest of that visit.

~

Later that summer, after my baptism in the cold, clear Flathead Lake, we went to visit Aunt Rose near Ronan. The farm was beautiful, the old house situated so that the sun filtered through the bedroom windows to wake you up, and then, late in the day, warmed the living room and kitchen when the family was huddled over books or stretched out playing cards on the hardwood floor. The windows of old, wavy glass gave the air a greenish tinge, so that wherever you were you felt like you were underwater in that house.

Aunt Rose greeted us with dull eyes and a half-smile, though she loved my mother and once told her that she was the only one of her sister-wives who didn't look down on her. My mother apologized for our visit, patting Aunt Rose's hand and saying, "We won't stay long. I know how hard it is to have company when you're at your wit's end."

My mother and I went to the kitchen to help Aunt Rose prepare lunch. But the kitchen and pantry shelves were bare, with only a few withered potatoes and a nearly empty sack of weevil-ridden cornmeal. My father went to the car and hoisted sacks of flour and powdered milk on either shoulder. Then he lugged in a five-gallon can of honey and a bushel of apricots he had picked from our orchard in Utah. My mother pitched in and helped Aunt Rose make bread. We ate lunch sitting at the table on two plank boards propped on twenty-gallon drums. We ate hot scones made from the rising bread dough, with honey and a bowl of half-ripened apricots that crunched when we bit into their green-orange flesh.

"I'm so glad it's almost canning season," my mother said cheerily. "We just ate the last of our bottled fruit—it got us through the winter, though." She paused, but Aunt Rose said nothing. My mother tried again. "How have you been, Rose? I hear it's been a hard winter, and you with all these little ones—I don't know how you got through it alone."

Aunt Rose said nothing. My mother kept trying to get conversation started, but as quickly as the talk began, it died. My mother, who still battled her own depression, finally gave up.

Lorinda had to wash dishes, so I helped. Then she led me to her "secret place," a hollow in the hillside that she had dug out and furbished with an old quilt. The sweet smell of grass growing in rich soil surrounded us. Lorinda stretched and sighed. She patted the quilt beside her and I stretched out, too. We were silent awhile, our breath fluttering the exposed white roots, a soft rain of silt falling onto our cheeks and hair.

"Did you get your period yet?" she asked.

I didn't know what she meant. I pretended I hadn't heard.

"You don't know about your period, do you? It's what happens when you get to be a woman. You bleed between your legs. Here. It means you can have babies."

When she pointed at the Y of my thighs and groin, something in me trembled and broke loose, moving me with it. I felt part of everything at once, yet separate, as well. And frightened. Would I bleed until my life spilled out? Was that happening to Lorinda, who seemed paler and thinner than the last time I had seen her? I wondered if she was going to show me the bleeding between her legs, or if she would show me her breasts again. Maybe I would show her mine, the nipples pale and pink as tiny, unripe raspberries.

After a minute Lorinda sat up and stretched her legs into the sun. "It's hot," she said. "Let's go down to the pond."

I was a good swimmer by then and insisted that we wear swim suits. We hid behind our towels in Aunt Rose's bedroom to slip on our suits, then rushed past the adults at the kitchen table. To my surprise, my father did not stop us or warn us to beware of the water. Then we were outside in a great bowl of green and blue. I was astonished at how warm the water was—not snow-cold like Flathead Lake or the artesian-fed pond back home in Utah. I waded out and began to swim while Lorinda dog-paddled near the shore. I swam back to her and stood still, watching as minnows nosed up to me and waterskaters slid frantically toward the shore. The pond was so full of life and the sky so full of light, I threw back my head and laughed for no reason. Ren watched from the grassy bank, his light hair like a halo around his head. Soon, Annette and Cassie waded in, yelling and splashing like three-year-olds, although both were older than I. As long as we stayed in the shallows, we had great fun playing tag, searching for stones, ducking underwater with our eyes open, looking down at green clouds of moss, looking up at light dappling the dark surface so that it was easy to believe that we were seeing into heaven.

And then Malcolm jumped right into the middle of our play. Lorinda retreated to the pond's edge. Malcolm moved his arms beneath the moss where we could not see them, then vaulted up with a splash, grinning and pushing himself after us, grabbing whatever he could. He caught my forearm with a fingernail, drawing a thin line of blood. I felt his hands slip over me, touching me where no one had touched. My vision tunneled into a dark whorl of rage. Satan does live in the water, I thought. A desperate willfulness boiled up in me. And a thrill of dismay I didn't want to feel. I pushed away, swimming backward and grabbing reeds to hoist myself onto the bank. Lorinda had already pulled herself out, and sat on the grassy bank watching. I sat beside her, breathing hard. A little blob of something—a clutch of fish- or insect-eggs—clung to my skin. I snorted with disgust and wiped the clear sticky stuff onto the grass.

Lorinda watched me with a knowing smile. We sat on the grassy bank in silence and watched Malcolm grapple with Annette. Anybody could see she wasn't having fun. He pushed her under and held her under by pressing down on her head. She flailed her way back to the surface, and snatched a draught of air. Then he was pushing her down again, pushing her under, sitting on her shoulders.

"Don't!" Annette gurgled, and Malcolm pushed her under again. Even though both could easily touch bottom, she was truly terrified.

Ren sprang from the pond's edge. Despite his fear of the water, he bobbed behind them, and in a move swift and graceful as tipping a basketball, he pushed Malcolm. Malcolm toppled head-first and splashed hard. Lorinda laughed out loud and clapped her hands. Annette headed for to the bank, gasping and sobbing. I glanced back toward the house, where my mother and father were talking with Aunt Rose. They were inside, paying no attention to us. Malcolm struggled to the surface and clumsily paddled toward Ren, throwing fists and laughing at the same time. Ren waded to shore and sat on the bank near the deep part of the pond. Malcolm blew water and giggled. "Come back, Sissy-boy!" he shouted.

"I don't know why you like the pond," I said to Lorinda. For the first time I felt completely separate from her. I walked to the farmhouse without looking back. After I dressed, I sat beside my mother as she crocheted and made one-sided conversation with Aunt Rose. I counted the hours till we would be on the road again, headed for our house in Nevada. I didn't relax until we were out of the Mission Mountains.

～

Three years later, my mother reported that Lorinda had gone down to Missoula to live with some strangers. They were not of our people, my mother said. "I wonder why your Daddy would let her do that. We've always been so wary of strangers raising you kids."

I wondered, too. But I couldn't formulate the questions that needed to be asked, couldn't put the puzzle in a frame. A few months later, Lorinda moved back to her mother's house, and I pushed aside the anxious feeling that came over me whenever I thought of her and Aunt Rose in that little farmhouse up north. But when my father came to visit the following August, he brought sad news, and directions to pack a few things. We were going with him to Salt Lake for a funeral. Ren, he reported impassively, had drowned in the pond.

As a doctor, my father had seen many beginnings and many endings. Through his great faith in the Mormon doctrine of eternal families, he accepted the death of his father, his mother, and his first child in the belief that we would all be reunited in the hereafter. Perhaps that was why he was so implacable as he spoke of Ren's death. But when Marie had drowned in the pond, he had held Aunt Melissa and wept into her hair. Why didn't he weep now? Why didn't his voice shake? He told us that most likely a cramp had taken hold, or the moss had roped Ren's arms and legs, held him down. But what I heard in his tone was disgust, as though something had been wasted.

My father remained impassive and impersonal throughout the funeral. Later I would excuse his manner as being part of his "doctor persona." But I wondered then, and I wonder now, what could have kept my father from grieving the loss of his child? I know that he loved each of us, including Ren. What had gone wrong?

Lorinda and I sat side by side on the pew. She sobbed brokenheartedly, and somehow I knew that she was crying for many losses. I held her hand, and I gave her my handkerchief, but my gestures were like pebbles thrown into a stormy sea. Lorinda seemed years older—had put on weight and wore her white-blonde hair in the manner of women in the group—pulled straight back in a bun, a style unflattering to her features. Tears coursed into the lines of her nose, over her lips, onto her chin. She whispered, "Ren was the good one. Is that why he died?" She looked into my eyes as if I might have the answer.

Later, after Ren was buried beside Grandmother Evelyn, Lorinda told me that she had been promised to her sister Gloria's husband. Lorinda would be his third wife. She didn't seem too happy about the arrangement. "He's old," she explained. "And very short. I'm taller than he is."

"Well, you're too young to get married. What about school? What about being a doctor, like Daddy?"

Lorinda shrugged. "I guess I'll have to give that up too."

"Well, I don't see why you have to give up anything. You're one of the smartest kids in the family. You could do anything you want."

Lorinda eyed me sadly. "You don't know anything, do you? Don't you see? Daddy *wants* me to get married. The sooner the better."

Later that year, when my father told Malcolm to move out, Lorinda decided to postpone her marriage. "I'm not sure I want to marry him," she said of her betrothed. "Daddy wants me to. But he reminds me of Malcolm."

Malcolm had moved to Wells, a town in Nevada not far from us; he lived upstairs from a hotel and whorehouse where he was the dishwasher and cook's assistant. One weekend Danny drove over to see him.

"It isn't right," Danny said later. "Daddy kicking him out like that."

"Maybe Daddy had good reason," I said.

"Like what?"

I shrugged. I didn't know how to put it into words.

We were all surprised when my father moved the rest of Aunt Rose's family to Wells, as though he wanted Malcolm to be in charge of them again. When Aunt Rose gave birth in the tiny house across the street from the row of red-light houses, Lorinda went to the neighbors for help. Even the whores were dismayed that Aunt Rose had not gone to the hospital, and they reported us to the police. Once again, Lorinda was in trouble. People in the family called her a blabbermouth and a liar. Perhaps to escape criticism, Lorinda surrendered to marriage.

Four years later, Aunt Rose died of heart failure. She had given birth to thirteen children over twenty-six years of married life. Lorinda seemed to accept the loss of her mother as inevitable, or perhaps she had done her grieving long ago. Although mascara streaked my face, I don't think Lorinda wept at her mother's funeral. She was expecting a baby and had shifted her center of gravity, moving in a vortex beyond our reach.

~

Years passed. I stopped going to the group's religious meetings and I saw the family only rarely. Still, Lorinda became the subject of gossip that reached even my distant ears. Some members of the family—people who had manufactured facts to protect the family just as Lorinda and I had—charged that Lorinda was a pathological liar. I remembered our fantasies as children and I thought perhaps their judgements about Lorinda were accurate. More time passed and then came one of those peculiar concurrences where life seems to be gathering loose ends to make a good, firm knot. Lorinda called and asked me to meet her at a health spa near my home. My father's death had left me with an unreasonable sense of responsibility for everyone in the family, and I asked Lorinda how she was getting along. As we did leg-lifts, she told me she had cancer. I confess, I didn't believe her.

"You don't look sick," I said bluntly.

"These little red spots," she said, pointing to the hematomas on her leg. "They're from cancer."

I pulled up my shirt and showed her two small red spots on my abdomen. "Does that mean I've got cancer, too?"

"Maybe." She looked though her thick glasses in that cross-eyed way and lifted her leg in perfect rhythm with me. A peculiar light radiated from her, the iridescence of a trout in spawning season. She surveyed me from head to toe without missing a beat. "You know about the Law of Chastity," she said after awhile. The no-nonsense tone of her voice demanded an honest response.

I forced a smile. "Are you asking about the circumstances of my marriage?"

She laughed silently, then shook her head. "In the Principle, if a woman is pregnant or nursing—or if she's beyond all that—she's supposed to lay off . . . sex, you know." She gave me a knowing smile. "So nobody gets jealous." Then she leaned over so that her leg lifted far out behind her, like a bird with long tailfeathers. "The people who brag about keeping the Law of Chastity are the ones who like sex the most. I'm not fooled."

She lay on her back awhile, doing sit-ups, grunting a little. "They say I've been deceived by the Evil One." She rolled onto her side and looked me in the eye. "I've been hurt. But I haven't been deceived."

During our aerobic workout she told me in sharp breaths that she was very young when Malcolm got to her, said that he started bothering her at the pond and everything escalated during the long, deep winter of Ronan. While we showered, she told me that she had eventually gotten pregnant, had given birth. She fell silent while we toweled off. Then, when we were dressed and headed for the street, she told me that the family in Missoula who took her in had eked a confession from her that the baby was her brother's child. They had called the state and petitioned to become the baby's foster parents.

"I haven't seen him since," she said, and turned her head so I couldn't see her cry.

I didn't know whether to believe her. In flashes I remembered the long-ago whispering of my father and mother over the dinner table, his hurried explanation that the Montana authorities were pressing him, he had to move Rose and her children to the little house not fifty miles from us, and my mother's protests that Rose's children would talk and get us all in trouble.

But my father had moved them to Nevada anyway, and in less than a year the word was out about the polygamists in Wells. Rose's baby came, Lorinda talked, and soon the sheriff was knocking at our door in Elko, asking my mother questions. We had to move again. Malcolm had disappeared into the gambling halls of Winnemucca—a place Danny called the armpit of the world.

I can only guess why Lorinda told me what she did that day at the spa. Perhaps she suspected I would be fertile ground for what others regarded as her pathology, both of us impaired after a childhood of lies, in our ability to discern the truth. Or perhaps she trusted our history as playmates and our shared status as black sheep, spilling out her story because she could contain no more secrets. Or perhaps she wanted her due as a sister—to have me listen and believe her. But I failed her; I only half-believed, which is the same as not believing at all.

❧

A few years after our visit to the spa, Lorinda disappeared. She had earned a nursing degree and was the only breadwinner for the three families of a husband who spent his days roaming labyrinths of religious doctrine instead of making a living. Then I learned that she was a patient in the hospital where she had worked as a nurse. Some people said she did have cancer; others said she had a nervous breakdown. My mother told me that she was getting psychiatric care, even though her husband had warned her to "trust not in the arm of flesh."

Lorinda pretended to be asleep when I visited. A film of sweat shone on her pale face. I kissed her damp forehead and took in the rancid smell of fear. I leaned down and whispered an apology: "I'm sorry I didn't believe you. Don't give up on yourself." After awhile I tucked the cold hand I'd been holding under the covers. A few days after her release, she disappeared, leaving her children in the sketchy care of her sister and sister-wife, Gloria.

A year after Lorinda's disappearance, my mother and Aunt Emma received an envelope from Lorinda, postmarked Florida, and I went to visit them, hoping that we could straighten things out and bring her home. Aunt Emma reported that the letter was full of "outlandish stories." When I asked for details Aunt Emma said she couldn't remember anything significant Lorinda had said, only that she was thankful for their succor when Aunt Rose died. When I asked to see the letter, no one could find it despite the pristine order of the duplex my mother shared with her twin sister. Then my mother confessed that Lorinda had written that she would die if she came back to Utah.

"Can you believe that?" my mother said.

"What does she mean—that she could be killed, or that she'll die because of family burdens, or what?"

"Lorinda always did exaggerate," Aunt Emma said.

My mother tucked her lips in a small, tight smile. "Exaggeration seems to run in this family."

It was time to get to the bottom of a few things. "Why did she leave, then? She was working so hard for her family!"

My mother and Aunt Emma sat in silence looking intently at their hands.

"Tell me something, will you? Why did Lorinda go to live with those people in Missoula? Remember, back when she was a teenager? Why did Daddy move Aunt Rose to Nevada?"

My mother and Aunt Emma stared at me. I couldn't tell if they were confused or dismayed. I had always distressed my loved ones this way—bringing up incidents everyone wanted to pretend not to know, or confronting realities they wanted me to think about in another way.

Aunt Emma clucked her tongue and shook her head, as though she didn't know what to do with me. I traded the question for another.

"How did Ren drown?" My gaze darted from Aunt Emma to my mother and back again.

The women looked at each other. Aunt Emma spoke. "He fell off a raft at the deepest part of the pond. Right after dinner. We taught you kids not to go swimming too soon after eating."

"I heard that he got tangled in the moss and panicked," my mother said. "He never did learn to swim."

These speculations seemed insufficient, just as they had when my father first offered them. I remembered the furious blinking of Ren's eye. I remembered his lanky teenaged body. What had weighed on him until he went under? What had made him helpless in water—and in life?

"What if it was something else?" I prodded.

"Satan lives in the water," Aunt Emma said. "Your daddy always said that."

"Rulon wouldn't go swimming without his garments on," my mother added. "And he was a good swimmer."

I sighed, unable to press the issue of Ren's death any farther.

In her letter, Lorinda had asked if she and Aunt Emma would continue being her "mothers" since her own mother was gone.

"What will you tell her?"

"We'll tell her, of course." Aunt Emma said stoutly.

I thought of the trust my mother had invested in me, of the connection between one person believing what you say and having the courage to speak out.

"If Lorinda tells you about her life, will you believe what she tells you?" I asked. The alarm in their eyes told me I'd asked for too much. I sighed and kissed them good-bye. You could not find more tender and dedicated mothers anywhere on earth: Praying for me as I made my descent into monogamy. Praying for Lorinda until she surfaced again. Searching for us as we counted our moments of hell like so many pomegranate seeds.

I drove across town thinking of Ren and Lorinda. I thought of Aunt Rose's sad eyes and her slow half-smile. Snow dusted the freeway. It was almost six months until Memorial Day, but I turned east toward the cemetery where our family burial grounds are located. Midway between the pine grove and my father's headstone, I stepped over the cement slab with Ren's name on it. A few plots waited to be filled by members of my family but there would not be room for everyone. There would not be room for me—especially since my place in the family has been questioned. But Ren was in his place. For an instant, envy invaded my heart. I closed my eyes and remembered the last time I had seen him, his anxious, eye-twitching smile as he tried so hard to be a good brother, an acceptable member of the family. Opening to the light, then as quickly shutting it out. Innocence frozen in time.

What had happened that evening he drowned? The pond gaping at the night sky. Four or five sisters swallowed, one at a time, in refracted starlight as his desire to protect them was thwarted. The schism between ethic and impulse too wide and too deep to cross. Had he known about Lorinda, witnessed the sexual abuse of other sisters? Perhaps he had tried to force Malcolm away or been forced himself—perhaps he had seen and felt too much, so filled with experience he could not take another breath. The good brother, wrestling a dark angel in a murky world. Perhaps a cramp struck and he could find no rock to stand on. And the fear of water took him down.

Or—I could barely think it—had his life been taken? Though I suspected Malcolm was capable of violating his sisters, I could not imagine him taking a life. He had never fit the family profile, did not know how to be an adequate scion of patriarchy but sad and sick as it all seemed, I felt that Malcolm had craved his own stolen childhood. Perhaps he had tried to gain some control over his own life and some relief from the expectations imposed on the oldest son of polygamy by invading the bodies of his sisters and stealing their innocence.

I moved to my father's bronze headstone, thinking thoughts I didn't want to think. That my father, the good doctor, must have known about it all along. If Lorinda had carried her brother's child, what torments had my father lived through? He'd had the knowledge to perform an abortion but he was bound by his doctor's creed, his spiritual calling, his intractable devotion to life. Lorinda said she had given the baby to a foster family. But ironically, that's what my father had scattered his family to avoid: giving the babies to strangers. How did he feel after running and hiding to preserve our solidarity, traveling wearily from state to state, year after year, only to have the trouble erupt inside the family? I bent and touched the bronze words: *Father; Husband; Teacher; Friend.* How would the dark seeds sown in his garden of light be manifested?

Aunt Rose's stone is smaller than my father's. But her carved name deepens over time, while the raised bronze letters of my father's stone lose their edge, becoming rounded and soft. Despite her passive ways, Aunt Rose's life had become an embodiment of resistance. Like Demeter in search of her daughter, she would not give up, would not release her daughter to eternal darkness even when the earth turned cold. In a dream she had come to me from the shadow world to insist that something be said, that we sound an alarm before other daughters are lost, even knowing that the ancestral weave may unravel as the pattern of abuse is torn from its genetic spindle.

If I were asked, what would I tell Lorinda's daughters about why their mother left them? What could I tell them that is real and true? Nothing they haven't already learned. Unhappy truths: Brothers can't always be trusted. Mothers can't keep their daughters safe. Pluto waits to draw them down where they must be content with pomegranate seeds instead of the whole fruits of life. Perhaps all I can give them is this story with a few facts. Each will have to do her own sorting to decide what is wheat, what is chaff.

"By their fruits ye shall know them." My father read it to us straight from the scriptures. From this I have learned to check reality, because results don't lie. I know why Lorinda went to Florida: Her daughters and sons were running wild. Her husband smiling into his chin and

reciting some obscure doctrine that women are born to give men pleasure. No matter what they say about Lorinda being a pathological liar,
somewhere the seeds were planted; the family orchards are bearing
their harvest and some of it is bitter.

I fumble in my pocket for a tissue, in my heart for some wisdom.
Nothing there. The truth is cold, a peach frozen in January.

Sister-Wife

I WONDER IF I HAVE THE RIGHT to tell Alma's story, even though hers is a singular story and some good may come of telling it. Alma's story reflects the human dilemma, the dissonance of our idealism against hard reality. In a family that aspires to godlike perfection, Alma's apparent insufficiencies became a reminder that life doesn't always look the way we want it to look. Our people pride themselves in serving divine will—a particularly incontestable form of hubris which tends to separate and isolate rather than unify, yet Alma's ordeal speaks of humility and vulnerability, opening a plot of common ground where we all struggle to understand why we are here. She broke that ground while tracking her own shadow, and in claiming her dark side became somehow perfect in the sense of whole, or complete.

I wasn't there for most of this story, but I know the people well. Alma and I are sisters—half-sisters, really, but because my father insisted that in the Principle of Plural Marriage we were all one family, we called each other sister and meant it. Alma has other sisters, like Karen, who is seven years her senior, an imperious beauty with a magisterial disposition. But none is so like Alma as I am. Born less than a year apart, both lacking birth certificates that could be used against our parents in court, we mirrored each other's age, temperament, and coloring, as well as the angst of doubting our right to be here.

Alma began a lifelong obsession with horses the night our mothers wrapped us in blankets and stuffed us into the big backseat of the green Hudson. Another raid was brewing; we must escape the authorities that could take us from our mothers, the forces that could put our grown-ups in jail—events that had happened to our people in the World War II years before Alma and I were born. When we returned from Mexico three months later, Alma was nearly dead of dysentery. That brush with death got her hooked up with a tall sorrel horse she named "Babe." She wasn't strong enough to hoist a saddle, so she'd leap from the fence and hang over his bare back and kick one leg across. Then, clutching his long mane, she'd streak across the bare fields. Aunt Melissa said it was a caution: ladies rode sidesaddle for a reason, and Sally should stop that girl before it was too late. But Aunt Sally gave her daughter what she wanted. In fact, everyone gave Alma what she wanted, everyone except her older sister, Karen. A fierce love burned between the sisters, as if Karen intended to train Alma's frailty to strength. Karen reminded Alma that in the United Order she could not really own a horse, it would belong to everyone, and Alma should let the boys ride horses and get started on her hope chest like other girls in the family.

In 1955, as the McCarthy reign of terror ended and the Cold War mounted, another polygamous roundup scattered my father's family to the four winds. Alma left Babe with the neighbors and after a brief sojourn with us in Nevada, Aunt Sally headed north, Karen and Alma in tow. My mother and Aunt Emma established a home in Nevada while our father closed the doors to his naturopathic office and went into hiding. But Alma and I wrote faithfully to each other, postcards in first-grade printing and later, neat penmanship on pale pink paper.

A few years passed before the political focus shifted to foreign policies in places like Cuba and southeast Asia. We returned to Utah and

Alma began dating a feisty young man from our religious group. Tag had grown up on a ranch in Montana that was gradually being settled by our people into a township made up of ten-acre parcels, each family with its own sustainability, the way Brigham Young had said it should be. Tag knew how to ride horses and drive a tractor and make hay. He was attracted to Alma, and she to him. At least once a month he made the long journey past Yellowstone Park and through the badlands of Idaho to be with her.

He was free-spirited, and the brethren worried about him. Karen— who had been married for four or five years by then, and knew something about men—said Alma could never keep such a wild horse in hand. Aunt Melissa predicted Tag would one day leave the group, and some said Alma was too tender to survive out in the world where the natural man rules and hearts are godless.

The year I graduated from high school, Karen played the part of indulgent older sister and gave a slumber party for the teenaged girls in my father's family. Karen's husband, Caleb, had spent the years of their marriage furbishing a strong brick dwelling with apartments upstairs and down. His second wife lived in the basement with her new baby and took care of Karen's three little children that night as we popped corn and put on our pajamas and told stories about the old days. Yet my stomach cramped all evening, not from food or excitement, but because I felt ill-at-ease with my own sisters. By then I was questioning everything, dating outside the group, and the mothers whispered that I was becoming worldly. Perhaps my jaded view stained the innocence of our girl-talk that night, but our remarks seemed barbed with darker, sharper truths than those spoken aloud. Alma left the room to take a phone call, and when she returned, Karen spoke pointedly.

"See how he can't go a whole evening without calling? It isn't right for a man who's going to live the Principle to be so gone on one girl."

"You think he has a weak character?" Alma asked.

"You're meant for someone like Caleb—someone who can take a

firm hand with you." Karen's voice carried the authority of all older sisters.

"But if she loves Tag . . ." I started. Both sisters turned to look at me. I had the awkward sense that I'd broken into a conversation that had been going on for years.

The next time I saw Alma—it was a year or more later—she showed me her hope chest full of linens edged with hand-crocheted lace and embroidered flowers, crafted while I was writing papers for my classes at the university. I wondered what had happened to Alma's love of horses. She told me that she and Tag had broken up for good and she had decided to become Caleb's third wife. The wedding ceremony would be secret and I was not invited.

I had jumped the fence around our religious group by then, and people I had known all my life called me a troublemaker. So after a glass of lemonade, we hurried off in opposite directions. The next time I saw Alma and Karen, the occasion was my own baby shower—a shower thrown by big-hearted Aunt Sally who must have known that my due date was a mere eight months beyond my wedding. Alma was happy for me, seemed happy for everyone. She occupied the back bedroom of Karen's house; she was a sister-wife. And that is where Alma's story really begins, a story that in many ways excludes me. I know of some details through other family members, through the words Alma and I shared when it was over, and through the knowing that defies time and space—the knowing of the heart.

As potential Mothers in Israel, we had inherited the legacy of Sarah, who laughed when a messenger from God told her she would have a son in her old age and gave birth to Isaac. In our little field, a woman's raison d'etre was to raise a righteous seed unto the Lord. What good was a woman among plural wives if she could not bear children? The childless women in our group often became strange and witch-like, with their herbs and their sorrow. Some stood in meeting and made prophecies that were discounted before they were heard. A barren woman was at best a perpetual child, and at worst a creature to be pitied.

When Alma did not conceive, Aunt Melissa blamed it on bareback riding and lifting heavy saddles. But the infertility was more likely due to the staph infection she caught while assisting in our father's office during the first year of her marriage. The infection rampaged through her body and none of my father's herbs contained it. Eventually he forsook the naturopathic way and used the auxiliary degree in medicine that allowed him to practice in Utah; he prescribed purging antibiotics that left Alma pale and bedridden. She lay in the back bedroom, waiting for the tide of her life to turn.

But the tide did not turn. Seven years after our father was killed, the year the banks of the Great Salt Lake obliterated bird refuges and submerged the newly reconstructed Salt Air Resort, Alma and I met in a Greek restaurant near our father's office. We ordered food with names we could not pronounce; we mused sadly that the doctor's domain had become an insurance agency. By the time we met, Alma had made her decision and there was no changing it.

On the basis of our shared history, I imagine Alma on that night when everything became clear for her. In my mind's eye, I see her arriving after work to help with the birth of Karen and Caleb's ninth child. I imagine her lapsing into a moment of pretense that the eight children bathed and dressed and kneeling before the fireplace are hers.

"We say our prayers to the fire," Joseph, the youngest, says in his self-satisfied way.

"We don't pray to the fire, Joseph," Alma says, uneasy because she sees in him a familiar strain of self-righteousness. "We pray facing north—and we pray to God."

"But how do you know God is north?" Rachel asks. "I thought he was straight up." She points past her red curls at the ceiling.

"Rachel, five minutes don't pass without you asking impossible questions." Alma sighs and straightens her long, lean frame. "We kneel facing north because that's where the Lost Tribes will come from when they rescue the remnant of Israel in the Last Days. Also, your grandfather says that the City of Enoch will return to earth from the North Star, near Kolob, where God lives."

As I imagine the scene, I wonder if Alma believes the litanies she recites for Karen and Caleb's children. I think she must have clung to belief in something—otherwise, how did she get through that day?

"Caleb!" she calls as though she is his mother. "Caleb, we're waiting!" Then to Rachel. "Get your father for prayers."

Perhaps Joseph leans against her, asking, "Where's Mama?" and Alma strokes his hair. "Your mama is having a baby." Then Caleb enters, that distant gaze in his cobalt eyes. He kneels before the fireplace, back to everyone, the family patriarch doing his duty.

"Hush, now," Alma whispers to the children. "Fold your arms."

Caleb gives her a bemused smile, then speaks in a deep trombone: "Our dear Father in Heaven." And the other voices chime in: "Our dear Father in Heaven."

Caleb prays for rain. He prays for peace. He prays that dear Karen will be delivered safely. He prays that the Lord will bless dear Alma with the desire of her heart.

And after each plea, the children echo, "Please bless dear Alma with the desire of her heart."

Alma clenches her arms and holds her body rigid. Perhaps she can feel the wind in her mind or sparks crackling behind her eyelids. At last the prayer is over and the children file up to kiss Caleb and Alma good night. And Rachel says shyly, "Will you tuck us in, Aunt Alma?"

She nods, feeling Caleb's sticky gaze on her. At last the children are folded in, neat and silent as eight white sheets on linen shelves. Alma descends to the kitchen and mixes bread in the blue porcelain pan. The cool batter salves her nerves. From the back bedroom float the voices of Karen and Caleb. They have phoned the midwife, and now they are choosing a name for the baby. As always, Caleb has left things for the last minute—something Alma complains about when the girls at the sewing shop where she works are chatting over lunch. She tells them that he bought her gold wedding band only an hour before he slipped it on her finger. She doesn't tell them that it is the third wedding band he had bought, or that she has sister-wives. She could lose her job over that. She smiles wryly, remembering the ceremony where Karen took Alma's hand and offered it to Caleb and he covered both their hands with his and then pushed the gold band onto her ring finger. Back then the band had been too tight. Now her fingers are so thin the ring swivels; it could easily be lost in the bread dough.

Karen mews weakly from the bedroom. "Alma, what are you doing in there?" This morning Karen's voice had been strident on the phone. "I want you to be here when this baby comes." The hint of something behind Karen's firm words, something Alma has prayed for and dreamed of for years now hovers almost palpably.

"I'll be in as soon as I've set the bread to rise," Alma calls back. She reaches into the flour bin. She is as at home here as anywhere, had once decorated and lived in the back room where she will stay tonight. Caleb put those walls up when she agreed to marry him. Karen had chosen the wallpaper.

After her long bout of sickness, Alma had moved to an apartment. Now she is a guest, "Aunt Alma" come to delight the children with molasses cookies she has too much time to bake, and little trinkets she can afford because she has no children of her own.

Of course, she has every right to be here. Each month she turns her paycheck over to Caleb who manages their family's United Order. Karen's needs are great. Alma's needs are small: the tiny apartment, a few clothes, the little she eats—although she is better about eating, now. Alma gets dry satisfaction from providing for her older sister, who has given her so much—sewed her wedding dress, handed down shoes and half-completed diaries, and shared her husband. "I'm a hand-me-down girl," she thinks, then stops to reframe her thoughts.

She pushes the dough away, then pulls it toward her, tugging it apart with each movement of her arms, shaping it into something palatable and nourishing, something to replace the dark anger that nearly eats her alive.

~

At first, time at the apartment complex where she dwelt among divorced people and old couples had been luxurious: on her nights with Caleb, they played chess, read poetry aloud, slept in until seven. Perhaps his face softened during those mornings alone, whispering over cantaloupe and hot biscuits, sharing stories of his boyhood and choosing names for babies to come. But the babies didn't come.

"Alma, I forgot to wash the bedroom with disinfectant." Karen would have roused her sister from her reverie by now.

Alma hears her, rinses the dough from her hands and dries them carefully. She draws a bucket of warm water and pours a pine-smelling disinfectant that turns it milky; the fragrance of birth. In her childhood, fundamentalist houses filled with this smell signaled the advent of a new brother or sister or cousin, and now nieces and nephews. The smell brings tears to Alma's eyes. She pauses at the door of the bedroom, puts down the bucket and closes her eyes until the tears are gone. Then, with a deep breath, she enters.

Caleb's rawboned frame roosts at the bottom of the bed as he softly reads scriptures. Karen sits against the pillows, her dark hair spread across white pillowslips embroidered with pink roses and edged with handmade lace. Alma had worked those sheets and cases for a month and given them to Karen for Christmas. Karen had smiled tearfully and vowed to use them only for special occasions, which left Alma to imagine what those occasions might be.

That was a memorable Christmas, the same Christmas she had ended up in the hospital. Alma was strong enough by then to work twelve-hour shifts, but she had been fasting for seventy-two hours and Christmas bore down like a vise—the children opening their stockings, Karen's announcement that a new one was on the way. The queasiness in Alma's stomach rose to her heart. Just as they were sitting down to Christmas dinner, Alma rushed from the house, leaving her coat draped on the hall-tree and Karen openmouthed beside Caleb at the head of the table. Alma had run to her little car, had driven through the cold empty streets until it started snowing and she could no longer see. She only vaguely felt the bump of the other car, the door pressed against her hip, the cold windshield soothing her forehead like the cool cloth the mothers had used when she was so sick in Mexico.

In Karen's bedroom, Alma presses a cloth dipped in ice water to her sister-wife's forehead. But Karen removes it and sits up. She fixes Alma with her bright eyes and interrupts Caleb's reading to ask, "Are you all right, Alma dear?"

Alma laughs and shakes her head. "You're the one in labor!" She turns away and takes a cloth from the bundle of oven-sterilized towels. Caleb begins reading again, his voice like soft thunder. Alma washes the headboard and footboard and the dresser with disinfectant, drying the wood as she goes. She wipes the knickknacks and the frame of Grandmother Evelyn's picture. Perhaps she remembers how, when we were children, Grandmother Evelyn was always complaining about our noise. Yet, once in awhile she would pull us onto her lap to examine the baby dolls we carried everywhere, then tell of the days when she had ridden her mare bareback through the Star Valley countryside.

"I was a happy girl," she'd say.

"What happened?" we'd asked.

Grandmother would dip her white head, then raise it. "Too much to do. I had my own children, and when Charlotte died, with her seven that survived, I raised sixteen in all. Don't make overmuch of babies, my girls. Babies don't always bring happiness—and they always bring work."

Now Karen speaks into the deep silence. "Caleb, Alma and I need to have a little talk."

"Alma . . ." Karen begins after Caleb leaves, "each time I've given birth, I've wanted . . ." her face bleaching white as bone, ". . . wanted to have the strength to . . . do this. Before it was just too hard. And we hoped that you would still . . . be able to . . ." Karen swallows. "But now . . . with no chance for you at all . . . I worry about you . . . and I've been so blessed—"

She stops as pain grips her face, then surprise. Then she says matter-of-factly, "My water just broke. I hope the midwife hurries."

Alma starts up. "I'll send Caleb for her."

Alma tells Caleb to hurry the midwife, then brings fresh sheets and helps Karen into a fresh nightgown. She glances out the window, toward the drive. "I wish they would hurry," she says to no one in particular. Anxiety for the midwife mixes with relief that Caleb is out of the room. Just Alma and Karen, sisters, after all is said and done. Karen can't help the way she is; she was born to organize other people's lives. And neither can Alma help wanting to be free of other people's fences. Sweetness rises in her breast as she goes down the hall and puts the wet nightgown and pillowslips and sheets into the washer. The fluids of her sister's body and her sister's baby stain the white cotton. She pours in a little bleaching powder. When the washer begins its cycle, she returns to the bread rising in her sister's kitchen. The yeasty smell opens her head; the bubbles in the dough she kneads effervesce in her heart; she is grateful to perform the tasks of love in her sister's home tonight.

The practice of marrying sisters is not considered peculiar among our people. My own mother and her twin sister were married to my father and since the bonds of twinness were never severed, they became Siamese twins of the heart. Uncle Lawrence had married three sisters; even with the law watching him they had lived together in the same house and reared each other's children. Some men said it was easier to live the Principle if the women already knew how to live together, how to share.

When her babies came too fast for her to take care of them, Aunt Rose had shared her family with Aunt LaVerne, who was itching for responsibility and heartbroken that the Lord had not blessed her with children. And everyone knew the Johansen family, held up as a model of the Principle at its best, where the wives had not been sisters, not even relatives, but became the best of friends. The younger woman had given birth to seven children, while the older woman waited. When the last son was born, he became his father's favorite, and the boy and the older wife shared a bond that deepened as he grew. The boy's mother didn't interfere in his upbringing. According to the story passed through our group, when the youngest boy died in a motorcycle accident, the biological mother comforted her sister-wife as any sister would comfort a mother who lost her son. Although Alma had seen the two women at weddings and funerals, their legend preceded them, made people stand apart and stare at them, so often were they held up as the example of true sisterly love.

Sisterly love. It doesn't always look the way you think it should look. Alma watches the bread rise and listens. No sound from the bedroom. Perhaps the pains have stopped altogether. She gathers a slab of shortening and smooths it with her fingers inside twelve blackened tins. Aunt LaVerne had waited twelve years for her firstborn. Aunt Emma had waited eighteen years for her second, the entire family on its knees every day to pray for her relief. But in Alma's case, time and prayers have made no difference. She knows now it does no good to hold it against God or Caleb, or Karen, for that matter. She takes a deep breath, lifts the dough and throws it on the board. She can easily forgive Karen—perhaps she can even forgive Caleb, if she can forgive herself. What will she forgive herself for? For riding horses? For getting sick? For being barren ground where seeds will not take root?

She rolls the dough into a smooth sphere. Once she had believed that if she was careful enough, had faith enough, all problems could be anticipated and solved. First she tried the herbal teas: althea, uvedalia, camphor, camomile. Then the powders, roots ground between mortar and pestle, sometimes moistened into salves: squaw root, birch bark, ergot. Then the exercises and the massages. Our father did everything he knew—used every chiropractic correction, every diathermal and ultraviolet machine. He referred her to people inside the group and gave her the names of colleagues in the medical community. The midwives of the religious group told her everything they knew about healing and fertility. Sister Slater told her that the problem was that her womb sat at an odd angle. But if she drank the teas diligently, if she put her faith in the Almighty, if she lay perfectly still on a slanted board afterward. . . . And so she did, trying to fall asleep on the ironing board, all the blood rushing to her head, Caleb snoring in the bedroom.

Caleb didn't want her going to doctors outside the group. Faith would be enough, he said. Their lives would prove that the Lord uses weak things of the flesh to accomplish His purposes. So she began fasting. Once a week for twenty-four hours, on her day off, she denied herself food and even water, spending most of the day on her knees in prayer. After two years she had increased the fasts to forty-eight hours, and six months later, to seventy-two. A three-day fast culminating at Christmas dinner preceded the accident.

She doesn't remember the crash and I have only the barest information, gleaned here and there. I know that Alma came to gradually. Perhaps Karen stroked her face like a mother with a sick child, saying, "Don't worry, darling, it's all right." A siren shrilled so loud it seemed to be coming from inside her body.

They rushed her into the emergency room strapped to a stretcher, Karen squeezing her left hand, and stroking her face, not minding the blood on her hands. By this time, Alma had concluded that she was in labor, in the throes of an abnormal birth that had forced them to the hospital. She was oblivious to the huge lump lifting the hair on her brow, of the blood trickling across her left temple, was aware only of wrenching contractions. Soon there would be a child, the girl she had dreamed of named after her mother. That was all she could see, feel, believe, and so it must be true.

Alma throws the perfect ball of dough down and punches it to shatter the silver image of herself on the hospital cart. But the image is not a glass to be broken, not an illusion. Like boiling soup it bubbles up, irreducible and searing and real.

As she shapes the dough in Karen's kitchen, she hears herself calling out, "Hurry! It's time!" And Karen's martyred smile, and the emergency nurse running cold hands across Alma's arching stomach, then snapping on a milky glove to search beneath the sheet, then gazing into Karen's sad eyes while she, Alma, pleads for good news.

The emergency personnel took her into a room with doors that closed, strapped her to the bed, pried her fingers from Karen's, and left her wild-eyed and talking to the great white light which broke over her in waves like the white hot pain in her head. At last, the resident physician arrived, his white coat too big for him, his voice like warm milk.

"I'm Dr. Monroe. I'm getting you out of this," he said, unbuckling one strap, then the other. He lifted the sheet; his fingers gently probed. Then, sitting on the bed, brown eyes like soft earth drawing Alma down from her hot, white ride, he said, "Alma, you are not having a baby. Do you understand that? Tell me what's causing you so much pain."

And then the storm of weeping, while the young man rocked her like a baby. The blurting of secrets she had sworn to keep. About the Principle, about Caleb, about Karen.

The young doctor sat still and silent for a long time. "Maybe if you and your husband could go away alone for awhile—"

Alma shook her head and blew her nose, hard. "They think I'm jealous. And I am. And I have no right to be jealous."

"Every woman has the right to be jealous," he said softly.

"Not of Karen. I love Karen."

"What do you mean, then?"

Hot tears ran down her cheeks. "When we were married, my father asked, 'Why do you enter into this covenant?' and I knew I couldn't say 'Because that's what I'm supposed to do.' That isn't reason enough.

Our people serve God. And so I gave the right answer: 'To raise a righteous seed unto the Lord.'" Her voice thinned to hard wire. "It's the only good reason to live the Principle. And I can't fulfill it."

The young doctor sighed. "Let me talk to your husband. Things can be done. Amazing advances in fertility research."

Alma pressed a hand against her flat stomach. "He says we must have faith," she said.

"Medical intervention requires faith, too," the doctor said. "I'll talk to him." And then for no apparent reason, he laughed. And Alma thought of Sarah, mirthful in the face of the impossible.

Now she breaks the big ball of dough into twelve parts to shape the white loaves and set them in their black tins and cover them with cheesecloth. She stares out the window into the empty night, her reflection shimmering back at her like a mirage.

Caleb had visited her in the hospital. Her head was swathed in gauze, but her eyes were bright. She introduced him to the young doctor, gesticulating in a frantic dance of fingers, her heart rising in a joyous wave.

"Please, Caleb," Alma begged when Dr. Monroe left.

Caleb shook his head and blushed. "The problem's not with me, Alma. I have children."

She bit her lip and turned her face away. She stared at a painting of a woman in her white nightgown, holding her baby at the window. She stared at it until Caleb went away.

So began her lonely visits to the fertility clinic, the humiliation of tests that lit up her insides for the camera and then the medications and much later, the exploratory surgery, finding what blocked the way. And the bills, requiring longer hours at work and an extra job. At the hospital she was always alone—even when her mother and Karen were there, she felt an aloneness so deep and long it seemed to have begun with her own birth.

Caleb came to visit her when she was recovering from one surgery.

"Why did you come?" she asked.

"You are my other rib," he said gently.

"Then I'm a broken rib." She gritted her teeth to hold back the tears.

"Don't worry, Alma. You still have one ovary. God can do any-thing—even if there were no ovaries, He would bless you with a child if you had enough faith. Think of Sarah of Old. Think of Aunt LaV-erne, who waited twelve years and Aunt Emma who waited eighteen years for a child."

And she pulled back from him and looked him straight in the face. "They've done everything they can for me, Caleb. Now they need your help. There's a process that increases the chances fifty percent. They've done it with cows and mares for a long time. Artificial insemination."

Caleb flushed. "Alma, we are not animals."

"But Caleb—you have children. You don't know what it's like. . . ."

"We must have faith. We must fast and pray."

This made her shriek. If she had been stronger she'd have gone after him with her nails. "We! I have had faith! Enough to let them cut me open!" She pulled herself up, ignoring the stab of pain and grabbed his hand. "Please, Caleb. Dr. Monroe says it's simple. They just take you into a little room, and give you a little jar and leave you alone. No one will see. No one will even know!"

A look of revulsion crossed his face and he backed away. "God would know."

And that was when her heart sank into the red sea of her rage. When she spoke, her voice was authoritative. "I'm not the one who has no faith." And her mouth closed like a dead bolt.

That was when she truly began to live alone. She attended counsel-ing sessions with a kind, strong woman who urged Alma to stand up for herself, to do everything possible to fulfill herself. She endured more surgeries. And when the surgeries didn't change anything, she applied to adopt as a single parent. But the adoption worker knew her name and launched an investigation; when they found she was part of a polygamous family, they terminated the process.

She visited Dr. Monroe one last time to say good-bye. There was no need to come back, with nothing left inside for him to fool with. Dr. Monroe promised that if he came across a baby through "channels," she would be the first to know.

"You'd do that for me?" Alma asked. "Why?"

"Because I want you to be happy."

Alma gathered her things in a whirl, banging her hip on the corner of the desk as she backed out the door. "Thank you," she said. "But I'm going to . . . make myself happy."

And she had made herself happy. She found other seeds inside herself and saw them sprout and flourish. Her work took on a new dimension as she moved from tailoring to sewing wedding gowns. She began to enjoy coffee breaks with the seamstresses, drinking hot lemonade while they smoked and stirred sugar into their black coffee. Wednesday afternoons, she took classes in dressmaking and fashion design. At night, at a drafting table set up in the corner of her apartment, she designed wedding gowns and trousseaus and maternity dresses. Each had an old-fashioned flair. She bought a stereo system and a sound library of Mozart, Beethoven, Chopin to keep her company as she worked. Caleb's infrequent visits interrupted her concentration. Even on the nights he slept at her apartment, she stayed up late, the light of the drafting table throwing her magnified silhouette on the wall.

"Come to bed, Alma," Caleb would say.

"I've things to do," she murmured.

"Don't lose sight of that which is truly important," he intoned, as if reading from the scriptures.

She said nothing. Perhaps she had lost sight of what was truly important. But children's clothing—long crinolines, calicos, pinafores—spun in her mind. Someday she would sew her creations. Her name would be finely embroidered at the neck of every garment.

For a time she held back her checks from the United Order to buy a trailer and some land. Then she moved to a rural district outside the city. She adopted a wild filly through the Adopt-a-Horse Program. It was absurdly easy. The officials didn't check for polygamous heritage; they only checked the size of the acreage, and made her sign a paper promising not to sell the horse to a glue or dog-food factory. She named the filly Spirit. And gradually, the sky became vivid, the wind stronger, water so very clear. Trees and flowers seemed limned in rainbows of light. She came home from dressmaking to work with Spirit, gentling her to hackamore, then bit and bridle, walking the horse with the weight of the saddle, then a bag of feed, and then, finally, her own body. Astride the filly, Alma was whole.

But now, she knows that Karen will offer up this unborn child, a sacrifice to sisterhood, and Alma's fine balance wavers. Karen wants to change the balance. Caleb wants to change the balance. Perhaps even God wants to change the balance. The dark window washes with headlights. The midwife hurries in with her little bag of instruments, Caleb behind her. Alma ushers the birdlike woman to the bedroom and meets Caleb at the bedroom door.

"I wish it was you, Alma," he says.

She steps back. "Don't, Caleb. I'm fine. Really, I am. And so are you. Now get in there where you belong."

Always before, Alma had stayed in the room during Karen's birthings, standing at the foot of the bed as if trying to learn the miracle by heart. But tonight when Karen calls to her, Alma brings a cold towel for her forehead, ice for her cracked lips, then disappears to the kitchen to test the bread's golden crust, warm waves filling the house like good will. She doesn't want to watch Karen's face or the little head crowning. She wants to be strong enough to accept what is real, to serve others as she can, like these loaves of bread, plain and simple, or dressed up with honey and fresh milk—something honest, something true. And when the midwife calls, "Come quickly, Alma, it's time!" and Caleb's soft rumble, "Alma, quick—you'll miss it!"

Alma calls back, "As soon as I get this bread out of the oven." And then the baby's burbling cry, and it is too late.

Later, when the loaves are turned out of their tins and the crusts swathed in butter, when Karen and the baby have been bathed, and when the midwife has bestowed a shadowy kiss and "I'm just sorry it wasn't you, Alma," as the grandfather clock strikes the midnight hour, Karen's voice drifts down the hall. "Alma . . . Alma, darling. Please come here."

And so Alma gets up from the table where she has been staring out at the night, and she walks down the hall.

"Alma . . ." Karen reaches for her.

Alma kisses her sister's supple cheek. "Giving birth seems to make you younger," she smiles.

"Alma . . ." Grimacing with an after-pain, Karen grips Alma's hand for a moment, then takes the small white bundle and holds it out. "Take this." Alma takes it, holds it close, peers at the little face.

And then Karen's voice, a strange mix of light and pain. "I want you to have her—name her—keep her as if she were your own."

Alma looks at Karen, then back at the baby. She forces herself to breathe slow and deep. Her own? Her sister's child. Her husband's child. Almost like her own.

Now, looking down at the tiny, wrinkled face, she is filled with a temptation strong as starvation. Something to fill her life. She looks past Karen's strangled smile.

If ye be the son of God, turn these stones into bread. She could take it, keep it, let the world witness her worth.

Alma holds the baby close; the warmth fills her chest and spreads into the cavity of her womb. "As if she were your own." Perhaps a flicker of recognition flits through the baby's blank blue eyes. There is no "as if." Things are or they are not. And in that instant she knows: something of this child really does belong to her. Just as something of Joseph and Rachel, of Karen and Caleb and even Dr. Monroe—in some way everyone belongs to her.

She looks at her sister. There's no use pretending that she can do things Karen's way. The Lost Tribes aren't coming to rescue her. On earth we must rescue ourselves, must reach with open arms to receive salvation. We must permit ourselves to be refined into something irreducible, something worth offering to God.

"Karen, thank you. But it wouldn't work." A surprising triumph lifts her voice and her heart. She holds out the baby. "She's beautiful, Karen. But she's yours—yours and Caleb's."

"But . . . what will you do?"

"Live my life, Karen. It's precious—precious as that baby's."

Openmouthed, staring, Karen takes the child, her tears suddenly gone.

Alma notices that her heart still beats strong, and that the feeling of fullness has not left her. Illusions take up a lot of space. When they are gone, life flows in.

As she walks down the hall, Caleb stops her. "Did Karen tell you? Isn't it a miracle—her willingness to give so unselfishly?"

Alma smiles. "She told me. But Karen has already given too much. Besides . . . don't you know, Caleb? The miracle has already happened."

He smiles, not because he understands, but because he thinks he should smile when she is smiling.

Alma decides not to spend the night there—no matter how it strikes everyone else. She floats on a draft out the door of the wonderful old house. There she stands, looking up. From habit, she searches out the Pole Star then throws her arms skyward.

"Thank you," she says, surrendering to countless bright holes in dark blue blanket of sky.

～

The last I heard, Alma had left Caleb and was creating a life separate from the religious community that spawned us. She had become a member of the official Church of Jesus Christ of Latter-day Saints and seemed fulfilled in making her contribution to the human family. Besides using her talents on behalf of children and families, she is a caretaker at a rehabilitation hospital, drawing on deep wells of patience and compassion. Karen stayed with Caleb for the sake of her own children as well as others in the polygamous community. She has formed a committee that interfaces with social services and medical groups in the larger community to see that the women and children of polygamy get the help they need. Both Alma and Karen have recently graduated from universities with honors, two of a handful of our father's twenty-five daughters to receive college degrees. Alma was fifty-two, and Karen was pushing sixty. Both have said, "I feel like my life has just begun."

Speaking of Isaac

"NEVER SPEAK OF HIM AGAIN," Uncle Anthus said after we buried Isaac. He said it the way he always made prophetic pronouncements for our people, as though he was declaring the right path, and no other route would do. His attitude typifies the fundamentalist belief that there is only one way to see things, one right way to live. And for those of us who have been born into this splinter from the early Mormon church, the right way means living the Principle of Plural Marriage. I believe Uncle Anthus means to preserve our peculiar lives but I could not reconcile myself to his dictum regarding Isaac. According to Uncle Anthus, I am a trouble-maker, and he doesn't know how to deal with me—just as I have never known how to deal with myself when I'm asked to withhold the truth. I have never deliberately set out to break faith with him or with any-one in the group and there's a trembling now I have never felt before, as though I am treading on forbidden ground, as though I am about to encounter something I have always been afraid to face.

Part of it is the fear of not knowing, the human inclination to link the unknown to my own mortality. And in Isaac's world, Isaac's con-sciousness, there are many unknowns. I don't know what he thought, or how he felt, or why he did what he did. I don't know how to tell this story. I know before I have begun that I will not find the one right way to tell it, and that no human vessel will contain the heights and depths of Isaac's life. All I can do is tell what I know. And one more thing: I cannot *not* tell it. Out of respect for him, I must speak of Isaac.

I was three years old. We lived all together then, in the compound of houses overlooking the farm in Salt Lake County that summer, just before my fourth birthday. The air stuck like pinesap to our skins, and we longed to go swimming. I sat with my brothers and cousins in the shade of the orchard. Then we moved to the stream where the dark water uttered a cool promise. Yellow jackets hummed in the willows, angry with the heat and stir of sunlight. We children wanted desperately to jump into the water, clothes and all, but after the series of green-willow switchings already received that summer, we had learned to ask. My brother Danny carried the request to my mother, but Aunt Emma met us at the kitchen door. Then we remembered, it was her day off.

"No," Aunt Emma said. "You can't go swimming."

"Why not?" we whined. "It's hot. The stream is so cool."

"No," she said. "You'll get cramps."

"We only get cramps after eating," we said.

"We're having lunch in half an hour," she said.

"Well, let us go for half an hour, then."

"No," she said.

"Why not?" we said. "It's so hot."

"You'll get polio. Then you won't be able to walk."

"Daddy said that polio is only in public pools and in the irrigation ditch. This is the stream. The stream is full of snowwater."

"That's right," she said. "The snowpack is melting, the stream is too high. You'll drown."

"Please," we said. "Pretty please."

"No," she said. "Not while I'm in charge."

The next day was hotter and stickier still. The birds drifted into somnolent silence and bugs ruled the heat, the bumblebees lurching from flower to flower. We longed to go swimming and thought with despair of yesterday's exchange. Then we remembered that Aunt Emma was at work and that my mother was in charge of us—of me and my brothers and Aunt Em's children, Isaac and Ramie.

"Please let us go swimming," I wheedled, tugging at my mother's skirt. I was her only daughter, her baby, and the odds were on me to get my way.

My mother smiled. "You want to go swimming?"

"Yes!" I jumped up and down.

"She can't go unless I go," my mother said to the older ones. "She's too little to go swimming alone."

"We'll all go," Saul said quickly. "You can come with us."

Everyone agreed. My mother even packed a picnic lunch for us to eat after we swam so that we would not have to wait an extra hour.

The water was delicious. Soft cool fingers of moss stroked our skin; minnows nibbled our toes; water skaters slid up and said hello. The trees waved at us from overhead, mottling the light as we moved through corridors of earth and sky. But I did not know how to swim, and cried because I wanted to reach the waterfall that fell into a pool of sunlit water beyond the deep end of our swimming hole. I wanted more than anything to feel it splash over my face and body.

Isaac heard me crying. He came back to carry me out to the place where even he could not touch bottom. "Put your arms around me," he said. I clasped my hands around his neck and he spread his arms wide. We glided over the water like a large, pale swan until we laughed in the sparkle of waterfall and sunshine. Joy was its name.

My brothers Saul and Isaac were only three months apart, born to twins and to the same father. At the time they married my father, the twins were conjoined at the psyche and the temptation to play out their rivalry was overwhelming. A daily game of control and be controlled, of comparison and denigration resulted.

To always be racing each other was not something Isaac or Saul wanted, but competition and comparison were thrust on them as surely as the religion that had spawned us. When the boys ran, they could not simply run side by side; someone always encouraged them to race. When they wrestled, Isaac was always pressed to win, though he was delicate in some ways. When the boys were baptized, a new campaign began to exhort Isaac toward righteousness, to be the most righteous boy a boy could be. And when the boys turned twelve and received the priesthood, he was urged to be more holy, to be the best young man a young man could be.

The pressure didn't end there, but extended to secular spheres. Everything from fishing trips to school grades became grist for the competition. When Isaac and Saul graduated from junior high school, Aunt Emma did not know that Isaac was slated to sing on the school program. He had not said a word to his mother about it, although my mother was in on the secret and played the piano for him. I think Isaac believed the performance would placate his mother and set him apart so that he would not have to out-race, out-fish, out-wrestle Saul. After the first wave of indignation because my mother had participated in a surprise, Aunt Emma basked in Isaac's golden voice.

After that first performance, whenever my father requested music, Isaac was urged to step up. Saul drifted into a backdrop of outdoor games or retreated to the attic window where he drew pictures or tied flies for fishing. Isaac became the family performer, emissary to a hard-hearted world, proving that our peculiar clan had merit. My father and Aunt Emma often pointed to Isaac as the shining example, what we should all strive to be. Isaac stared at his shoes and a pink stain spread from the collar of his white shirt to his cheekbones. Meanwhile, Saul who often came home with mud to his knees, his church shoes ruined, Saul with his habit of brooding in the attic where he drew wild creatures, was held as an example of how not to be.

After a time Saul's fiercely independent spirit took over and he dropped out of the competition altogether. The lines of fundamentalism are so uncompromising, Saul with his earthbound ways could only be the villain. He stopped attending our religious meetings. Isaac was left by himself to meet Aunt Emma's and my father's expectations and he bore the onus of eldest son alone. His quest was difficult, seeking the goal of perfection, his only landmark the Cross. With Malcolm long since out of the running, and now, with Saul gone astray, no reassuring sense of proximity, no infusion of the untamed could alleviate the lonely stoicism of Isaac's post.

Aunt Emma read Bible stories to us, of Isaac and Ishmael, of Jacob and Esau, of Joseph and his brothers. As one son was blessed over the others, she always looked meaningfully at Isaac. She never looked at Saul. It was as though she had forgotten he was there.

Saul became the prodigal son. He disappeared into the world, went to college, drank beer, ran with women. He wrote a long letter to our father, disenfranchising himself from the system of sacrifice, martyrdom, and personal renunciation that had engendered him.

Meanwhile Isaac grew in the priesthood and in the official church. When it came time for me to be baptized into the Church of Jesus Christ of Latter-day Saints, Isaac was the one who performed the baptism. His arm around me as we entered the baptismal font made me feel at home; his hand over mine as he eased me under the water and lifted me up again—the entire ritual seemed part of a huge, sensible design. Once again, he underwrote my entry into the larger community along a path that I could trust. Before long, he married an easygoing Mormon girl with a sweet nature resembling my mother's. He worked hard, became a father, then a teacher. I babysat their young children on an occasional night until Isaac moved his little family to California and showed no inclination to leave the official church or to take another wife.

Aunt Emma mourned. She developed symptoms of her sorrow: stomach cramps, back trouble. Each week she fasted and prayed for a full twenty-four hours on her day off work. On those days she wrote long, passionate letters to Isaac urging him to "choose the right." After years of his mother's fasting and praying and letter-writing, Isaac came home with his wife and several children in tow. It isn't easy to give one's life over to the way prescribed by someone else, but Isaac did so as earnestly and as lovingly as he did everything else. He did his best to honor his mother and his father. First he rounded up my wayward brothers, Saul and Jake and Danny. One night Saul and Isaac took over my bedroom and talked long and earnestly. Isaac never raised his voice. Saul never raised his. At one point, Saul spoke in a voice clear enough that it could be heard beyond the door.

"You think the leaders of the group are men who care about Christian love and brotherhood. But someday, Isaac, you'll find that what matters to most of them is ego and power."

Isaac was silent for a time before I heard his soft baritone paving the way for understanding. At the end of the discussion, they came to an agreement: Saul would continue in his way and Isaac would continue in his. But they would preserve their brotherhood through mutual respect. It was as though they had wrestled with angels. No one was sure that anyone won, or that winning was the point. But both of them felt stronger, and each felt the love of the other.

Within a year Isaac married two women whose husband had died. He became father to their children and he moved his burgeoning family to the bitter cold of Montana where, in one of his apocalyptic moods, my father had purchased land. One of the new wives had teenagers, and the oldest, named Carlos, was bitter about his father being so quickly replaced, and he began to get in trouble. Isaac determined to love the boy anyway, just as he did everyone else.

Isaac visited my father and tried to mend my father's relationship with Saul. "I had a dream, Father," he said respectfully. "I was wrestling with Saul. I felt nothing but love from him and for him. I am sure he can be won to the Lord." My father nodded, and for the first time in many years, the shadow of skepticism did not cross his face when Saul's name was mentioned.

Occasionally Isaac visited my mother. He sat at her table and drank Postum and let his mask of cheerful idealism fall. He spoke of the dreariness of life in Montana. He spoke of the new wives and of his fear that he was failing. He seemed to miss the long, predictable nights in the arms of his first love. He spoke of the harsh practices of the brethren on the ranch who were as unyielding and intolerant as Montana winters. Isaac told her about one incident, when food was stolen from the United Order storehouse, and how the brethren had punished the thieves by holding them in a dugout for five days giving them nothing but bread and water. Carlos had been the ringleader, and the brethren called Isaac in: they wanted him to do something about the boy's rebellious ways.

Carlos had let his hair grow long and since deer-hunting season had begun, Isaac made a deal with Carlos. "If you want to go hunting with me," he said, "you must let me cut your hair." Isaac took scissors and a plastic tablecloth into the kitchen, clothes-pinned the cloth around Carlos's neck. As he was about to cut a shank of Carlos's long black hair, the boy pulled a knife. In seconds, Isaac was on the floor, bleeding, a kind of sacrifice to the righteousness of the brethren.

Isaac wavered between life and death at a Missoula hospital. As Isaac went into surgery, the entire group fasted and prayed for his life. He lost one kidney and the other threatened to shut down. My father, perhaps recognizing that he had offered Isaac up by insisting that the son pursue his father's contract with God, vowed that he would give up his only vice, the family game of pinochle, if Isaac would be healed. As I look back, it seems that this may have been Isaac's time to die—it would have been a genuine sacrifice for all of us—but we were unwilling to let him go. Or pehaps my father's offering was the ram in the thicket that saved Isaac's life.

After we summoned Isaac from the grave and cheated him of his martyr's death, nothing seemed to go right for him. One of his plural wives measured him against the husband who had died in the car wreck, and she left. Isaac might have felt somewhat unburdened; instead, he felt like a failure. Another of his plural wives bickered, his first wife walked in clouds of confusion. Fault-finding made his homes unwelcome places.

When my father was murdered, perhaps no one was more bereft than Isaac, whose identity was so firmly tethered to my father's. At the funeral, the heavy mantle of my father's authority fell on Isaac, as the oldest righteous-living son. He was now principal at the school in Montana, but the priesthood council criticized his slow, soft way of dealing with reprobates. They wanted the rod of discipline. The natural man, they reminded Isaac, was an enemy to God. Isaac did his best to shore up his gentle nature, to rule with a firm hand.

Isaac's eyes filled as he told my mother of his heartache. "I keep telling them, 'Just love them. All the children need is love.' But they don't agree."

That winter of 1983–84 I began thinking about Isaac every day. I can't say why, exactly. Just that I would be cooking dinner, and he'd be on my mind. Or I'd wake up thinking about him. Or I'd be holding one of my children, and I'd see Isaac in the profile. I had heard he was coming to visit sometime during the winter holidays, and I made up my mind to see him then.

Around Christmas my mother told me he was sick, he'd had some kind of a breakdown, and she was worried. He'd been fasting too much, doing too much, living like he was on borrowed time. I phoned Aunt Emma and attempted to make arrangements to see him but she was limiting the number of visitors to those who were especially close to him. Obviously she did not count me among them. I discounted anything I might have done to cheer him. Instead, I took this to mean that I was not welcome, since I was a woman too selfish to live the Principle of Plural Marriage.

The morning Isaac left Salt Lake to return to the cold north, he came to say good-bye to my mother. He held her and kissed her and thanked her for being a wonderful aunt and mother to him. And then, as he started out the door, he stopped.

"Aunt Ella, Saul was right."

"Why, what do you mean, Isaac?"

He shook his head, stared at the floor.

"Just tell Saul that he was right."

My mother reported this peculiar conversation to me, and chills ran though me. I felt I must do something. But what could I give Isaac? He had taught me to walk, taught me to speak. He had carried me. What did I know that would carry him through this? And then I realized: I had learned the value of speaking honestly, regardless of who was listening. As I thought how lies choke out life and lead to death, I decided to talk to Isaac. I wanted to let him know that it was time his penchant for sacrifice ended.

The challenge was more than I'd imagined. Each day I tried to work up the courage to call Montana and tell the truth. As I put out my hand to pick up the phone, my heart froze: my sentences disassembled, the words went cold. I wrote Isaac's name on my calendar. The day came and went. Again, I wrote on my calendar "Call Isaac." If I made myself call him, perhaps I would know what to do and say. Perhaps I would find a way to say it without causing damage, without treading on the bones of my father, without hurting Isaac, who was already hurting too much.

That morning, the morning of the third time I wrote his name on my calendar, the phone rang early, waking me. I picked it up and heard the hollow buzz of long distance. No answer, only the hollow line. I thought of the cold north, but I did not think of Isaac. I could not imagine Isaac calling and not saying, "Hello, darling. How are you?" as he always had done.

When I came home from my writing class that day, my husband met me at the door. With exquisite tenderness he took me in his arms. I have sad news, he said. Your brother Isaac shot himself this morning. My husband held me for a long time and listened while I blamed myself for not acting on what my spirit knew. No ram had appeared in the thicket this time. It would be a long time before I felt clean again.

It was forty below in the Bitterroot Mountains the morning of Isaac's funeral. They had to pick-axe the frozen ground, carve out a hole. We gathered at the ranch, determined to be cheerful in Isaac's name. We knew that he loved us. We knew that we loved him. We had faith that somehow the big rip in the sky would be mended, through a seamless recognition that all individual knots must someday be undone and woven together into one great whole.

But then came the speeches. The brethren took this opportunity to make a stand about liberalism, about selfishness, about suicide. As his children and his longtime wife mourned, the brethren of the priesthood condemned Isaac. They did not dwell on the many kindnesses he had offered every person there—the roofs he had patched, the gardens he had sown, the chimneys he had cleaned. They did not mention that each month he mailed fifty of his hard-earned dollars to the Children's Defense Fund while managing to clothe and feed his own. They did not speak of his tenderness toward all children—including Carlos, whom he forgave freely—and toward the children who had been his students. The brethren justified their righteousness. They justified their apathy. They justified their position.

Brother Mitchell Dean spoke of how Isaac had been led astray and was under the influence of the Evil One, and justified himself for refusing to respond to Isaac's request for a blessing the night before he killed himself. Saul sat beside me, his angry muscle working. Danny's hands were closed in two fists. I wept as I watched the faces of Isaac's children, crushed and betrayed.

That night, we gathered to break bread together, as is our custom when we have lost a loved one. I could not eat with them, thinking of Isaac's children who had been told that their loving father had betrayed everything he stood for. Then Brother Mitchell Dean commanded me to return to the fold.

I turned an angry gaze on him, and my back stiffened. "Why would I want to do that?"

"Because you must keep the Lord's commandments."

"I'll keep the commandments as I understand them, thank you."

Aunt Emma stepped up. "But dear, we want you to be with us forever. There's only one way you can do that. We don't want to lose you, too."

I took a deep breath. "Aunt Emma, you've suffered so much, I don't want to add to your heartache. But if there's only one way here, then count me out. Let me be the lost lamb and let the Lord track me down."

Her eyes filled for the hundredth time that day. "But we love you."

"Yes," Brother Mitchell Dean said. "We love you."

"Then really love me," I said. "Stop pretending. And stop pretending to love Isaac. Really love him. Accept what he did and love him anyway."

"The doctrines say . . ." I felt Brother Mitchell Dean adopt his argumentative stance.

"I've had a bellyful of doctrines today." That quickly I'd been snared into the old game of be right and make wrong. "And not one word had the breath of life in it. I don't want to play the doctrine game."

"But we need you," Brother Mitchell Dean insisted. "We need your strength."

I looked at Aunt Emma. I looked at Brother Mitchell Dean. "My strength doesn't come from doctrines or the one right way. It comes from love and you can have it without bringing me back. Just stop judging!" I left the gathering full of judgements of my own, my composure dissolved in tears.

～

Mine were not the only words in defense of the way Isaac lived, and mine was not the only refusal to judge the way he died. People stood in religious meetings and spoke fervently, trying to restore the love and respect lost at Isaac's passing, trying to heal the wounds made at the funeral. To stop the furor, Uncle Anthus stood in the priesthood council meeting and gave the edict: "We will never speak of Isaac again."

Isaac's wife and his mother and my mother wept. They had lost him once, lost him twice. Now they were losing him again.

Never speak of Isaac again? When words are life, a balm in Gilead that reaches beyond the grave? How can this be acceptable among a people who believe in the literal truth of "In the beginning was the Word . . ."? Never to speak of Isaac was a death beyond anything I'd experienced.

Of course, I have never taken the one right way. I have always been a problem to my father, to my mother. But they have loved me even when they have not approved of me. And now I'm breaking the decree of Uncle Anthus, who has never known quite what to make of me. He has inferred that I am a liar. Certainly I have lied. But not about my father's blessing on my writing, nor about my life's purpose. He has inferred that I do the work of the Devil: I know I have been the pawn of evil; the day I let my young husband go to Vietnam, I became a minion of the dark, but I struggled with the help of God and of my father to make our way back to the light. I do not pretend to be right-eous or saintly, for I know that at any given moment I could succumb to schemes instead of visions, to lies instead of truth. But in this case, silence would spawn a bigger lie—a revocation of life before the eyes and mouth are stitched shut. And so I insist: it is wrong not to speak of Isaac, for silence is the death within death that none of us deserves. And so I call on Uncle Anthus, on everyone, to speak of Isaac. Let us learn from Isaac's life and from his death how we let someone so pre-cious slip away. Let us acknowledge that we did not love him like Christians, that we did not love him like a brother. And that he was too pure to wear the cloak of our hypocrisy.

As for me, I'm still mapping my own heart. It's one of the ways I talk with God. On the map is a shrine, a place that is holy. At this shrine I speak of what lives, what matters, what endures. And now I am speaking of Isaac.

I have a dream now and then that comes to me unbidden on lonely nights when my heart pounds hard and I am afraid it will suddenly stop. In the dream, I am deeply asleep, with only the drum of my heart in my ears. Then the drum stops and I am alone in the dark. I stumble forward, calling out for my mother, my father, my husband. Then I am crossing a wide, bright river. I am afraid, and still very much alone although the land on the other side is beautiful, and along its shores move the people I love. I am wading through waters of light. On the other shore I see them, but I do not know how to cross. My faith is weak. I don't know how to swim. And then Isaac comes for me. He picks me up. "Put your arms around me," he says. I cling to him. And like a white swan we glide until we reach the other shore.

Holding Grace

UNCLE ANTHUS ACCUSES ME of doing the work of the Devil. He has said it just that way: "She is doing the work of the Devil," and he said it from the pulpit, too, with my mother and the rest of the family listening as he implied in his prophet's voice that I am lost to the powers of darkness. I'm struck by how much Uncle Anthus looks and sounds like my father, with his white mane and upright carriage, his voice thinned by yearning, so very like my father who has been gone for twenty years now, right down to his habit of clenching his fists and squeezing his eyes shut as if I have caused him physical pain. This resemblance, as much as anything, both startles and wounds me. I don't want to admit that his judgement hurts, but it does. I have lost too many members of my family, even in a family that had members to spare. Further losses seem unnecessary and unfair.

Uncle Anthus doesn't understand the work I do. Over the years, my husband and I formed our own communications training company, aiming to build a healthy and inclusive community through honesty. Several of my brothers and sisters took our seminars, facing lifelong fears and the deeply rooted practice of lying to keep peace. I was enormously proud of them for confronting painful truths and having the courage to change their lives. After awhile, three of my father's wives also enrolled. Before she took the seminars Aunt Sally had confessed, "I just want my life to end so I can go to the Other Side and be with Rulon." After she completed the course, she found a new lease on life. A few years later she married again, a man she had admired all her life who happened to be my father's cousin. They married in the LDS temple, which outraged the brethren of the fundamentalist priesthood council.

Some of the people who completed our seminars subsequently left the religious group, maintaining they'd never really believed in the Principle, they'd only lived that way because of their parents' wishes. Some of the women, including a couple of my sisters, found self-respect and left their husbands, citing abuse or neglect. Many of my nieces and nephews left polygamy and joined the official Church. We worried that our Utah program might be regarded as the "fundamentalist training" thus jeopardizing the heterogenous, cross-cultural education we had delivered in cities all over the world. Then enrollment from the polygamous sector abruptly stopped. I soon found out why: Uncle Anthus had declared, from the pulpit, that I was doing the Devil's work. My mother sat at the piano during his speech, fighting back tears.

Uncle Anthus can't see how these sad and frightened fundamentalists come to our communication seminars, then four days later show up in Sunday school full of love and light and a sense of well-being. To them, Uncle Anthus says plaintively, "Why didn't you come to me? Maybe I could have helped you."

"I don't know why you think you need this when you have the Gospel," Uncle Anthus told the priesthood council member who completed our series of seminars, then enrolled his five wives and all of his adult children. Brother Parley says we've helped him reclaim his children who had gone to the ways of the world, with drugs, smoking, and drinking. I understood the children's predicament. How could you grow up and leave home when you had two choices: to stay in an environment where you must be a perpetual child, or live a life of rebellion? The girls were doing heaven knows what, as Brother Parley told me, and the boys were in trouble, too, although he did not worry so much about them. I remembered my own claustrophobia and the ensuing revolution.

This Devil's work, as Uncle Anthus calls it, is not in any way opposed to the Gospel of Jesus Christ. It is the work of telling the truth. Some people call it human development. Others call it transformation education. I like to describe what we do this way: We teach people to discover what really matters to them, their basic purpose in being. Then we urge them to focus on what matters until it is manifested. We show them how to refine the raw emotions of fear, blame, shame, and anger into rocket fuel to reach their dreams.

In spite of the fulfillment of my own dreams (a monogamous marriage that has produced four beautiful children, plus two rewarding careers), I live every day with the sense that I have let my siblings down. This translates into a fear that I will be denied access to them in the eternities. You know the story of Isaac. We were enrolling people in our first seminar when he plunged into depression. I could have trusted what I knew and shared this forum for expressing himself. The opportunity to be honest without being judged could have saved his life. But I didn't want to be criticized by Uncle Anthus and other people I love, so I stood by while Isaac fell apart and took his own life. Contrary to what we urge our students to do, I did not interrupt entropy.

But this story isn't about Isaac or Uncle Anthus or me. It isn't even about the religious group. This story is about the context in which things happen, which is also how other things are disallowed. It is about contexts that sustain monogamy and contexts that sustain polygamy. It is also about the context set in our communications seminars, where everybody aims to get what he or she wants without hurting anyone else, a context of win/win. But mostly, it is about my lost sister, Grace.

As I've said, Katherine Handy was the only one of my father's wives to be his only wife. She (and perhaps, for awhile, he) thought she would always be his only wife. There was a baby girl who died the day after she was born. Then a son, Sherwood, who one day became a doctor like his father and his grandfather. Then a daughter, Patricia, a sweet little girl who would grow into a small, soft woman married to a marriage and family therapist. And then came Grace, who was only three years old when my father and Katherine separated. Once my father had committed himself to polygamy, Katherine refused to let him see the children.

Throughout my childhood, I asked questions about that missing family, imagining those absent siblings who were no longer children but older than Saul and Isaac. I thought of what my father said, that regardless of who our mother was, we were all members of the same family, and I felt the urge to examine the hole their leaving had created in our lives. I wondered how they had lived without our father, and then I wondered what I had missed. I imagined reunions with my oldest brother and sisters, whose pictures I had never seen. When I was a teenager and rebelled against my father's strict ways, I sometimes tried to fool myself into believing that the older children were the lucky ones, since he had not overshadowed their lives with his unreachable example of moral uprightness and spiritual excellence. We grew up. My father grew older. Still we did not hear from the first family.

Then, in the late seventies, we had news of Sherwood through Isaac who had moved to California and found himself in the same stake, or religious district, as our oldest brother. The two men met and formed a friendship. My father and Aunt Emma pressured Isaac to draw on the trust he had established to persuade Sherwood to reconcile with our father. Perhaps Isaac sweetened Sherwood's bitter feelings, but he also reawakened dormant anger.

As I've already described, on his parents' fiftieth wedding anniversary, Sherwood traveled across the Mojave to upbraid his father but ended up sharing sorrow and restrained love. Afterward, father and son exchanged some correspondence. Then Katherine's "Guardian Angel" poured out words long withheld and Rulon wrote back, addressing that angel. Ultimately, the letters did little to reconcile them, being too much like the letters each had written in their hearts over forty years of separation. Neither wanted to be wrong about those long-ago choices, considering the prices they'd paid.

Then Aunt Emma wrote to Katherine, long letters that went unanswered for many years. Such a peculiar nicety, writing to a husband's first wife; such an extraordinary attempt at reclamation of missing persons. But Aunt Emma took this task on willingly, persistently. When my father was assassinated, Sherwood was invited to be a pallbearer. Katherine sent a sympathy card to all the sister-wives and their children (a landmark event!) having written in a frail, wavering script, "To know Rulon was to love him."

These seven words signaled a supreme triumph for Aunt Emma. The lost had been found. Aunt Emma continued her correspondence until Katherine died. Then she started writing to Grace, the youngest of Katherine's children, who responded but refused to meet anyone in the family.

In 1984, during the time I was becoming a communications trainer, I got a phone call from one of Katherine's grandchildren who had read something I had published. The young man had called, not to inquire about the family, but to ask about his grandfather's estate. I had to laugh. I told him that I had inherited a tie tack, mother of pearl, worth about four dollars. I invited him to check with Aunt LaVerne, my father's legal wife, if he wanted to know the particulars of my father's estate. That phone call from a faceless nephew was the last I heard of my father's first family for many years. During the civil case my family brought against Rena Chenowyth, I met briefly with Patricia, my oldest sister, a small, gentle woman, who explained that she dared not become too familiar with her father's other families for fear of betraying her mother. She warned me that Grace, the youngest of Katherine's children, wanted nothing to do with her father's other families. Patricia asked that I not share her address or phone number with other family members. I respected her wish that our contact be limited.

~

Then, nearly fifteen years after we started communication training, I was completing the first day of a seminar and as I stood behind the table gathering my papers, a handsome student in his early thirties came to me and said, "I think I'm your nephew. Well, your nephew-in-law, really. My wife is your father's granddaughter. By the first wife."

I was surprised, thinking that perhaps Uncle Anthus had lifted his edict, or that one of them had moved out from under his thumb. "Which of my brothers is her father?"

"Her mother. Your sister. By your father's first wife."

"That's not possible. " I snapped my briefcase and prepared to leave. "LaVerne has only sons."

"No . . . I mean the *first* wife. The one who left."

My mouth gaped. "Your wife is Katherine's granddaughter? Who is her mother?"

"Grace. My mother-in-law. Your sister."

"Trainer altitude"—a phrase that reminds us to keep a professional distance from our students—vanished. I covered my mouth with my hand. "I . . . can I meet her?"

The next night I met Grace's daughter, Alaina, who was about to graduate from the first seminar. With her dark hair and eyes, Alaina looks very little like my father's family, except for her height. She is beautiful and exotic and statuesque, a treasure that any aunt would be proud to claim. What benevolence, that I could meet one of Grace's children under such loving circumstances.

A few moments later when I met Grace, I knew that things had come full circle. We held each other and I realized we had been given a second chance at relationship. As it turned out, Alaina had persuaded her mother to take our seminars. Soon after this, my two youngest children suddenly lost their teenaged disregard for the work their parents do and decided to take the seminars, too. So Clarissa and Brett joined the same training group as Grace.

Small like her mother, but light-haired like my father, Grace's eyes are his shade of blue. She has his fierce intelligence as well as the emotional strength I always associated with his doctor persona. But, like me, Grace was withheld in spirit, something I once attributed to the shyness that goes with living polygamy. Despite her reserve, Grace was polite, even warm, sizing me up without seeming to do so. She made subtle, penetrating jokes as we compared our lives, the paucity of family relationships in hers, the paucity of material goods in mine. And I was so excited to see her, yet afraid I would scare her off, I did my best to restrain myself.

I became Grace's trainer, not once but twice. When she graduated from her last seminar, I set up a meeting for her with Aunt Emma. Grace wanted to meet and thank Aunt Emma for her correspondence in person. A quiet joy rose in me. Perhaps, at long last, I could really do something for Aunt Emma who had done much for me and many others, and who had suffered long, having watched our father die, having lost her only son to suicide, and who now, without career or husband, rode the knife-edge of aplastic anemia, her life jeopardized by every infection that came along.

Grace and Aunt Emma visited for an entire afternoon. I believe that both were fulfilled in that conversation. Before Grace returned to Los Angeles, she and I vowed never to lose each other again.

~

Four months later, just before her seventy-ninth birthday, Aunt Emma went to the hospital. An infection raged through her, and no antibiotic could stop its progress. My mother was there, and so was Eileen, Aunt Emma's miracle child, born eighteen years after the promise that she would one day be a Mother in Israel once again. My oldest daughter, Erica, left her post as a labor and delivery nurse to sit at Aunt Emma's head. At one point, I begged Aunt Emma not to leave us. A shadow passed over her eyes, the familiar irritation that I was once again interfering in something she needed to do. In a kind voice, Erica told me that I had interrupted Aunt Emma's concentration.

"See? She's looking at someone or something. Maybe she's following the light. She doesn't want to stay here anymore." Then, adopting the same soft urgency she used with birthing mothers, Erica coached Aunt Emma to slip her skin and give birth to her spirit. A beauty, a mystery beyond words, to see my daughter midwife my mother's twin into eternity.

At my invitation, Grace and her husband flew out for the funeral. When the speeches had been made and the songs sung, I took Grace by the elbow and led her toward Uncle Anthus, who had positioned himself at the doorway of the RCA meeting hall to console people.

"Here comes the troublemaker," Uncle Anthus said, speaking, of course, of me.

Even though there was a teasing note in his voice, both of us knew that he meant what he'd said. Perhaps I had stirred up trouble. For him. For the group. For my father. For my husband. But I had done one good thing. I had brought Grace home.

"This is Grace. Katherine's and Daddy's youngest daughter. Grace. Remember?"

His eyes filled. "I haven't seen you since you were four years old," he said wonderingly. He cupped her face in his hands, looked deeply into her eyes, then held her close. Then he looked at me, it seemed, with new vision. A moment of realization, so precious, an understanding that we are in one another's lives to fulfill some ultimate purpose. And then the moment was gone. People were crowding behind us, wanting to shake Uncle Anthus's hand, and those who had heard that Grace was present, pressing to meet her. I felt eclipsed once more, but in a good way. Holding Grace, bringing her home, that was a win for all of us.

The Mark of My
Ancestors Revisited

 EVERYONE NEEDS A NEW SCRIPT for living. Otherwise we are condemned to repeat the mistakes of our parents and grandparents. Who knows the extent to which we are programmed by our DNA, how precisely our behaviors, our attitudes, even our tastes are determined by the powerful genie in the lamp of ancestry? But I believe in free agency (a belief passed on by my parents and grandparents as basic to the Gospel of Jesus Christ) and I have used this birthright to write a new script—a script of monogamy instead of polygamy, a script of assertive being instead of martyred or victimized being, a script dedicated to living rather than dying a little bit at a time—the "death of a thousand cuts." This need to redefine myself has released a flood of words. At first I wrote fiction, practicing Mormon logic, finding ways of telling the truth without laying out the facts. When one of my stories was accepted for publication, I went to my father to explain. It was about six months before he died.

"Some of the characters may seem familiar, Daddy. But I promise to keep the family secret."

He smiled and closed his eyes, his face weary, the lines deep; for a moment I thought he might have drifted off. Then he looked me full in the face. "This book you're writing . . ." he began. My eyes widened. I hadn't told anyone about the book; it was a secret I kept in my bureau drawer. "It must *not* be a novel. People need to know that these things really happened—what our lives have been. It must be the truth."

I flushed. "I aim to tell the truth. It's just . . . sometimes it's easier . . . when you use fiction to tell it." I tried to smile as I served this little slice of sophistry. He should know about sleight of hand, this way of escaping controversy and prison bars and bullets.

He shook his head. "It needs to be biography. Based in reality."

Perhaps he knew that in charging me to tell the truth, he was blessing my life with freedom from a childhood of lies. Perhaps he also recognized that in allowing his story to be told, the unassailable myths surrounding him would be altered. But his face was earnest when he said, "The book must be a biography. Facts *and* truth. Letter *and* spirit."

I tried to fulfill his request that I present the Allred family as "a good and saintly people." But I have known all along that bloodline is no guarantee of saintly behavior. Now I also know that religious fixation in a physical world can lead to insanity. I read the papers and knew why the Lafferty brothers had murdered their sister-in-law and her eighteen-month-old daughter, slitting her throat from ear to ear because she refused to live the Principle, in a horrible echo of the Blood Atonement rites I'd once heard described following a priesthood meeting. I lived through the violence of the LeBarons, which didn't stop when Ervil went to prison, didn't stop until his sons were convicted of murdering four "lambs of God" in Texas, while more of Ervil's followers were arrested for running an automobile theft ring in Arizona.

I know that my father's group has its own lunatic fringe. Even when I was a child I knew that some of the men in the group who talked long and hard about Christ-like love were actually jockeying for power and position. Now I can see how far they will go: some have inflicted emotional, physical, and spiritual abuse; others have committed crimes: theft, sexual abuse, neglect of their wives and children. I wonder about my father's role in this. While I have no doubt that he loved his wives and children, I think there were times when he loved his vision of a family kingdom more than the reality of family life. And perhaps there were times when his vision was reduced to plots and schemes, his family members to mere players on the stage he set. Perhaps our family commitment to the Principle of Plural Marriage became a deus ex machina, my father the wizard behind an emerald door, directing his sons, brothers, and followers who blew their apocalyptic smoke in order to gain the upper hand, especially with women and children.

For many years I have carried the knowledge that righteousness can seed destruction. Three days before my father was murdered, I saw him at my mother's house. She was sick with a kidney infection, and he stopped by to assure himself that the antibiotics and cranberry tea were working. He praised me for taking care of my mother. Then he peeled a ripe peach and fed my younger daughter, Maya, slices of it from the tip of his carefully-honed pocketknife. He kissed me good-bye and went outside. From the kitchen window, I watched him go. He stopped on the lawn and took my older daughter, Erica, by the shoulders. "Remember who you are," he said. He held her face in his hands and looked into her eyes and said again, "Remember who you are, my darling." "I will, Grandpa," she responded in her high, clear voice. That was the last time I saw him.

There are times when I must stop and listen carefully in order to remember who I am. A cacophony of resistance and self-righteousness echoes through the labyrinths of my experience and I am once again reduced to wishing that I had been born in a "normal" home, with one father, one mother, and a handful of relatives living in the mainstream. Then I remember that tyranny can be found everywhere—not just in patriarchy, not just in polygamy. Sometimes, when it gets to be too much, Jess and I put on waders and head for deeper rivers. He ties a fly on my line and I pull out an occasional rainbow or brook trout or some fish whose ancestry can't be traced. He reminds me that although life is often dangerous, it is rarely as serious as people make it out to be. It is always flowing, always changing, always creating something new. If I peer into the river long enough, I can see everyone there, my mothers shining with gifts of love, my brothers and sisters and their children glimmering below the surface of sunlit waters, dark undersides casting shadows in the deep. And there, in the shallows, the whores and cardsharps of Nevada swim alongside the Baptists and Latter-day Saints, and I know that they are my kin, all of us spirit-children of the same spirit-parents. One day, if these deeper, wider streams survive, I will pull out a pure and perfect Utah cutthroat, a direct descendant of Lake Bonneville. I will give thanks to the Upper Deep Creek for feeding my wider, deeper river. And I will name the fish Sarah and give her back to the water. Perhaps she will spawn; perhaps not. Catch and release—the exercise of true love. It's something I learned from my father because even though it was so hard for him to do, he did it anyway. He remembered that I came to him from another place, so he charged me to be who I am then let me go. He freed me to carry these stories of a rare and ancient breed over the rapids into the wide river beyond the fall. I know who I am, and although the family birthprint has faded, I still carry the mark of my ancestors.

Acknowledgments

I AM GRATEFUL TO MY MENTOR, David Kranes, who urged me out of secrecy into print, and to Harold Moore, who encouraged me to keep writing. Thanks especially to Teresa Jordan, who helped me resurrect certain stories, and to Hal Cannon, who helped me sing them back to life. Sally Smith banished writer's block with a snap of the fingers. Thanks to Judith Kitchen for her clear sight and generous spirit, and to members of my various writers' groups: Dawn Marano, Kristen Case, Wendy Rawlings, Susan Sample, Kate Woodworth, and Heather Hirschi. Also thanks to Lawrence Coates, Kristen Rogers, Pam Carlquist, Ron Molen, Elyse Lord, Deborah Foss, and Joanne Bloom. Thanks to those who were there at the beginning: Gloria Skurzynsky, Ivy Ruckman, Barbara Williams, Phyllis Barber, and Lorraine Henriod. Thanks to Martha S. Bradley for sharing her expertise. Thanks to Wendy Weil for having faith in me. I am especially grateful to Carol Houck Smith, high priestess of literature, whose vision graces many books and many lives.

Thanks to those family members who have made journals and records available so that authenticity is served, particularly Byron Stout, Owen Allred, Arnold Allred, Rhea Allred Kunz, and my father,

Rulon Clark Allred. Thanks to all my siblings, particularly the two brothers who helped open the doors to freedom. Special thanks to Forrest, Kathleen, and Judy for trusting me with their mother's story and for allowing me access to their lives. Thanks to Bill Hughes for helping me to find my voice.

My deepest gratitude goes to those who have loved me even when I say things they don't want to hear: my mother, my father, my children and grandchildren, and especially my husband, who has heard and seen everything, yet stayed to see what's next.

Support from the Utah Arts Council, Writers at Work, the Desert Writers Workshop, the Squaw Valley Writers Workshop, and the Vermont Studio Center has been invaluable, providing time, conducive environments, and inspiration to write.

Sections of this book first appeared, in slightly different form, in various publications and anthologies, listed below with grateful acknowledgment:

Lodestar: "On the Perch"

The Stories That Shape Us, edited by Teresa Jordan and James Hepworth: "Sister-Wife"

A New Genesis: A Mormon Reader on Land and Community, edited by Terry Tempest Williams, William B. Smart, and Gibbs M. Smith: "Messages from the Aerie"

The Crossroads Anthology, edited by Heather Hirschi, Ariana-Sophia Kartsonis, and Brenda Miller: "Manna in the Desert"

The Best of Writers at Work, edited by Christopher Robbins: "Remember Who You Are"

Bibliography

Books and Articles

Allred, Byron Harvey, Jr., *A Leaf in Review*. Caldwell, Idaho: The Caxton Printers, Ltd., 1933.

Bradlee, Ben, Jr., and Dale Van Atta. *Prophet of Blood—The Untold Story of Ervil LeBaron and the Lambs of God*. New York: G.P. Putnam's Sons, 1981.

Bradley, Martha S. *Kidnaped From That Land*. Salt Lake City, Utah: University of Utah, 1993.

Kunz, Rhea A. *Voices of Women Approbating Celestial or Plural Marriage: Volume One— My Sacred Heritage*. Draper, Utah: Review and Preview Publishers, 1978.

Kunz, Rhea A. *Voices of Women Approbating Celestial or Plural Marriage: Volume Two— Treasured Memories*. Draper, Utah: Review and Preview Publishers, 1985.

LeBaron, Garn Jr. "Mormon Fundamentalism and Violence: A Historical Analysis." www.exmormon.org/violence.htm, 1995.

Porter, Perry L. "A Chronology of Federal Legislation on Polygamy." www.xmission.net/plporter/lds/chron.htm, 1998.

Journals

The Life and Times of Byron Harvey Allred, Sr.—Based on his personal Diaries. Compiled by Byron D. Stout.

Indian Territory Mission: The Missionary Journal of Byron Harvey Allred, Jr. Compiled by Arnold Allred, Hamilton, Montana: Bitterroot Publishing Company, 1981.

History of the Life and Acts of Byron Harvey Allred, Jr. Compiled by Owen A. Allred.

Memoirs of Katherine Handy Allred State

Autobiography and Journals of Rulon Clark Allred